LOUIS

LOUISIANA LEGACIES

READINGS IN THE HISTORY OF THE PELICAN STATE

EDITED BY

Janet Allured
Professor of History
MCNEESE STATE UNIVERSITY

&

Michael S. Martin
Associate Professor of History
DIRECTOR, CENTER FOR LOUISIANA STUDIES
UNIVERSITY OF LOUISIANA AT LAFAYETTE

ADVISORY EDITORS

Light Townsend Cummins
Austin College

Judith Kelleher Schafer
Tulane University

Edward F. Haas
Wright State University

WILEY-BLACKWELL

This edition first published 2013 © 2013 John Wiley & Sons, Inc.

Edition history: Harlan Davidson, Inc. (1e, 1995)
Harlan Davidson, Inc. was acquired by John Wiley & Sons in May 2012.

Wiley-Blackwell is an imprint of John Wiley & Sons, formed by the merger of Wiley's global Scientific, Technical and Medical business with Blackwell Publishing.

Registered Office
John Wiley & Sons Ltd, The Atrium, Southern Gate, Chichester, West Sussex, PO19 8SQ, UK

Editorial Offices
350 Main Street, Malden, MA 02148-5020, USA
9600 Garsington Road, Oxford, OX4 2DQ, UK
The Atrium, Southern Gate, Chichester, West Sussex, PO19 8SQ, UK

For details of our global editorial offices, for customer services, and for information about how to apply for permission to reuse the copyright material in this book please see our website at www.wiley.com/wiley-blackwell.

The right of Janet Allured and Michael S. Martin to be identified as the authors of the editorial matter in this work has been asserted in accordance with the UK Copyright, Designs and Patents Act 1988.

Library of Congress Cataloging-in-Publication Data

Louisiana legacies : readings in the history of the Pelican State / edited by Janet Allured & Michael S. Martin ; advisory editors, Light Townsend Cummins, Judith Kelleher Schafer, Edward F. Haas.
      p. cm.
   "Edition history: Harlan Davidson, Inc. (1e, 1995)."
   Includes bibliographical references and index.
   ISBN 978-1-118-54189-0 (pbk. : alk. paper) 1. Louisiana—History. 2. Louisiana—Biography. I. Allured, Janet. II. Martin, Michael S., 1972–
   F369.L886 2013
   976.3—dc23
                              2012037670

Cover image: Cypress swamp © Damir Frkovic / Masterfile
Cover design by Simon Levy

Printed and bound in Malaysia by Vivar Printing Sdn Bhd

1 2013

CONTENTS

EDITORS' PREFACE

Although all of the articles in this volume were written by scholars of Louisiana history and originally appeared in peer-reviewed journals or books published by academic presses, the essays we chose to include in this reader are not only written in an accessible style but tell compelling stories that any student of history will find intriguing. The collection may be used as a supplement to the standard college-level textbook, *Louisiana: A History*, but even the casual reader will find the essays entertaining as stand-alone pieces that offer an in-depth examination of Louisiana's storied past. Heavy on social history, the collection also includes important pieces on the antics of Louisiana politicians, from the Longs to their latter-day counterpart, Edwin Edwards.

Some of the essays are classics, so well-written, with subjects so intriguing, that they continue to enlighten and entertain modern students of history. Carl Brasseaux's glimpse into the moral lapses of French colonial Louisiana and Joseph Tregle's piece on the mythical "Creole" of Louisiana, for example, still generate lively classroom discussions, decades after their original publication. Other articles represent new themes, cutting-edge research, and novel interpretations. The convoluted and constantly shifting history of gender and race in Louisiana law and custom; the state's propensity for violence and murder; its music, food, and indulgent cultures, and its marketing of the same, are relatively new subjects of scholarly inquiry. The volume concludes with a balanced, thoughtful piece on a timely and controversial subject, the state's long disregard for protection of the natural environment. Written by renowned environmental historian Tyler Priest and his student, Louisiana native Jason Theriot, the final article examines the many variables responsible for coastal erosion and wetlands loss.

As editors, we selected pieces we know will be appropriate for and stimulating to undergraduates and a more general readership. To increase the book's accessibility, we removed footnotes and some of the supporting data that is typical of scholarly articles, letting the narrative flow and allowing the focus to fall where it should: on the drama of the story and the explorations of ideas. Those who are interested in pursuing the scholarship further are encouraged to consult the original publication, the citations for which are given on the first page of every selection.

The essays in this collection are grouped in parts that proceed chronologically; the themes of each part are emphasized in an introduction that provides a brief overview of the period, the substance of the individual articles, and some ideas to ponder while reading. "Questions to consider" follow each individual essay, designed for instructors who may assign them in an undergraduate Louisiana history class.

We hope you find these pieces as entertaining as we do. We invite you to contact us with feedback about how we might improve the next edition of this volume.

Janet Allured
Professor of History
McNeese State University
Lake Charles, LA 70609
jallured@mcneese.edu

Michael S. Martin
Associate Professor of History
Director, Center for Louisiana Studies
University of Louisiana at Lafayette
Lafayette, LA 70504
docmartin@louisiana.edu

PART ONE

LOUISIANA'S COLONIAL CONTEXT

Although Europeans had ventured into the lower Mississippi Valley in the century and a half before their arrival, the Le Moyne brothers, Pierre and Jean-Baptiste, led the expedition that would establish the first permanent European settlement in the region in 1699. The Le Moynes, better known by their aristocratic titles of Sieur d'Iberville and Sieur de Bienville, are considered the founding fathers of the French colony of Louisiana, and their actions there set in motion a collision of cultures and populations with far-reaching effects.

The colony of Louisiana held only a tenuous place in the imperial designs of the French monarchy. As such, it remained underdeveloped from a European mercantilist perspective, and historians for centuries deemed it a failure. Daniel Usner, however, chooses to evaluate French colonial Louisiana on the basis of its internal economy, and he shows how a "frontier exchange economy," made up of small-scale, personal interactions actually fostered cross-cultural contacts. In describing American Indians, Europeans, and Africans on the edge of European empires engaging in day-to-day exchanges, Usner emphasizes the fluidity, rather than rigidity, of the boundaries between their lives.

Carl Brasseaux's essay on the moral climate of French colonial Louisiana shows how the Louisiana settlers, situated as they were on the periphery of the French empire, ignored—sometimes unintentionally, but often purposely—the moral strictures of the Catholic Church and the colonial governments. Brasseaux shows that this disregard for traditional morality, manifested most often in extramarital sex, drunkenness, and gambling, reflected in part the makeup of the population of Europeans who ended up in Louisiana, notably the convicts, prostitutes, and soldiers. But it was also a characteristic transmitted to the colonists by the *coureurs des bois*, French trappers who lived either on their own or among the Indians much of the time. Brasseaux's essay points to the fact that once established as the norm by the 1720s, the permissive morality became so ingrained in the colonial psyche that it was handed down to succeeding generations of newcomers to the colony.

The Louisiana colony became a dominion of the Spanish empire in 1763, although Spanish authority was not truly consolidated until the rule of General Alejandro O'Reilly in 1769 and 1770. Over the three decades that followed, the Spanish governors of Louisiana instituted a series of reforms to bring Louisiana into line with the Spanish imperial system. Among these reforms were the institution of liberal immigration policies, designed to grow the colony's population in order to increase its agricultural output to enhance its position as a buffer between New Spain (with its capital at Mexico City) and the English North American colonies along the eastern seaboard. As a result, immigrants from around the Atlantic world established themselves in the lower Mississippi Valley. Some of these peoples came to Louisiana by choice, such as the Acadians or the Canary Islanders, others by force, such as the African and Caribbean slaves.

Among the most notable groups of immigrants to Louisiana during the era of Spanish control, and perhaps the most surprising, were the English speakers from the British colonies. They arrived in increasingly large numbers in the 1780s and 1790s. Some of them, like Oliver Pollock, the subject of Light Cummins's essay, came even earlier. Pollock, a financial backer of the patriot cause during the American Revolution, established himself in the area of the lower Mississippi Valley then known as West Florida in 1769. Between that year and 1824, under the British, Spanish, and American governments, he amassed landholdings and created substantial plantations, made considerable profits as a merchant, lost most of his personal wealth as a result of his support for the American cause, and then reemerged as a major economic player in the region. Cummins contends that Pollock is representative of other Anglo immigrants to Louisiana before the American Revolution.

THE FRONTIER EXCHANGE ECONOMY OF THE LOWER MISSISSIPPI VALLEY BEFORE 1783

by Daniel J. Usner

E ven the most devoted historians of Louisiana are quick to point out that the colony in the Mississippi Valley constitutes "a study in failure" or "a holding action" in comparison with the English colonies along the Atlantic seaboard. Louisiana suffered from a low priority in the mercantile designs of both France and Spain. Immigration and population growth proceeded slowly, exportation of staple products to Europe fluctuated, and subsistence agriculture predominated over production of cash crops. But Louisiana's sparse populace and tentative transatlantic commerce can actually be used to the historian's advantage, allowing one to turn more attentively to dimensions of economic life that have been neglected in the lower Mississippi Valley as well as in other colonial regions of North America. Studies of economic change in North American colonies concentrated for a long time on linkages with home countries and with each other through the exportation of staple commodities. Historians are now turning to economic relationships that developed within regions, with greater attention to activities not totally dependent upon production for the Atlantic market.

Here I will examine the formation of a regional economy that connected Indian villagers across the lower Mississippi Valley with European settlers and African slaves along the Gulf Coast and lower banks of the Mississippi. The term *frontier exchange* is meant to capture the form and content of economic interactions among these groups, with a view to replacing the notion of frontier

From *William and Mary Quarterly* 44 (April 1987): 166–192. Used by permission of the Omohundro Institute of Early American History and Culture.

as an interracial boundary with that of a cross-cultural network. . . . Small-scale face-to-face marketing must be taken seriously, especially for understanding how peoples of different cultures related to and influenced each other in daily life.

. . . [T]he lower Mississippi Valley is here defined as an economic region that was shaped by common means of production and by regular forms of trade among its diverse inhabitants. . . . In 1763 the lower Mississippi Valley was partitioned into the Spanish province of Louisiana and the English province of West Florida. The latter colony, therefore, must be included in any study of the region's economy. The persistence of frontier exchange across the political boundary can too easily be overlooked when Louisiana and West Florida are treated separately.

The focus of this study falls not directly on familiar economic settings—the fur trade for Indians and plantation agriculture for blacks—but rather on the interstices in which people exchanged small quantities of goods in pursuit of their livelihood. A brief summary of how the formal network of towns and outposts took shape is accompanied by an outline of population changes in the lower Mississippi Valley. Then the reader is asked to follow more closely the multiple directions of interaction through which deerskins and foods circulated from group to group. Over most of the eighteenth century, exchanges of these two kinds of products contributed strongly to the notable fluidity of social relations among lower Mississippi Valley inhabitants. It must be emphasized, however, that exchanges occurred under, and often despite, very unequal social conditions because a colonial elite worked steadily to enforce bondage upon black Louisianians and West Floridians, dependency upon Indians, and subordination upon a mixed lot of white settlers. . . .

I

Sent by France late in 1698 to establish a military post near the mouth of the Mississippi River and to forestall Spanish and English advances in the region, naval captain Pierre Le Moyne d'Iberville encountered dismal prospects for what he hoped would become a colony. Already overextended imperially and facing shortages of food at home, France was not prepared to deliver supplies with any regularity to the Gulf Coast. Like many other nascent colonial ventures before it, Iberville's isolated outpost therefore depended heavily upon trade with neighboring Indian villages for its survival. Soldiers and sailors either purchased food directly from Indians or acquired peltry from them to exchange for imported grains and meats. During the second decade of the eighteenth century, this trade expanded from localized exchange with villages near the Gulf into an extensive network of interior posts that not only facilitated the movement of deerskins to the coast but functioned as marketplaces for the exchange of food. . . .

To advance trade up the Red River, a French garrison occupied a post near the Caddo village of Natchitoches in 1716, and a subsidiary trade station was established at an upriver Indian town called Upper Nasoni in 1719. Only twenty miles southwest of Natchitoches, the Spanish, who had been gradually edging toward the Red River, constructed a military post at Los Adaes in 1721. Louis Juchereau de St. Denis, who became commandant of French Natchitoches in 1719, had already been trading in this area for several years—with both Spaniards and Indians. In 1721 a small detachment of soldiers from the Yazoo River garrison joined a group of about one hundred settlers at the lower Arkansas River. . . .

A decade of immigration and slave trading to Louisiana, attended by death for hundreds of Europeans and Africans, resulted by 1732 in a population of only about 2,000 settlers and soldiers with some 3,800 slaves, at a time when the number of Indians of the lower Mississippi Valley, though rapidly declining from disease and war, was still in the range of 30,000. Large-scale immigration from Europe stopped by the mid-1720s, and only about 400 black slaves reached the colony between 1732 and the 1760s. This slow growth of population—to approximately 5,000 slaves, 4,000 settlers, and 100 free people of color—meant minimal encroachment on Indian lands: most settlers and slaves lived along the Gulf Coast and the Mississippi River below its junction with the Red River. Trade relations with the Indians developed more freely because, for a time at least, the region's tribes were not markedly agitated by French Pressure on their territory.

At first, given the scanty and erratic supply of trade goods from France, Louisiana officials relied on distribution of merchandise among Indian leaders in the form of annual gifts. In doing so, they accommodated by necessity to Indian protocols of trade and diplomacy. For the Indians, exchanges of material goods represented political reciprocity between autonomous groups, while absence of trade was synonymous with a state of war. Because commerce could not operate independently from ritual expressions of allegiance, such formal ceremonies as gift giving and smoking the calumet had to accompany economic transactions between Indians and Europeans. Conformity to these conventions recognized the leverage of such large tribes as the Choctaws and Caddoes on Louisiana's commerce and defense. They were essential to the initiation of the network of trade for deerskins and food—both items important to the success of Louisiana—against the threat of English competition from South Carolina and Georgia.

Even so, the formation of this network did not occur without costly conflict. Only after a long war against the Chitimachas, which provided Louisiana with many of its first slaves, did the French secure the alliance of all Indian tribes in the Mississippi delta. While small tribes like the Chitimachas confronted French power directly, conflict between larger Indian nations was fueled by intercolonial competition. In the 1720s Choctaw and Upper Creek villagers helped the French thwart British expansion to the Mississippi River, while the Chickasaws and Lower Creeks fought against them to protect English traders still operating within the Louisiana hinterland. The most explosive crisis came in 1729 when, after a decade of deteriorating relations with encroaching settlers, the Natchez Indians waged a desperate war against the French. Meanwhile, a push by Louisiana officials and planters for the production of tobacco and indigo provoked resistance within: as the volume of these exports rose during the late 1720s, so did the level of slave rebelliousness. A Negro plot was discovered in New Orleans shortly after the Indians destroyed the French plantations at Natchez, and many of the slaves taken captive there assisted the Natchez in their ensuing, but losing, defense against the Louisiana army. Dealing with a black majority within the colonial settlements, and living in the midst of an even larger Indian population, officials employed greater vigilance and harsher coercion as time went on.

Toward mid-century, chronic shortages of merchandise and English intervention nearly turned the Choctaw nation, a bulwark of Louisiana's security, against the French. The benign policy of gift giving could go only so far in mitigating the effects of unreliable imports upon the deerskin trade with

Indians. Unable to divert the powerful Chickasaw nation from the English because of inadequate quantities of trade goods, French officials resorted to a strategy of intimidation and debilitation, employing Choctaw warriors on major campaigns and in continuous guerrilla raids against Chickasaw villages. Participation in this conflict through the 1740s, which was motivated by the need to avenge enemy hostilities as well as to fulfill obligations to the French, took its toll on the Choctaws. Rebellion by a pro-English party within the nation broke out in 1746, costing the Choctaw people much suffering and death in what became a violent civil war waged to preserve their alliance with French Louisiana.

Louisiana's frontier exchange economy survived the Choctaw revolt, with the exportation of deerskins steadily increasing alongside that of tobacco and indigo. Demographic and geopolitical changes that began in the 1760s, however, portended greater challenges to the trade-alliance network. Immigration into the lower Mississippi Valley resumed after Great Britain drove French settlers from Nova Scotia in 1755. By 1767, seven years after Spain obtained Louisiana from France, more than a thousand of these Acadian refugees reached the colony, forming new settlements along the Mississippi about seventy miles above New Orleans and at Atakapas and Opelousas on Bayou Teche. From 1778 to 1780, two thousand "Islenos" migrated from the Canary Islands and established their own communities, along the Mississippi and Bayou Lafourche below New Orleans. In 1785 seven ships carried another 1,600 Acadians from France to Louisiana. Meanwhile Great Britain was accelerating colonization on the eastern side of the river, having acquired West Florida by the Treaty of Paris in 1763. Settlers from the Atlantic seaboard, many with slaves, increased the colonial population of West Florida to nearly 4,000 whites and 1,500 blacks by 1774. An even larger influx occurred after the outbreak of the American Revolution as loyalist refugees sought asylum in the Florida colony and settled mainly in the Natchez area. By 1783, when Spain gained sovereignty over West Florida and control over both sides of the Mississippi, the colonial population of the lower Mississippi Valley approached 16,000 Negro slaves, 13,000 whites, and over 1,000 free people of color.

By the 1780s, the Indian population in the region was, for the first time, becoming outnumbered by colonial inhabitants, while the colonial economy shifted toward greater dependence upon expanding commercial agriculture.

Consequently, Louisiana officials exerted tighter political control over interethnic exchange in order to concentrate slave labor on cash crops and to reduce the mobility of Indian villagers. The frontier exchange economy did not fade from the lower Mississippi Valley, however, for efforts continued to be made into the nineteenth century by many old and new inhabitants to perpetuate small-scale trade across heightening racial divides.

II

Before 1783 the deerskin trade . . . encouraged widespread participation in a network of diffuse exchange from Indian villages to colonial port towns. Indian customs and French commercial weaknesses, as already seen, required a formal sphere of trade-alliance relations, but many people across the region also relied upon informal and intimate forms of cross-cultural trade. . . .

[T]he Indian trade in lower Louisiana was shaped by a complex of . . . circumstances. A small number of colonial troops with minimal support from the crown had to be dispersed among a few select posts. Intertribal conflicts and English trade with Indians in the region determined when and where French stations were constructed and, furthermore, continued to be destabilizing influences on Louisiana's trade. The irrepressible eastward flow of beaver skins from the upper Mississippi Valley to Canada also affected the trade network in Louisiana, making the Lower valley a separate, predominantly deerskin-producing, trade region.

The economic and political importance of the Indian trade to Louisiana is evidenced by the close attention that officials paid to the details of its operation. The overall interest of colonial administrators centered upon the interference and competition of English traders, but particular measures were required for regulation of the region's internal commerce as well. In order to maintain stable relations between traders and villagers, governments in all North American colonies administered tariffs or rates of exchange. In 1721 the Choctaws and the French agreed to trade at the following prices: a quarter of an ell (one meter) of woolen cloth called *limbourg* or one axe for four dressed deerskins; one blanket or tomahawk for two dressed deerskins; and two-thirds of a pound of gunpowder or twenty gun flints for one dressed deerskin. As the cost of European manufactures rose and additional goods entered the regional economy, new tariffs were negotiated from time to time by colonial and tribal leaders. Although much of the trading occurred at varying rates, depending upon local conditions and individual circumstances, official tariffs represented colonial accommodation to Indian insistence that trade be contained within the political sphere of relations. Once it established rates of exchange, the Superior Council of Louisiana had to contend with complaints from traders and Indians alike about inadequate supplies or inappropriate prices. Operating between a fixed ceiling of rates set between tribal and colonial governments and a rising floor of costs charged by import merchants, the traders tended to have, as noted in the minutes of a meeting in December 1728, "a greater share in the complaints that have been made about the high price of the goods than the Indians themselves." For their part, Indian representatives bargained for better exchange rates by repeatedly comparing the expense and quality of French and English merchandise.

Despite attempts by groups of merchants and officials to monopolize Indian commerce, the deerskin trade involved many colonial inhabitants as well as Indians. Even during the demographic and agricultural expansion of Louisiana in the 1720s, settlers relied upon deerskins, acquired directly or indirectly from Indian villagers, as a means of buying imported goods. . . . Many settlers and even slaves exchanged something for deerskins once in a while, and innumerable colonists passed in and out of the deerskin trade as a temporary means of livelihood. Others made a lifetime occupation from seasonally trading imported merchandise for peltry and other native products. The identities of some professional traders among the Choctaws offer informative glimpses into the business. Marc Antoine Huché grew up among the Choctaws, was hired in 1721 as interpreter for the company at "five hundred livres per year with two rations for himself and his wife," and traded for Mobile commandant-entrepreneur Bernard Diron d'Artaguette. . . .

After 1762 the number of traders operating in Indian villages increased with the growth of the colonial population, and their ethnic composition became more English. By the mid-1780s, Spanish officials estimated that five hundred traders, employees, and transients were living in and around Choctaw and Chickasaw towns, while nearly three hundred more operated in Creek towns. Considered "vagabonds and villains" by colonial administrators interested in orderly commerce, many of these men married Indian women and became affiliated with specific villages. . . . The children born to this generation of traders and their Indian wives belonged to the clans of their mothers, and some became important tribal leaders by the beginning of the nineteenth century.

Most deerskin traders learned to speak the language of the tribe with whom they dealt. As emphasized by an anonymous chronicler of the Choctaws' trade with Louisiana, who may have been a trader sometime before the mid-1730s, "it is necessary to know their language well." Many traders probably spoke Mobilian, a trade language or lingua franca, instead of or in addition to distinct tribal languages: "when one knows it," noted Lt. Jean François Benjamin Dumont de Montigny, "one can travel through all this province without needing an interpreter." Antecedents of Mobilian may have existed in the region before European contact, but economic relations with the colonial populace of Louisiana undoubtedly accelerated and expanded its usage. . . . Based upon the western Muskhogean grammar of the Choctaw, Chickasaw, and Alibamon languages—all mutually unintelligible—Mobilian served as a second language, mixing with wide variation lexicon and phonology derived from both Indian and European speech. Well before the mid-eighteenth century, Mobilian became familiar to colonists and Indians west of the Mississippi River. All Caddo villages, as reported by Antoine Le Page du Pratz, contained someone who could speak this "Langue vulgaire." Mobilian was a convenient second language for many settlers and slaves as well as traders to use among Indians, and through the nineteenth century it continued to be spoken by Indians, Negroes, and whites in southern Louisiana and eastern Texas.

Among the goods exchanged for deerskins, liquor was the most volatile item. As in other colonial regions, alcoholic beverages in Louisiana functioned both as a lubricant for expanding Indian commerce and as a stimulant for satisfying military and other colonial personnel. Louisiana and West Florida governments tried to control this commerce, but the very frequency of ordinances regulating trade in liquor reveals its ever-widening use among Indians, settlers, and slaves. In 1725 the Louisiana Superior Council attempted to remedy abuses caused by the "many persons here who have no other trade than that of selling brandy and other drinks at exorbitant prices and even grant credit to all the soldiers, workmen, and sailors." Beginning in 1717, innumerable orders were issued prohibiting the unauthorized sale of liquor to

Indians and slaves, whose consumption of it, officials feared, would increase chances of violent rebellion. By mid-century a cheap rum called *tafia* became the region's most popular drink and a convenient medium of exchange. The English government in Pensacola attempted to restrict Indian traders to fifteen gallons every three months, which was considered a necessary amount for their purchase of food from Indian villagers. But in 1772 several Choctaw chiefs bitterly complained about the quantity of rum that "pours in upon our nation like a great Sea from Mobille and from all the Plantations and Settlements round about." Traders sometimes watered their rum, four kegs of which could buy a Choctaw pony during the 1770s, and encouraged excessive consumption among Indians in order to make more profitable bargains for their deerskins. Peddlers and tavernkeepers persistently violated their licenses by selling tafia and *eau de vie* to soldiers and slaves as well as to Indians.

Deerskin traders and other peddlers played a dynamic role in the frontier exchange economy. While immediately helping distribute the produce of Indians, slaves, and settlers, they performed a long-term economic function. Indian hunters required an advance in goods before they pursued the winter season's thickly furred animals, forcing traders to wait until spring for their pay. In response to this seasonal pattern, traders acquired goods on credit from town merchants and obliged themselves to pay with interest within a year. By extending larger amounts of credit to more inhabitants of the area and by dealing more frequently in dry goods and export commodities, itinerant traders contributed to the commercialization of marketing in the lower Mississippi Valley. . . .

III

The frontier exchange economy also involved trade in foodstuffs. Colonists in Louisiana, though ill supplied from home, were at first reluctant to labor to feed themselves by growing crops; fortunately for them, Indians were able to produce more than they needed for their own use. Thus there developed a lively trade, though one less visible to historians even than the diffuse trade in deerskins. While sailors and soldiers from France, with some Canadian coureurs de bois, were constructing the colony's first fort at Biloxi Bay, the Pascagoulas, Mobilians, and other coastal Indians eagerly swapped surpluses of corn, beans, and meat for axes, beads, and other useful items of European manufacture. During the first decade of the eighteenth century, colonial officials regularly sent parries up the Mobile and Mississippi rivers to purchase maize from Indians. In order to facilitate their trade with the French, some villages relocated closer to the coast and planted larger volumes of grain. The Houmas, for example, abandoned their town several miles east of the Mississippi and settled downriver along the west bank near Bayou Lafourche, where they became reliable suppliers of food to both travelers and settlers. In 1708, when the colony consisted of 122 military men, 80 Indian slaves, and only 77 settlers (24 men, 28 women, and 25 children), "everybody," according to special commissioner Martin d'Artaguette, was asking for gunpowder "to trade with the Indians for the things we need." Through sales of venison to these people, Indians who hunted around Fort St. Louis were acquiring guns, each musket worth ten deer by 1710.

The availability of Indian produce tempted some officials and colonists to profiteer in the sale of food. Louisiana's first political conflict, in fact, centered upon accusations—not entirely false—that the Le Moyne brothers engrossed "the meat and other produce that the Indians have brought to Mobile," trading with the king's merchandise and marking up the price of food for their own profit. Far away from France, where local governments and traditional constraints still protected buyers of food from profiteering middlemen, colonial merchants and administrators tried to intercept corn and game from Indian suppliers and resell the food to consumers at exorbitant prices. The Superior Council assumed responsibility for fixing the price of basic food items beginning in 1722, when buffalo beef was set at eight sous per pound, cattle beef at ten sous per pound, a quarter of a deer at four livres, poultry at three livres apiece, and eggs at fifty sous per dozen. Such regulations, however, never stopped commandants of military posts from attempting to monopolize food supplies and other goods delivered by neighboring Indian villagers.

Many *habitants*[1] of Louisiana preferred direct exchange with Indians for their subsistence, which proved easier than learning how to produce their own food from the soil and wildlife of an unfamiliar land. Trade with Indians for food also allowed a degree of freedom from the pressures inherent in colonial

---

[1] Habitants refers to Louisiana's colonists.

agriculture, causing alarm among colonial officials and merchants who hoped to build a colony that would export some profitable staple. Although general commissioner Marc-Antoine Hubert found the soil along the rivers and bayous to be "of surprising fertility," he lamented in 1716 that "the colonists of the present time will never be satisfied with this infallible resource, accustomed as they are to the trade with the Indians the easy profit from which supports them, giving them what they need day by day like the Indians who find their happiness in an idle and lazy life." Another observer found in France's feeble commitment to colonizing the lower Mississippi Valley the reason why inhabitants had for two decades "done nothing else than try to get a little trading merchandise to obtain from the savages their sustenance, consisting of Indian corn, beans, pumpkins, or small round pumpkins, game and bear grease." The Indian trade, by deflecting colonists from agriculture, thus helped frustrate early efforts to integrate the region into the world market for the benefit of both the colony and the mother country. What looked to officials like laziness was really a testimony to the vitality of the exchange economy.

When the Company of the Indies sent a flood of immigrants to Louisiana between 1717 and 1721, dependence on Indian supplies of food actually expanded. A food crisis was created as seven thousand settlers and two thousand slaves disembarked on the Gulf Coast without adequate provisions. Malarial fevers, dysentery, and scurvy combined with hunger to kill hundreds of French and German immigrants and Bambara and Wolof[2] captives. Soldiers and workers employed by the company were sent to live in nearby Indian villages, and shipments of corn were sought from interior tribes.

Like the deerskin trade, food marketing followed a more open and diffuse pattern than colonial administrators desired. Although France treated Louisiana as an importer of flour, alcohol, and a few more luxurious foodstuffs, supply lines were too tenuous and shipments always too small or spoiled for habitants to rely upon external sources for grain and meat. Colonists accused merchants who exported flour from France of shipping inedible and short-measured supplies. The Illinois country also proved to be an unreliable source of wheat for the colonists downriver. Therefore, Indian villages and colonial settlements within the lower valley came to depend upon a regional network of

---

[2] Bambara and Wolof refers to West African peoples who arrived as slaves during the eighteenth century.

exchange, in which food surpluses were periodically traded in bulk to areas in short supply, and smaller-scale transactions regularly occurred among Indians, settlers, and slaves.

The generous system of distributing land to settlers in Louisiana helped stimulate a domestic market in corn, rice, and other produce. In order to keep colonists in the colony and to encourage agriculture, France offered settlers moderately sized tracts of free land, usually with five arpents of river frontage and forty arpents deep from the bank (200 square arpents or 170 acres). "A man with his wife or his partner," wrote Father Paul du Poisson in 1727, "clears a little ground, builds himself a house on four piles, covers it with sheets of bark, and plants corn and rice for his provisions; the next year he raises a little more for food, and has also a field of tobacco; if at last he succeed[s] in having three or four Negroes, then he is out of his difficulties. This is what is called a habitation, a habitant; but how many of them are as nearly beggars as when they began!" Settlers who failed to make their habitation productive depended upon food shared by kin or distributed through the market, while those who succeeded in farming maintained a diversity of crops that helped minimize their dependency upon the export-import economy.

The presence of numerous military personnel in the region and the fact that about 25 percent of Louisiana's colonial populace lived in New Orleans by mid-century especially stimulated cross-cultural food marketing. Corn, game, and other provisions consumed at interior posts like Natchitoches and Tombecbé came from neighboring Indian villagers who bartered for such trade goods as metalware, brandy, and cloth either directly with the soldiers or more formally through their officers. The government also purchased large quantities of grain for its troops from settlers along the Mississippi River. The Choctaws not only sold foodstuffs to the garrison stationed at Fort Tombecbé, beginning in 1736, but also carried corn, vegetables, and poultry to the Mobile market.

New Orleans and Mobile benefited from food crops and meats and even from such prepared items as persimmon bread, cornmeal, and bear oil that were sold by Indian communities in their vicinity. During the 1720s those Acolapissas, Chitimachas, and Houmas who had resettled closer to New Orleans continued to produce corn, fish, and game for city dwellers and travelers. On the Pearl River, between New Orleans and Biloxi, the Pensacolas, Biloxis, Pascagoulas, and Capinas furnished "an abundance of meat to all the

French who are near enough to trade for it." Of a group of Chaouachas who migrated from the lower Mississippi to the Mobile River outside the town of Mobile, Bienville declared that "their sole occupation is to produce corn by means of which they obtain from the French what they need." Other "*petite nations*"—the Alibamons, Biloxis, Pascagoulas, and Chahtas—migrated during the 1760s to the lower Mississippi, where they participated in riverside trade and the New Orleans market. In 1776 there were ten Indian villages, over 1,000 people altogether, interspersed among plantations along the Mississippi upriver between New Orleans and the mouth of the Red River.

Many of the several thousand African slaves shipped to Louisiana during the 1720s to expand commercial agriculture turned to small-scale cultivating and marketing of foodstuffs. As in other plantation colonies, the autonomous production and distribution of foodstuffs by slaves resulted from more than the economic interests of slaveowners. In addition to producing such export staples as tobacco, indigo, and timber, black Louisianians on both small and large grants of land, called *concessions*, grew food crops for their own consumption and occasionally for their owners to sell to other colonists. On their own time slaves attended to their personal subsistence needs and eating tastes. As director of a large plantation at Chapitoulas owned by the Company of the Indies (its population in 1731 included 230 slaves), Antoine Le Page du Pratz recognized this inclination and recommended that owners give "a small piece of waste ground" to their slaves, "engage them to cultivate it for their own profit," and purchase their produce "upon fair and just terms." He also prescribed this arrangement as an alternative to the dances and assemblies held by slaves on Sundays, where he suspected they traded stolen goods and plotted rebellion.

Afro-Americans became aggressive traders in the food market of Louisiana. Many slaves were sent from plantations to the towns of Mobile, New Orleans, Natchez, and Natchitoches to sell poultry, meats, vegetables, and milk on their owners' behalf. They also sold foodstuffs and other items independently of their owners whenever and wherever possible. Although the colonial government intermittently enforced regulations upon slave peddlers, requiring them by 1751 to carry written permits from their owners, the open marketing of goods by slaves benefited too many people to be forcibly prohibited during the first half of the eighteenth century. The limited self-determination for slaves that stemmed from the production and trading of food had several advantages. It helped owners to maintain their slaves at a level of subsistence minimizing hardship, death, and rebellion; it provided consumers with a larger quantity and wider array of foods than would otherwise have been available; and it gained for slaves some means of autonomy from their masters. From these circumstances in the marketplace, not to mention those in colonial kitchens, came the heavy African influence upon Louisiana's famous creole cuisine.

Many slaves moved food in and out of the market with great resourcefulness. Pilferage became a means of protest against slaveowners, of supplemental nutrition within the slave community, and even of escape from bondage. . . . Throughout the eighteenth century, small fugitive camps fed themselves from plantation herds and storehouses, traded leftovers with other slaves, and even channeled goods into the open market. The fifteen or more inhabitants of one camp, discovered behind the Bienvenu estate in 1781, survived by killing stray cattle, by growing patches of corn and vegetables, and by making "baskets, sifters and other articles made of willow," which slaves on a nearby plantation sold for them in New Orleans.

Most day-to-day pilferage on plantations and in towns occurred without much official notice, but cases in which theft led to arrest and prosecution reveal the variety of ways that slaves illicitly exchanged food with other Louisianians. After Alexandre Boré discovered one hundred chickens and five quarters of rice missing from his plantation at Cannes Bruslées in 1753, one of his many slaves was flogged into admitting that he had traded them away for tafia. The settler who bartered with him, one Faussier of Chapitoulas, was sentenced to pay fifty livres indemnity to Boré as well as a fine of one hundred livres. Meanwhile, the pilferer managed to break his chains, steal a gun, and flee into the forest. On June 3, 1782, a twenty-six-year-old slave named Juan was arrested in New Orleans; his interrogation disclosed an ambitious flight financed by theft. He crossed Lake Pontchartrain to the city after raking from his owner a pirogue, a gun and ammunition, a shirt, and some sweet potatoes. On the way he stole turkeys and hens from the De La Chaise plantation and, after selling them in New Orleans, stole five more hens from a courtyard in town. Juan sold the hens to a Frenchman named La Rochelle for cash, with which he had intended to buy gunpowder.

Farmers as well as slaves from the surrounding countryside brought grains, vegetables, fruits, and poultry to the multiethnic market at New Orleans. German immigrants who settled above the city during the 1720s, numbering about fifty families in 1726, became a notable group of food provisioners. "They bring every day to the market," observed one contemporary, "all kinds of produce to the city." When raids by Choctaw rebels caused them to flee from the "German Coast" to the city in 1748, New Orleans became, as Gov. Philippe de Rigaud de Vaudreuil reported, "deprived of the comforts that those settlers provided for it by their industry and their thrift." These very independent farmers, who eventually returned to their settlement, were later joined by Acadian refugees who settled just north of them and proved especially active in growing corn and rice for the colonial market. Many French, free Negro, and Canary Island families also provisioned the New Orleans vicinity from their gardens and fields. While individual transactions were usually small, collectively they amounted to a substantial volume of provisions. In August 1770, Spanish officials complained that New Orleans was suffering corn and rice shortages because upriver farmers found it more profitable to sell their produce to the English in West Florida. The marketing of both food and deerskins defied trade barriers that were being raised by officials along new political boundaries.

Venison, wild fowl, and other products of hunting, fishing, and gathering made up another set of widely marketed foods. Slaves hunted, fished, and collected edible plants both for their own use and for their owners' kitchens. The Houma, Chitimacha, and other Indian communities dispersed among the plantations, as noticed by Bernard Romans in the 1770s, "serve as hunters, and for some other laborious uses, something similar to subdued tribes in New England." Within the colonial towns lived professional hunters and fishermen who like Aougust Savan, a free mulatto of New Orleans, supported their families by selling food on the levees and streets. In 1770 a traveler observed that along Lake Pontchartrain behind New Orleans, at the mouth of Bayou St. John, there were "Fishermen and Fowlers and when unemploy'd in that Business they gather Wood & burn it into Charcoal." During the winter months Indian villagers dispersed into small hunting camps of ten or so families. . . . These Indian camps, spread along the Alabama, Mississippi, and Red river drainages, were principally occupied with producing for the deerskin trade, but they rarely neglected to exchange venison, bear meat, and tallow for am-munition, cloth, and drink with settlers and travelers whom they encountered during the hunting season.

For a long time domestic beef was scarce and expensive in Louisiana; early attempts to build herds from imported livestock proved fruitless. But a regional network of cattle trading gradually developed and, like other kinds of food exchange and the deerskin trade, involved extensive interethnic participation. In the 1720s French traders and Indian villagers around Natchitoches began moving horses and cattle eastward, down the Red River. The Caddoes, expe-rienced horsemen since the mid-seventeenth century, when Spanish livestock herded by other Indians began to reach their villages, exchanged cattle and horses with the French and other Indians. The Tunicas and Avoyelles, situated near the junction of the Red and Mississippi rivers, became important middle-men in the livestock trade; Le Page du Pratz praised the latter group "for the services they have done the colony by the horses, oxen, and cows they have brought from New Mexico." The amount of beef available to Louisianians was increasing by the mid-eighteenth century, and some settlers were operating meat and dairy farms at Pointe Coupée, Barataria, and other places near New Orleans. By 1766 the average number of cattle on each farm along the lower Mississippi River was approaching fourteen head. Meanwhile the settlement of Bayou Teche by Acadian farmers also expanded the livestock trade. Along with Atakapa and Opelousa Indians in southwest Louisiana, Acadians acquired cattle from the Trinity River area and started raising their own herds on open grazing lands.

Slaves participated in this livestock network as drovers, herders, and dairy producers. When Joseph LeKintrek and Daniel Bopfé formed a livestock-raising partnership at the German settlements in 1741, seven of LeKintrek's slaves—three men, two women, and two children—accompanied his cattle to the new *vacherie*, where they also tended sheep, hogs, and poultry. In 1783, when New Orleans merchant Jean Baptiste Macarty purchased 180 head of oxen from the settlement of Atakapas, he employed a crew of one Indian, one Negro slave, and a few whites to drive and ferry the animals over the tricky drainage of the Atchafalaya Basin. As in the case of hunting and peddling foodstuffs, bringing beef to the colonial market provided slaves with greater freedom of movement and closer contact with colonists and Indians than existed in plantation labor.

IV

The participation of Indian villagers, black slaves, and white colonists in fur and food marketing discloses closer interaction and greater cultural exchange among them than historians of colonial regions have generally portrayed. In this respect, trade in the lower Mississippi Valley generated economic roles and ethnic relations similar in flexibility and fluidity to those recently discovered for blacks in early South Carolina and Virginia. Clearly, Indians did not just hunt, blacks did not just grow crops for export, and whites did not merely choose to become either subsistence farmers or staple planters. However, a complex of forces circumscribed economic and ethnic relations and minimized the leveling potential of frontier exchange. The institution of slavery, European class divisions, racism, colonial policy, and violent conflict all contributed to the building of racial barriers in Louisiana and West Florida, especially after the demographic scale tipped unfavorably for Indians. The transformation of the lower Mississippi Valley into an agricultural export economy, which accelerated during the last quarter of the eighteenth century, further intensified the hierarchical stratification of both race and class.

Changes in the deerskin trade implemented by Spain after 1783 signaled that the network of frontier exchange stitched by inhabitants over the previous decades was beginning to ravel. Indians of the large interior nations, who had close ties to many traders, entered this period with high expectations of further commerce. Following the withdrawal of Great Britain from West Florida, the Choctaws, Chickasaws, and Upper Creeks negotiated new trade tariffs with the Spanish government in June 1784. The deerskin trade, however, rapidly slipped under the control of a few merchant houses. The English firm of Panton, Leslie and Company, with Spanish authorization, began to monopolize trade with Indian villages east of the Mississippi. On the other side of the river, Natchitoches traders and settlers likewise gave way to better-financed and more-organized merchants. Accelerated commercialization of the frontier exchange economy inexorably upset its traditional customs and patterns. Most notably, traders carried ever-larger quantities of rum into Indian villages, the distribution of gifts occurred less often, and the tribes fell into chronic debt to merchant houses and thereby became more vulnerable to pressure against their land.

Sheer demographic force explains the gradual marginalization of Indians in the regional food market. As settlers increased in number and grew their own crops, the volume and variety of foodstuffs provided by Indian communities declined. Scattered bands of Louisiana Indians concentrated on bartering venison and bear oil with travelers and settlers mostly during winter months. The declining political power and economic importance of Indians also manifested itself in the formal sphere of relations, where gifts of food had customarily bound parties into a reciprocal relationship. A reduction in the level of inter-colonial rivalry for Indian allegiance after 1783 diminished the willingness of Louisiana officials to share food with visiting Indians. Food thus became more strictly a market commodity just as the role of Indians in the marketplace was diminishing. Indians responded to this breakdown in food-giving protocol by committing acts of banditry against the livestock and crops of settlers.

The role of slaves in food exchange was threatened by general changes in the region's economy. By the 1780s a large number of people in New Orleans had become professional peddlers or *marchands* who bought foodstuffs from producers and resold them to consumers. Increasing commercialization and the growing volume of trade made traditional price tariffs issued by the government less effective. "The peddlers are moving around in different parts of the City," reported the Cabildo, "and their wares cannot be inspected by the officials and for this reason they sell the goods as well as the spoiled commodities at an arbitrary price so they will not lose anything in their business." Accordingly, in September 1784 the government established a marketplace and required food marchands, both free and slave, to rent stalls. Slaves sent daily to sell "vegetables, milk, wild fowl, quartered venison and mutton" for their owners continued "to enjoy the liberty to sell their commodities in the City as they did before." Farmers bringing their own produce to town were allowed to sell directly to the public for three hours, after which their goods had to be sold at wholesale to the licensed traders. The formation of an institutionalized marketplace in New Orleans, with fees to be paid and goods closely watched, contributed to the gradual relegation of black producers and peddlers to a subordinate status in the food market. Without either an owner's permit or an official license, slaves found it more difficult to trade openly. One visitor to New Orleans in 1797 observed that blacks vended "to raise a scanty pittance" from small stalls located between the levee and the first row of houses. But he found that most "were obliged to account to the master for the profits of the day."

By the end of the eighteenth century, the frontier exchange network was rapidly being superseded by the commercial production of cotton and sugar. Even so, people living in the region did not wholly relinquish older forms of economic exchange. Even after the large tribes of the deep South were removed, Indians continued to peddle foodstuffs and other goods along the Mississippi and in Mobile, Natchez, and New Orleans. Hundreds of Louisiana Indians—Choctaws, Houmas, Chitimachas, Tunicas, and others—camped on the outskirts of New Orleans, usually during the late winter, and peddled in the city an array of foods and food-related items: venison, water fowl, and other game; such manufactures as baskets, sieves, and cane blowguns; and kindling wood, wild fruits, medicinal herbs, and such culinary spices as filé, a powder ground from sassafras leaves and used by Louisianians to make filé gumbo. Indian families also seasonally traveled Louisiana's waterways during the nineteenth century, trading the same kinds of goods with both planters and slaves.

Afro-Americans resorted to surreptitious forms of exchange to compensate for their deteriorating trade opportunities. In violation of ordinances adopted in the early nineteenth century by the Orleans and Mississippi territories, many residents continued to exchange goods with slaves as well as Indians. Some of the very middlemen whose appearance marked the marginalization of slaves in the food market were willing to buy items from them. Peddlers called *cabateurs*, who traveled the waterways in pirogues and bought all kinds of produce for the New Orleans market, became infamous for their illicit trade with slaves. They were frequently accused of encouraging Negroes to steal from their owners, but pilferage by slaves had long been part of their resistance and survival under bondage. Observing the plight of the marketer who was also treated as marketable property, Charles Robin aptly explained why slaves bartered with caboteurs: "True, the Negroes do have chickens and pigs of their own, but they can sell nothing without the permission of their masters. It is better for both the buyer and seller to do without permission."

Economic life in the lower Mississippi Valley during the eighteenth century, in which many later subsistence activities and adaptive strategies were rooted, evades historians who seek only strong commercial institutions and growing export values for their evidence. Within an extensive network of coastal towns and interior posts stretching from the Alabama River to the Red River, the region's inhabitants participated in a cross-cultural web of economic relations. When one follows the movement of deerskins and foodstuffs through this network, the importance of small-scale trade among diverse groups of people comes into focus. Louisiana was indeed an extraordinary North American colony, imposing even less demographic and commercial pressure upon the continent than did French Canada. But the backcountry of England's Atlantic seaboard provinces, as well as Canada and New Mexico, also passed through a long period of frontier exchange. The form and content of interethnic relations discussed here, and made more visible by Louisiana's history, can be profitably explored at the obscure crossroads and marketplaces of other colonial regions.

Questions

1. Usner uses the term "frontier exchange economy" throughout his essay. What is the "frontier exchange economy," and why is it significant?
2. What effects did the relatively slow growth of European and African populations during the first half of the eighteenth century have on the relations between those groups and American Indians in the lower Mississippi Valley?
3. What were the cultural and economic effects of the deerskin and food-stuff trades?
4. What effects did the end of the "frontier exchange economy" have on slaves, American Indians, and Europeans in Louisiana?

THE MORAL CLIMATE
OF FRENCH COLONIAL LOUISIANA,
1699–1763

by Carl A. Brasseaux

Throughout the period of french rule in Louisiana (1699–1763), Catholic missionaries were consistently unsuccessful in their efforts to dictate the colony's moral values. Indeed, clerics repeatedly lamented [*sorrowed*] that their European- and Canadian-born parishioners had little regard for their religious message, and even less respect for the dignity traditionally accorded their station in France. Because of the impotence of the traditional arbiters [*empowered per.*] of morality, the moral tone of French Louisiana was initially determined by Canadian immigrants who constituted the backbone of early colonial society. These settlers brought to Louisiana a social and cultural heritage markedly different from that of their French confreres. These differences stemmed in part from the frontier environment of New France, which afforded colonists far greater personal freedom than was accorded their counterparts in the mother country, and partly from their intimate association with Indians. In the seventeenth century, Canadians were in almost constant contact with Native Americans, and, as William J. Eccles has noted, it is thus "hardly surprising that the Canadians early adopted much of the Indian way of life and became imbued with some of their characteristics." [*QUOTE ↑*]

The result was a socio-cultural metamorphosis of New France society. Many young Canadians of the late seventeenth century preferred the life of

Originally published in *Louisiana History: The Journal of the Louisiana Historical Association* 27 (Winter 1986): 27–41. Used by permission of the Louisiana Historical Association.

fur traders in the wilderness, "where their parents, the *curés*, and the [government] officials could not govern them," to the *habitant's* mundane and ordered existence. The wilderness, however, offered other liberties unavailable in church-dominated New France. According to Jesuit missionaries, when not engaged in fur trading, which actually occupied only a small portion of their time, hundreds of *voyageurs* annually devoted the bulk of their energies to travelling "drinking, gambling and lechery." Indeed, quick to exploit the Indians' relative promiscuity, these adventurers—many of whom were married to white Canadiennes—reportedly employed Indian women instead of men on trading expeditions because of their willingness to work for lower wages, to perform menial tasks, and to gratify the Canadians less utilitarian needs.

The example of the uninhibited traders effectively undermined the efforts of Catholic missionaries to impose upon the natives the asceticism of Counter-Reformation Catholicism. Though outraged, the beleaguered priests found themselves unable to curb effectively the excesses of the Christian renegades. In the wilderness areas of the Mississippi Valley frequented by these adventurers at the dawn of the eighteenth century, missionaries lacked all but moral authority over the *coureurs des bois*, who had abandoned their own moral code for the Indians' relatively permissive mores, and, when they attempted to use this authority to guide the wayward Catholics, priests found their admonitions to reform held little persuasive power. In fact, not only did these Canadians openly live "in debauchery" with women of friendly tribes, but they also raided indiscriminately villages to "obtain slave concubines." Some coureurs des bois also worked to discredit the missionaries in the eyes of their potential Indian converts, thereby extinguishing the religious threat to the frontiersmen's way of life.

The example of the coureurs des bois was not lost upon the early Louisiana colonists, with whom they were in frequent contact. Indeed, the young Canadians deposited at Biloxi by Iberville in 1699–1700 quickly emulated their role models when thrust into the frontier setting of the French Gulf Coast. Father Paul du Ru, writing in March 1700, complained that the Biloxi Canadians, who grudgingly attended his services, were "boisterous" and disrupted Mass. Such sacrilegious demonstrations soon paled by comparison to subsequent improprieties as the French elements of the colonial population were seduced by the promiscuous moral climate established by the Canadians. Canadians and their French confreres exhibited what was, in the opinion of many Louisiana clerics and administrators, an unhealthy interest in Indian women. The soldiers' preoccupation with *les sauvagesses*, however, could hardly have been surprising to anyone, as Biloxi was a backwater military outpost populated primarily by bachelors from 1699 until 1704, when twenty-two French girls were dispatched to Louisiana at the insistence of colonial officials. This influx failed to satisfy the garrison's need for women, and those soldiers fortunate enough to find French brides soon had cause to regret their decision, for their mates often proved not only homely, but also prone to constant nagging about frontier conditions. Leery of the consequences of domesticity, many members of the garrison remained bachelors, and these men—officers and enlisted men alike—seized upon any opportunity to visit friendly Indian villages.

Trappers, who appeared at intervals in Biloxi and, after 1702, in Mobile, quickly exploited the soldiers' continuing demand for female companionship by establishing a black-market trade in sauvagesses seized in the interior and sold to members of the garrison as slaves. By 1710, the acquisition of female slaves had become so pervasive, and the sexual exploitation of the Indian women so flagrant that Commandant Jean-Baptiste Le Moyne de Bienville and Commissaire Nicolas de La Salle, who could agree on nothing else, both insisted that the colonial ministry send French women as brides for the garrison's numerous bachelors. But no ministerial action was immediately forthcoming, and the abuse continued.

When twelve girls, entrusted to the care of Mme. Antoine de La Mothe Cadillac finally reached Louisiana aboard the *Baron de La Fauche* in 1712—the first of several projected shipments of *des jeunes filles de bonnes familles*—Louisiana officials anticipated the establishment of a more stable society, in which familial responsibilities would force *les colons* to settle down and become productive citizens. Such was not to be the case, however. The prospective brides were not only unattractive, but they had also acquired a rather dubious reputation upon landing, as rumors of their seduction by the ship's officers and passengers circulated throughout Mobile. Only three are reported to have found husbands. This incident, and the waning economic fortunes of colonial proprietor Antoine Crozat, prevented the continued immigration of French women into the predominantly male settlement.

Frontier values thus continued to prevail in the tiny Louisiana colony, much to the chagrin of the provincial clergy. Venting his frustration in a

lengthy memoir to the colonial ministry, Father Henry de La Vente, the pastor
at Old Mobile, noted in 1713 or 1714 that

> the principal source of the public and habitual lack of religion in which
> they have languished for so long is not being able to . . . , or not want-
> ing to bind oneself to any woman through a legitimate marriage. They
> prefer to maintain scandalous concubinages with young Indian women,
> driven by their proclivity for the extremes of licentiousness. They have
> bought them under the pretext of keeping them as servants, but actually
> to seduce them, as they in fact have done.

Pregnancies frequently resulted from these illicit unions, and, according
to one observer, many parents strangled their half-breed infants, apparently
to avoid detection by the civil authorities, who frowned upon miscegenation.

The problem of Indian concubinage was soon overshadowed by the influx
of several hundred French criminals brought to Louisiana by forced immigration between 1711and 1720. The most conspicuous of the approximately
1,300 deportees were 160 prostitutes and 96 teenaged débauchées from Paris's
La Salpêtrière house of correction for women; by 1721, this group had come
to constitute 21 percent of the colony's female population. Though some of
these women found husbands in the colony and settled down to productive
lives, becoming, in the process, the matriarchs of prominent Louisiana "first
families," many of these débauchées reverted to their only means of gainful employment to support themselves in the colony. Prostitution was nothing new to
Louisiana, but it had been confined to isolated cases, such as a Frenchwoman
on Dauphin Island who, Cadillac noted in 1716, "sells herself to all comers,
the Indians just like the whites." The impact of the former inmates from the
maison de force, however, was felt throughout lower Louisiana. Indeed, soon
after their arrival, the problem of Indian concubinage vanishes from administrative correspondence, and never again would it create a moral controversy
in the colony, despite the dramatic growth of Louisiana's garrison after 1717.

This is not to say that Indian concubinage became a mere memory. To
the contrary, enslaved concubines remained a fixture at such frontier posts as
Fort Tombecbé and Natchitoches. Nor was interracial concubinage confined
to isolated military garrisons. Louisiana's experiment with Indian slavery had

proved largely unsuccessful by 1720, prompting the colony's proprietary government to seek a new labor source. In the more rapidly developing areas of the colony where Frenchmen displaced the local Indian population, particularly the emerging plantation area immediately above and below New Orleans, African slaves, whose arrival coincided with that of the white deportees, supplanted their native American counterparts. The pattern of exploitation of African women in the agrarian settlements paralleled closely that of Indian women by frontier garrisons, and, by 1763, the colony contained a significant and rapidly growing mulatto population. These abuses, however, were rarely reported, because the agrarian and military posts were generally commanded by bachelors who often shared the guilt of their subordinates.

Far more conspicuous were the public displays of debauchery in the capital and major posts. Scandals were so widespread and so disruptive that Louisiana officials, at the insistence of clerics, attempted unsuccessfully to establish a *maison de force* (house of detention) at New Orleans. Public promiscuity was symptomatic of the instability of the many loveless marriages of convenience forged in the colony. Broken marriages were unknown in Louisiana prior to 1719, but in the 1720s and 1730s they became commonplace, despite the efforts of some priests to settle amicably domestic quarrels. In suits for separation, promiscuity, dissoluteness, and physical abuse figured prominently as legal grievances. When plaintiffs were able to substantiate their charges, which was generally the case, the colonial judiciary consistently approved requests for the separation of bed and board, and the ease with which these suits could be prosecuted and won by disgruntled spouses further undermined the social institution upon which Louisiana's continued development hinged.

The flurry of suits to dissolve marriages in the colony is an accurate barometer of the lax moral climate in frontier Louisiana society. In the austere religious climate of late seventeenth- and early eighteenth-century France, Frenchmen of the lower social orders—from which the vast majority of Louisiana's colonists were drawn—were compelled to attend Mass on Sunday, to conform to the prevailing standards of church decorum, and to pay homage to the local priest. . . .

[Such compulsion] suggests moderate religious apathy among the common Frenchmen, and the criminal background of thousands of forced emigrants to the Mississippi Valley reveals an even stronger disregard for the precepts of the Church. When transported to an area in which the clergy maintained only a shadowy presence, these transplanted French Catholics felt free to exhibit their formerly suppressed feelings toward the Church. Indeed, Louisiana immigrants quickly discovered that traditional moral constraints (particularly peer pressure and the threat of arrest by self-righteous officials) did not exist on the Franco-American frontier, and many French men and women consequently practiced only selective adherence to traditional, or "official" morality. It is thus hardly surprising that common law and bigamous unions were widespread, even among the social elite. . . . Mme. Baudin, wife of the government storekeeper at Balise, created a scandal by her extramarital affairs "with several officers" at the post. Charles D'Arensbourg, commandant at Côte des Allemands, publicly maintained a concubine despite the opposition of the Church.

As in the case of D'Arensbourg, the admonitions of the clergy were generally ignored. The Church's lack of influence in early Louisiana stemmed from a combination of factors. First, the Catholic mission was chronically understaffed. Second, the very modest administrative stature of the vicars general, who constituted the leading religious officials in Louisiana until the 1790s, effectively limited the amount of influence that the Church could exert on local civil functionaries. Third, the moral fiber of the priests themselves was often suspect, as seen in the child sired by Father St. Cosme and Father Beaubois's attempts to seduce Governor Etienne Périer's pretty French-born *domestique* while administering the sacrament of confession. Moreover, Louisiana's vicar general acknowledged, in 1725, that many priests sent to Louisiana had been "interdicted in their [respective French] dioceses and had fled to Louisiana to avoid punishment for their disorderly lives." The clerics' serious character flaws tended to diminish the Church's moral authority in the eyes of the colonists. Fourth, throughout the period of French colonization, the clergy was far more concerned with its creature comforts, material possessions, and political prestige than with its spiritual mission. Priests rarely ventured from the security of their presbytères and thus Catholics in all but the most densely populated posts lacked religious services. Finally, the Louisiana missionaries generally viewed their assignment to Louisiana as a most distasteful form of exile and, soured by their personal frustrations, these clerics developed abrasive personalities which alienated many of their parishioners.

Most colonists consequently were at least apathetic, if not openly hostile, toward the clergy. In the first decades of Louisiana's existence, clerics encountered a remarkable lack of enthusiasm among the colonists for church construction. Churches at old Mobile, Dauphin Island, and New Orleans were either not completed or delayed because of popular apathy. No church was built in New Orleans, for example, until nine years after the post's establishment. During the interim, however, numerous cabarets and billiard halls had been erected, and they flourished to such an extent that the bulk of the town's population assembled at these establishments instead of the church services held in makeshift quarters. Nor would attendance improve after construction of St. Louis Church. Commenting upon the situation, Mother Tranchepain noted in 1728 that, in the colony, "religion is little known and practiced even less."

It was difficult for the priests to exercise any moral authority when the churches were empty. Ecclesiastical sources indicate that only half of the Catholics living in proximity to the colonial churches actually made their Easter duties, and extant documents also imply that a far smaller number of parishioners attended Sunday services. Indeed, Father Raphaël complained in 1725 that there was practically "no difference between the holy days of obligation and Sundays and work days, between Lent and Carnival, [between] the Easter season and the rest of the year." This situation would persist throughout the French period. The numerous military and economic crises faced by the colony in succeeding years should have constrained many Louisiana Catholics to seek solace in religion, particularly in the chaotic war years of the 1750s and 1760s; yet, after 1725, church attendance declined steadily. This is not to suggest, however, that Catholics were remiss in observing the sacraments deemed necessary by their faith for salvation. Baptismal and marriage registers particularly are replete with entries in all French colonial-era parishes along the Gulf Coast. Yet, the fact remains that between 1699 and 1763, the Church failed to attract a majority of parishioners within commuting distance of chapels to compulsory weekly services.

Many of those who attended Church services were hardly more pious than those who frequented the taverns on Sundays. Attorney General François Fleuriau, his wife, and the wife of Superior Council member Perry ran afoul of the clergy for laughing and creating a disturbance in church. After repeated warnings from the church warden and himself, Father Hyacinthe, the officiating priest, ordered Fleuriau and his companions to leave church. The women refused to leave; other members of the congregation rose to denounce the priest; and Fleuriau "arose in anger and commanded the Father to shut up and continue the Mass, upbraiding him loudly in church for what he styled affectation." In another episode, the officers of the colonial garrison, who had been relegated to the choir loft by the rental of pews by the New Orleans pastor, demanded that pews be provided their wives in the front of church, as befitted their status. When the priest refused, the officers "chased him into the church and pursued him even into the very sanctuary, raising a scandalous tumult in these sacred precincts. . . ." Intimidated by their effrontery, the pastor conceded one pew, but the officers, still dissatisfied, moved the lectern from its customary side of the altar to the opposite end of the sanctuary just before Mass over the next several weeks to torment their nemesis.

The clergy was hardly content with this state of affairs, but they lacked the administrative machinery to alter the situation. The colony's secular leaders, moreover, were not always sympathetic to the wishes of Church officials, who often were less than diplomatic. Father La Vente created a sensation in Old Mobile by refusing to permit Bienville, the acting colonial commander, to serve as a child's godparent because of his alleged misconduct with a recently arrived Frenchwoman; the missionary then submitted to the humiliated commandant his proposals for dealing with the problem of Indian concubines. It is hardly necessary to note that La Vente's plan was never implemented.

Even Cadillac, Bienville's moralistic successor, appears to have been alienated by the colonial clergy, and though he paid lip service to the church's ideals, he made no genuine effort to alter the colony's lax moral climate. Finally, Father Raphaël de Luxembourg, the zealous Capuchin superior in the 1720s, attempted to browbeat members of the colonial council into promulgating regulations designed to curb the excesses of the secular population. Raphaël's efforts met with a singular lack of success until his appeals to France created a demand for change from the directors of Louisiana's proprietary company. As a consequence, in 1725 and 1727, the Superior Council, Louisiana's chief judicial and quasi-legislative body, adopted ordinances prohibiting talking in church during Mass, gambling and drinking in cabarets during divine services, and requiring pregnant women to file an official declaration regarding their condition with the nearest judicial officer. These ordinances merely succeeded in placating the irrepressible Father Raphaël, but, because of their lax enforcement, did nothing to resolve the colony's festering moral issues. In fact, despite the moralistic image projected by Governor Périer in the late 1720s, the colonial government did not attempt to reform local society until after Louisiana's retrocession to the Crown in 1731.

Pursuant to the wishes of the colonial ministry, Bienville, who assumed command of Louisiana for the third time in 1732, and *Commissaire-ordonnateur* Edme Salmon launched an official crusade in 1733 to rehabilitate the colonial population. Chevalier de Louboey was officially reprimanded for his scandalous affair with Mme Garnier. Then Salmon, who observed that the common Louisianian was a drunkard and gambler "who spent on Sunday all of the money he had earned during the week," pushed through the Superior Council measures banning all forms of gambling and prohibiting the sale of liquor at the times of divine services. Though these ordinances, like their predecessors, were subject to lax enforcement, the show of resolve on the part of the Crown, and particularly the disciplinary action taken against Louboey, forced the general population to exercise greater discretion in their indiscretions.

This is not to suggest that Louisiana's moral climate changed substantially after 1733. While it is true that conservative agricultural communities based on traditional European morals emerged in Mobile and on the German Coast and other river settlements near the colonial capital (though even here scandals were not unknown among prominent French families), frontier morality continued to flourish throughout French Louisiana. The numerous marriages to legitimize children of townspeople, the many suits for separation, and scores of administrative reports indicate that sexual promiscuity continued unabated, though less conspicuously. Soldiers dispatched to the frontier openly engaged in debauchery with Indian women and, less frequently, with white women in isolated posts. French military agents among the Southeastern Indians were notorious for "raping" Indian women, and, indeed, the Vaudreuil Papers strongly suggest that the deterioration of Franco-Choctaw relations stemmed directly from soldiers' sexual crimes. According to Chief Tatoulimataha (Red Shoe's brother) the anti-French activities of his sibling in the mid-1740s were precipitated by broken French promises and the provocative behavior of Gallic "chiefs [officers] and other Frenchmen . . . who behaved badly towards them [Choctaw chiefs] and their wives."

The sexual exploits of French military personnel in the field were apparently matched by those of the soldiers in the New Orleans garrison. Despite the government's moralistic policies, royal physicians were compelled to open a hospital at New Orleans for victims of venereal diseases in the late 1730s. This institution closed apparently by 1740; however, it was resuscitated in 1756 as other venereal strains were introduced into Louisiana by new recruits in 1751–1752, and by virtue of the soldiers' libertinage they spread to epidemic proportions.

The recruits of the early 1750s created other problems in Louisiana. Gambling, for example, had been a problem of long standing in the colony. As early as 1723, the Superior Council had banned all games of chance involving sums in excess of 100 livres. Additional regulations were promulgated in 1725, and gambling was prohibited altogether in 1733 and again in 1744. As the repeated issuance of these regulations indicates, gambling was never driven entirely from the colony; indeed, by the early 1750s, gaming tables were publicly displayed in New Orleans. But gambling was not considered a major problem until after 1753. By 1753, small fortunes were being won and lost at faro tables in New Orleans. Responding to public complaints Governor Louis Billouart de Kerlérec made a concerted effort to close the "gambling dens" located "in all parts of the city," but, because the gamblers, including many prominent military officers, "never play[ed] two consecutive nights in the same place" and because of vocal public opposition, he was unsuccessful. He therefore attempted, but failed, to beat them at their own game by opening a government-run casino at New Orleans during the carnival season.

In addition to patronizing the illicit New Orleans gambling dens, the French recruits of the 1750s—primarily "professional deserters" arrested in France and exiled to Louisiana—were so given to "unrestrained debaucheries of liquor and women" that Governor Kerlérec, writing during the Seven Years' War, considered his garrison "more dangerous to the colony than the enemy itself." The many *libertins* in the garrison obtained their liquor and apparently prostitutes from a large, ostensibly unemployed class of *gens sans avoue* in New Orleans. Composed of the aging male forced immigrants of the 1720s, these individuals operated for decades unlicensed "cabarets" in "the rear of the City." Usually working under cover of darkness, these black market distributors of wine and *guildive* also plied their trade among Indians and slaves, who often

THE MORAL CLIMATE OF FRENCH COLONIAL LOUISIANA, 1699–1763   35

stole articles from townspeople to barter for liquor. When the garrison was withdrawn from Louisiana in 1763, the latter groups became the dealers' principal market, and the shift in emphasis produced an unprecedented rash of burglaries in New Orleans. Reacting to the problem in typical fashion, the Superior Council adopted an ordinance summarily banishing the culprits, but, as usual, no effort was made to enforce the decree.

The fact that the forced immigrants of the 1720s would figure so prominently in the last major moral controversy of the French period clearly reflects the persistence of the permissive moral climate established at the dawn of Louisiana colonization. Embracing the moral code forged in the wilderness by coureurs des bois, Louisiana's independent, anticlerical, and hedonistic pioneers effectively resisted the limited moralizing influence of the Catholic clergy while creating a frontier society that reflected their newly acquired values. Their influence is seen most clearly in the rapid conversion of French immigrants to their way of life. Moreover, contrary to popular belief, these libertines and the less conspicuous male deportees had a lasting impact on colonial Louisiana. Indeed, the influx of hundreds of forced emigrants into Louisiana under the Law regime momentarily inundated the colony with persons of dubious moral fiber, and their presence in the colony seriously retarded the moderating influences that demographic growth and the concomitant expansion of governmental and religious authority would normally have had in the area. Indeed, the evidence suggests that this sociological maturation made significant strides only in the densely populated farming belt immediately above and below New Orleans and perhaps in Mobile, but, even in those areas, the emergence of a local mulatto population indicates that the population's sedate appearance was only superficial. In the other areas of the colony, including the capital, the colonists were only somewhat less discreet.

The pervasive colonial permissiveness was sustained by the limited influence and worldliness of the Catholic clergy. Rival orders feuded constantly over territorial rights and local ecclesiastical preeminence. Moreover, clerics rarely ventured from their presbytères, and, by the 1760s, they were devoting, according to their Spanish successors, an inordinate amount of time and energy to the administration of their large landed estates. Finally, the priests' lack of diplomacy in promoting their designs usually only succeeded in alienating their few genuine adherents. It is thus hardly surprising that the number of New Orleans Catholics attending Sunday Mass fell from less than 50 percent in the mid-1720s to under 25 percent at the end of French rule. The percentage of Catholics attending Church services on holy days of obligation was even smaller.

In the absence of moral constraints normally provided by the Catholic Church and reinforced by weekly homilies, a frontier morality developed as successive waves of Canadian and French soldiers and settlers deviated at will from traditional values. Irreligion was often manifested in criminality. Gambling, public drunkenness, and sexual promiscuity were commonplace in the colonial capital and all of the frontier posts in lower Louisiana and would remain so for decades after the departure of the colony's French garrison in 1763. The persistence of these problems reflects the pervasiveness of the region's frontier values among the civilian population. Thus, in terms of morality, Louisiana in 1763 differed little from the turbulent colony of 1723. . . .

Questions

1. Describe the "frontier morality" that emerged in French colonial Louisiana.
2. What were the peculiar circumstances that the frontier environment created that allowed for the creation of new social and cultural forms in a place like colonial Louisiana?
3. If most of the early colonists of the lower Mississippi Valley defined themselves as Catholics, why were Catholic clerics unable to exert moral authority over them? How would you say the relationship between clergy and laity differed then as compared to now?

OLIVER POLLOCK'S PLANTATIONS: AN EARLY ANGLO LANDOWNER ON THE LOWER MISSISSIPPI, 1769–1824

by Light T. Cummins

Oliver pollock provided timely assistance to the rebel cause as the congressional commercial agent at New Orleans during the American Revolution, thereby earning the historical reputation as the "Financier of the Revolution in the West." In 1776 and 1777, he shipped gunpowder from Spain and Cuba via the Mississippi River to George Washington's army. He also superintended the supply efforts which provisioned the expeditions of James Willing and George Rogers Clark. Although studies of his patriot efforts during the Revolution abound, no historian has heretofore examined in detail Pollock's personal business transactions in the Mississippi Valley. This article will survey the landholding career of Oliver Pollock as an Anglo merchant and planter who came to the region prior to the Revolution, who owned extensive lands in British and Spanish territory, and who retained these holdings under the subsequent rule of the United States. His experiences and activities in this regard were typical of a larger group of Anglo settlers who came to the lower Mississippi as landowners in the years prior to the Revolution. They were the vanguard of Anglo-American settlement in Spanish colonial Louisiana. . . .

[W]hen Oliver Pollock arrived in the lower Mississippi Valley during 1769, he carried with him citizenship as a subject of King George III and took full advantage of this status in West Florida. British West Florida and

Originally published in *Louisiana History: The Journal of the Louisiana Historical Association* 29 (Winter 1988): 35–48. Used by permission of the Louisiana Historical Association.

Spanish Louisiana shared a common boundary in the years between the Peace of Paris (1763) and the American Revolution, when the holdings of Great Britain thereafter became Spanish territory. Prior to the military conquests of Bernardo de Gàlvez in 1779, the east bank of the Mississippi north of the Iberville River (located between Baton Rouge and New Orleans) was part of British West Florida. The entire west bank of the Mississippi and the Isle of Orleans, which included the city, along with land on the east bank south of the lberville, belonged to Spain. To the British authorities in the West Florida capital of Pensacola, Pollock was, prior to the Revolution, only one of many Anglo merchant-planters trading along the Mississippi and Gulf coast except, unlike some of the others, he had been more fortunate in cultivating support and acceptance from the Spanish government at New Orleans.

During his business career in the region prior to the Revolution, Pollock received land grants from the West Florida authorities, operated plantations in English territory, later had some of his British titles confirmed by the Spanish after the revolt, and maintained these plantations until his death in 1824. In addition, various members of his family moved into the area and secured additional land. The Pollock family's landholding history in lower Louisiana seems to have been illustrative of other British-era proprietors who stayed in the region to live under the Spanish and then the American government. Indeed, Pollock's descendants continued to live on their holdings along the Mississippi River for generations. . . .

Pollock came to the Mississippi Valley in 1769 on the heels of the military expedition led by Spanish general Alejandro O'Reilly, who was sent to reassert Spain's control over Louisiana after the abortive governorship of Antonio de Ulloa. Pollock, representing the Philadelphia firm of Willing and Morris for whom he had been a correspondent for six years at Havana, clearly sought to curry favor with O'Reilly, an individual he had first met years before in Cuba. Pollock visited with O'Reilly on the Spanish flagship while it lay at anchor below New Orleans. Based on these discussions, O'Reilly, even before arriving in New Orleans, awarded Pollock a contract to supply the city with flour. This arrangement provided Pollock with the firm base upon which he established over the next few years a successful merchant house which operated both in Spanish Louisiana and British West Florida.

The Spanish government (especially under the regime of Luis de Unzaga) tolerated Anglo merchants like Pollock . . . because it had no alternative if the colony's economy were to continue functioning. These persons travelled freely between Spanish Louisiana and British West Florida. They imported needed commodities into Louisiana and insured capital migration into the Spanish province. . . . Pollock speedily opened a lucrative trade between the Mississippi Valley and Philadelphia via the Gulf of Mexico and Atlantic. In addition, he frequently travelled throughout West Florida and maintained a residence there as well, although he made his primary home in New Orleans where he operated a merchant house.

Between 1769 and 1775, Pollock received several major grants of land in British West Florida under the terms for awarding such to subjects of King George III. As well, he bought land from other British grantees who wished to sell. In all, he owned four large tracts of land in West Florida in addition to lots in several of the English towns. One of his earliest grants from the British government was made in 1769 for four hundred acres on the Tangipahoa River some thirteen miles north of Pass Manchac. Other than this grant, however, Pollock favored land on the Mississippi River because of its obvious financial value and geographic convenience to New Orleans. He secured two tracts from the British in this district: acreage immediately south of Baton Rouge upon which today stands part of the campus of Louisiana State University and a second holding on the east bank of the River across from Pointe Coupée. Both of these properties had improvements on them, including houses, and Pollock operated them as plantations during the British period.

During the early 1770s, Pollock also interested various of his business colleagues in securing lands in British West Florida. Robert Morris and Thomas Willing, the Philadelphia merchants for whom he served as corresponding agent, secured two grants on the Mississippi from authorities in Pensacola. Pollock organized these tracts as working plantations and hired a resident manager, Alexander Henderson, who operated them for the firm of Willing and Morris. Henderson had thirty-four slaves on these two tracts and successfully grew rice prior to the Revolution.

These plantations, located immediately adjacent to the river, were well suited to the method of rice cultivation employed on the lower Mississippi during this era. Their fields could be conveniently flooded by constructing a small system of levees. Rice was sown as bedding plants in time for the spring floods, the high water from which flowed into the paddies through diversion canals. After the water had stood for approximately two weeks, it was drained from the young plants into neighboring swampland by means of secondary ditches. Once the rice matured a second flooding from the river covered the crop until shortly before harvest time. Slaves then cut the rice with sickles, bound it into bundles, and thrashed it by hand. Although rice production satisfied the local market, it never became a significant crop because of the need for intensive labor and the limited amount of land suitable for growing it. In addition, many colonists considered it an inferior food reserved for slaves and the poorer classes. Nevertheless, the growers of rice found a steady market for it in New Orleans. Pollock served as financial manager for the Willing and Morris rice plantations, kept their accounts, and operated as their factor in New Orleans. By the mid-1770s, however, he fell into controversy with Henderson, the overseer. Both men accused the other of mismanagement and with falling rice prices, Thomas Willing attempted unsuccessfully to remove Pollock from active management in this venture.

Pollock found greater favor with members of the Willing family other than Thomas. James Willing, a younger brother of Morris's partner, became Pollock's most significant associate in Mississippi River plantations. Young Willing came to the region at Pollock's invitation. The New Orleans merchant had become convinced that the most important and potentially valuable land on the Mississippi between Baton Rouge and Natchez could be found at Tunica Bend. Here the river made a sharp turn where two bayous, Tunica and Spring, entered the Mississippi on the east bank. Moreover, the two small streams joined at the foot of a hill which was high enough to be safe from flooding. Land at Tunica Bend had early attracted the interest of various individuals who had passed through the region. Rufus Putnam visited the bayous in 1772 while on a trip through West Florida. He was most impressed with the site, which he noted in his journal would be the perfect location for a settlement. A later traveler described the area as "a rich and hospitable country." British grants made in the late 1760s deeded this area in two separate tracts to Henry Fairchild and General Frederick Haldimand. Pollock proposed to James Willing in 1772 that they create a partnership to purchase and develop this land.

Willing secured the hilly area along Spring Bayou from General Haldimand and, by late 1772, was engaged in the growing of rice and corn. He built a magazine on the high ground and opened a small trading post on the bank of the river. Pollock purchased the tract to the north along Tunica Bayou from

Henry Fairchild. Both partners built houses for themselves on the property, which was managed as one plantation. For a time during the late eighteenth century, Spring Bayou temporarily became known as Willing's Bayou, thereafter taking the name of Pollock's Bayou, a designation by which it is still known today. Pollock purchased Willing's land shortly before the outbreak of the Revolution and combined the tracts into one holding which eventually became known as the "Old Tunica Plantation." Here Pollock planted indigo and regularly made crops of rice, tobacco, and vegetables. Vessels passing on the Mississippi routinely stopped to purchase supplies and foodstuffs at the small trading post. A cousin from Pennsylvania, Hamilton Pollock, arrived in the mid-1770s to live at Tunica Bend and oversee the operation of the plantation. This arrangement would continue until his death in 1814 with the exception of a period during the 1780s when wartime debts removed the Pollock family from control of Old Tunica Plantation.

The plantation became locally known for its indigo crop. During the 1770s, in fact, the entire area along the river north of Baton Rouge became an important area for indigo production. The planters at Pointe Coupée, for example, made a total of 50,000 pounds of dyestuff in 1775 while most producers on both banks of the river had plantings which yielded at least seventy-five pounds of refined indigo per acre. Since indigo dye usually sold for a dollar per pound, this represented an attractive crop for most planters. In addition to Pollock and his plantations, the holdings of Isaac Monsanto, Maurice Conway, Benjamin Farrar, John McCarty, and Patrick MacNamara all produced large crops of the blue dye. Many Englishmen of the era, including the author Captain Philip Pittman, considered Mississippi Valley indigo to be superior in quality to that grown in the Carolinas and the West Indies. Old Tunica Plantation continued to prosper with this crop to the close of the Spanish period, although demand for the dyestuff outside Louisiana lessened by the end of the century because of Spain's restrictive trade laws.

By 1776, Oliver Pollock had thus emerged as one of the most prosperous merchants and landowners in the lower Mississippi Valley. He invested in lucrative ventures and had ample capital for various business transactions. From his base at New Orleans, he operated an extensive mercantile network and also bought real estate in Spanish territory. He purchased a house on present-day Royal Street in New Orleans at public auction in December 1777, reselling it to James Harris less than three months later. He also secured land during 1769 to the north of New Orleans in Spanish territory, including a tract which would in a later era, become part of Elmwood Plantation. The American Revolution changed for all time Pollock's economic position when he became the most prominent supporter of the rebel cause in the Mississippi Valley. He used the safe residence extended to him in Spanish territory by a succession of governors to support the Americans. In so doing, Pollock lost his own personal fortune in the process.

His landholdings in West Florida however, remained intact. In spite of the rebel activities of some West Floridians, the British apparently made no move to expropriate lands from pro-American partisans. The 1779 campaigns of Bernardo de Gálvez, at any rate, removed the British from the Mississippi and ended this risk. The Mississippi River district of British West Florida fell to Spanish control. Although Governor Gálvez did nothing to legitimize British land titles in Spanish law, all Anglo landowners who remained in the region retained at least de facto control of their properties until the policies of Governor Esteban Miró formulated between 1785 and 1787 permitted legal reconfirmation.

Financial losses caused by his support of the Americans, however, forced Oliver Pollock to return to the Atlantic Coast at the close of the Revolution and in the process, he lost many of his landholdings to creditors. By 1781, his personal debts in Louisiana had become considerable: he owed the Spanish government 74,087 *pesos* which had been borrowed in the name of the Continental Congress while he found himself in debt for an additional 29,440 pesos to various New Orleans residents. Pollock declared bankruptcy in early 1782 and liquidated many of his assets and personal possessions in an effort to satisfy his debts. By February of that year, he had assigned to individual creditors his slaveholdings, his residential property in New Orleans, and the Mississippi River lands near Baton Rouge and Pointe Coupée, while Old Tunica Plantation became the property of Carlos Trudeau. In late April of 1782, he left Louisiana and returned to the United States. He saw this trip as the only way by which he could personally lobby Congress to repay the loans he had negotiated in New Orleans on its behalf. His absence from Louisiana would last six years, take him to a Cuban prison, and have both Congress and the state of Virginia question his claims for reimbursement.

The period of Oliver Pollock's absence from the lower Mississippi Valley, however, did not mean that he was completely forgotten. Thomas Patterson had Pollock's general power of attorney in New Orleans and continued to negotiate disputes with the creditors. In addition the elder Daniel Clark acted as correspondent for Pollock in various business dealings directed from Cuba and the Atlantic Coast. Pollock maintained a credit account with Clark, whom he already owed money stemming from Revolutionary War debts. Having secured a partial repayment from Congress and Virginia, Pollock returned to Louisiana in 1788. He arrived in New Orleans shortly after the disastrous fire of that year. Taking advantage of increased demand for supplies needed for the rebuilding effort, Pollock sold building materials to local residents. He also convinced the Cabildo to make belated purchase of a pump fire engine which he had imported from Philadelphia. As well, Pollock engaged in trading slaves all along the river in order to generate additional capital. By May of 1790, he had settled all of his overdue accounts with the individual creditors at New Orleans, although he still owed money to the Spanish government.

The profits from these transactions permitted Pollock to begin buying land along the Mississippi once again. In the wake of the fire, he purchased several town lots in New Orleans and constructed houses on them which he sold at a profit. He also regained legal ownership of the Old Tunica Plantation in 1789 when he repurchased it from Trudeau. The cousin, Hamilton Pollock, returned to the plantation, immediately began a series of improvements, assembled a slave crew, and resumed agricultural production at Old Tunica. Oliver Pollock also purchased other plantation lands in the Feliciana district. He bought one thousand acres along Bayou Sara. As well, he sought reconfirmation of his earlier British title to the Tangipahoa River property under the terms of the 1785 decree. Other members of the Pollock family also secured property during the 1790s in the area as part of an Anglo-American influx into the region. Hamilton Pollock was granted one thousand acres on the southern part of Bayou Sara while Thomas Pollock, a nephew, secured a nearby tract. George Pollock, a distant cousin, received a large grant on the Amite River.

Although various family members remained in the area, Oliver Pollock returned to the United States in 1791, and there he lived for the next twenty-eight years. He first resided in Carlisle, Pennsylvania, and, after the death of his first wife, he moved to Baltimore, where he remarried. Old Tunica Plantation, however, continued as an important family asset, along with the lands owned by Hamilton, Thomas, and George Pollock. As well, shortly after the Louisiana Purchase, Pollock's eldest daughter Mary, her husband, Dr. Samuel S. Robinson, and their children moved to present-day Wilkinson County, Mississippi, a few miles north of Tunica Bend at a location then in the United States. They made frequent visits to the Old Tunica Plantation in Spanish Territory from their home in nearby Pinckneyville and, with the passing of Hamilton Pollock in 1814, they undertook management of the plantation. By this time, the "Florida Parishes" region of southeastern Louisiana had become heavily populated with Anglos and was in the process of breaking away from Spanish control. Cotton as well had become the major crop at Tunica Bend. The increasing volume of steamboat traffic on the river also provided the opportunity for additional profit. The Pollocks and Robinsons built a levee at the foot of Tunica Bayou and opened a woodyard.

Old Tunica Plantation eventually encompassed considerable improvements. A cluster of buildings stood along the north bank of Tunica Bayou on the eastern edge of the plantation, well away from the Mississippi River. Here could be found a modest home with ample open porches on both the front and back sides, a washhouse, a kitchen building, a log smokehouse, and related structures. The house at this location, still standing and today known as the Trudeau House, was built as a raised Creole cottage, although it mixed freely the architectural features of Spanish, French, and Anglo styles. Set on a large hill, it had a view of vessels passing on the river, while it was situated to take advantage of summer breezes on its wide galleries. The Robinson family, which included Pollock's daughter and grandchildren, resided temporarily in this home before establishing permanent resident in Pinckneyville. In 1813, the Pollock family sold the parcel of land upon which this complex stood to a neighbor, Phillip Alston, and concentrated their operations nearer to the river at the mouth of Tunica and Pollock bayous.

Along Pollock Bayou just east of the river could be found the overseer's quarters which were occupied by Hamilton Pollock from the 1790s until his death in 1814. This home, less opulent than the Trudeau House, had been constructed by Oliver Pollock prior to the American Revolution as his personal residence on the property. This building served as the plantation headquarters during Hamilton's lifetime and was surrounded by various slave cabins, cotton barns, and corncribs. A small group of buildings also existed at the site where the two bayous flowed into the Mississippi. A few lots at this location had been sold over the years to various individuals by the Pollocks, thereby creating a small, rude settlement known as "Viejo Tunica." This consisted of the general store and woodyard owned by the family, along with several private residences and related outbuildings. The Pollock family, in addition to engaging in planting directly, also rented parts of the plantation to various persons. In 1817, for example, Washington White, a local farmer, cultivated approximately eighteen acres of corn while Oliver Ratliff, another tenant, farmed a fifty-acre tract on the south side of the plantation. The Pollock family usually rented land for six dollars an acre in the late 1810s. The Tunica Bend district, of which the plantation was a part, along with the holdings of other planters in the area had become by this time one of the most populated stretches on the river between Baton Rouge and Natchez. As a traveler noted, the area was "a handsome settlement, extending about twelve miles along the east side of the river."

Oliver Pollock returned to the lower Mississippi in 1819 upon the death of his second wife and there he lived out the remaining years of his life. He maintained his legal residence at the Pinckneyville, Mississippi, home of his daughter. This town apparently had little to offer him. "Pinckneyville," as one observer of the period recorded, "is a straggling village of ten houses, mostly in decay, and some of them uninhabited. It has a little church, a tavern, a store, and a post office." Pollock therefore preferred to stay on the Old Tunica Plantation whenever possible. He also owned a home in nearby St. Francisville, where he occasionally resided.

Although a man in his eighties by the early 1820s, it seems that Pollock still had the inclinations of an entrepreneur. He and some of his children laid elaborate plans for the development of a major townsite on the plantation where Bayou Tunica entered the Mississippi. His heirs continued these efforts after Pollock's death in December 1824. They eventually filed town plans with the state of Louisiana and in 1829, offered lots for public sale at Tunicaville, the main thoroughfare of which bore the name Pollock Street. Although the settlement eventually received a post office, it never prospered and the Pollock family realized little profit from the venture. They also became involved in a title dispute regarding the plantation which stemmed from Pollock's wartime debts to Patrick Conway and Alexander Baudin. A final resolution in this matter did not come until the late 1820s, when they gained a clear title. In financial need, they sold parcels of the plantation to other planters, although they kept some of the original holding for themselves. A grandson, Oliver Pollock Robinson, lived on part of the property until the Civil War. Other Pollock descendants also maintained homes in St. Francisville and at the nearby hamlet of Bayou Sara.

As well, in the mid-1830s, the Pollock family initiated a series of complicated legal claims which sought to regain titles of the British-era land grants which Oliver Pollock had assigned to creditors as part of his 1782 bankruptcy and which he had been unable to resecure during his life. Dr. Robinson, Pollock's son-in-law, argued before the commissioners of the General Land Office that his father-in-law's Revolutionary War debts had been incurred in the name of the United States government and that the use of the plantation lands as collateral in the 1780s had been illegal. Nothing resulted from these efforts, however, since they were obscured and eventually dismissed among the thousands of Louisiana land claim cases which came before the United States General Land Office and its commissioners in the antebellum era. Nevertheless, Oliver Pollock's descendants continue to the present-day as residents along the Mississippi River, although they sold their remaining interest in the Old Tunica Plantation and moved to the Natchez area after the Civil War.

The story of Oliver Pollock's land tenure in the Mississippi Valley seems to have been fairly typical of a larger group of Anglo settlers who came into the region prior to the American Revolution. Like Pollock, others of them and their families developed traditions of land tenure in the lower Mississippi Valley which endured across the shifting eras of domination by Great Britain, Spain, and the United States.... As a group, they have been largely forgotten by history. They were the opening wedge of the Anglo-American influx into the lower Mississippi Valley in the decades prior to the Louisiana Purchase.

Questions

1. What roles did early Anglo settlers like Oliver Pollock play in Spanish colonial Louisiana?
2. What attracted Anglos to colonial Louisiana during the late eighteenth century, and why were they welcomed by the Spanish colonial government?
3. How did the colonial-era plantations created by planters such as Oliver Pollock differ from the stereotypical plantations of the antebellum period?

PART TWO

WOMEN, RACE, AND CLASS
IN EARLY LOUISIANA

Women played important roles in Louisiana history from the beginning, but they were often omitted from the historical narrative because of a lack of sources. While men, even poor ones, often turn up in the historical records as heads of households, property and business owners, and members of military units, relatively few women appear in such records. In addition, unless they were fairly wealthy and reasonably well-educated, women seldom generated the kinds of documents—such as diaries and letters—that historians typically rely on to discover the past. To get at the history of women, then, researchers tend to look in the only place where sources for them might turn up: criminal records. The articles in this section by Kimberly Hanger and Judith Schafer are based largely upon such records. As you read these works, consider how the paucity of sources for women might affect our understanding of them and of their role.

In several places in this reader a recurrent theme emerges: the difficulties of establishing an agreed-upon set of rules about race in Louisiana. Racial boundaries, rights (or the lack of them), and privileges were complicated by the presence of a relatively large group (as compared to other southern states) of mixed-race people who were not enslaved. From the beginning of European settlement through the end of the Civil War, Louisiana law prohibited marriage between people of different races. Yet illicit sex occurred regularly, usually between white men and black women, and produced a population of free people of color who became culturally and demographically significant in Louisiana. As Hanger discusses in her article, free people of color occupied an undefined and anomalous position, "the middle section of a three-tiered hierarchy in which they were not truly free or slave, often not pure black or white." Hanger looks at the ways in which free black women in Spanish New Orleans challenged their second-class status and refused to conform to Spanish notions about gender and racial hierarchy.

Spain acquired Louisiana from France in the Treaty of Paris of 1763 and ruled it until the Louisiana Purchase of 1803; by the late eighteenth century, New Orleans, the largest city in northern New Spain, was a thriving, dynamic, multi-cultural port. The population was roughly evenly divided between free people (including free people of color, known as *libres* in Spanish New Orleans) and slaves. Like all port cities, New Orleans had a significant transient population consisting mostly of men who lived there for a few months while on business but whose families lived elsewhere. This large cadre of men without their wives present produced a cultural acceptance of mistresses and second families of illegitimate children. Frequently, the mistresses were free women of color, sometimes referred to as *placées*.

Footloose men with wads of money in their pockets also contributed to a thriving prostitution industry, for which New Orleans grew infamous. Long after the Spanish had turned over control of Louisiana to the United States, and for decades after Louisiana achieved statehood in 1812, the prostitution industry continued to flourish, as Judith Kelleher Schafer's article makes clear.

Schafer, a legal historian, writes about a sensational case that drew overflowing crowds into the courtroom to hear the trial of a respectable riverboat pilot, Abraham Parker, accused of murdering a prostitute. Like many other men, Parker lived part of the year elsewhere (in Tennessee, where he had a wife and children) and part of the year in New Orleans. He was apparently in the habit of frequenting the brothels, and on the night he shot Eliza Phillips dead, was quite drunk. Schafer's story about the nature of the prostitution business in New Orleans is intriguing on many levels, including the fact that the brothel where the crime occurred was run by a slave woman who turned over the profits to her absentee white master. Consider how the power of class and gender determined the outcome of this case.

In the essay by Sara Sundberg we leave New Orleans and look at the life of a woman in rural Feliciana Parish, Rachel O'Connor, a plantation mistress. Rachel and her husbands (she married twice) benefitted from moving to the area when it was sparsely populated and still under Spanish control, because the Spanish handed out land grants freely to women as well as men in an attempt to increase settlement. When both her husbands and her sons pre-deceased her, Rachel was left with significant debt and a large plantation, complete with many slaves, to run by herself. To wriggle out from under the debt burden, she sold the plantation to her half-brother, David Weeks, in an agreement that allowed her to remain on it and manage it. Because she continued to rely on Weeks's advice, she wrote to him frequently. In those letters, her life's story has been at least partly preserved.

DESIRING TOTAL TRANQUILITY—AND NOT GETTING IT: CONFLICT INVOLVING FREE BLACK WOMEN IN SPANISH NEW ORLEANS

by Kimberly Hanger

Colonial new orleans was a community, like so many others in Latin America, in which the upper sectors desired to maintain order and *"toda tranquilidad"* [total tranquility], preferably by way of legislation if necessary. Challenges to this tranquility came from those groups considered marginal and thus often subordinated, oppressed, and made generally unhappy with the status quo, among them workers, women, soldiers, slaves, and free blacks (*libres*). Free black women—the focus of this paper—drew upon multiple experiences as members of several of these subjugated groups: as women, as nonwhites, sometimes as former slaves, and usually as workers, forced by poverty to support their families with earnings devalued because they were gained doing "women's work." But they did not suffer silently. Condemning the patriarchal order, racist, sexist, authoritarian society in which they operated, libre women vigorously attacked it both verbally and physically, employing such elite-defined legal and illegal methods as petitions, judicial procedures, slander, insults, arson, and assault and battery. With these tools and others they tried to topple a tranquil, balanced world unfairly weighted against them. In an ideal world Spanish societies were to be highly stratified by race, gender, wealth, and legal status, where every member was cognizant of her or his proper place. New Orleans, however, was not and never has been part of an ethereal, ideal world, not for its libre citizens or any others. Although perhaps viewed by the crown as a peripheral town on Spain's northern frontier,

Originally published in *The Americas* 54 (April 1998): 541–556. Courtesy of the Academy of Franciscan History.

by the late eighteenth century the "city that care forgot" was actually a vibrant port with people moving in and out, establishing relationships across racial and class boundaries, and generally challenging any kind of stable social order. The only nucleus to boast the title of *ciudad* [city] in all of northern New Spain, New Orleans had a resident population that grew from about 3,000 to about 8,000 during the era of Spanish rule, with a large transient population adding to this number. The percentage of free blacks rose from ten to twenty percent of New Orleanians over the same period; two-thirds were female. The rest of the population was about evenly divided between whites and slaves, with varying numbers of *indios* [Indians] and *mestizos* [mixed-race] residing in and around the city. Insecure of their status within this cosmopolitan, fluid, multiracial, and multiethnic society, members of the upper echelons and the royal and ecclesiastical bureaucracy tried to maintain social control through legal channels that defined proper behavior. Law and custom purposefully delineated differences among Spain's subjects, constructing and maintaining inequalities based on race, religion, occupation, gender, wealth, and lineage; from the Spanish perspective it went against nature for all persons to be equal. Within the Spanish legal system privileges were equated with rights, with various corporate groups accorded *fueros* (privileges) and people of different classes and races readily identified by the clothes they could wear and activities in which they could engage.

When changing conditions threatened the social hierarchy, officials acted to restore order, harmony, and a sense of justice among inhabitants. For example, in an attempt to exercise some control over the multitude of troops, ships' crews, free blacks, and slaves who converged on New Orleans during the American Revolution, the attorney general asked the *cabildo* (city council) to forbid libres and slaves from wearing masks and mimicking whites during the carnival season. With so many strangers in the city, officials found it difficult to identify the race of masked revelers. A few years later Governor Esteban Miró admonished libre women not to don fancy headdresses, plumes, or gold jewelry; he reserved these items for white ladies of quality. As they had been accustomed to in past years (but had evidently strayed), "*negras, mulatas, y quarteronas*"[1] had to wear their hair flat or, if in a coiffure, covered with a

---

[1] This refers to those who were of full-blooded African ancestry (*Negras*), half-black (*mulatas* or mulattoes), and one-fourth black (*quarteronas* or quadroons).

kerchief. Officials and white elites also attempted to "divide and conquer" the free black and slave population. They feared that libres would incite desires for liberty among slaves and thus corrupt a seemingly docile labor force. During the tumultuous decade of the 1790s the actions of libres came under ever increasing scrutiny, as the racial warfare that swept Saint Domingue exacerbated always-present anxieties about sympathetic collusion between free blacks and slaves. When order did break down and disputes arose, governing bodies and the legislation they created tried to mediate between competing interests to reach an acceptable compromise, while taking into account the status of each party. The art of arbitration thereby restored "total tranquility" in the name of public interest. Whenever possible, parties on both sides of the issue were encouraged to reconcile their differences and act according to acceptable rules of conduct, whether the case was heard before a civil, criminal, or ecclesiastical tribunal. Even though there was a shortfall of qualified lawyers working in the far reaches of the Spanish empire, the concern for justice and legal procedure persisted. . . . Judges working in the Spanish legal system conducted thorough investigations. Through interpreters they compiled detailed testimony, most of which in Louisiana was given in French, and occasionally in English or Native American and African languages. While questioning followed a pattern, everyone—slave and free, rich and poor, female and male—was accorded a voice. Plaintiff, defendant, and witness could expound at length, about matters directly pertinent to the case or not.

Many of the individuals who tested the boundaries of elite-defined acceptable behavior—and whose voices thus echo from the historical past— were free blacks. Their position within New Orleans' hierarchy was not well defined, and in fact, most libres did not choose to be demarcated as a separate group, preferring instead to be admitted to and accepted by white society. They desired that the distinctions between themselves and whites be dissolved altogether, claiming to be "free like you" and asserting "a universal equality among men," with only "their method of thinking, not color," differentiating them. Free black women would extend that equality beyond the confines of gender.

Nonwhite, female, and often poor, libre women were the frequent subjects of oppression within this system. They were often condemned as "lewd" and "licentious" in New Orleans and throughout the Americas. One late eighteenth-century observer of New Orleans lifestyles, Claude C. Robin, de-nounced the many white men who were tempted to "form liaisons with these lascivious, coarse, and lavish [libre] women" and subsequently were "ruined." He, however, blamed the women for such sinful practices, as did New Orleans physician Paul Alliot, who believed that free black women inspired "such lust through their bearing, their gestures, and their dress, that many quite well-to-do persons are ruined in pleasing them." When accused of repossessing a slave he had donated to his former concubine (the free *parda* Magdalena Canelle, mother of his two *cuarterona* daughters), don Luis Beaurepos dismissed Canelle's claims due to the fact that her "only proof to ownership rests on the sworn word of some *mulatas*, libertines like herself."[2] The objects of this derision, however, did not perceive themselves as such and resisted efforts to denigrate them as women and nonwhites. Like all libres living in slave societies, New Orleans free women of color operated from an undefined, anomalous position, the middle section of a three-tiered hierarchy in which they were not truly free or slave, often not pure black or white. Libre women were also trapped in a patriarchal society that valued males more than females but that did not afford them the paternal protection due the weaker sex because they ostensibly did not possess honor and virtue, attributes only accorded whites. Caught in between the interests of officials and residents, of white, libre, and slave men, free black women fought oppression on a daily basis and sought to assert their identity, in part by striving to attain what was important to them: freedom for themselves, friends, and relatives; stable, long-lasting unions that produced children and cemented kin networks; prosperity for themselves and future generations; and respect as hardworking, religious members of the com-munity. In general, they faced an uphill battle.

Most of the above were goals that white citizens also espoused. Ironically, in seeking to attain what whites had—and thus argue for a measure of equity —libres had to come together as a group with their own agenda. They thus promoted their distinct identity. Although conservative compared to modern civil rights leaders, New Orleans libres challenged the racist ideology of he-gemonic whites, increasingly so during the revolutionary last decade of the

---

[2] *Parda* referred to a light-skinned free black, *cuarterona* to someone who was one-fourth black.

eighteenth century and first decade of the nineteenth century. To protest their subordinate status within New Orleans society and at the same time create an identity that emphasized their contributions to that society, free black women and men often used cultural expressions and political actions, such as carnival balls and parades, protests, petitions, and civil suits. Libre women wanted to reform, not revolutionize, a system that condemned them outright for being nonwhites and women and failed to recognize their worth except as measured by skin color and gender. Rejecting race and sex as a basis for placement in the social hierarchy, libres like Maria Cofignie (whom we will meet in the following pages) made an appeal for individual or group efforts and achievements. They emphasized what made them good citizens: concern for family, hard work, honest business transactions, orderly conduct, church attendance, property accumulation. The played on the sentiments of the court as poor, laboring mothers whose primary responsibility was to their families, thereby using and reinforcing the image of women as domestic caregivers, while at the same time revealing the powerful economic roles they played as household heads and breadwinners. In pursuit of their rights as women and free person, they flaunted gold jewelry, headdresses, and clothes that only whites were supposed to wear as they strolled down the streets and along the levee and bayou promenades in the evening; operated businesses that competed with those of libre and white men and exercised economic power by accumulating substantial estates of urban and rural properties and slaves; brought before the justice system spouses and strangers who abused them; and hurled insults and occasional blows at whites who belittled them or questioned their rights in public social spaces.

A few cases will help illuminate the efforts libre women made to assert their rights, struggle against subjugation, and disrupt the "total tranquility" New Orleans officials desired. The first is that of María Pechon, a free *morena*, who in 1776 charged don Patricio Macnemara, an influential Irishman, with assaulting and wounding her and her son Francisco, a free pardo.[3] According to the testimony that María, Francisco, and several white and free black witnesses presented, the mother and her twenty-year-old son had been returning from New Orleans to their plantation several miles downriver and had to stop

---

[3] *Morena* refers to a dark-skinned free bnlack woman.

for the night along the way. At about ten o'clock they arrived at the Tixerrant plantation and asked permission to stay in one of the slave cabins. A few moments later, Macnemara, who owned a neighboring plantation, burst into the cabin. He demanded that the Pechons produce either passes from their master if they were slaves, or their acts of emancipation to prove they were free. When Francisco (perhaps too haughtily to suit Macnemara) replied that "I am free and have no need of a pass," and "I am on a voyage and cannot carry it in my pocket," Macnemara struck him twice and dealt a third blow to María, who came between them to protect her son. Macnemara and his slave bound Francisco and carried him weakened and bleeding to his plantation, despite the protests of a free black witness, the Tixerrant boys, and one of Macnemara's white servants. Although threatening to punish Francisco further, Macnemara released him the next day after having his slaves guard him overnight. The Pechons returned to New Orleans, where they rented a house and hired a doctor and a slave to care for them.

María demanded restitution for this unprovoked, unjust attack on her and her son, a blatant disregard for their rights as propertied free persons. At the very least, she sought monetary compensation for expenses incurred in treating their wounds, and probably would have preferred a public apology from don Patricio. The case is incomplete, but she likely received neither given Macnemara's close ties to influential government figures. Nevertheless, María valiantly pursued justice through legitimate methods, thereby proving herself the more honorable party. She stated that Macnemara's allegations of deception were false; he knew that she and Francisco were free, as did all the other persons who were present at the time of his assault. María drew attention to the fact that "it is not the custom for free blacks to carry with them in their hands their acts of emancipation when they traveled, because the fact that they are free is well known to everyone." She further appealed to the sentiments of the court as a mother who instinctively tried to defend her son, an act that was "only natural among free people, to defend themselves against those who would kill them, or tie them up, or beat them; not only is this natural among the free, but among slaves as well."

Even in a deferential society like New Orleans, there were limits beyond which libres and slaves could not be pushed without retaliation. María was well aware that she lived in a bounded place, but she and other libres argued that these boundaries gave them some protection as well. A threatened, insecure Macnemara had transgressed the unwritten rules that governed behavior in this complex community. He had insulted the Pechons by treating them as slaves, when everyone knew them to be free persons. Because Macnemara's image of the Pechons varied from how they viewed themselves, his words and deeds denigrated them. Fortunately for him—and for many other powerful, connected men like him—he possessed the means to avoid paying for his transgressions.

Although Spanish society valued and rewarded people of other cultures for imitating and striving to be like Spaniards, who along with most Europeans considered themselves to be superior beings, María Pechon and other ambitious libres definitely challenged New Orleans' race, class and gender hierarchy. She wanted to be treated as an honorable, well-to-do, free *vecina* (propertied citizen), regardless of her color. While continuing to stress their importance as mothers who protected and provided for their children, independent, property-holding libre women nevertheless defied prescribed gender roles, prompting males threatened by their actions to petition for redress and restoration of order. In 1797 don Fernando Alzar and Co. together with fifty other *mercaderes* (shopkeepers, retail merchants) asked the Cabildo to prohibit the activities of increasing numbers of women—slave as well as free black— who daily sold merchandise on the streets and in other parts of New Orleans and even on plantations in the countryside. Lamenting that such practices detracted from their livelihood, the supplicants appealed to the mercy of the cabildo: they had to pay exorbitant rents for their shops and at the same time try to feed their families. In addition to playing a prominent role in local marketing, libre women owned and rented out urban property at rates higher than their proportion of the total and even free population, and at rates much higher than white women although not as great as white men. For example, a census of the third district of New Orleans taken in 1796 listed the proprietors and tenants of each house. While comprising only about one out of seven of all residents and one of five free inhabitants, free black women owned almost one-third the houses in the district. Comparable figures for white women were less than one of ten total residents, one of eight free residents, and about one-eighth of homeowners, less than half that of libre women. The rents libre landladies could exact in New Orleans' tight housing market occasionally earned them the ire of white tenants who found the tables of exploitation turned and themselves helpless. . . .

In addition to acting independently through their control of economic resources, libre women resisted race, class, and gender exploitation by exhibiting behavior deemed antisocial by the dominant white society and in contradistinction to prescribed gender roles. One of their most effective weapons was the hurling of "*palabras injuriousas*"—"insulting words" or slander in legal parlance—sometimes accompanied or provoked by physical attacks. Frustrated with a patriarchal, racist society that discriminated against them both as nonwhites and as women, libres occasionally lashed back at their oppressors with venomous tongues. Anyone could be accused of slander, but libres in particular were targeted because the law demanded they show respect for all whites, their actual and symbolic former "masters." One woman who resented this preferential treatment for whites and the humiliating behavior expected of libres was María Cofignie (Coffiny), a free mulata. In May 1795 don Pedro Favrot, a captain of the fixed regiment, brought charges against Cofignie for insulting his daughter Joesefina. According to the testimony of white neighbors who witnessed the incident, Cofignie's young pardo son was playing with some children on the sidewalk in front of the Favrot home on Conti Street. They told the *pequeño mulato* to leave them alone, he threw dirt in Josefina's face, and the other children chased him to his mother's house on the same street, whereupon Cofignie furiously confronted the señorita and referred to her as a "hija de puta" (daughter of a whore or a prostitute)—a definite insult. Berating Josefina for threatening her son, Cofignie decried the actions of Josefina and other persons of French descent like her, who "just because they are white, believe that we [libres] are made to be scorned, spurned, and slighted. I am free and I am as worthy as you are; I have not earned my freedom on my back" (i.e., as a prostitute). These egalitarian sentiments upset the white witnesses and the Favrot family, who considered Cofignie's pronouncements "the most vile atrocities that were as outrageous . . . as those that have caused a revolution" in France and its Caribbean colonies. Like libres in Saint-Domingue, Cofignie "talked of the whites in general with disdain and great contempt."

By accusing Cofignie of criminal behavior in a public arena, don Pedro sought to quell these inflammatory ideas and restore the reputation of his daughter and wife, the former insulted to her face and the latter by implication labeled a whore. He ably played the part of the influential patriarch defending the honor of his female charges. As a nonwhite single mother of illegitimate children, Cofignie had to rely on her own efforts; according to the Hispanic code of values that prevailed in New Orleans, she had no honor and was left unprotected and vulnerable. Although she probably enjoyed more independence than the Favrot women, she also had greater responsibilities. After more than two months of languishing under house arrest (the women's prison had been destroyed by fire in December 1794) without any sign of a resolution to the case, Cofignie pleaded with the court to release her so that she could work to sustain her family. She claimed to be "a miserable poor person burdened with . . . four children" and four months later would give birth to another. While repeatedly denying the charges brought against her, Cofignie reluctantly accepted Favrot's proposal to drop the case in exchange for humbling herself and apologizing to señora and señorita Favrot. She had no choice if her family were to keep from starving. Cofignie's independent spirit, like that of so many libres, was restrained by material necessities. Libre women also attacked one another, but each party usually was of a different phenotype, with darker women most commonly the aggressor. . . .

The numerous complaints that filled the dockets of the Spanish New Orleans judiciary offer a rich resource for glimpsing into the daily lives, values and worldviews of the city's residents. . . . They reveal that verbal and physical conflict commonly ensued in public spaces where insulting and humiliating behavior could be witnessed and thus have maximum impact. María Cofignie [and others] assailed those whom they perceived as their persecutors on the city's streets, either in front of their own or the other party's home. Others like María and Francisco Pechon made sure that there were witnesses to the incident even if it occurred indoors. Additional confrontations took place in taverns, billiard parlors, dance halls, and marketplaces or along the roads that lined the levees and canals surrounding New Orleans. Conflict also usually erupted between persons of different statuses trying to "put" the other party in his or her "place" or even lower on the social scale: white v. libre, male v. female, light phenotype v. dark, regular army v. militia, Spaniard v. French Creole. . . . Such threats to one's identity and honor and the corresponding response disclose much about societal values, at least as defined by the dominant group. On an individual level, insults meant something because they diverged from the targeted victim's own perception of him or herself. María Cofignie had not earned her freedom by prostituting herself, señorita Favrot was not the daughter of a whore, María and Francesco Pechon were not slaves, and libre women in general were not lewd and lazy. . . .

Testimony and events that surrounded the Cofignie, Pechon, and other cases reveal the discrimination, desires, and frustrations many libre women experienced in New Orleans' patriarchal, hierarchical society. These defendants expressed in words and deeds what most free blacks probably felt like doing on an almost daily basis but were hesitant to act upon due to such retribution as Cofignie was subjected. Through various forms of political action and cultural play, in both covert and overt ways, they and other libre women resisted oppression based on their race, sex, and status. Most opted for peaceful resolution rather than revolutionary equality, as eventually did María Cofignie when she decided to sooth the wounded pride of the Favrot family and save her children from starvation, rather than fight for an assessment of her worth based on merit instead of race.

Nevertheless, free black women did pose a threat to a social hierarchy defined by patriarchy, European ancestry, and wealth, with fortunes primarily made through land and slave ownership. They were the subjects of discrimination as women, nonwhites, and slaves or the descendants of slaves. White women and slaves envied their relative economic independence, their greater choice of marriage partners, their relationships with white men. Crown and church officials and white elites tried to restrict free blacks' choice of clothing and jewelry, access to property, type of occupation, and social activities by the way of regulation and taxation. Libre women, in turn, resented being treated differently and subjected to greater scrutiny because of their race, gender, or former slave status. Their rage and exasperation erupted in both public and private spaces—on the city's streets, in its markets, along its promenades, within its individual residences—despite official efforts to maintain total tranquility.

Questions

1. Explain the title of this piece. What did the authorities in Spanish New Orleans want and why, and how did free black women resist?
2. What evidence does the author use to support her thesis? How might those sources affect her interpretation?
3. What did elite whites in New Orleans think about the character and behavior of free women of color? How did the women see themselves?
4. What did the free women of color want, according to Hanger?
5. In what ways did libre women have more choices than white women and slaves?

A FEMALE PLANTER FROM WEST FELICIANA PARISH: THE LETTERS OF RACHEL O'CONNOR

by Sara Brooks Sundberg

E arly louisiana census tables never listed Rachel O'Connor's name under the occupational category appropriate for planters—that of "Agriculture;" yet, Rachel O'Connor, a twice-widowed planter in antebellum West Feliciana Parish pursued that occupation for more than twenty-six years. In March 1831, she reported to her brother that her nearly 700 acre plantation, Evergreen, produced 187 bales of ginned cotton that season, exceeding its previous record of cotton production by at least twenty bales. Along with this news O'Connor reported on the health of the plantation's flock of laying hens and the cost of pork for the plantation's inhabitants, including over seventy slaves. In sum Rachel O'Connor explained, "the work of the plantation is going on very well." Rachel O'Connor's remarks, typical of the progress reports she mailed to her brother about Evergreen Plantation, are part of a remarkable collection of 157 letters Rachel penned to her brother and his family between 1823–1845. The letters are published in *Mistress of Evergreen Plantation, Rachel O'Connor's Legacy of Letters 1823–1845* edited by Allie Bayne Windham Webb.

Rachel O'Connor's letters, along with correspondence related to her between other members of her family and fragmentary pieces of information from public records, provide enough information for a microhistory of

Originally published in *Louisiana History: The Journal of the Louisiana Historical Association* 48 (Winter 2006): 39–62. Used by permission of the Louisiana Historical Association.

O'Connor's life. . . . In her family values, work roles and cultural attitudes she is typical of pioneer, female, slave-holding planters in West Feliciana Parish. Her life story illuminates the rules women lived by in the largely male world of commercial agriculture in the early South and the contributions female planters made to that world. Claiming, developing, and preserving Evergreen Plantation for future generations, Rachel O'Connor left her imprint on the land and people of Evergreen Plantation as surely as she did on her letters.

Rachel O'Connor and her second husband, Hercules, qualify as pioneer settlers on the Southern cotton frontier. The couple settled on the Louisiana frontier in 1797 when West Feliciana Parish, then known as Feliciana, comprised part of Spanish West Florida. Rich deposits of loess soils and the region's moderately dry and mild climate made Feliciana attractive to southern pioneers eager to make their fortunes growing cotton, corn, and sugar cane. . . . The area quickly developed into cotton and sugar plantations dependent upon slave labor and by 1800 the frontier of settlement—defined [by the U. S. Census Bureau] as two people per square mile—reached the area in and around Feliciana and then moved on.

Rachel and Hercules O'Connor located their Feliciana plantation just ten miles from the landing at Bayou Sara, a site favorably situated on the Mississippi River between Natchez and New Orleans. They were part of a sizeable Anglo American population that sought to capitalize on the region's agricultural promise. The region attracted settlers of means, but it is not clear whether as a newly married couple the O'Connors qualified as part of this group. Rachel already owned land in the Attakapas district in southwest Louisiana. The couple may have owned land but little cash. In 1835, looking back on their early years in Feliciana, Rachel recollected, "We began the world very poor when we came to this place [Feliciana] the 5th of June, 1797. We had only provisions to last us two days and had to trust in Providence for the next."

Despite their limited beginning, Rachel probably expected that she and her husband would prosper. After all, her step-father and mother prospered through land owning and planting on the frontier. Rachel O'Connor's widowed mother married William Weeks when Rachel was just four years old. Weeks owned several thousand arpents of land in the Attakapas district along Bayou Teche and the southwestern Louisiana coast and in Feliciana where the family lived. Rachel O'Connor came of age among families who became successful through claiming land and planting on the frontier.

Rachel O'Connor and her first husband, Richard Bell, took advantage of Louisiana's land-owning possibilities when Bell made a land claim of some 400 arpents on Grand Cote Island, along the coast in the Attakapas region near her step father's, William Weeks, much larger land claim. Bell may also have bought or claimed land nearer Bayou Teche in the Attakapas region. He died in 1792 leaving Rachel with an infant son and land in Attakapas. The eighteen-year old land-owning widow gathered up her infant son and returned to her stepfather's home to live after her husband's death. William Weeks, by now a widower, lived in Feliciana, and it was there, five years later, that Rachel O'Connor met and married her second husband, Irish immigrant Hercules O'Connor. A letter to Hercules O'Connor from a friend, James Corrie, who lived in Ireland, congratulated O'Connor on his good fortune in a marriage that "I expect is to your welfare and future happiness. . . ." Corrie acknowledged the roots of O'Connor's success in America when he concluded his letter of congratulations with inquiries about his own chances for land and marriageable widows.

Liberal land policies on the part of the Spanish government made it possible for pioneer families, like the Weeks and O'Connor families, to claim land and settle in Attakapas and Feliciana. Both Rachel and Hercules O'Connor made land claims in Feliciana. Rachel O'Connor filed the first of her two land claims in Feliciana under her maiden name of Rachel Swayze in 1797, probably shortly before her second marriage. The Spanish Governor confirmed the claim for 276 arpents of land (about 234 acres) in 1798. The United States government reconfirmed her claim in 1819. This claim was not contiguous with Hercules O'Connor's larger claim of some 500 acres. The O'Connors eventually sold Rachel's claim to William Weeks. Rachel O'Connor claimed another parcel of land on behalf of her young son, James O'Connor. This land situated adjacent to Hercules O'Connor's claim was "improved" or cultivated as the law required. "My papers convinced them [the land office] that the land was granted in 1803, and that it had been surveyed the second time in 1804, and improved in 1807 and 1808," Rachel remembered. The United States government confirmed the claim in 1826. Together, Rachel and Hercules O'Connor claimed nearly 700 acres in present-day West Feliciana Parish, excluding land they sold to William Weeks.

Land claims made by married women, like Rachel O'Connor, were not an uncommon occurrence in the frontier South. Fifty-two women like O'Connor filed original land claims or purchases in what later became West Feliciana Parish. Altogether their claims amount to about 5 percent of all land claims or purchases in the parish. This percentage is consistent with female land claims in Georgia and North and South Carolina during their colonial periods. As these numbers suggest, Rachel O'Connor was part of a widespread minority of female landowners in the early south. In West Feliciana Parish, women's land holdings averaged some 452 acres, although the size varied considerably. Like Rachel O'Connor, many women added their claims to those of their husbands in an effort to expand the size of family plantations. As the years went by, the government gradually restricted the number of acres pioneers could claim, making women's claims even more essential to building family fortunes.

Female landowners were usually not alone on their land. They came to Feliciana with their husbands, or were about to be married as in Rachel O'Connor's situation. They did not realize complete ownership or assume full management responsibilities of their family's land until they were widowed. By 1830, 10 percent of the original women filers now listed themselves as heads of household with twenty slaves or more, including Rachel O'Connor. In other words, they were widowed, female planters. Given the fact that some of the women who made original land claims and purchases died or remarried, making them difficult to trace, the total percentage of original landowners who became female planters could be considerably higher. Over the years the number of female slave-holders in West Feliciana increased as the population grew. By the end of the antebellum period women accounted for an average of 17 percent of heads of household with twenty slaves or more. These women were all widows. The numbers of slave-holding widows in West Feliciana Parish mirrored a trend in female slaveholding throughout the southeast, with some areas registering percentages as high as twenty percent.

The neighborhood around the O'Connor's plantation filled rapidly. But, pioneer conditions lingered on in the frontier's wake, especially for farmers who began planting with meager resources, such as the O'Connors. Rachel O'Connor always referred to the "good old home" they built in modest terms. Their house, likely built from locally-obtained cypress wood, did include a wide gallery and the plantation estate would, eventually, include numerous outbuildings. The couple also brought slaves.

The O'Connor family improved their homestead, increased their number of slaves and planted cotton for twenty-three years until Hercules O'Connor died in 1820, apparently from alcoholism. Rachel O'Connor is conspicuously silent about her life with Hercules O'Connor. She does not lament the anniversary of his death in her letters, as she does the deaths of other family members. Hercules O'Connor's alcoholism undoubtedly stressed their relationship and his illness may have forced her to take over management of the plantation before his death. There was no one else in her immediate family to turn to after Hercules O'Connor's death because her eldest son, Stephen Bell, had died earlier in the year. Her younger son, James O'Connor, like his father, succumbed to alcoholism. Rachel O'Connor signed an interdiction order barring James O'Connor from handling his own affairs probably because of his disease. He died in 1822. Rachel O'Connor's grief over the deaths of all of her family within the space of just two years must have been devastating. Years later, reflecting upon this time in a letter she evoked the stoic faith that sustained her through their deaths, "It is our duty to submit to the will of Providence, ... Otherwise we may draw on ourselves double sorrows, the latter I accuse myself of. In time past, had I been more resigned at first, I don't think my misfortunes would have been so severe. . . ."

And yet, O'Connor's faith was not all that sustained her through this time of loss. When her first husband died, the then eighteen-year-old Rachel Bell and her infant son retreated to her step-father's home to live and to work caring for her siblings. This time, after the death of her second husband, Rachel O'Connor might have turned to her prosperous, half-brother, David Weeks, for a safe and secure home. But, the forty-six year old widow owned a house, land and slaves on a plantation she had struggled with her second husband to develop for more than two decades. She stuck to the land.

Without immediate family to assist her on the plantation the decision to stay on the land could not have been an easy one for Rachel O'Connor. She relied on extended family for emotional support and financial advice, especially from her half-brother David Weeks, a successful sugar planter in the Teche country in southwestern Louisiana. She helped to care for David Weeks when she lived in her step-father's home, and her eldest son, prior to his death, journeyed to Grand Cote Island with Weeks to establish a plantation. Rachel's O'Connor's affection for David Weeks and his wife Mary and their children is evident in her letters. Most of her surviving letters are addressed to them. Thus, it is not surprising that Rachel O'Connor turned to David Weeks for assistance when she encountered serious legal difficulties that endangered the future of her plantation and slaves.

The death of Stephen Bell, Rachel O'Connor's eldest son, in 1820 began an ordeal of economic and legal difficulties for Rachel O'Connor that persisted almost until her death in 1846. Her troubles began when she accepted Stephen Bell's succession and agreed to pay his debts, including a substantial debt owed to the partnership of William and David Flower. O'Connor paid some of the debt owed to the firm, but in 1822 William Flower wanted to retire from business and settle his accounts. He brought suit against Rachel O'Connor in 1825 in the Third District Court in West Feliciana Parish for payment of Stephen Bell's debts. O'Connor countered the suit with two arguments; first, she claimed her signature was fraudulently attained because Stephen Bell's estate had not been inventoried. Second, she claimed that she was a married woman at the time she accepted her son's succession and entered into the agreement to repay Flower. Louisiana law, according to her lawyers, required married women to have the consent of their husbands before making such agreements. O'Connor claimed she did not have the consent of Hercules O'Connor when she signed the agreement.

Rachel O'Connor's defense highlights important differences between Anglo common law operative in most other parts of the United States at the time and the Louisiana Civil Code. Under the 1825 Civil Code women in Louisiana could legally own and manage their separate or *paraphernal* property. This was not true in most other states where the common law concept of coverture denied women legal identity and placed their property under their husband's ownership and control. Even a woman's separate property usually became liable to her husband's debts and his management. Rachel O'Connor had been raised in Louisiana which meant she grew up under the civilian legal tradition. Nevertheless, her ethnic background was English. Anglo families in Louisiana sometimes disregarded the civil law provisions more liberal to women in favor of restrictive common law principles. It is not clear whether Rachel O'Connor really did not understand her rights to manage her separate property or whether she chose to ignore them or whether she pleaded female dependency to protect herself from William Flower's litigation.

Regardless of her intent, probate records demonstrate that she actually did have Hercules O'Connor's consent to accept the succession and that the couple requested and accepted the inventory of Stephen Bell's estate. As Rachel O'Connor alleged, only her signature appears on the agreement to repay Stephen Bell's debts to William and David Flower. In any case, Flower appealed his suit against Rachel O'Connor all the way to the State Supreme Court, and won. In 1830 the Court ruled that when Rachel O'Connor accepted Stephen Bell's succession it became part of her *paraphernal* assets, or separate property, which she could administer without her husband's consent. Thus, the agreement she made with Flower obligated her to pay her son's debts.

Shortly after the Supreme Court's decision Rachel O'Connor sold her plantation and nineteen slaves to David Weeks for $23,675.00 to protect these assets from William Flower. She did not, however, immediately release the mortgage. She held David Weeks' notes for the plantation along with a notarized agreement from the sale that guaranteed that she could remain on the plantation and manage it during her lifetime. Flower did not believe Weeks' purchase of Rachel O'Connor's plantation was real. He persisted in his efforts to collect debts owed him by Stephen Bell, including seizure of some of O'Connor's cotton and slaves in lieu of payment. Just before the sheriff arrived to seize her cotton and slaves Rachel O'Connor released the mortgage on her plantation. She pleaded with David Weeks to assert his ownership, "either come yourself, or empower some person to act for you. . . . or you may depend, all will be lost, which indeed I cannot bear to think of." David Weeks eventually asserted his ownership of the plantation, counter-suing William Flower for damages.

The two men and their lawyers battled one another in court for the next ten years. Flower claimed that the sale of Rachel O'Connor plantation to David Weeks was a fraudulent, "simulated sale" designed only to avoid payment of Rachel O'Connor's debts. Flower was right. The Weeks family's intention was to keep the case in court as long as possible. Finally, in 1836, the State Supreme Court agreed with Flower. The Weeks heirs, having apparently exhausted their legal appeals, paid a court settlement in 1837 worth nearly $13,000. The payment included interest accrued back to 1825.

Rachel O'Connor's reliance on David Weeks for help and advice concerning legal matters and plantation affairs is evidence, according to some historians, that female planters were not truly heads of households. Caught in a web of expectations comprised of nineteenth-century prescriptions for woman's sphere and domesticity, southern women did not possess the skills or inclination to plant or manage their own affairs. . . . Rigid patriarchy resulted and that meant that even if women mustered the courage to manage plantations they usually did so only until they could pass along the responsibilities to elder sons or other male heirs.

This interpretation of the experiences of female planters like Rachel O'Connor ignores the fact that planters, both males and females, relied upon kin for advice and financial help. . . . It was not unusual that Harriet Flowers Mathews, O'Connor's neighbor, managed an eleven-hundred acre cotton and sugar plantation on the banks of Bayou Sara for several years after the death of her husband, then mortgaged the plantation to her son-in-law and daughter during the financially depressed years of the late 1830s and early 1840s. Mathews protected her plantation with the help of kin, just as O'Connor did, insuring the availability of capital from family to run the plantation, while still managing it herself and keeping it within the family. Male planters utilized relatives in similar ways.

Moreover, many widows remained actively involved in managing their plantations even after it appears their male heirs came of age. Fifty-four percent of all the female planters in the 1820 census reported white males living on their plantation who were twenty-five years old or over, the age young men would be most likely to take over full management of their widowed mother's affairs. West Feliciana Parish probate records indicate that a clear majority of the female planters who reported white males, presumably kin or white overseers, living on their plantations continued to be actively involved in legal matters pertaining to their plantations; buying and selling property, acting as executrixes of estates and so on. . . .

It is true that women's participation in business affairs placed them at odds with legal principles codifying their subordination. The Louisiana civil law code, like common law statutes, included provisions that legally sanctioned women's inferior status. Yet, unlike common law, the Civil Code recognized women's legal identity and it allowed women a greater share, one-half instead of one-third under common law, of property accrued during marriage as well as the ownership and management of separate property as already discussed. Of course, women still could not manage the community property of the marriage without their husband's consent and, as Rachel O'Connor's case illustrates, there was often confusion about whether women could legally administer their separate property, independent of their husbands.

And yet, the limited sphere of Louisiana women's property management may not have always been rigidly followed. Historian Joseph McKnight found that throughout regions like Feliciana, where Spanish civil law still influenced behavior, women acted independently. They also joined with their husbands in economic activities even though the law did not require their participation. West Feliciana Parish notarial records indicate many women did obtain the necessary permission to manage family property while married. Nevertheless, unfettered legal freedom to manage one's affairs came to women only as widows or single women.

The assertive, public behavior required for management of plantations could discourage women from acting on their own behalf. In a letter to her brother David in 1834, Rachel O'Connor acknowledged that "a Widowed mother cannot manage her affairs as a father; they are afraid to speak for themselves." Yet, in her own life she confronted her fears. In another letter to her brother nine years earlier O'Connor explained that she wanted to clear her son's claim on a parcel of land and the law required her to appear at the busy, local land office to do that. "I am at present very well and I expect much smarter than you would think until after I have told you of a journey that I have late taken out to St. Helena Court House, where the land office is kept, for the purpose of securing the 240 acres of land that formerly belonged to my poor James . . . . I considered it one hour of time and wished for you to be here, and then finally concluded to go myself if I lived to do so and started with no other than Arthur [her slave]. . . ." Even before James' death, she demonstrated determination to save family property when she arranged for him to be legally "interdicted," effectively barring him from managing his own affairs. Finally, it was Rachel O'Connor, working with her lawyer, who dealt with the sheriff when he seized Evergreen Plantation cotton as security against the debt William Flower claimed she owed him. Rachel O'Connor wrote letters urging David Weeks to act and sent legal papers for him to sign. To save the property she wrote "I could ride Big Black 30 miles a day with all ease one day with another, while I am frightened." In the end, Flower won the court case against Rachel O'Connor, but Rachel O'Connor prevailed anyway. With the help of her half brother and through her own assertiveness and determination she kept her plantation intact, managed it until her death and passed it on to Weeks family heirs in her will.

O'Connor's knowledge of plantation operations is, perhaps, the best indication of her willingness to assume the responsibilities of the plantation. Modest in her own assessment, Rachel's letters to her brother claims, "So, my dear brother, you can see I am still trying to creep along slowly with the help of good friends bestowed by a kind *God*." Yet, in 1824 at the age of fifty she hired an overseer only because she felt too ill to carry on alone, "Since I have been so poorly, I have hired an overseer at 25 dollars per month for two months, if he behaves well not otherwise."

Like other female planters Rachel O'Connor employed slaves as overseers. She claimed to trust them more than the white overseers she hired over the years, "I have lost poor Leven one of the most faithful black men ever lived— he was truth and honesty and without a fault that I ever discovered. He has overseen the plantation nearly three years and done much better than white man ever done here and I lived a quiet life . . . ." O'Connor . . . frequently expressed frustration with white overseers, among other reasons, because they would not mind her command to stay away from female slaves.

Rachel O'Connor defies the image of the plantation mistress hopelessly out of touch with plantation affairs, dependent upon an overseer and unable to control her slaves. At the age of fifty-five she still went about her rides through the cotton fields on horseback, monitoring the progress of the plantation. She dutifully reported to her brother on "his" plantation affairs. "The last of your crop is pressed. It made forty more bales, one hundred and eight bales the whole crops of cotton, and they commenced hauling it to the river this morning."

She frequently defers to David Weeks in business affairs but there is no indication he restricted her management in any way, including purchases for the plantation. "Your new horses plough charmingly and as gently as dogs. The one that I bought for $25 behave [sic] quite well . . . ." Even more compelling evidence of David Weeks' trust in his sister's management is the fact that O'Connor communicated directly with the New Orleans cotton factor, who negotiated sales and purchased supplies for her. In later years, when the heirs of David Weeks proved less reliable than David Weeks in meeting O'Connor's financial obligations concerning the plantation, she scolded them, "Whoever I send the cotton to must consider themselves bound to send me such necessaries as I write to them for and to pay any drafts that I may draw on them to carry on the farm. Otherwise my liberties would be less than a common overseer". . . .

West Feliciana Parish widows demonstrated authority in handling plantation affairs. Harriet Flowers Mathews instructed cotton factors concerning the sale of her crops. Eliza Lyons, O'Connor's nearest neighbor and close friend did the same. Eliza Lyons instructed factors about all four of her plantations. Letters Lyons received from her factors indicated they valued her approval. "We have before us your returned letter . . . . From a remark in it . . . . we have feared you did not approve of what we did with the business . . . we hope you will agree with us." Eliza continued to manage plantation affairs even after her marriage to her third husband in 1840. Her management built upon a strong example. Eliza Lyons' mother, Lucy Pirrie, established the tradition of independent action when she made original land claims in West Feliciana Parish and managed affairs concerning her plantation for a time following the death of her husband.

With the exception of Eliza Lyons the personal autonomy exhibited by female planters in this study emerged out of the experience of women like Rachel O'Connor, slave-holding widows who came to the region as pioneer settlers and who resided on economically viable plantations. For the widowed women of means surveyed here, it is reasonable to suggest that their plantations, in a sense, supplanted the role of marriage. In a society that valued women's dependent, domestic role, women's status came from marriage. . . . Plantations provided the means through which widows could achieve economic security and status. Moreover, the responsibilities of ownership and management of plantation property provided widows an opportunity to refashion their identities, redefining their usefulness and roles within their families. . . .

Plantations provided Rachel, and other women like her, economic and personal security. Even so, the loss of so many of her family left her, at times, desolate "I am alone," O'Connor admitted to her brother in 1823, "and the night's too long to venture to bed early knowing it is but seldom that I can sleep so long, ..." She felt affection and obligation toward her two orphaned nieces raised at Evergreen. She also expressed attachment to particular slaves who worked Evergreen Plantation. When David Weeks requested she send some of her slaves to work for his brother-in-law, Frederick Conrad, on Cottage Plantation, she complied with reluctance, "I sent Dave, Eben, Harry, Littleton, and Frank. Pray write to Mr. Conrad to be careful of them. They were born and raised here with me which causes me to love them better than I had ought, but my heart must remain as it pleased God to form it." Some of the slaves on Evergreen Plantation may have been special for Rachel O'Connor, but her relationship with them also reflected their status as chattel property. Slaves were an investment for O'Connor. She bought, sold and physically punished them. As a female planter she cared for her investment by nursing them when they were sick and making sure they were clothed and fed. She rewarded their childbearing, an event economically beneficial to the plantation, by giving each female slave extra clothing when she gave birth.

The plantation itself provided O'Connor comfort and meaning. "My good and comfortable old Home is so precious to me, that when my times comes, it is my desire to Die here, . . ." O'Connor claimed to want to improve and expand her holdings only as a legacy for her brother's family. But her personal pride in her accomplishments on the plantation is evident. She expressed particular joy in her garden, which she worked herself: "I love the garden and cannot be content out of it. I have my house yard covered with evergreens, and now call it by that name." Her garden included vegetables, which she sold for much-needed cash, but her letters also comprise a virtual catalog of plants useful for landscaping—scarlet lights, pinks, butter and eggs, lark spurs, and yellow roses. Pioneer settlers like Rachel O'Connor sought to cultivate and reshape their natural environment as means of improving and controlling it both economically and aesthetically. At a time when there were few organized scientific or agricultural societies in the South, women, like O'Connor, who shared planting tips and seeds with their friends and family, played a vital, though informal role, both in agricultural development of the South and in the development of a characteristically southern landscape. According to her niece, Rachel took great "pains" with her yard, but the fields absorbed her attention as much as her gardening. In 1844 she crowed that Evergreen Plantation is "in first rate order" and the cotton was nearly all planted. But, it was her new orchard of 400 fruit trees that was her "*idol*", and Rachel wondered whether it was right to take pride, as she did in her "earthly treasures."

Rachel O'Connor planted, harvested and shipped cotton to market for nearly twenty-five years. During the economically depressed period between 1830 and 1840, O'Connor shipped an average of 125 bales per year to New Orleans, just a few bales less than the average for female planters in West Feliciana Parish in the much more prosperous year of 1850. In the twilight years of her life, O'Connor became increasingly handicapped by ill health and loss of her hearing. Her brother died in 1834 and, for a time, she feared she could not recover from his loss. She continued to manage the plantation for another eleven years, even encouraging David Weeks' heirs to purchase more land for her to manage. "Cotton brings a good price now," O'Connor advised the executor of David Weeks' estates and "I don't think you should be afraid to venture the price of the lands. It is near here and will be a great advantage. . . ." Her attitude toward management and expansion of the plantation is best expressed in a letter she wrote to David Weeks' heirs in 1835, "I have a great desire to manage for the best the time I have to live, and by adding some more land to this place, would afford me much fairer chance of doing so."

In 1844 David Weeks' heirs displayed their impatience with her continued residence on Evergreen Plantation. They may have also worried that because the State Supreme Court declared the sale of the plantation fraudulent in 1836, she, or other members of her family on her mother's side, might attempt to claim the plantation after her death. As early as 1836 Rachel tried to persuade the Weeks' heirs to return her property to her without success. In 1844 she signed a second conveyance reconfirming her sale of the plantation and slaves to David Weeks two decades earlier. The Weeks family legally owned most of the plantation. But O'Connor could rightfully claim to have built Evergreen and to have devoted most of her adult life to it. She desired only to remain on the land with her slaves, managing everything as she had always done. Rachel O'Connor died on May 22, 1846, after a difficult and painful surgery to remove a tumor from her breast. A testament to her hard work, frugality and management, O'Connor's estate, not counting the property she sold to her half brother sixteen years earlier, appraised at just over $33,000.

What can we say about Rachel O'Connor within the context of her female peers? We know that her experience as a female planter was not un-usual, particularly in an agriculturally-rich area like West Feliciana Parish.

Female planters represented a significant percentage of early nineteenth-century planters in West Feliciana Parish as well as in other areas of the South. . . . Their experiences were, however, shaped by gender. Women like Rachel O'Connor assumed traditional female tasks of household management, including providing food, clothing and nursing care for their slaves, as well as overseeing production on the plantation. We also know that even though widows enjoyed more legal autonomy than their married counterparts, female planters faced formidable obstacles in the management of their property. The male dominated legal and business world that defined women as subordinate made it especially useful for female planters to act interdependently with male kin or other relatives. To fully appreciate female planters' authority in the management of their plantation it is useful to eliminate autonomy as a requirement for women's exercise of authority. Rachel O'Connor acted with authority in regard to Evergreen, even though she acted in concert with her brother and his family. They shared a mutual interest in preserving the plantation.

Rachel O'Connor labored within the patriarchal system as it existed within the slave-holding south. . . . The authority Rachel O'Connor exercised in the management of her plantation ultimately derived from her personal commitment to a job well done and the resulting success she had as a planter. It is fitting that the plantation O'Connor helped to build through her land claims and purchases, hard work and gritty fortitude could provide the opportunity for her to exercise her capabilities so fully and acceptably and that it could provide her a measure of economic and personal independence. . . .

Rachel O'Connor earned the designation of planter, even if census tables do not specifically assign her that role. In fact, through her letters we catch a glimpse of Rachel O'Connor seated at her "old desk" writing, and as she does, expressing her own idea of herself as a female planter. . . . The last line in Rachel O'Connor's final letter in 1845, penned shortly before her death, reads "I have one hundred and two bales of cotton pressed which will be in N. Orleans by the time you receive this." Her words are an appropriate way to remember "Rachel O'Connor—that is as a female planter in West Feliciana Parish."

Questions
1. How common were female planters like Rachel O'Connor in Louisiana?
2. How did the common law system prevalent in the Anglo states differ from the Louisiana Civil Code in regards to married women's control of property?
3. What problems did O'Connor encounter in running the plantation? Which of those problems might have been encountered by any plantation manager, and which were difficulties that resulted from her gender?

THE MURDER OF A "LEWD AND ABANDONED WOMAN": *STATE OF LOUISIANA* v. *ABRAHAM PARKER*

by Judith Kelleher Schafer

S tate of louisiana v. abraham parker, a long forgotten and never officially reported appeal of an 1851 criminal prosecution for murder, provides an excellent illustration not only of the way historians can use court records and public trials to illuminate not only the workings of the law, courts, and attorneys, but to view the larger implications of what one case can reveal about antebellum attitudes about crime, law enforcement, the criminal justice system, race, gender, prostitution, class status, and cultural values. This obscure case also demonstrates the richness and variety of legal history as it sheds light on the business of prostitution and the relationship between prostitution, gender, and slavery in New Orleans before the Civil War.

As police Lieutenant Michael Hughes walked his beat in the pre-dawn darkness of a mild but muggy New Orleans morning in May 1851, he heard "quick footsteps" of a man "padding along in his stocking feet." Attracted by the sound, Hughes spotted a partially dressed man running headlong down Poydras Street toward the Mississippi River. The policeman finally caught the fleeing man, whom he recognized immediately as Abraham Parker, the pilot of the riverboat *C. E. Watkins,* and asked him what difficulty had occurred to cause him to run down the street half-dressed in the middle of the night. Parker stated that he had done nothing, that he was only going to his boat, and to allow him to pass. After repeated questioning on the part of Hughes and staunch assertions that "he had done nothing," Parker finally admitted—"with

Reprinted with permission: *The American Journal of Legal History* 44 (January 2000): 19–39.

considerable embarrassment and hesitation"——that he had visited a woman in a house of ill-fame somewhere on Basin or Bienville streets, that some persons had attacked him and stolen his clothes, and that he had to flee for his life. Hughes later testified that Parker "appeared very much excited," and Hughes, considering Parker's unusual appearance and the time of night, decided to take him to the Watch House for further questioning.

Not long after Parker arrived at the Watch House with Officer Hughes, several persons burst in and reported the murder of a woman in a house of ill-repute on Gravier Street between Circus and St. John streets, some distance from Basin or Bienville streets. Officers arriving at the scene had found a pair of boots, a hat, a coat and a pistol in the adjoining yard. Muddy footprints tracked over the back yard fence, which had two pickets broken off at the top, as though a person had climbed over them in haste.

Once inside the house, the officers found the bloody body of Eliza Phillips on the floor in the middle of the room, shot dead. When they returned to the Watch House, Hughes asked Parker if the hat he had found belonged to him. Parker did not answer, but when Hughes handed him the hat, he placed it on his head. The police officer then conducted Parker to the Orleans Parish jail to await a hearing on the incident. After a post-mortem examination, the coroner concluded that Eliza Phillips died of a gunshot wound "which passed through the chin of the deceased, came out through the neck, and again passed into the body," stopping finally at Phillips' third rib.

City newspapers reported the case with headlines such as "Another Horrible Murder" and "A Woman Murdered in Gravier Street." One reporter described Phillips as being a "degraded woman . . . in the habit of living with some dissolute character who aided her in extorting money from her visitors." According to this journalist, if Phillips, a twenty-five year old English woman who had resided in the city only briefly, had not had the "bold aspect and visible depravity which characterize her class, she would be considered handsome." The reporter's characterization of Phillips as "bold" sharply contrasted with conventional views of ideal white women that emphasized virtues such as softness, deference, timidity, and meekness. In comparison, this writer described Parker as a man well-known in New Orleans, about thirty-five years, "middle sized and robust," a man "from whom better acts might be expected, than those for which he has become a criminal," an upstanding man who had a wife and children in Tennessee. The local press would continue to emphasize Phillips's status as a "degraded woman" and her murder as just "another of those frequent occurrences," while it portrayed Parker as a respectable husband and father throughout the preliminary hearing and subsequent trial. As it turned out, the highest court in Louisiana would base its decision in this case on the same assumptions.

James Caldwell, the Recorder of the Second Municipality, conducted the preliminary hearing on May 12, in front of a standing-room-only crowd. Those who could not find space in the courtroom not only sat on the window sills within the chamber, but tried to hear the proceedings from outside of the building's open windows. Eugene Suchet, Phillips's "bedfellow" and almost certainly her pimp, testified first. With minor variations, all other testimony corroborated Suchet's description of the events of the night of May 7 and the early hours of May 8. Toward the end of an evening of drinking on the town, Abraham Parker and an unnamed and never identified male friend decided to visit a brothel at 211 Gravier Street. The owner of the property, Sumpter Turner, a partner in the tobacco brokerage firm of Turner and Renshaw, entrusted the actual management of the brothel to his slave Eliza Turner, who also sold coffee and perhaps liquor in the front room of the house. Parker entered the house, put his arms around Phillips, whom he had obviously known previously, and "said he would like to go into a room with her, to which she consented." They walked together into a back room. Almost immediately Phillips emerged and showed the slave Eliza "a piece of money"; the slave gave her approval to "go ahead" and Phillips returned to the back room. After some time, Phillips came out of the room and walked out into the street. Parker went out into the front room dressed only "in his socks and drawers," sat down, and talked for some time with his friend. Phillips became angry when she returned to the coffee room and found Parker still there, undressed. "G__d d__d you, why don't you put on your clothes and go?," Phillips asked. Parker responded that she could "go to Hell," it was none of her business, and not to touch his clothes, and threw them on a chair in the front room. As she did so, Parker's watch fell on the floor, shattering the crystal. Infuriated, Parker said, "D__d you, I told you not to touch my clothes."

As he began to dress himself, the "partly drunk" Parker accused Phillips of stealing a Tennessee ten-dollar bill from his vest pocket. Phillips called Parker a "damned liar" and denied taking the money. Parker drew a loaded pistol from his breast pocket and said to his friend, "the d__d bitch" had taken it. He then struck Eliza on the back of her neck with the back of his hand, a blow sufficiently powerful to propel her into the next room, saying "Get it G__d d__d you, or I will shoot you . . . and everybody else in the house." Parker's unidentified friend tried to quiet him, suggesting that they leave the house. At this time, Eugene Suchet entered the room and immediately tried to mollify the "somewhat intoxicated" Parker by assuring him that if Phillips had taken his (Suchet's) money that he would certainly "slap her face." When Phillips denied once more having the bill, Suchet told Parker that he did not believe that she had stolen his money. Infuriated, Parker replied, "God damn you, you are taking up for the woman. I'll shoot you." Phillips continued to deny that she had the bill, and at his friend's suggestion, Parker took a candle and went into the bedroom to search for the money. When he did not find it, he took hold of Phillips and told her he knew that she had the bill, "and that he was bound to have it, that he had treated her well, and that she ought not to have robbed him." Phillips opened her purse to show that it contained only the two dollar and fifty cent gold piece that Parker had given her for her services, a few other pieces of silver change, and a receipt for her weekly room rent of nine dollars, signed by the slave Eliza. Once more, Phillips asked Parker to leave the house. At this, Parker cursed again, raised his pistol, put it to Phillips's neck, fired, and ran out the back door. Phillips "lingered a few minutes in dreadful agony, and then died." A thorough search of the dead woman's clothing and the house at 211 Gravier failed to produce the ten-dollar bill.

Local newspapers reported that Parker "appeared somewhat affected during the proceeding but heard evidence with perfect calmness." The crowd that packed the Recorder's courtroom for the three-day hearing exhibited "the most lively interest in the proceedings." Randell Hunt, a well-known local attorney, served as counsel for the accused at the preliminary hearing. While Hunt did not deny that Parker had shot Phillips, he hinted that the gun had fired accidentally. His most strenuous defense of Parker lay in his insistence that Eugene Suchet's character was so depraved that no one could or should believe him, even under oath. Hunt called Suchet "an infamous scoundrel living upon an unfortunate woman . . . a dissolute and corrupt vagabond."

Recorder Caldwell agreed, stating publically that if the case depended on the testimony of Suchet alone, he would immediately discharge the accused, "for, unsupported, he would not believe a word Suchet said . . . the manner in which he lived stamped him with infamy." Under cross examination, Suchet claimed that he worked as a blacksmith when he could find work, but that illness had prevented him from finding work for the past six months. He said he had known Phillips when she lived in a house on Perdido Street, and that she had moved to the house at 211 Gravier two or three weeks before her death. Suchet admitted that he owned no property, had no income and that he had lodged with the deceased almost every night for the last six months. Although Caldwell professed disgust at Suchet's boasting that he had lived off of Phillips, the Recorder stated that he felt duty-bound to send the case to the First District Court for trial for murder. The grand jury found a true bill against Parker for murder on May 30. Parker pleaded not guilty on June 4, and the clerk of the First District Court set the case for trial on June 17.

Located in the Presbytère, one of the buildings flanking the St. Louis Cathedral on Jackson Square, the First District Court of New Orleans shared the rat-infested firetrap into which the building had degenerated with four other district courts and the Supreme Court of Louisiana. Just three weeks before the trial of *State* v. *Parker*, the grand jury complained that the constant noise of drays passing by the open, first-floor windows of the First District Court, interfered with jurors hearing important testimony at criminal trials. The building, ordinarily crowded by witnesses, attorneys, accused criminals, hangers-on, fruit vendors, spectators, civil litigants, and the clerks and judges of six separate courts presented an unusually hectic scene on the first day of the trial of Abraham Parker: "It was crowded in every part by an anxiously expectant multitude, and hundreds who could not obtain admission crowded to the windows and every attainable spot from which sight or hearing of the proceedings could be obtained." Local newspapers noted that the reputation of the counsel for the defense, the "social position of the accused, and the awful crime with which he was charged," created an interest "seldom exceeded in criminal prosecutions." Judge John Larue presided over the trial. A hardworking member of the bench who kept his docket up to date, Larue had made a reputation as a fair but tough jurist who handed down stiff sentences, "offering terrible prospect[s] to evildoers." The legal community considered Judge Larue "a man of rare natural abilities" who united "high legal attainment and a ready familiarity with the jurisprudence of Louisiana and the principles and practice of criminal law."

By the time the trial began, two attorneys had joined Randell Hunt on Parker's defense team: John Randolph Grymes and John Blount Robertson. . . .

The District Attorney, Mortimer M. Reynolds, opened the trial by summing up the facts of the case and the applicable law. He then presented a series of witnesses who essentially restated the testimony given at the preliminary hearing. After Reynolds's questioning of Eugene Suchet, Randell Hunt cross-examined him, and forced Suchet to admit that he had no income and that Eliza Phillips supported him. When Reynolds objected to this line of questioning, Hunt told the judge that he wished "to show the idle, dissolute, depraved character of the witness." Judge Larue sustained Reynolds's objection, stating that Hunt had taken "more latitude in denunciations of the witness than could be permitted." Hunt then proceeded to introduce witnesses to undermine Suchet's credibility; one witness testified that he would not believe Suchet under oath and that "he knew fifty people who would not believe him under oath either." This witness asserted that "Suchet had been in the habit of supporting himself by extorting money from persons who visited women of bad repute with whom he associated." Hunt then began a series of leading questions concerning the character of Suchet, such as "Is he not idle and vicious, etc.?" At this, Suchet asked for the protection of the court. Reynolds objected to the tone of Hunt's inquiry, and the judge, after considerable discussion among the attorneys, ruled that Hunt could introduce witnesses as related to Suchet's reputation for "truth and veracity" only. The attack on Suchet functioned as a way to attack Phillips herself. By condemning Suchet because he lived off the income of a "lewd" woman, Parker's attorneys avoided directly slandering a woman who, after all, had been brutally murdered during an argument over a ten-dollar bill. In doing so, Parker's attorneys attempted to convince the jury that Phillips's death was not worth ruining the life of the "respectable" Abraham Parker. . . .

Grymes and Hunt then introduced witnesses to prove the good character of the defendant. One testified that he had known Parker for seventeen years on the river, and that he had a wife and children in Tennessee: "He has always borne a good character." The captain of the *C. E. Watkins* also vouched for

Parker's character, but on cross-examination, he admitted that after a fight in Cincinnati, authorities had charged Parker with manslaughter: "I heard that he was surrounded and cut his way out. I have seen him fight men. I heard that one man he cut in Cincinnati died… and again I heard he had not." Hunt and Grymes' men introduced "a host of witnesses" who testified as to the "excellent character of the accused." When Reynolds objected, Judge Larue ruled that Hunt and Grymes had to confine their character witnesses to testify only to the accused's general reputation for "peace and quietness."

In a one-hour closing statement, which the *New Orleans Bee* described as one of his most "masterly efforts," Reynolds attempted to minimize the damage done to his principal witness by arguing that other witnesses had corroborated much of Suchet's testimony, including the fact that Parker had admitted that he had gotten into some difficulty with a woman on the night of the homicide. To those who had alleged that Suchet's association with "lewd women" made it impossible to believe him, Reynolds posed this question, "Was it a greater offense for him to seek the association of such women—a single man without wife or children—than it was in the prisoner at the bar [Parker], who though husband and father, so cohabited with such women?" Reynolds warned the jury that the defense attorneys would play on their sympathy for Parker's wife and children, but that the jury must remember that the defendant "ruthlessly sent a lonely and unprotected woman to her last account, without a moment's preparation, and though she was a fallen creature; though she led a life of shame, she was equally under the protection of the law as the chastest in the land."

Randell Hunt captured the "undivided attention" of the large and excited crowd of spectators in his two-hour closing statement: "Mr. Hunt was particularly severe in the animadversions on the testimony of Eugene Suchet." In what one newspaper described as a "terrible excoriation," Hunt attempted to discredit Suchet's testimony as "wholly false and groundless." Although he had presented no evidence at trial to substantiate his charge, he closed his attack on Suchet with a cheap shot, accusing him of stealing the ten-dollar bill, thus causing Phillips's death. Hunt then characterized Parker as "a man brave and humane … when he visited this woman it was not with a feeling of enmity, but the very contrary." Although Hunt admitted that Parker had sex with the deceased in "a moment of looseness and levity," he claimed that Parker had shot Phillips quite by accident. In closing, Hunt appealed to the sympathy of the jury, "which was a touching specimen of forensic eloquence. . . ."

The District Attorney had the final say. He argued that "the law presumed the homicide to be malicious by the fact that the prisoner carried about with him a loaded pistol, and used it fatally, without sufficient provocation" to commit "a cruel and unprovoked murder."

Judge Larue then charged the jury, in "an impressive and impartial charge," warning them not to bow to outside influences such as "the excited crowd attending the trial" or the testimony of the friends or enemies of the accused or the deceased. The judge reminded the jury that the defense had conceded that "a woman has been murdered," and the jury had to decide whether her death resulted from an accidental or an intentional act. "You must judge of this by common sense, by the rules that govern your judgment in every day transactions, your own heart and testimony. A better rule I cannot lay down for you." Judge Larue then explained the difference between murder and manslaughter to the jury, but he did not comment on the testimony. The jury left to deliberate at 1:40 in the afternoon. Unmoved by the defense's attempt to smear Suchet and sanctify Parker, the jury returned at three o'clock with a verdict of "guilty of manslaughter." Although Parker had employed some of the most talented attorneys in New Orleans, and despite the withering attack on Suchet, and indirectly on Phillips, the jury did not buy the defense's explanation of events and remained unconvinced by their tactics. Reynolds's powerful indictment of a legal system that might excuse a married man who bought sex from a prostitute and then shot her with a loaded, concealed weapon impressed them more than the smear tactics of the defense. Apparently Reynolds convinced the jury that a prostitute, even one who had allowed herself to become subordinate to a slave, could not be denied the protection of the law simply because of her occupation. This argument must have resonated with the jury, because they found Parker guilty.

The jury's decision may also have reflected class conflict in New Orleans. Exemptions for jury duty were so extensive that "the material of which the Juries are likely to be composed, is considerably depreciated . . . [although] the nature of jury service eminently calls for the most intelligent and upright men." Generous exemptions often led to "fruitless attempts to empanel juries." Those who remained to serve came from a social class more likely to sympathize with the victim than with the upper-class Parker and his expensive attorneys.

On the following day, Judge Larue sentenced Parker to twenty years in the state penitentiary and a fine of $1000, not an unusually severe sentence for manslaughter. Parker's attorneys immediately applied for bail, which Larue set at $15,000. Parker posted bond the same day, and left the courthouse, free on bail. He would never serve a day for his sentence.

Judge Larue refused a petition for a new trial on June 22 and the defense attorneys appealed to the Supreme Court of Louisiana. Hunt and Grymes filed several bills of exceptions, asserting that Larue had violated the rules of evidence by restricting the testimony concerning the character and misdeeds of Eugene Suchet. . . .

The Supreme Court rendered its decision on February 23, 1852. Ruling that Judge Larue had erred in restricting the defense to proof of Suchet's general reputation for "truth and veracity" alone, the high court held that the defense "should have been allowed to offer general evidence as to the general character of the witness impeached," to allow the State to inquire as to how the witnesses learned of his character. . . . The justices sent the case back to the First District Court for a new trial with instruction to Judge Larue to admit evidence of Suchet's bad character and testimony to prove Parker's high morals.

By the time that Abraham Parker's new trial began, Judge Larue no longer presided over the criminal court. [The Louisiana Constitution of 1852 made all positions on the formerly appointive state bench elective. Though Judge Larue was elected to that position in a landslide, he nonetheless chose to resign, citing an inadequate salary.] When the new trial began, one of Parker's attorneys, John Blount Robertson, now presided over the new trial. Robertson had won the special election called to fill the position created by Larue's resignation.

Three and a half years passed before the First District Court of New Orleans called Parker to stand trial again for the homicide of Eliza Phillips. The long delay occurred because the prosecution . . . could not or would not find the necessary witnesses to retry the case. Although no record exists of the new trial several New Orleans newspapers reported that it began and ended on January 31, 1855. The clerk called the names of the witnesses, but none appeared, and "it being apparent to the court that they could never appear," the district attorney entered a *nolle prosqui*, and the judge dismissed Parker. . . .[1] Largely forgotten by 1855, two of the three newspapers that reported the case's dismissal gave Phillips's first name as Isabella instead of Eliza and reported her address incorrectly, although still in the district where many prostitutes resided. Printing allegations as facts, the *Delta*, echoing Grymes's false assertion in his closing statement, reported that Parker, fearing assault by a number of persons, accidentally fired his gun. In the end, corrupt men who held the reins of judicial power subverted justice in favor of a man of their own class.

Although the case did not proceed to trial, as a former member of Parker's defense team, Robertson should have recused himself. . . .

Abraham Parker never served a day for the killing of Eliza Phillips. It is not clear from the record whether he paid court costs. After his dismissal, city directories continued to list him as a riverboat pilot who rented a succession of rooms in New Orleans until 1889, when his name disappeared from the directory.

State v. *Parker* demonstrates the ability of court records to illumine the law and the workings of courts, attorneys, and judges, and to reveal societal attitudes about crime, gender, and class status. An 1817 ordinance of the city of New Orleans made renting rooms or lodging to any woman "notoriously abandoned to lewdness" an offense punishable by a fine of fifteen dollars for each twenty-four hours the offender, after receiving notice from the mayor, continued to furnish housing to such women. The following year, the Louisiana legislature passed a law prohibiting keeping a brothel or face a fine or imprisonment at the discretion of the court. State law did not make prostitution a crime, but the city ordinance made "any woman or girl notoriously abandoned to lewdness, who shall occasion scandal or disturb the tranquility of the neighborhood" subject to a fine of twenty-five dollars or one month in jail. An 1845 city ordinance made it illegal for such women to drink in cabarets or coffee houses or face the same penalty. Eliza Phillips's living arrangements demonstrate that police, recorders, and judges enforced these laws sporadically, when they bothered to enforce them at all. Phillips rented a room in a building that housed several prostitutes. The owner of the building, a prominent

[1] *Nolle Prosqui* means the prosecutor dropped the charge for lack of evidence.

white businessman, profited from this arrangement while his slave managed the brothel. Her arrest the morning after Phillips's death and subsequent appearance before Justice of the Peace Jacob Winter on a charge of keeping a brothel ended in a quick dismissal. Although no evidence exists that the slave manager sold liquor in the house, she did sell coffee to the public, further violating city ordinances. As no law specifically made selling sex a crime, most of the city's recorders charged so-called lewd women brought before them as vagrants, although they had residences and did not therefore fit the legal description of vagrants. . . .

A reading of Louisiana law prohibited brothel-keeping and acting as "lewd and abandoned women" and even a cursory view of the enforcement of these state statutes and city ordinances makes it clear that neither lawmakers nor the public sincerely wished to eradicate prostitution. Only a few dozen cases charging people with keeping a brothel came before the First District Court of New Orleans in the 1850s, and almost all of these case records indicated that the prosecutor filed a *nolle prosqui* dismissing the case before the matter came to trial. The scarcity of these cases on the criminal docket contrasted sharply with local newspapers' reports of dozens of arrests of so-called lewd women and operators of brothels each year. Unless prostitution caused a public nuisance or disturbed otherwise "respectable" neighborhoods, the authorities allowed the profession to exist and even flourish in antebellum New Orleans. A contemporary writer noted that men in New Orleans went quite openly to houses of prostitution. This writer estimated that prostitutes occupied at least three-fifths of the dwelling rooms in certain parts of the city and that an "immense number" of regularly established brothels operated quite openly: "it is not unusual to see the windows and doors of almost every house as far as the eye can recognize them, filled with these girls."

State v. *Parker* also illuminates societal attitudes about prostitution and gender. Antebellum New Orleanians regarded prostitution as a women's offense, although women could not commit this act alone. No evidence exists of prosecution of their customers or even newspaper accounts that reveal the names of such men. The *Parker* case record and the local newspapers demonstrate a notable lack of sympathy for prostitutes in general and Eliza Phillips in particular. Newspapers constantly refer to her as a "degraded woman," and cannot even admit that she appeared attractive without qualifying the statement by mentioning "the visible depravity that characterizes her class." Reports of arrests of prostitutes often refer to them sarcastically as "*Nymph de Pavé*," literally nymphs of the pavement.

The trial record in the *Parker* case also rejects the double standard that applied to men and women. Although many men in antebellum New Orleans supported wives who earned no wages, the defense attorneys used the fact that Suchet did not work and allowed Phillips to support him as one of the most damning pieces of evidence against his character. Newspapers described Parker as a socially prominent, "robust" man without qualification and commented that "better acts might be expected of him." Although antebellum society characterized Phillips's status as "degraded" by her occupation, Parker's availing himself of her services only constituted "a moment of looseness and levity." Parker even bragged that "he had been good to her," when in reality he used her for his own gratification. The very fact that the defense attorneys successfully got their client off without punishment by using a defense stressing Parker's respectability and Phillips's degraded status reflects society's attitudes about men, women, and prostitution. Parker's status as a husband and a father by its very nature implied good character in antebellum New Orleans society. That the defense attorneys could unblushingly assert that Parker was a man of "pure morals" who would never hurt a woman, when he had spent an evening carrying a loaded, concealed weapon while drinking on the town, committed adultery by purchasing sex from a prostitute, and in a fit of drunken rage killed her, speaks volumes about society's attitude. Only the judge and the district attorney mentioned at trial the plain fact that Parker had shot Phillips, and that she deserved the protection of the law regardless of her occupation.

State v. *Parker* also opens a window on slavery in New Orleans. Louisiana law and city ordinances prohibited anyone from operating a brothel, but clearly the slave Eliza Turner managed the brothel at 211 Gravier Street. . . . Louisiana law forbade teaching slaves to read and write, but the rent receipt found in the dead woman's purse bore the slave woman's signature. And the slave woman's speedy dismissal on the charge of keeping a brothel indicated that her owner may have pressured the justice of the peace, or even bribed him to release her. The facts of this case also demonstrate that Turner broke several other state statutes and local ordinances. The Black Code prohibited slaves from selling "any commodity whatsoever," but Turner sold coffee and perhaps liquor in the front room of the brothel. Masters of slaves who sold goods could suffer penalties of a fine not less than fifty dollars and jail time of not less than one month. A city ordinance also prohibited slaves from living away from their owners, but obviously Turner lived at 211 Gravier, and her owner did not. Finally, the law did not allow white women "abandoned to lewdness" to live in the same house as women of color or for women of color to rent rooms to such white women. Eliza Phillips violated not only the law, but also racial etiquette by allowing a slave woman to subordinate her. But in New Orleans, slaves not only ran brothels, they also sometimes worked in them as prostitutes. The *Picayune* reported that the slave Louisa kept a brothel, "the resort for slaves of an abandoned character." Police found two slaves there with passes from their owners and baskets of flowers "to hide their evil deeds." The slave women either convinced their owners that they sold flowers, or the owners knowingly allowed them to work as prostitutes and collected their wages. A week before Phillips's murder, six free women of color came before the Recorder Joseph Genois for keeping "disorderly houses which were frequented by lewd women." Obviously statutes and ordinances against these practices were ordinarily honored only in the breech.

Finally, *State* v. *Parker* reveals something of the business of prostitution. Parker paid Phillips two dollars a month and female servants made between eight and twelve dollars a month; Phillips paid rent of nine dollars a week to the slave Eliza. At least two other prostitutes lived at 211 Gravier, since police found them in the house just after the murder. Even if only three prostitutes worked in the house, the owner of the property, Sumpter Turner, would have collected over one hundred dollars a month from his slave manager, not counting any profit she may have made from the sale of coffee or liquor, if she sold liquor. A number of wealthy New Orleans businessmen profited from renting to prostitutes. The merchant John McDonogh made a practice of purchasing houses in fashionable neighborhoods and renting the premises to a brothel keeper. Recorder Caldwell himself rented property to so-called houses of ill fame. Sumpter Turner realized an above-average profit from the establishment at 211 Gravier Street. The *Picayune* estimated the average monthly rental for such establishments at thirty dollars.

State v. *Parker* is but one illustration of the variety and vitality of legal history. The character in this drama about whom we know the least, Eliza

Phillips, led a brief life that ended in a violent and untimely death. Nearly one hundred fifty years later, there remain important historical lessons to learn from her death.

Questions

1. How does Schafer use the case of *State* v. *Parker* to illustrate class differences in New Orleans?
2. What was the ultimate outcome of this case?
3. What does the case reveal about societal attitudes regarding gender and prostitution?
4. What does it reveal about slavery in New Orleans?

PART THREE

TRANSFORMATION OF THE LOUISIANA "CREOLE"

❧ ☙

When the United States purchased Louisiana from France in 1803, the territory's inhabitants—after more than a century of French and Spanish colonial rule—had no tradition of republican government or democracy. English would now be the official language, and alien American customs, laws, and governance would define the new order. The arrival of Anglo settlers and officials naturally produced some resentment on the part of Latin-descended, or "Gallic," natives. White Louisianians responded by developing a romantic mythology about the Creole past. Although "*Creole*" traditionally described any Louisiana native, without regard to race or ethnicity, white Louisianians sought to redefine the term and claim it for themselves. Whites propagated the notion that Creoles had been charming, sophisticated, educated, and refined aristocrats of Latin ancestry. Joseph Tregle debunks those myths in an engagingly written classic essay about early New Orleans society. He provides evidence that the term Creole was used far more broadly than Louisiana whites claimed, and that the Creoles of lore were not the aristocratic sophisticates later generations alleged.

In the second essay, Justin Nystrom uses the term *Creole* to describe a mixed-race woman, Louise Marie Drouet, as well as her father, a white man. Nystrom's article details the complications inherent in defining lines of racial hierarchy and social identity in New Orleans at a time of social and political upheaval. The story of Louise Marie Drouet is set against the backdrop of the Civil War (1861–65) and Reconstruction (in Louisiana, Reconstruction began in 1863, but in the rest of the former Confederacy in 1865, and lasted until 1877). The end of slavery threw the three-tiered system of race relations described in Part Two into doubt and caused whites in Louisiana to distance themselves even further from people of color. The Republican-dominated Louisiana government of the Reconstruction era allowed mixed-race marriages for the first time, and thus the chance to legitimize offspring of interracial unions. This in turn caused hostility from whites who saw their mixed-race relatives as a threat to their inheritance. Nystrom follows the case of Louise Marie Drouet, caught up in this transition as she fought her white relatives over a modest portion of her father's estate.

EARLY NEW ORLEANS SOCIETY:
A REAPPRAISAL

by Joseph G. Tregle, Jr.

Most of the south has been content with one Lost Cause, one romantic memory of a time gone by in which it has been possible to linger with mixed emotions of pride in the perfection of the past and regret for its passing. But in that most distinct of southern states, Louisiana, where loyalties have so often been confused, even the Confederacy has been unable to dominate the nostalgia of the people, and, indeed, the commiseration felt by Louisianians for the death of the antebellum South has been as nothing compared to their mourning over the fate of the Creole.

A veritable cult of the Creole has grown over the years, propagated by historians as well as by journalists, by scholars as well as by the often pathetic present-day representatives of this supposed tradition, confused but happy in their knowledge that once their kind had ruled these lands along the Mississippi with a grace and charm long since lost to the modern world. For those who look so longingly to the past, these old Latin ways and forms have taken on the character of a superior culture, doomed to be crushed in the eventual day of Anglo-Saxon uniformity.

But when dreams distort historical truth, it is necessary, though perhaps futile, to challenge them, and it is the purpose of this paper to re-examine the nature of New Orleans' early population, to restore some proper focus in

Joseph G. Tregle, Jr., "Early New Orleans Society: A Reappraisal," *Journal of Southern History* 8 (February 1952): 20–36.

which to view the society of the city and of the state. It was perhaps inevitable that misunderstanding should spring from the confusion that was Louisiana in the 1820s. Nowhere was this confusion more striking than in the crossroad of the world that so dominated Louisiana life, the metropolis of New Orleans.

The population of the city in the 1820s was divided into groups and shadings of groups, whose suspicions, resentments, and hatreds fed on the isolation from each other occasioned by differences of language and tradition, and battened on the familiarity bred by inevitable competition for political and economic power. The largest single group in the community was the *ancien population*, the descendants of the French and Spanish colonial settlers, about whom so much has been written and so little has been explained. Romantic folklore, filial pride, and uncritical if effusive writings have hidden these people behind a mythological fog which even today it is socially dangerous to try to penetrate. There are few things clung to so tenaciously or taught so vehemently in New Orleans as the doctrine of the Creole, which might be summed up as the religious belief that all those who bore that name were Louisianians born to descendants of the French and Spanish, that they were almost uniformly genteel and cultured aristocrats, above the lure of money, disdainful of physical labor, and too sensitive to descend into the dirty business of political and monetary struggle with the crude Américains, though they were influential enough to engulf the barbarism of the latter and give social and artistic tone to the city.

Nothing so infuriates the apostles of the Creole myth as the widespread belief in some outland quarters that the term implies a mixture of white and Negro blood,[1] and they insist with an air of finality and aggressiveness that no Creole has ever been anything but a native white Louisianian descended from the Latin colonial stock. Even the descendants of the Acadian migrants from Canada are ruled out of this select society—they may be Cajuns, but never Creoles, for who has ever heard of a lowly Creole? Poor, perhaps, but never lowly. Only on one point is there any compromise, and that is in the willingness of the elect to admit that "Creole" may be legitimately used as an adjective to classify any number of things as native to the state, so that one may

---

[1] In 1952, when this article was published, the polite term was "Negro," as used by this author, rather than "African American."

speak correctly of a slave as a "Creole Negro," for example, if never simply as a "Creole." Some latitudinarians will even concede a place to those such as the scions of the German settlers who came into Louisiana under John Law, or to post-Purchase French migrants, since all these eventually become identified with the Gallic culture of the community. But the more frequent insistence is on the narrower definition.

It must be admitted that these Creoles of fancy are a charming and thoroughly delightful people. After all, they possessed physical and moral qualities, if we are to believe the tradition, which placed them among the favored of Providence. Their girls were models of beauty and feminine virtue, protected from the crudities of life by a rigid and almost incredible family supervision and training, yet the very epitome of those social graces and accomplishments which make for the delight of men. The women were deferential wives and mothers, arbiters of style and behavior, mistresses of gracious households. And who would not recognize the men—the dark and lithe youths, handsome, gallant, and brave, educated in France or select American colleges, and equipped with an electric pride which sparked at the slightest contact and led inevitably to numberless duels, generally of the gentlemanly kind involving slender swords and as little vulgar gore as possible; or the older, dignified, and chivalrous aristocrats, wise in the ways of the world, urbane and courtly, the very soul of honor and hospitality.

Their great accomplishment, we are told, was to know how to live. Not for them the rush and greed of the grasping American, whose god was the dollar and who had little time or inclination for the joys of the theater or the appreciation of beauty. It was breeding, never money, which counted with the Creole of tradition, and family pride made it impossible for him even to consider an economic pursuit which required the removal of his coat or the laborious use of his hands. He could be a banker, of course, which was eminently respectable, a professional man, a planter, or even a merchant, if on a large enough scale. But it should occasion no surprise that he fell farther and farther behind in the economic race with the Yankee—no man of his sensibilities could be expected to care enough for mere money to chase it with the almost frightening determination of a John McDonogh, or to allow the bothersome details of business to interfere with the serious things of life such as the theater, the opera, the ball, or the hunt. One could not be expected always to have an eye on the Americans! Thus life for the traditional Creole had few sharp edges—he moved in the circles of his society with gentility of manner and an awareness of all the subtleties of good living which could only have come from his noble lineage. Paragon of style, judge of good wine and fine food, connoisseur of handsome women, he was to the manner born.[2]

The only serious fault with this hallowed doctrine of the Creole is that it does demonstrable violence to historical truth. It is abundantly clear that in the 1820s and 1830s "Creole" was generally used in Louisiana to designate any person native to the state, be he white, black, or colored, French, Spanish, or Anglo-American, and used not as an adjective but as a noun. Thus the terms "Creole" and "native" were interchangeable, and if one wished to speak only of those Latin Louisianians who could trace their ties to the soil back to colonial days, the only precise form for so doing was that of the "*ancien population.*" It is true, of course, that since the great preponderance of Creoles were of this original stock it was not at all unusual to find "Creole" being used as a more convenient term than "ancient population," especially when one considers that the Anglo-American Creoles were neither numerous enough nor generally old enough in the 1820s and 1830s to make necessary the more limited and accurate terminology during the heated racial conflicts in the community, and certainly it was realized that no one would think of considering the Negro as being at all involved in any of these factional distinctions among white men. Moreover, the *ancien population* almost universally insisted upon identifying their interests as those common to all *native* Louisianians, and they deliberately embraced the non-Latin native as one of themselves. There could be no question, therefore, of denying him the title of Creole. It follows naturally that the Acadians were likewise full-fledged members of this group, and there was certainly never any attempt in the press or the hustings to consider them in any other light.

The evidence on all these points is quite clear. Innumerable newspaper advertisements refer matter-of-factly to Louisiana-born Negroes as Creoles; Isaac Johnson, native of the Florida parishes, completely Anglo-American in speech and culture, was proud of his right to the Creole label; and Alexander

---

[2] In 1952 it was common to use the male pronoun when referring to a population that included women. Tregle's references to a Creole as "he" should not be construed to mean that all Creoles were male.

Mouton, Acadian Jacksonian from Lafayette, was certainly considered by his contemporaries as a major leader of the Creole group.

It was as a native Louisianian, as a matter of fact, that the Latin Creole primarily thought of himself, for he saw in that powerful and mystical bond which ties most men to the soil of their birth the principal justification for his determination not to become a forgotten man in his own land. The danger of that eventuality coming to pass was by no means slight in the 1820s and 1830s. For two other major groups in New Orleans and throughout the state had gradually come to dominate the affairs of the community to the growing exclusion of all others: the Anglo-Americans and the so-called "foreign French."

The Americans, of course, were of all kinds and from all places. They had come down into Louisiana principally after the Purchase to seek their fortunes in the rich acres of the new territory and in its markets, banks, courts, and thriving trading centers. There had been other Americans in New Orleans before 1803, to be sure, and they had generally been of a breed that was not easy to forget. Rough, violent, profane, and brawling, the floating adventurers, the river bullies, and the backwoods denizens come to market had made the American and Kentuckian names things to be feared and often detested among the citizens of the great port, who welcomed the trade but regretted the traders. One did not need the pride of the Creole of tradition to decide that he would have little to do with men such as these.

Louisiana folklore has, unfortunately, too greatly stressed this vulgarity and barbarism of the early Americans in Louisiana, and a part of the Creole myth would have it that for many decades the Creoles held aloof from the newcomers, confident of their own evident superiority, keeping alive the social, artistic, and cultural traditions of the community while the Yankee changed money in the temple. Nothing could be further from the truth, for it is a misrepresentation of both the Latin Creole and the Anglo-American types.

The plain truth of the matter is that the *ancient population* of the early nineteenth century, the Latin Creoles, were hardly the same sort of people met with so delightfully in the Creole myth. That they were charming in their way can hardly be denied, but theirs was a charm springing from simplicity, from a natural, sensate joy in life, and from the fervid and mercurial emotionalism of their temperaments, rather than the charm of a highly cultured or accomplished people. Many of them unquestionably possessed the courtliness of manner which had sprung from the days of the greatness of France and Spain, but the form had long outlived the substance of any aristocratic heritage. Illiteracy among the Latin Creoles was appalling, for example, and was certainly not limited to the less fortunate of their members. Even such men as Jacques Villeré and Bernard Marigny were notoriously limited in education, though both had spent time in France and were unquestionably among the elite of Creole society. At one time both of these men were charged, not by Anglo-Americans but by other Latin Creoles, with being unable to write a simple sentence. Marigny, indeed, the so-called "Creole of Creoles," is reliably reported to have eaten with his fingers instead of the more customary knife and fork.

Educational facilities had been severely neglected in the colony before 1803, and it was the rare exception rather than the rule for Louisianans to do much studying anywhere, France included, until well after the Purchase. Nor had their status as colonials allowed the Louisianians opportunity to develop any of the faculties which might have allowed them to compete on an even footing with those who moved into their country after 1803. They had known no banks under France and Spain, had had no opportunity to produce any commercial princes or political leaders of their own, and were by and large a people with little initiative and a limited awareness of the facts of nineteenth-century life. Provincial in outlook, style, and taste, the typical Latin Creole was complaisant, unlettered, unskilled, content to occupy his days with the affairs of his estate or the demands of his job, for it should be obvious that the average Creole was no more wealthy than the average man anywhere and worked where work was to be had. He lived in sensation rather than reflection, enjoying the balls and dances, betting heavily at table, or perhaps at the cockpit, endlessly smoking his inevitable cigar, whiling away hours over his beloved dominoes, busying himself with the many demands of his close-knit family life. Seldom a fashion plate, he was more often than not adorned in pantaloons of blue cottonade, coarse and ungainly in appearance and separated from misshapen shoes by a considerable visible stretch of blue-striped yarn stockings. A hat of no standard style and an ill-fitted coat with long, narrow collars and skirts usually completed the costume.

The women, fortunately, displayed greater taste in their dress, but were given to an ornateness which was more appreciated by the French than by the Americans. It must be stated regretfully, as well, that the Creole belle did not sweep all before her. To many she was beautiful, to be sure, with clear classic features and magnificent black hair, but others preferred the charms of her American sister, and even her admirers admitted that she generally ran to plumpness too early in life. As to her manners, some found them an interesting and gay mixture of small talk and flirtation, while others were left cold by the shallowness of young girls and matrons whose whole education consisted frequently of small instruction in dancing and music.

Even the romanticizers of the Latin Creole have seldom presented him as an intellectual, it must be admitted, which is just as well, since literature, art, and scientific knowledge actually had little appeal to the *ancien population*. Every library begun in New Orleans from 1806 to 1833, for example, seems to have been the product of Anglo-American rather than Latin planning. An observant Prince Achille Murat noted also that New Orleans in 1832 was a "striking contrast to all the other large cities," intellectual conversation being met with there rarely and the whole place containing only three libraries, "while the book-stores contain works of the worst description of French literature." But the prince had seen all of New Orleans, and he hastened to point out that if there was little conversation of note, "ample means are afforded for eating, playing, dancing, and making love."

It was as a patron of the theater, of course, that the Latin Creole is supposed to have demonstrated the most exquisite taste and refinement, but here again the historical record fails to substantiate any claim of such superiority. For all their love of the famed Théâtre d'Orléans, the native population was so sparing in its attendance in 1824, for example, that manager John Davis announced reluctantly that he would shortly be forced to close his doors, and such crises were by no means infrequent in the next decade. By the early 1830s, as a matter of fact, the enterprising James Caldwell had developed the American theater in the city to the point that even such rabidly French papers as the *Bee* had more or less come to slight the older but backward Orléans. As for the quality of presentation and performance, the French theater was hardly distinguishable from the American in a period in which all taste was seemingly execrable. If the Anglo-Americans rejoiced in the exhaustive antics of *Tom and Jerry*, the Latin Creoles had their Jocko, or *the Monkey of Brazil*. It is noteworthy, too, that the first real season of grand opera in New

Orleans was the work of the Englishman Caldwell, rather than of a French or native impresario.

It is reassuring to realize, moreover, that the Creole was not unlike every other New Orleanian where money was concerned—which means that he would grasp practically any means to acquire it. Wealth was the all-consuming aim of practically everyone in the community, and if the Creole's imagination was limited in devising new ways of growing rich, he could and did pursue the known ways with a passion and relentlessness which yielded nothing to that of the Yankee, even if he was seldom as successful. Political privilege, deception, trickery, even outright fraud, were no monopolies of the Anglo-Americans in business and trade. The Creoles played at that game, too, and as frequently fell athwart the law. It happened to Major Bartholomew Grima, for example. One of the best-known sons of a prominent old family, a dealer in crockery and glassware, the major late in 1825 forged the name of Nicholas Girod to $120,000 worth of notes, gathered his considerable ill-gotten gain, and quickly fled the city of his birth. Romance to the contrary notwithstanding, "breeding" and "gentility" felt the universal pull of the dollar. New Orleans in the 1820s was that kind of city.

And so we must take the Creole as he actually was, rather than as some would give him to us: a provincial whose narrow experience and even narrower education left him pitifully unprepared to compete for leadership with the Anglo-Americans and foreign French. He could surpass them in nothing but numbers. Generally illiterate, almost always politically naïve, genuinely uninterested in intellectual or artistic concerns, and not unduly fastidious in his theatrical tastes, the Creole was basically a simple man averse to change. He was no more an aristocrat than he was an Ottoman Turk.

But he was human, and he could not help but resent the Anglo-Americans and the foreign French, because they represented in many ways everything that the Latin Creole was not. Most of the Americans who settled in the state after 1803, for example, were a far cry from the ignorant roustabouts and backwoodsmen, who, though they might continue to plague the city during the busy season, were after all transients who played no part in the continuous life of the community. Those who came to stay were more often than not men of some ability and even greater ambition. They had seen the opportunities opened in the newly acquired territory of the Union, and they had flocked there to take advantage of them: young lawyers with their eyes on the many administrative jobs in the new territorial government, or very much aware of the demand for legal talent in the booming commercial and maritime concerns of the city; merchants anxious to share in the prosperity of the strategic position at the mouth of the Mississippi; thousands of junior clerks, with dreams of serving out an apprenticeship under those already established and then going on to enterprises of their own; physicians anxious to grapple with the notorious plagues of the "wet grave"; divines equally inspired to bring salvation to the people of this new Sodom; and planters to whom the rich soil of the state held out hopes for all those things which had not been forthcoming in the older settlements left behind. The very fact of their migrations was testimony to their initiative and independence; they were in a real sense a select strain of the American stock. Not, of course, that they were necessarily possessed of any greater refinement of spirit or higher sense of morality; they were no more aristocrats than were the Latin Creoles, and they as frequently succumbed to the lure of wealth and power. But they knew what they wanted, and they were as a rule better equipped to get it than were the native Louisianians. Better educated, more sophisticated politically, economically, and even culturally, the Anglo-American generally possessed an energy and inventiveness, an ability to devise new and better ways of doing things, which the Latin Creole usually found himself unable to match, though frequently able to copy.

It was inevitable that the Latin Creole should rapidly react toward these newcomers with feelings of envy, jealousy, and an overwhelming sense of inferiority. He naturally resented the Anglo-American assumption that the natives were too backward to understand the nature of republican government; he bridled when English was made the legal language of the community; and he fumed at the staid New England propriety which insisted he was headed straight for hell because he managed to enjoy himself on Sundays. He knew full well his own limitations in this struggle for supremacy, and he finally in desperation sought help from those who were closer to him in blood, language, and heritage—the foreign French—though these too he hated and feared for their superiority and their condescending manner. There was little else which he could do, however. Very few, indeed, were the Creoles who were leaders at the bar, and fewer still were those able to fill the important editorials chairs which so influenced public opinion—for such important tasks the natives were forced to depend on foreign talent.

The foreign French were not at all loath to make a bid for power in the state. Like the Americans they were generally men of at least some education and training, with initiative enough to have triumphed over disaster or misfortune in their original homes and with stamina sufficient to have brought them to this new world for the fashioning of new careers. They were frequently skilled in the intricacies of political competition; many were deeply versed in the law; and others were quite at home behind an editorial desk. Some of them, to be sure, were leaders of such outstanding accomplishment that they would have made their marks probably in any community of the world, men such as Etienne Mazureau, the brilliant lawyer and orator; Louis Moreau Lislet, the profound student of the civil code; or Pierre Soulé, the fiery political spellbinder.

They had been coming into Louisiana ever since the early days of the French Revolution, fugitives from the continental Terror, victims of Napoleonic oppression, *émigrés* from the conservative strictures of the Bourbon Restoration, escapees from the nightmare of slave insurrection in Santo Domingo. In Louisiana they found not only a safe refuge but a society with which they had much in common, including language, religion, mores, and law, and from the very beginning they had become a major force in their new community. It was evident, however, that they had failed to endear themselves to the Louisianians. Conscious of their general superiority, they had been quite free in their ridicule of Creole provincialism, criticizing local styles and deploring native backwardness. Never blind to their own advantage, most of them readily accepted United States citizenship, with loud avowals of loyalty, and yet they had more cause even than the Creole to hate the new Anglo-American settlers. For not only did these latter threaten a disruption of those Gallic forms and ways of life which the refugee had good reason to cherish, they were also the major competitors for that mastery of the affairs of the state which the foreign French were determined to enjoy themselves. It was a prize worth fighting for, and the Anglo-Americans soon felt the effectiveness of this leadership against them. These French, not the Creoles, were to be the most potent enemy, and as much as the Americans might detest this "foreign faction," they did it the honor never to underestimate its skill or prowess.

The other major foreign elements in the city's population, such as the numerous Irish and Germans, lacked the cohesion and leadership which made the foreign French such a power in the community. With little to build on except their own brawn, the Irish had turned to the boisterous life of draymen, canal diggers, or street laborers, some to suffer the indignity of expending themselves in competition with convicts of slaves, others to enjoy the freeman's privilege of dying in droves to push the New Basin Canal through pestilential swamps to the lake behind the city. All were subject to the ravages of the whisky which at least helped make such a life livable. The more stolid and phlegmatic Germans, meanwhile, contented themselves generally with less exciting and demanding tasks as butchers, hired hands, and mechanics. Some, however, found places on the police detail of the city, the New Orleans Guard, a notorious force of heavily armed gendarmes equipped with swords, pistols, muskets, and bayonets, whose frequent drunken and riotous violence made them as much a menace as a protection to public safety. The greater part of the Guard, however, seems to have been recruited from that section of the city's population which remained least integrated into the normal pursuits of the populace, the Spanish and Mexican residents of the Faubourg Marigny.[3] There in their retreat below the Quarter, apparently divorced from the interests of the rest of the city, these dark and silent people were wrapped in their own concerns, difficult to discern from the forbidding and dangerous-looking men who lounged endlessly along the levee, enfolded in their great cloaks of foreign design, with no seeming occupation except that of leisure.

A large part of the city's population, giving as much character and vitality to the community as the white group, were the Negro slaves and the free persons of color, whose relative numbers were estimated at 20,000 and 15,000 out of the overall 60,000 permanent residents of New Orleans in 1835. Their lot in a city which was continually reminding itself of its perilous exposure to racial conflict was unbelievably free and undisciplined. Slaves were seemingly masters of their own time in a great number of instances, free to come and go where and how they pleased. Hiring themselves out as draymen, laborers, and mechanics, they were frequently under no obligation except that of bringing

---

[3] A "faubourg" is a suburb. Faubourg Marigny is adjacent to the *Vieux Carré*, or French Quarter, and was originally a suburb but is now part of the city of New Orleans.

to their masters a fixed portion of their incomes, beyond which they were at liberty to establish themselves in separate dwellings in various parts of the city, to roam the streets at will, or to frequent their own gambling dens and public houses.

They made a picturesque sight, especially on Sundays, when they openly defied the rule which confined their gatherings to Congo Square, and were often to be seen, hearty and fat, fitted out in princely style in the best broadcloth and the finest of hats, headed for balls and carousals, raising their voices in joyous and carefree song to a reigning favorite—"Rose, Rose, coal black Rose." They loved to hire carriages for themselves on a Sabbath afternoon, and on the gala occasion when the Pontchartrain Railroad made its first run in 1831, slaves in hacks crowded around the road and even added to the congestion before the City Hall. One disgruntled white man went so far as to protest in 1836 against the nuisance of having to dodge the smoke from slaves puffing cigars in the streets, but little seems to have come from his complaint.

The whole behavior of the Negro toward the whites, as a matter of fact, was singularly free of that deference and circumspection which might have been expected in a slave community. It was not unusual for slaves to gather on street corners at night, for example, where they challenged whites to attempt to pass, hurled taunts at white women, and kept whole neighborhoods disturbed by shouts and curses. Nor was it safe to accost them, as men went armed with knives and pistols in flagrant defiance of all the precautions of the Black Code. Unquestionably, much of this independence might be traced to the clandestine familiarity which prevailed to a great extent between black and white in almost every part of the town. In Tchoupitoulas, Camp, Julia and New Levee streets, for example, were to be found houses in which both races, bond and free, caroused together in what might well be called intimacy.

The free persons of color were no less unrestrained and enjoyed a status in Louisiana probably unequaled in any part of the South. Members of this class were often to be found as owners of cabarets and especially of gaming houses where slaves and free Negroes might consort without interference from the authorities, even after the curfew gun. Many were artisans, barbers, and shopkeepers, and became so prosperous as to own slaves of their own and to acquire large holdings of real property in the Quarter. What objection there was to the presence of Negro dwellings in the midst of a white neighborhood, interestingly enough, does not seem to have stemmed from any protest against the Negroes themselves, but against their frequent inability or refusal to keep their buildings in the proper state of repair.

It was the free Negro women, actually, who proved themselves to be the most enterprising. Many, of course, burdened by age, ugliness, or a sense of righteousness, contented themselves with modest shops or presided over oyster, gumbo, and coffee stalls along the levee. But a large if undetermined number monopolized the task of accommodating the licentiousness of the male part of New Orleans, no mean ambition when it is remembered that perhaps half of the city's men were bachelors living in rooming houses or husbands whose wives were still in the North. Those of the women favored by nature set themselves up in bordellos all over the city, even in the most respectable neighborhoods, or roamed the streets in open pursuit of trade. . . .

Who could say then, in simple terms, what New Orleans was, this mixture of men and tongues? The roving Captain James E. Alexander had warned in 1833: "let no one judge of America from New Orleans, for it is altogether *sui generis* [one of a kind]." He could with all accuracy have said the same for the whole state.

Questions

1. What does Tregle mean by "*ancien population*" in reference to early Louisiana?
2. What is the myth of the Creole?
3. In what ways was the myth false, according to Tregle?
4. Besides the Creoles, what other ethnicities populated New Orleans? How would you characterize Tregle's descriptions of them? Explain.
5. Is Tregle's picture of the Creoles a flattering one? Why or why not?
6. Did the description of slaves in this article surprise you? Why?
7. In what kinds of occupations were the free people of color likely to engage?

IN MY FATHER'S HOUSE: RELATIONSHIPS AND IDENTITY IN AN INTERRACIAL NEW ORLEANS CREOLE FAMILY, 1845–1875

by Justin Nystrom

Born in 1847 to a free black woman in New Orleans, Louise Marie Drouet would face a degree of societal change unimaginable to the generation that had preceded her. The same could be said of her father, Louis Florange Drouet, and her first cousin, Edmund Arthur Toledano, both elite white men who had shared in the commercial prosperity of antebellum New Orleans. With the old order rendered obsolete by civil war, defeat, and emancipation, the task of reordering society fell on the shoulders of New Orleanians of all races and social standing. Until a new postbellum racial paradigm fully emerged, this societal reconstruction proceeded in an organic fashion. . . .

We will never know more than a handful of tantalizing fragments about the chain of events that brought Louise Marie Drouet into this world. Her father, Louis Florange Drouet, was a thirty-six-year-old bachelor from a prosperous white Creole family that had deep roots in the city. From what most people around him could gather, he had lived the quiet life of a wealthy merchant, owning and operating a building materials concern on Tchoupitoulas Street. When his father died in the spring of 1847, Drouet inherited a small fortune, including a great deal of commercial property in the warehouse district of Faubourg St. Mary. Among these parcels was a two-story

Originally published in *Louisiana History: The Journal of the Louisiana Historical Association* 49 (Summer 2008): 287–313. Used by permission of the Louisiana Historical Association.

frame house on the corner of Tchoupitoulas and Gaiènnie, and it was here that he had made his home.

One can only infer from his actions the sort of man L. F. Drouet was in everyday life, for he had a reputation as an intensely private man. Only one of his numerous relatives in the city ever came regularly to visit with him, and he seemingly had no close friends. Although he was quite wealthy, he lived modestly. Drouet's neighbors in the Faubourg St. Mary often noticed the Creole on evenings driving an open buggy alone through the streets around his home. Although few questioned his gentility and fine manners, he was painfully taciturn. Moreover, at a time of life when most men had long since married and started families, the reclusive Louis Drouet remained a bachelor and lived alone. There was another side to this eccentric man, however, of which few of his white neighbors were aware. Sometime in 1846, Drouet had entered a *plaçage* relationship with a twenty-year-old Afro-Creole woman named Elizabeth Bresson. Before long, he had negotiated the rental of a cottage on Constance Street, where he installed his young mistress.

Predominantly within the Creole community, *plaçage* consisted of an arranged sexual relationship outside the bounds of marriage between white men and typically free-born mixed-race women. Brokered between a female guardian of the young *placée* and the man to whom she would become a mistress, these agreements often involved significant financial support on the part of the man, including direct monetary support and living accommodations, typically a rented house. Custom dictated that the father would also financially support any offspring resulting from the union, but such plans could and often did go awry. Often, a *placée* came from a family where for several generations the women had served as mistresses to white men. . . .

Although she was only twenty years old when she entered the union with Louis Drouet, *plaçage* was already a way of life for Elizabeth Bresson. Two years earlier, she had entered an unsuccessful union with another man by the name of Samuel Morgan. Not long after she became pregnant with his child, Morgan left town and was never heard from again. Louis Drouet's offer not only rescued Elizabeth from financial jeopardy, but as the kept mistress of a wealthy white man, it conferred upon her a type of status peculiar to its time and place. As long as her relationship with Drouet lasted, this young free woman of color had her own home and a certain measure of independence. While one might wonder what role genuine affection played in the relationship, for Elizabeth Bresson, it was by necessity an economic decision.

It was only a distance of about ten blocks between the home of Louis Drouet and the cottage where he kept Bresson, but the difference was, quite literally, night and day. As 1846 turned into 1847, neighbors observed Drouet's carriage tied in front of the Constance Street cottage "every night and sometimes during the day." Soon, Elizabeth became pregnant, and, by July of 1847, she had given birth to a daughter. Drouet had visited his mistress frequently throughout the pregnancy and delighted in the birth of his child. Yet, when Elizabeth's brother William and a childhood friend carried Marie Louise Drouet to St. Louis Cathedral to be baptized, Louis Drouet was not in attendance. If he loved his daughter, he was still not yet willing to publicly proclaim Louise as his own. For all practical purposes, she belonged to another world entirely.

For some unknown reason the intimate aspect of the relationship between Louis Drouet and Elizabeth Bresson ended shortly after the birth of their daughter. Mother and child remained, however, very much part of Drouet's life. In addition to providing the customary financial support, he would often visit his daughter at the Constance Street cottage, though he no longer spent the night. Eventually, he asked Elizabeth to start bringing Louise to visit with him at his own home on Tchoupitoulas or at his feed store across the street. Even though Elizabeth had, as her brother put it, "got [another] man to support her," she continued to take Louise on monthly visits to her father.

Louise and her mother belonged to what scholars have described as the middle stratum of antebellum New Orleans' three-tiered racial caste system. This arrangement placed white Orleanians at the highest level, enslaved people of African descent at the bottom, and free people of color somewhere in between. Although this dynamic had taken root in other parts of the American South, it was in New Orleans, with its large and prosperous free person of color community that the middle caste came to play such a crucial role in the larger social pyramid. About half of the city's people who possessed some amount African blood were free, and their presence made a vital contribution to the overall racial dialogue in New Orleans. Unbeknownst to Orleanians of all colors, however, the world that Louise Drouet had been born into was already entering its twilight. The coming of the Civil War, emancipation, and the political turmoil of Reconstruction would eventually throw social conventions in New Orleans into a state of turmoil.

The last antebellum decade brought important changes to Louis Drouet's life, and, in time, these changes would heavily influence the fate of Louise, his mixed-race daughter. In 1852, he decided to rent out a portion of his mostly empty two-story home to a young German immigrant couple. Henry and Mary Schwartz were sober and industrious tenants, and they eventually became Louis Drouet's closest friends outside of his blood relations. The Schwartzes noticed the periodic visits of Louise and her mother, but remained discreet enough to not ask questions about the girl. Yet, through the grapevine, they came to know the truth. When Drouet's young slave boy Sam told Mary Schwartz that Louise was his master's daughter, she already had her suspicions. In a bout of uncharacteristic loquacity, Louis Drouet once commented to Henry Schwartz that Louise was not as "good-looking" as her mother. At no time, however, did he ever introduce Elizabeth or the child during their visits to any of his white friends.

Around the same time that the Schwartzes came to live with Drouet, another important person became a regular fixture in his life. L. F. Drouet's nephew, Edmund Arthur Toledano, was the only son of his sister Hyacinthe. Four years earlier, the young man had boarded the steamer *Falcon* in search of his fortune in recently-conquered California. Now back in New Orleans, twenty-two-years-old and undoubtedly much wiser, Toledano set about learning the far more practical mercantile trade from his uncle Louis. The young Creole had a head for commerce, and in time, he not only began handling all of Drouet's financial affairs, he had also established himself as an independent cotton weigher. Toledano had become his uncle's closest confidant to the point that if he ever missed his daily visits to the house on the corner Tchoupitoulas and Gaiènnie, his uncle would send for him. Despite the bond that had built between the two men, however, and indeed perhaps because of it, Drouet kept the knowledge of his secret affair across the color line from his nephew.

When Elizabeth Bresson died suddenly early in 1858, the relationship between Louis Drouet and his daughter necessarily changed. Her mother's death brought Louise's monthly visits to an end, and for the next few years, she went off to live with her great-aunt Fanny Porée in Jefferson Parish. Louis Drouet had not forgotten about his daughter, however. In early 1861, he sent for Fanny Porée. Drouet instructed her to take Louise to the St. Augustine Convent near the corner of Bayou and St. Claude in the heart of New Orleans' old Afro-Creole Tremé community. Here the Sisters of the Holy Family operated a boarding school for young women of color. For the next two years, Fanny Porée would make monthly visits to Drouet's home to pick up ten *piastres*. She would then carry this money to the convent, where, upon accepting the payment, a nun would write out a receipt for the illiterate Afro-Creole woman. Many of the convent's charges would have come from similar circumstances, and Louise's situation would have hardly surprised any of the sisters. St. Augustine's undoubtedly furnished Louise with a proper Catholic education and a secure environment, yet it must have also been a lonely time for the adolescent. Although she had been placed there at the request of her father, he did not visit her once during her stay. This was one more indication that while Louis Drouet was willing to fulfill his financial obligations to his daughter, he still feared what damage public avowal of her might bring upon himself and his white family.

It may have actually been Arthur Toledano's departure for the war in 1861 that had made Louise's placement into the convent possible. His daily handling of his uncle's business came to a temporary halt when he took command of Watson's Battery, a light artillery unit assigned to the Trans-Mississippi theater. If Louis Drouet had wanted to keep knowledge of his illegitimate daughter from his family, Toledano's absence certainly helped matters. This would also explain why he waited three years after Elizabeth Bresson's death to place Louise in the convent. Louis Drouet would not be able to keep this secret forever, however.

For Arthur Toledano, the war proved to be more about hardship than glory. Although they strayed far from southern Louisiana, seeing action at Shiloh and Corinth, it was at Port Hudson in the summer of 1863 where the Watson Battery had faced its most difficult duty. Just upriver of Baton Rouge, Port Hudson was a final Confederate stronghold on the Mississippi and its defense depended greatly upon the artillerists whose shot, grape, and canister mowed down repeated Union infantry assaults. Here 7,500 Confederates held firm against 40,000 Union soldiers for forty-eight days, all despite a determined siege and literally no receipt of reinforcements or supplies. Reduced to eating mules, cats, and any other creature unwise enough to pass within musket shot, Toledano and his men had endured a miserable time of it.

On the morning of July 10, 1863, New Orleans woke to a thunderous barrage from the Union flotilla that sat moored on the levee. As tendrils of smoke drifted over the French quarter, it soon became clear that the navy had fired a massive 100-gun salute to celebrate the fall of Port Hudson. The surrender of Vicksburg on the Fourth of July had sealed the fate of those who had so tenaciously defended the Mississippi's last citadel. In negotiating the terms of capitulation, the Union generals agreed to parole the Confederate enlisted men, but not the majority of their officers. Four days after the Federals' triumphant salvo deafened the Crescent City, Drouet's nephew boarded the steamer *Suffolk* at Port Hudson with the rest of the Confederate prisoners and began the brief downriver journey to the city of his birth.

The occupying Union forces had turned the upper floors of the massive United States Customhouse on Canal Street into a prisoner detention facility, and it was here that Arthur Toledano spent the remainder of summer.... By September, however, Union authorities had shipped Toledano and his comrades to Johnson's Island prisoner of war camp, a remote outpost situated on a dismally exposed island in Lake Erie's Sandusky Bay. When Arthur Toledano arrived there in mid-October, he was just in time for the first of two brutal Great Lakes winters. He would not leave until he finally took the oath of allegiance on June 11, 1865.

A surprise greeted Toledano when he finally returned home from Johnson's Island in October 1865. He found that there was a new resident living with his Uncle Louis—it was his first cousin, Louise Drouet. The dramatic chain of events that had brought Louise to live with her father had begun a month earlier when Louis Drouet's personal servant discovered her employer lying unconscious in the yard. Frightened, she cried frantically for help. Henry Schwartz, Drouet's long-time tenant, described what happened next:

> I went there and helped to take him up stairs in his bed. I remained there with him until eleven o'clock. He told me on that occasion that he was always sick and needed somebody to take care of him. He added, 'Mr. Schwartz, I am going to tell you something I have never told you. I have a daughter, she is in a convent.' I told him why he did not take her with him. He said it would be perhaps better for her to remain in the convent. He also told me that Louise's mother had another daughter but that he was not her father. He said, 'I know I was the father of Louise.'

I then told him that as long as Louise was his daughter he ought to take her with him, he having nobody else to take care of him. He said that he was afraid that people might talk about that. I told him that he ought to do it and let people talk.

A new equilibrium descended upon the Drouet house following the war. Edmund Arthur Toledano resumed his daily trips to his uncle's home, sometimes staying for dinner where he sat at the table with his uncle and his first cousin. Toledano, recently married, was periodically accompanied by his new wife on these visits. Louise now joined her father on his nightly rambles in his buggy through the streets of uptown New Orleans. They attended plays and circuses together, and the old Creole showered her with affection, which by all accounts she returned in full. When Louise went out visiting or on errands, neighbors could see her father anxiously waiting at the street corner for her return. Occasionally, Louise's half-sister Sylvanie Morgan would come to visit. It all seemed quite normal, particularly as the turmoil of war had so altered the composition of many households in New Orleans that such a change would have hardly elicited comment. To those who did not know any better, Louise undoubtedly passed for white.

Unfortunately for everyone involved, the profound societal changes that had brought this family together under one roof had also begun to threaten its very existence. The old three-tiered racial caste system that had ordered New Orleans society since its founding now faced collapse. Emancipation diminished the uniqueness of the city's free people of color by reducing the distance, at least in the eyes of the law, between former slaves and the Afro-Creole elite. That the black leadership class enjoyed material and educational advantages over the freedmen paled in comparison with an increasingly binary racial order. The diminishing status of New Orleans' free people of color also made their white relatives grow increasingly uneasy about acknowledging blood ties, for white Creoles in particular were already anxious about their own racial identity. Yet, in 1866, these changes had only begun to take place.

The collapse of the city's middle racial tier also led to an identity crisis for the antebellum free black population. There were several options available to this caste, and each held different risks and rewards. Some conspicuously proffered their services as the natural political leadership for the freedmen only to confront resistance from not only white Republican politicians who sought to harvest the fruits of victory for their own benefit, but also from the freedmen who remained skeptical of their social betters' newfound interest in their plight. Less conspicuously, others ebbed toward the single most attractive option left available to them, the option of crossing the color line. If they failed to retain their position as the black elite and if they failed to pass into white society, then the middle caste stood to fall to the lowly status of freedmen—a situation many found disconcerting. . . .

Louise Drouet may well have been completely oblivious to all of the great social, legal, and political changes taking place around her, but as a girl on the threshold of her transformation into womanhood, she undoubtedly found the stability of her father's house a welcome change. The dramatic upheaval in her midst mirrored her personal life. She was born into a world where her future prospects might include becoming a *plaçée*, much like her mother and her mother's mother had been. Living with her father exposed an entirely different path, the path toward becoming not just a woman, not just a mistress, but a lady. Perhaps over time, she might even cross the color line, assuming the role of Louis Drouet's *legitimate* daughter. But if this was her plan, the stakes were higher than she could have ever known. If she did not succeed at becoming white, she would become black, for the middle tier that she had left rapidly disappeared in a sea of freedmen. The world of the *placée* no longer existed, and there was simply no going back to the way things were before the war.

Prosperity accompanied Arthur Toledano's return to civilian life. Not everyone who had done well in antebellum days enjoyed a revival of good times, but the financial backing of the Drouet-Toledano clan undoubtedly aided this veteran. Certainly as a cotton weigher, it did not hurt to have strong family connections in the commodities trades. Between 1867 and 1871 Toledano took advantage of depressed real estate prices and bought several substantial uptown tracts including two square blocks of the present-day Garden District. The carpetbagger ascendancy clearly did not leave this savvy businessman financially prostrate.

Yet, if Arthur Toledano did not have any particular animosity for the Republicans who now ruled Louisiana, an incident that occurred in March 1871 probably changed his mind. The Louisiana Constitution of 1868 was certainly the most racially progressive document that the state had conceived up until that time. Among other things, this charter included provisions for ending segregation on public conveyances, and additional laws passed in 1869 strengthened the letter of the law, if not its enforcement. While many blacks simply chose not to force the issue, it did, on occasion, bring them into direct confrontation with whites who had taken it upon themselves to resist the new order. News of such incidents—in schools, barrooms, trains, and elsewhere, had periodically appeared in the papers by the time Arthur Toledano and his wife returned home from a visit to Carrollton.

It was about six o'clock in the evening when the in-bound street car pulled up to the Carrollton depot. Arthur Toledano and his wife Céleste waited for the driver to open the door, and then climbed up the steps into the wooden trolley car. As Toledano paid the fare, Céleste looked up and down the aisles for an empty seat, but did not find any. Just then, a man waved her over and graciously relinquished his own seat to her. Thanking the man, Céleste sat down and waited for the car to begin moving. In the seat next to her sat Jane Price, a twenty-nine-year-old mulatto domestic servant on her way home to the Lower Garden District.

After lurching several blocks down St. Charles Avenue, the already-crowded car stopped once more to take on additional passengers. One of these was a friend of Céleste's seat mate, and the two women waved to each other. Trouble began almost as soon as the car started moving again. Perhaps Jane Price was incensed that no gentleman yielded his seat to her friend, or maybe it was just a reaction against years of second-class citizenship. Whatever the case, Price crossed her arms high on her chest and began purposely elbowing Céleste Toledano in the face in the hope that she might force the white Creole lady to give up her seat.

Outraged by Price's actions, Arthur Toledano sternly warned her that he would give her five minutes to put her arms down. When Price replied that she "was as good as anybody having paid fare, she would do so as she pleased and sit as she saw proper," an enraged Toledano grabbed the woman's hand and jerked her elbow away from Céleste's face. Price promptly resumed her offending pose a second time and Toledano again pulled her away, this time threatening to throw her out the window if she tried it again. Jane Price remained undeterred and resumed elbowing Toledano's wife. When Arthur Toledano grabbed her by the wrist a third time, Price sprang up, struck him across the face, and ripped his collar loose from his shirt, all while cursing him repeatedly. This last torrent of oaths sent the other passengers into a fury and they angrily called for the driver to halt the vehicle. When it finally came to a stop, several passengers ejected Price and her friend.

As if the ride that evening had not upset Toledano enough, a few days later a Metropolitan policeman served out a warrant for his arrest. Jane Price had filed assault charges against Toledano for striking her without provocation. Fortunately for him, the witnesses who came forward on his behalf offered far more corroborative and detailed accounts of the affair than had Price and her friend. The recorder's court quickly dismissed the charges, but the whole experience must have been rather unsettling. Price's actions had struck at the most central fear held by white Southerners, the sanctity of white womanhood. Unable to protect his wife from such insults, Toledano had failed to fulfill his honorable duty as a white Southern man. . . .

Toledano's unpleasant confrontation on the streetcar was part and parcel of the deteriorating political situation in Louisiana. Between his ascent to office in 1868 and the zenith of his power in 1870, Louisiana's Republican governor, Henry Clay Warmoth, had built a surprising coalition of political supporters. As 1871 began, however, much of this coalition had begun to collapse. Rival members of his own party worked feverishly to undermine him from within. At the same time, former Confederates and otherwise Democratic whites who had once lent support to Warmoth grew increasingly uneasy about supporting the carpetbagger. Indeed, Toledano had likely known some of the men who had at one time supported the administration. The crumbling of Warmoth's coalition marked a turning point in this unstable chapter of Louisiana's political history and set into motion a variety of forces that would ultimately lead to bloodshed in the streets.

Arthur Toledano underwent a political awakening amidst this turmoil. Although he had suffered much during the war, it was not until forces much closer to home had conspired against him that Toledano finally took a public stand. On a January night in 1872, the forty-two-year-old Creole signed on as a supporter of a bizarre combination of Grant Republicans and Bourbon Democrats who had angled for Warmoth's impeachment. Although this movement failed almost as quickly as it had started, it would not be the last time that Toledano became involved with the volatile politics of Reconstruction.

For her part, Louise Drouet had to walk a fine line while carving out her new identity. The essential problem was that she was caught between two worlds. While Louise yearned for the privilege and belonging of white society, she was unable to fully relinquish her ties to the Afro-Creole community. As Reconstruction wore on, it became painfully obvious that she could not have it both ways.

Louise's most problematic relationship was unquestionably the one that she maintained with the widow of Pierre Laurent. This Afro-Creole woman had known her father well before the time of Louise's birth, and although she only had known Elizabeth Bresson by sight, may well have been part of the network that had brokered the *plaçage* union between the two. Louise began making regular visits to see the Widow.

If Louise had an alter ego during her stay at her father's house, it was another regular visitor, her half-sister, Sylvanie Morgan. Although Sylvanie was two years older than Louise, the critical difference in their lives had been the character of the relationship between their mother and respective fathers. Unlike Louis Drouet, Samuel Morgan had forsaken all responsibility to the offspring that resulted from his union with Elizabeth Bresson. Not only had this placed an economic burden on Sylvanie Morgan, it also eliminated her only direct link to the white world. By the time that Louise came to live at her father's house, Sylvanie had married an Afro-Creole man and soon thereafter had started a family. This did not, however, mean that Louise's sister had completely ruled out benefiting from her fair complexion. Not only did she maintain ties with white society through her frequent visits with her half-sister at the home of Louis Drouet, evidence suggests that Sylvanie hoped that she might one day successfully pass her own children into white society. Indeed, when she registered the birth of her eldest child, Sylvanie Morgan acquired a valuable asset towards her newborn daughter's new racial identity—a birth certificate that declared her child as white. . . .

Suddenly, in October 1872, an event took place that forever changed the balance of the Drouet household. Louis Drouet's health had always been fragile, and indeed, his poor physical condition was one of the initial reasons that he had made the bold decision to bring his mixed-race daughter live with him in 1865. Now, seven years later, Louise was one of the several people standing vigil over her unconscious father as he lay dying. When he succumbed later that night, Louise ran from the room in distress crying, "My father is dead!" As she sat sobbing in the evening air on the gallery, Arthur Toledano tried to comfort her. "Louise, you must not think all the good men are dead," he pleaded, "as long as [you] shall conduct yourself as you have been, I shall stand by you because I know you are the dutiful daughter of my uncle."

Louise had been "conducting herself" as someone with a mind toward crossing the color line and there were plenty of indications that Louise was well on her way to succeeding in this endeavor. Her sickly father's doctor, the grocer who lived across the street, and a young man who had lived in the house as a tenant for a little over a year in 1868 all believed she was a lawful daughter—and neither Louise nor her father had made any effort to disabuse them of this notion. When a census worker came to their Faubourg St. Mary home in the summer of 1870, he inscribed a "W" beside Louise's name in the column denoting race. After all, this young Creole lady even had an Irish domestic servant waiting on her. Indeed, not only had Louise been engaged in passing, her father, and to a lesser degree, Arthur Toledano had been complicit in the deception even if each had different motivations for establishing Louise's white identity.

Yet, in spite of all of Louise's efforts to blend in with the family—or perhaps because of them—she also had plenty of reasons to worry about her future after her father's death, for the family dynamics were now entirely different. The paternal nature of the relationship had now been replaced by a lateral connection with a host of cousins who viewed her not only as a rival claimant to their uncle's estate, but also as a mixed-race woman who was making a bid to become their social equal.

With the protective hand of her father removed, the relationship between Louise and Arthur Toledano also began to sour. It would be impossible to decide precisely what caused the greatest conflict between the two, mostly because there were several factors that fed upon each other. Louise continued to live in her deceased father's house for a while. . . . Of the seventeen nieces and nephews who stood to inherit from Louis Drouet, some were undoubtedly aghast that their uncle had ever taken Louise in. One of them, Alexis Drouet, who had worked as the foreman on his father's cane plantation in antebellum days, seems to have had no notion of Louise's right to the estate. Unlike Arthur Toledano, some of Louise Drouet's white cousins were clearly in need of cash and probably worried about her claim on the estate should the courts recognize her as a daughter and thus, under the Louisiana Constitution of 1868, a forced heir. Perhaps from his own convictions, perhaps goaded by his cousins, as executor of his uncle's estate, Arthur Toledano moved to disinherit Louise.

On the face of things, one might think that Louise Drouet had been dealt a poor hand in the coming struggle with her white cousins, but some surprising things happened when she decided to fight for her legacy. By far, the biggest of these surprises occurred when Louise secured the legal services of Charles Magill Conrad & Son. C. M. Conrad, Sr. had been Millard Fillmore's Secretary of War, a signer of the Confederate constitution, and a member of the rebel legislature. Charles M. Conrad, Jr. was the brother-in-law of Davidson Bradfute Penn, the Redeemers' candidate for lieutenant governor in Louisiana's disputed election of 1872. As stated in his brief, Conrad & Son had decided to take Louise's case *pro bono* when "a friend who pitied the helpless condition of the orphan" had brought her plight to their attention. Now they would represent a penniless mixed-race woman in her quest for justice against a Confederate veteran. Clearly Louise had made a positive impression on people who moved in very influential circles. When direct negotiation with Toledano failed to bring about an "amicable settlement," Conrad & Son filed suit against the succession of Louis F. Drouet.

Many of the events that followed seem to have had far less to do with money and legal procedure than they did with fundamental issues of identity, human relationships, and community standards of fair play. Although Louis Drouet left behind a substantial estate, his only daughter had not sought a large inheritance. Instead, she prayed for $50 per month in alimony, an amount that would provide sufficient income to survive, but could scarcely be construed as the basis for luxurious living. More importantly, an award of alimony from her father's estate would serve as an acknowledgement of not only her paternity, but also of her relationship with her father's living relatives. For these heirs, the social stigma that such alimony represented far outweighed the financial consideration of Louise's request. If she were to win her case, Louise was unlikely to become her cousins' social equal, but the victory would nevertheless serve as a perpetual reminder of the Drouet clan's blood ties across the color line.

Conversely, the motivation of Louise's white supporters begs analysis. Perhaps their own conception of Louise was that she was, in fact, more white than black and that within the standards of the law *and* the custom of the community, she should be entitled to recognition by the estate.

Conrad & Son seemed particularly driven by what they characterized as the "peculiar ill grace" on the part of Toledano's legal arguments. The defendants' attorneys posited that the Constitution of 1825, the law in place at the time of Louise's birth, dictated her claim to her father's estate. Dismissing the Louisiana Constitution of 1868, they asserted that because Louise could not produce any legally-recognized documentation of her paternity, and because she was an illegitimate person of color, she could not legally inherit from her father' estate. Should this legal theory fail to prevent the court from ruling in Louise's favor, Toledano's lawyers also included an exception based on legal procedure, arguing that in this instance, the law did not allow her to sue the estate's administrator for alimony payments.

In court, Arthur Toledano seemed particularly obsessed with proving the dubious assertion that Louise was not the child of his uncle Louis. All of the witnesses called by the defense were nephews and heirs to the estate of Louis Drouet. In succession they lamely suggested that their uncle never said anything about having a daughter, but had to admit that they visited him infrequently, if ever. Toledano, who knew better, hinted that Louise was more of a servant than a member of a family and denied ever having dined with her. He suggested that if Louise had in fact been his uncle's daughter, Louis Drouet would have provided for her with a legal will. Toledano claimed that he had urged his uncle to do just that, pointing out that all of his heirs were "provided for," but that his uncle was so superstitious about death that he had refused to discuss the matter. According to Toledano, Drouet ended one such conversation with "*après moi, le déluge*," an apocryphal quote attributed to Louis XV and translated literally as "after me, the flood," but meaning, in essence, that he did not care what happened to Louise once he was gone. In response to the assertion that Louise's upbringing as a lady and weak constitution prevented her from making a living, Toledano acidly replied, "she can work." Contradictory at several junctures and teeming with malice, this testimony was not a credit to his character.

In contrast, the plaintiff's witnesses paraded to the stand one after another. White men such as Henry Schwartz, Louis Drouet's longtime tenant, described the affectionate familial bond between Louise and her father, and he was not alone. His fifteen-year-old son William directly contradicted Toledano's assertion that he and Louise never dined together—as did three other witnesses. Under cross examination, Toledano's testimony began to reek of perjury. A steady stream of both black and white witnesses unmistakably established Louise's paternity and praised her conduct as a dutiful daughter.

Conrad's able counsel brought initial results. Judge Antoine Tissot of the Second District Court, himself a white Creole who had once been a Confederate officer and a member of Governor Warmoth's militia, awarded Louise the alimony she had sought. Yet, it was not to be. Toledano successfully appealed the case to the Louisiana Supreme Court, a body which had actually enjoyed a reputation during Reconstruction for favoring the legal rights of minorities. Unfortunately for Louise, the higher court agreed with the defense's assertion that the remedy sought by her counsel was wrong, and that Louise Drouet could not in this circumstance sue an estate's executor for alimony. Seemingly, in seeking the wrong remedy, Conrad had failed her. In spite of the fact that many members of white society who had supported her cause, this interpretation by the Louisiana Supreme Court may have also been a manifestation of what legal scholar Virginia Dominguez characterizes as a postbellum culture of resistance to the rights of children born to mixed-race unions. As Charles Chesnutt opined, "in these matters, custom is law." Indeed, the custom that allowed for Louise's disavowal had trumped the surprisingly strong tempering force of compassion within the community. Whatever the case, Conrad & Son undoubtedly recognized the futility of pursuing Louise's claim any further.

The trial and resulting judgment seemingly reaffirms the notion that white Creoles became increasingly self-conscious of their interracial relatives as Reconstruction wore on. Yet, the fact that such an unusual collection of defenders came to the aid of this Afro-Creole woman also defies the conventions of a racist culture. Louise Drouet's supporters had been moved by her character, and the weight of their testimony demonstrated that she had made her father's final years happy, indeed, happier than he had ever been. When the seventeen nieces and nephews of Louis Drouet had moved to not only disinherit their uncle's only child, but to also deny her modest appeal for alimony, it had apparently struck the community as a grossly dishonorable act. Thus, Conrad & Son took her case, and a string of white men and women joined her Afro-Creole relatives and friends in an effort to correct such an outrage. Toledano and his white cousins may have ultimately won the suit, but they had lost immeasurably in the eyes of their peers. Their tight-fisted disavowal of Louise Drouet seemed to confirm all of the rotten things Anglo New Orleanians muttered about white Creoles when behind closed doors. It also demonstrated that racism had its limits, even in racially-charged times. More importantly, the case suggests that even in the waning years of Reconstruction, Orleanians remained divided over what place the former middle racial caste should occupy in society.

The courtroom drama of Louise Drouet and Edmund Arthur Toledano was but a small episode in a much larger ongoing crisis in the interracial Creole world during Reconstruction. This crisis was about both cultural and racial identity, and the tangled familial web of the Toledano-Drouet clan demonstrated the inexorable link between the two. For ostensibly white Creoles such as Edmund Arthur Toledano, the presence of a woman so intimately linked to both Afro-Creole society and his own bloodlines was a source of great anxiety—not so much for her mere existence, but for the fact that the relationship had become so very public. If the case of Louise Drouet is any indication, disowning loyal Afro-Creole relatives meant running the risk of censure within the larger community. Embracing them brought into question one's own racial "purity," particularly amidst the whispers uttered by some Anglo-Orleanians intimating that even self-identified white Creoles might not be the genuine article. As racial politics intensified, white Creoles grew increasingly sensitive about the subject of their heritage.

When the Louisiana Supreme Court overthrew Louise Drouet's lower court victory in April 1874, her legal battle had been fought and lost. Arthur Toledano's struggle against the social changes brought by Reconstruction continued, however. When the White League emerged in New Orleans during the summer of 1874, it offered the embittered Creole one more opportunity to not only take a swipe at the Republican government that had done so much to undermine his world, but also to take part in a campaign that promised to restore his reputation for personal virtue and honor within the community. The League was a paramilitary extension of the state's conservative Redeemer element, and it sought to take by force what they had failed to accomplish at the ballot box. As July blended into August and then September, the White League recruited young men to its cause, purchased arms, and drilled its members in preparation for a future insurrection that they would someday unleash against the Republican administration of carpetbag governor William Pitt Kellogg.

The day of the White League's rebellion finally came on September 14, 1874. Early that Monday morning, Edmund Arthur Toledano had grabbed his rifle and left his Garden District home. By nine, he had joined dozens of other White League volunteers at Eagle Hall, not four blocks from the house on Constance Street where his cousin Louise had been born. By that afternoon, Toledano's company had been ordered to the levee to do battle with the Metropolitan Police. For the White League, the day would be one of victory, but E. A. Toledano would not be so lucky. As he ran toward his opponent's position on the levee, a bullet slammed into Toledano's body and jerked him to the ground. Lying amidst the debris and dung of draft animals, he quickly bled to death.

After Arthur Toledano's death at the "Battle of Liberty Place," the Orleans Parish probate court assigned his widow Céleste as administrator of Louis Drouet's estate, a role she did not seem particularly desirous of fulfilling. Toledano's death undoubtedly complicated the proceedings, but there also seemed to be interminable disagreement between the surviving heirs as to the proper course for selling off the assets. By 1875, several of the heirs had successfully moved for the auction of the house on the corner of Tchoupitoulas and Gaiènnie as well as Drouet's other real estate holdings. In the end, legal expenses, taxes, and the passage of time had all served to fritter away the estate to such an extent that in the end, each of the remaining heirs received only about $800 apiece.

When Louise lost her case against the Drouet clan, she also lost all her aspirations of climbing New Orleans' social ladder, and in the end, she shared the fate of many who had once belonged to the middle racial caste of antebellum days. When the tide ran out on Reconstruction it stranded Louise in its wake, her rights as a citizen diminishing ever more with the passage of time. After leaving her father's home, Louise lived with her Uncle William and Great Aunt Fanny Porée until 1878, when she married a politically connected Afro-Creole man named Edouard Phillipe Ducloslange, a plasterer by trade. The following year, Louise gave birth to the first of four daughters. By 1900, her surviving children worked as seamstresses—an occupation that Arthur Toledano had suggested that she take up to support herself instead of praying for support from her father's estate. Louise Drouet died in New Orleans in 1914 at the age of sixty-seven. By that time, the descendants of the free Afro-Creoles may have retained some sense of cultural heritage, but they had been largely absorbed into a binary racial system that classified them as black. The world that Louise Drouet left behind was fundamentally different than the one into which she had been born.

As a postscript, Louise's half-sister, Sylvanie Morgan Duvernay, continued in her pursuit of passing her children into white society. Of her nine offspring, one for certain finally succeeded in this endeavor, but it required first a move to Mobile and then to Cleveland to finally accomplish the task. If his children had any notion of the dramatic times that their great-grandmother, Elizabeth Bresson, had witnessed as a *placée* in antebellum New Orleans, they never shared it. For their father, Eugene Duvernay, it was a story that he undoubtedly preferred to keep in the misty past.

Questions

1. Define *plaçage*. How common were *plaçage* relationships and why?
2. Nystrom argues that the changes brought about by the end of slavery and Reconstruction helped to produce the court case of *Drouet* v. *the Succession of Drouet*. Do you agree with him, or do you think that this court case might have happened at any time in Louisiana history? Explain your answer.
3. What is your reaction to the outcome of the case and Drouet's subsequent life?
4. What does Nystrom suggest about why white Creoles became zealous in claiming the term Creole for themselves and redefining its historical meaning?
5. How is the term "Creole" used in general parlance today? What does the term mean to you? What explanations can you offer for the recent shifts in meaning?

PART FOUR
VIOLENT LOUISIANA

❧ ☙

The Civil War ravaged Louisiana. It left thousands of the state's young men dead or wounded, its landscape scarred by battles and marauding, its economy in a shambles, and its social and political structures in disarray. Sown within that devastation, however, were seeds of hope, especially for the freedmen and freedwomen, recently emancipated and for the first time able to exert authority over their own lives. Those hopes seemed destined for realization at the beginning of the Reconstruction Era, but they would soon be dashed.

Increasing black assertiveness—socially, economically, and politically—engendered stiff white opposition in the years after the end of the war, and that opposition became increasingly violent as the 1860s became the 1870s. The single deadliest confrontation of the Reconstruction era occurred in the tiny Red River port town of Colfax in 1873. There, hundreds of whites and blacks engaged in a pitched battle on Easter Sunday for political control of Grant Parish. The battle turned into a massacre, in which dozens of blacks were rounded up, after they had surrendered, and summarily executed. Joel Sipress shows in the first essay of this part that the whites who perpetrated the Colfax murders were not necessarily conservative extremists. Rather, many of them had been political moderates until they felt their own authority threatened by radical black politics. That threat led to a brutal retaliation on a horrifying scale.

The period after Reconstruction, typically known as the Bourbon Era, saw no lessening of the violence in Louisiana. Lynchings, urban riots, and massacres remained commonplace, and, as Samuel Hyde shows in his essay on feuding in the Florida Parishes, violence became an accepted means of establishing order in some areas of the state. Hyde claims that this was especially true in places like the Piney Woods regions of southeastern Louisiana, where the pre–Civil War wielders of power failed to reestablish their authority after Reconstruction. The displacement of those old authorities invigorated contentious political contests in the Florida Parishes, as new leaders and their followers tried to fill the power void. The ensuing factionalism led to bitter, often personal and long-lasting, feuds.

The Bourbon Era also saw the emergence of increasingly effective attempts to limit black political participation through disfranchisement and social equality through segregation. With those legal strictures came new efforts to divide Louisiana's social, political, and economic systems into white and black compartments. The solidification of a two-tiered racial structure in the state belied its racial and ethnic diversity, leaving groups who fell somewhere between black and white—Creoles of color and recent European immigrants, for instance—suddenly constrained by those labels. Being defined as one or the other brought with it sometimes grave consequences.

According to Alan Gauthreaux, the surge of violence against Italians that emerged in the late-nineteenth and early-twentieth centuries reflected their classification as "non-white" by the political and social leaders of Louisiana. Seemingly uninterested in white supremacy, the Italians disavowed racial solidarity with people of similar skin pigmentation, and they willingly and uncomplainingly labored at jobs typically relegated to the black population. Thus, Gauthreaux posits that white supremacists in New Orleans and else-where targeted Italians as surrogates for blacks in enacting their violence, usually in the form of lynchings. This was particularly evident in the aftermath of the Populist political insurgency in the state, which threatened to unify blacks and other "non-whites" into a powerful voting bloc that might threaten white supremacy.

The violence waged against the Italians, like that waged against the freedmen in Colfax and in the Florida Parish feuds, was not simply a manifestation of racial or personal hatred. It was rooted in the political and economic contexts of the day as well.

"I WOULD RATHER BE AMONG THE COMANCHES": THE MILITARY OCCUPATION OF SOUTHWEST LOUISIANA, 1865

by Michael G. Wade

If the immediate post-civil war experience of southwestern Louisiana is any indication, then the federal government's failure to continue and reinforce the military occupation of other Southern locales after 1865 might represent another of the lost opportunities of Reconstruction. In many respects, the challenges faced by occupation troops in southwestern Louisiana in the latter half of 1865 were the same ones that plagued both Radical Republican politicians and their Democratic successors after Redemption. Furthermore, given the chaos, violence, and deprivation which characterized this time and place, many of these problems were perhaps best resolved, or at least mitigated, within the context of military control.

Southwest Louisiana is the region stretching from Franklin in the east more than 150 miles to the Sabine River in the west, and from the Louisiana coast about ninety miles north to Washington, Louisiana, comprising a total area of roughly 1300 square miles. For the most part a low-lying prairie, the region's sugar-producing eastern half contained most of its population. New Iberia, headquarters for the Union occupation, was located more or less in the center of the eastern section. The region's many bayous, which drained south to the coastal marsh on one side and back to swamps on the other, traditionally had presented problems for travelers and served as havens for outlaws.

Originally published in *Louisiana History: The Journal of the Louisiana Historical Association* 39 (Winter 1998): 45–64. Used by permission of the Louisiana Historical Association.

Part of this region had come under Union control in 1863 as a result of Gen. Nathaniel P. Banks' Teche-Atchafalaya campaign early in the year and Gen. William B. Franklin's Great Texas Overland Expedition that fall. Banks had hoped to cut the Red River supply line to the Confederate's Mississippi River stronghold at Port Hudson, while Franklin's operation was designed to quell Confederate resistance in East Texas and to discourage further French ambitions in Mexico. News of Banks' approaching forces caused massive slave defections, giving planters and invading troops their first real inkling of the postwar labor problem. Both Union campaigns failed, but not before the Union and Confederate armies, foraging off the surrounding countryside for several months, denuded the once-prosperous sugar plantations and farms.

Many French-born planters of the region, claiming to be neutral foreign nationals, discovered that this did not protect their property or aid their later efforts to recover damages from the federal government. At Madame Charles Olivier's plantation, just east of New Iberia, a provost guard commanded by a Captain Ellis of the 174th New York, sequestered all of the family's provisions. The records of the French and American Claims Commission, containing the petitions of over 700 unnaturalized French residents of Louisiana, even allowing for exaggeration of Union avarice and omission of Confederate depredations, offer ample testimony of the impact of war on the citizenry of the region. Nor were the oaths of allegiance many signed necessarily sufficient to forestall the loss of all their belongings. An admittedly partisan report to Confederate Gov. Henry Watkins Allen, writing about a St. Mary Parish neighbor of Charles Olivier, pointedly concluded that "We have already seen how poor Borel (who had taken the oath of allegiance) fared when he applied to General Banks for his last horse—his last means of support; others fared no better."

This lament was supported by the boast of George Hepworth, who was with Union forces in the Teche: "Never did an army make cleaner work than ours. . . . Our boys drove to the rear every pony and mule, every ox and cow and sheep. They did not leave, on an average, two chickens to a plantation. Wherever they encamped, the fences served as beds and firewood." On October 3, 1863, as he moved his forces up Bayou Teche, Gen. William Franklin remarked that this formerly prosperous region was "a country utterly destitute of supplies, which had been repeatedly overrun by the two armies." This situation only worsened when Franklin encamped his forces on the outskirts of

New Iberia for the winter. Northern forces would continue to skirmish with units of Gen. Richard Taylor's army in the region until the Confederates finally gave up the fight.

With military occupation came a series of measures which created a labor system that represented a transition between slavery and freedom. General Banks's free labor policy specified set wages and outlawed the whip, but required freedmen to sign yearly contracts which bound them to their plantations. It is not surprising that planters, workers, and many Republicans were displeased with a system based first and foremost on the military's definition of economic stability and social order. Planters balked at the prohibition of corporal punishment and the insistence on wages. Black workers and concerned Republicans resented the continuation of gang labor and other contractual restrictions as all too redolent of slavery. Banks's labor regulations, of course, affected only the portions of south Louisiana under his control, and, by the end of the war, Union forces occupied a somewhat smaller region than they had in 1863. . . .

From late spring to the installation of newly elected state and local officials in November 1865, contingents of Federal troops were responsible for overseeing the early phases of transition from war to peace in Southwest Louisiana. The small detachments, which occupied towns like New Iberia, would face serious problems. The war had temporarily dismantled the old planter-dominated political order, leaving a power vacuum which a host of competing interests sought to fill. Planters, freedmen, discharged Union veterans, former Confederates, speculators, jayhawkers, and other citizens all sought to turn the situation to their advantage. In the countryside, roving bands of die-hard Confederate guerrillas preyed on travelers, freedmen, livestock, and inoperative sugar mills. Lawlessness flourished even in towns since most locales lacked any semblance of civil government. Confidence men abounded, vice was unrestrained, and street brawls were commonplace.

Furthermore, wartime Union Army efforts to revive the state's agriculture had failed. The military's mandated labor system, imperfect as it was, had disintegrated after Appomattox. Freed slaves, destitute farmers, deserters from both armies and mustered-out soldiers at loose ends roamed the countryside. Although the formal surrender of the Confederacy's Trans-Mississippi Army did not come until June 1865, the informal exodus from that force had been going on all spring. Some vagabonds looked for work, others for anything that was not tied down or guarded. Travelers in St. Mary and St. Martin parishes reported that roads had fallen into such disrepair that they had actually disappeared in some places. Damaged levees caused flooding problems that spring, and again in 1866. The country was dotted with plantations, large and small, shorn of fencing, stock, provisions and equipment. Cattle and other creatures could not be kept away from growing crops. Some crops could not be grown. Antislavery journalist John Trowbridge reported that, in St. Mary Parish, "seed-cane was not to be had; and to recommence the culture an outlay of capital was necessary, from which no such immediate, bountiful returns could be anticipated as from the culture of cotton." Iberia Parish resident Emilien Landry, when asked years later about the condition of the Appoline Patout plantation out on Isle Piquant prairie a few miles east of New Iberia, replied simply that "it was naked." Landry's statement could have described many of the area's plantations.

While many whites in the Teche region resented the military occupation, many also recognized that it was indispensable to the restoration of order, a prerequisite for economic recovery. Freedmen needed protection from vengeful whites. Planters wanted the military to require recalcitrant blacks to work. Law-abiding people of all political persuasions desired protection of their persons and property from thieves and swindlers. Townspeople in the region demanded an end to street violence. Those who were destitute saw the occupation forces as a potential source of provisions.

Even more pervasive, and significant, than resentment was resignation. Republican journalist Whitelaw Reid toured the South in May and June of 1865. He concluded that "the National Government could have at that time prescribed no conditions for the return of the Rebel States which they would not have promptly accepted. They expected nothing; were prepared for the worst; would have been thankful for anything." Reid blamed President Andrew Johnson's North Carolina proclamation for fostering resistance to federal direction of Reconstruction. Against this backdrop of growing obstinacy, a major question was whether or not the size and composition of the occupation forces was sufficient to the task of restoring order, much less initiating reform.

Col. Charles Ledyard Norton entered New Iberia on June 1, 1865, with five companies of the 98th Colored Infantry, a total of 228 men. After establishing an encampment on Bayou Teche just north of town, this twenty-eight-year-old Connecticut Yankee, a graduate of Yale, described New Iberia as being in "a state of complete anarchy" when he arrived. St. Martinville and Vermilionville (present-day Lafayette), he said, at least had some semblance of civil government. His African American contingent was responsible for a region stretching south to the coast, north into St. Landry Parish, east to Franklin, and west to the sparsely settled, untamed region beyond Vermilionville and Abbeville, [including Imperial Calcasieu Parish]. His orders were to curb organized brigandage and other breaches of the peace, to enforce the transitional labor system devised by Gen. Nathaniel Banks, and to cooperate in the restoration of civil authority according to the late Abraham Lincoln's Ten Percent Plan. Predictably, Norton reported that the small size of his force made it impossible to enforce order over any distance, since "beyond the immediate vicinity of U. S. troops lawlessness prevails to a great extent."

Norton reluctantly began organizing white patrols of loyal citizens and paroled Confederates. He admitted that, given the existing racial antagonisms, such a move represented a "dangerous temptation to the exercise of tyranny over the blacks." However, without the presence of U.S. cavalry troops, he considered the mounted civilian patrols "the only means of preserving property from marauding parties of both colors." With this in mind, he empowered the mayor of St. Martinville to establish an interim police force to maintain order and preserve property, cautioning him against extreme measures "unless parties have evidently been guilty of some criminal act or depredation." Repeated guerrilla marauding around St. Martinville ceased after the mayor formed mounted patrols of local citizens and paroled soldiers. Norton reported that the civil appointments made by Gov. James Madison Wells were helpful, but only so long as their authority was reinforced by a military presence.

A week later, Norton reiterated his need for cavalry. "White cavalry is needed as a mounted police because negro soldiers, except under the eye of officers, can seldom be trusted to deal with men of their own color, tho they cannot be excelled in maintaining order among white planters." He might have added that local whites were more likely to respect the authority of white troopers. Referring to General Order Number 23 regarding labor relations on plantations, Norton indicated that most freedmen neglected their duties, and that it was difficult to get his black troops to enforce labor regulations if other blacks were involved. A few days thereafter, Norton observed "that a mounted force is necessary not only to maintain order, but [also] to keep up communications must be evident when the extent of the country and the character of the inhabitants is considered."

Norton reported that although the number of loyal persons was very small, the Americans and paroled soldiers were inclined to accept the new order, and the Creoles were at least respectable people. However, he regarded the Acadian population as "wholly treacherous." What exactly led him to his low estimate of the Acadians is unknown, but Norton's opinion of them was partially formed by his experience in rendering aid to destitute families. He reported that great care was being taken to help only the needy, but "The Acadian inhabitants will many of them swear to anything in order to obtain rations. Oaths will not hereafter be regarded by me except in special cases." Though this sort of duplicity might have been expected of any groups, regardless of ethnicity, Norton was not alone in his opinion. Lieut. Lorenzo Cook, stationed in Breaux Bridge, wanted to be transferred back to the Great Plains. Asked why, he replied, "I would rather be among the Comanches than among these ignorant priest-ridden people [Acadians]." Cook's prejudice was part of a larger, and widespread, reluctance to be policemen. Historian Joseph G. Dawson observed that, following the end of organized hostilities, "Impatient volunteers, sweltering in the Texas heat and Louisiana humidity, announced that they had enlisted to fight Johnny Rebs, not police rural towns, chase jayhawkers, guard cotton depots, or patrol the Mexican border." These were held to be jobs for the regular army or, as it happened in New Iberia, for colored troops.

Referring to the general composition of the population, Norton said that "there are the usual three classes, namely planters, negros [sic] and poor whites." While he may have had, or developed, some appreciation for family ties, religion, ethnicity, and political affiliations as factors complicating his assignment, these considerations do not appear in Norton's communiqués. Nearly all of the difficulties, he said, arose out of mutual suspicions between planters and freedmen. He reported that, in nearly all instances, freedmen either refused to work or neglected their duties. In some cases, they responded to orders with insolence and, in one case, "a negro [sic] drew a knife on his employer who in turn shot the negro [sic] (not seriously hurting him, however)."

When asked by planters what they should do when blacks refused to work, even for wages, Norton replied that they must inform recalcitrant freedmen that they could work on plantations for wages or for the government for nothing. Following orders from his superiors, Norton generally returned blacks who left plantations bound for his headquarters. Norton requested further instructions regarding a "rigid system of free labor." He said that this and the reorganization of civil government were the pressing needs of the region.

After a month, Norton was able to report that jayhawkers did not often venture within thirty or forty miles of New Iberia, although the Bailey Vinsen gang had pillaged two stores in Franklin, paused to shoot at local citizens, and then escaped the troops Norton sent to arrest them. General lawlessness was the rule in regions not in the immediate vicinity of Federal troops. In almost all cases, the trouble seemed to involve former Confederate troops.

His estimate of the Acadian population notwithstanding, Charles Norton was a conscientious and fair man whose priorities were the well-being of his troops and law and order. Norton earnestly tried to get adequate shelter for his soldiers, with middling success. He required that all keepers of retail establishments report to his headquarters and show their licenses or other authority for doing such business. To reduce public drunkenness and street fights, Norton ordered all places of business and amusement closed on Sundays. He demanded that law-abiding citizens be treated with respect and held himself and his troops strictly accountable for their own behavior. Norton brought charges against some of his troopers who fired at family members on the François Darby plantation. When a detachment of enlisted men wrecked a local establishment, Norton recommended that the damage estimate "may be justly slapped against the joint pay of [the] officers and men, including myself."

If Norton believed a complaint to be unwarranted, he did not mince words. When a New Iberia citizens' petition alleged disrespectful conduct by units of the 78th Infantry and the 3rd Rhode Island Cavalry, Norton challenged them to cite a single case of such behavior "which has not been promptly punished when brought to my notice. I beg leave to state also, that disrespect on the part of citizens toward my soldiers has been punished with equal promptness." The colonel also noted that he had repeatedly offered leading citizens assistance in promoting the welfare of the community. He thought that the petition was occasioned by the irritation that local whites felt at seeing their former slaves in United States Army uniforms. In a later report on an incident where black soldiers speaking to black servants over a fence were ordered away by the owner, Norton observed that the intolerance of black soldiers by some whites would be absurd except that it threatened to become serious.

Perhaps because he commanded so many black soldiers, Norton experienced considerable difficulty in getting his troops properly provisioned, housed, and equipped. Two weeks after his arrival, he requested that a competent quartermaster be sent to his post and that either a post bakery be established or a supply of soft bread furnished. "I have only one officer for each company," he wrote, "and it is more than one man can do to attend to his company and at the same time manage a Quartermaster's Office." On July 24, he reported an "urgent need for clothing and camp and garrison equipage." Norton said that these supplies were available in Brashear City (now Morgan City), about forty miles to the east, but the Quartermaster there was unwilling to turn them over. Furthermore, Company B of the 2nd Rhode Island Infantry was housed in former slave quarters. Other units may have fared worse, because Norton wrote that "as the rainy season is at hand I most earnestly request that the troops at this post be provided with shelter of some kind." There were other challenges as well. In early August, Norton approved the hiring of two civilian clerks for duty in the Quartermaster Department, one at $100 per month, because he could locate no enlisted man who could write.

Norton's biggest challenge, however, was the outlying areas of his command. He recommended that cavalry be stationed in Vermilionville and between that town and Opelousas, "the fifty miles between Washington [La.] and Vermillion[ville] being wholly unprotected." He wondered that the area south of Vermilionville had not been occupied and suggested that troops occupy Abbeville. Norton described the area west of the Vermilion River stretching to the Texas line as very unsettled and a traditional "retreat for desperadoes and outlaws." Until the 1880s, much of that vast grassland was sparsely settled country which featured herds of half-wild cattle and a history of vigilantism. His opinion was that a company or two of cavalry should at least visit the Calcasieu and Sabine River country out near the Texas border.

Norton's apprehensions about the region west of the Vermilion River proved to be well-founded. In August, he wrote of increased disorder in those regions to the north and west of New Iberia still unoccupied by U. S. troops.

He said that troops would be necessary "unless the State Authorities exhibit an efficiency which has not yet appeared." He further recommended the creation of a "Home Colony," a relief center which would attend to the large numbers of black children and infirm freedmen who had no visible means of support.

Norton apparently received some cavalry support in July, and three companies of the 3rd Rhode Island Cavalry arrived from Napoleonville in Assumption Parish a bit later. He would need them because conditions just twenty miles to the west of New Iberia had also worsened. On September 11, citizens of Lafayette Parish complained that two men had been murdered there and that a gang of "desperadoes" was threatening the lives of citizens. The next day, Norton dispatched Capt. O. A. Avery with Company B of the 3rd Rhode Island Cavalry to investigate and to assist local authorities in establishing a police force. Avery made three arrests and turned the suspects over to civil authorities in Vermilionville. He then proceeded farther west to investigate reports of disturbances there. Avery reported a great deal of disloyalty in the Calcasieu River region and nothing in the way of political reorganization. Norton wrote to Captain B. B. Campbell that, so far as he could learn, no law had ever existed there.

Abbeville, twenty miles south of Vermilionville and twenty miles west of New Iberia, was also troubled. In October 1865, Norton characterized it as still:

> entirely unsettled. . . . The town is subject to constant disturbance from a party of wild young men who assault negroes [sic] and disturb the peace generally…the negroes have told them that by so doing they will enslave themselves again. No negro [sic] will believe the statement of a southern man to the contrary. A large part . . . work as little as possible though I think the planters are apt to exaggerate the number.

Even in these troubled towns, Norton's concern was for order and fairness. Ordering Lieuts. Charles Scott and James Riley to occupy Vermilionville and Abbeville respectively, he reminded them that the reestablishment of civil government was a top priority.

Scott and Riley were to render all possible aid to local authorities and to arrest citizens only to enforce respect for the army or at the request of civil officials. They had no authority to approve labor contracts. Norton advised them to give only their best advice, to settle minor disputes fairly, and to put vagrants, whether black or white, to work on the public streets in order to induce them to seek other work. Within ten days, Norton was able to report that both towns were quiet and that the inhabitants were "well-disposed" to the new order. Restoration of civil authority in the back country, however, was proceeding more slowly because of its distance from military posts.

Washington, Louisiana, approximately five miles north of Opelousas, also came under Federal control. There, local freedmen who had enlisted in the Union army were organized into an occupation force. In July, Norton ordered Captain Avery to establish a courier detail to operate between New Iberia and Washington. Couriers from his post were to meet the messengers from Washington in Vermilionville once a week to exchange dispatches. He established a similar system, to operate three times a week, for communication with Franklin. Though the task was by no means complete, by early fall, Norton had restored some measure of civil order to his jurisdiction, particularly the eastern half.

Unfortunately, Norton's military occupation ended soon after the November 6, 1865, election. He reported that the election was quiet and orderly, and that "the inhabitants are said to be exultant over the anticipated removal of troops but I think that a short experience of the disorders which are sure to follow our departure will convince the better portion of them that a military force is still required here." In preparation for their departure, Norton ordered the withdrawal of his troops from Abbeville and Vermilionville. Acts of violence followed, especially cases of abuse of blacks, and Norton wrote that while he intended to bring the accused parties before civil authorities, he doubted "whether even the form of a trial can be obtained much less a just sentence."

These would prove to be prophetic words. Following the November elections and President Andrew Johnson's December announcement that the Union was restored, the incidence of violence against blacks increased markedly. In March 1866, Lieut. W. H. Cornelius, the Freedman's Bureau agent in St. Martinville, reported the Gustave Vincent, a young black boy, was peppered with birdshot by St. Cyr Wiltz for the offense of crawfishing on his land with two white boys. Some weeks later, Onesiphore Delahoussaye shot Joseph Gralan "for some trifling offense" and apparently was allowed to escape by local authorities. In May, a white man listed only as McRae attempted to rape a St. Martin Parish black resident, Pamela Castille. According to the agent, McRae was "arrested but permitted to escape."

In summarizing the violence in Louisiana over a two-year period ending on February 20, 1867, a Bureau representative recorded 86 freedmen killed and 230 injured in violent confrontations. Only two blacks had been killed by other blacks and just one white person had been murdered by a freedman. According to the report,

> In no instance . . . has a white man been punished for killing or ill-treating a freedman. In some few cases the guilty parties are in jail awaiting trial but the majority have either been justified by a Coroner's jury, acquitted or admitted to Bail. . . .

The Knights of the White Camellia, first established in St. Mary Parish in 1867, and led by Alcibiades DeBlanc, were probably involved in much of the violence. Secretive and sworn to maintain white supremacy, their influence was widespread. It was said, apocryphally no doubt, that every St. Landry Parish white man save one was a Knight, and that the solitary nonconformist was excluded only because of senility.

Judging by Col. Charles Norton's experience in southwest Louisiana, and by what followed his departure, Federal troops were removed just as some semblance of order was beginning to be restored. The climate of violence and the lack of respect for civil authority in the two decades following their departure has been amply documented by historians. The continuous, long-term presence of Federal troops in southern towns, despite ingrained American suspicions of military government, might have been a less arduous and more effective way of restoring the South.

The best time to secure the peace and shape the South's future was 1865, with the military helping to fill the vacuum in the political and social order. Then, Union troops had the moral authority of the victors. Furthermore, as historian Hans Trefousse observed, the South was prostrate, expected the worst, and was inclined to submission to its conquerors. In Louisiana, Unionist Judge Rufus K. Howell estimated that loyalists were about as strong as their opponents. At a minimum, this would have provided a substantial core of citizens inclined to be supportive of a firm hand. There were similar or even more favorable reports from all over the South. President Andrew Johnson's announcement of lenience on May 29, 1865, produced an almost immediate conservative recalcitrance with regard to enforced changes in the Southern way of life. It also demoralized Southern Unionists as they saw former foes restored to political power. President Johnson's continuing interference with Republican Reconstruction plans meant that conservatives could bide their time as the Charles Nortons and their troops served out their all-too-brief occupations, secure in the knowledge that they would soon be back in charge of local affairs. It seems likely that Norton and his peers elsewhere in the South drew much the same conclusion, and that it had a deleterious effect on their enthusiasm for the occupation. According to Trefousse, "It is at least conceivable that in the winter of 1866-67, an adjustment might still have been made. Southern cooperation for a Reconstruction program might have been won had not the administration interfered."

By 1867, however, occupied towns and their hinterlands had made significant adjustments and, emboldened by the president's opposition to the Fourteenth Amendment, viewed the army as agents of the despised Radical Republican faction in Congress. At the risk of stretching a point, the cases of post-World War II Germany and Japan—where American military occupation and political direction was immediate, continuous, and effective over much greater distances—perhaps provide some cause for optimism about the salutary effects of a more rigorous military presence in the postbellum South.

If such an occupation had been sustained in Southwest Louisiana, the troops could have curbed violence and unreconstructed white efforts to restore blacks to some semblance of servitude, as they did when the military quashed the Opelousas Black Code in 1865. Blacks thereby would have been protected from many of the excesses which followed in 1866 and 1867. Whites might well have benefited from a greater measure of law, order, and political honesty, which they said that local Radical governments failed to provide. The sugar industry, southwest Louisiana's economic mainstay, did not recover fully until 1880. This recovery might have come sooner had federal policy not changed after 1865 and again in 1867. . . . As it is, the prospect of what an ongoing military support of civil administration might have wrought in the postwar South remains, along with the elusive forty acres and a mule for freedmen, one of the great might-have-beens of postbellum Southern history.

Questions

1. What were the physical costs of the war to southwest Louisiana?
2. What problems did the new system of labor that replaced slavery present for both whites and blacks?
3. Why was southwest Louisiana lawless in 1865?
4. What difficulties did the federal commander, Norton, face in trying to keep order?
5. What happened after the withdrawal of the federal troops?
6. What does author Michael Wade think would have worked better? Do you agree? Explain your answer.

FROM THE BARREL OF A GUN: THE POLITICS OF MURDER IN GRANT PARISH

by Joel M. Sipress

Easter sunday, 1873, found about 150 black men, many armed with shotguns and rifles, encamped at a former plantation stable in Colfax, Louisiana. The stable served as the Grant Parish Courthouse, and the men had come to defend it. They found themselves besieged that Sunday morning, outnumbered and outgunned. For over a week, white conservatives intent upon smashing black political and military power in Grant had been pouring into Colfax. For more than two years, conservatives had been locked in a bitter struggle with radical Republicans for control of the parish. On April 13, 1873, that struggle was settled by force.

The battle began shortly after noon. For two hours, conservatives exchanged shots with black radicals entrenched behind crude breastworks. The conservatives opened fire with a small cannon that they had commandeered from a Red River steamboat, but to no avail. Searching for an avenue from which to attack, a scouting party discovered that the radical line could be outflanked by crawling along the riverbank. They also found a gap in the levee through which they could fire the cannon.

Around mid-afternoon, the cannon opened fire . . . while thirty men, led by a former plantation overseer, charged up from the riverbank. The freedmen's

Originally published in *Louisiana History: The Journal of the Louisiana Historical Association* 42 (Summer 2001): 303–321. Used by permission of the Louisiana Historical Association.

line broke in a panic. Routed, some tried to escape to the river or the nearby woods. A portion of the conservative forces set out in pursuit and slaughtered all they caught. About sixty other freedmen retreated into the courthouse itself. For about an hour, the assailants fired upon the former plantation stable. The freedmen shot back through the building's window cracks. Finally, the conservatives forced a black man taken prisoner earlier to set fire to the courthouse roof. The building ablaze, men poured out to surrender, only to be met by a deadly volley.

About forty black men were taken prisoner during the Colfax battle. . . . [T]he conservative forces' commander visited and promised to free the captives in the morning if they would stop their "damned foolishness" and return home to tend their crops. After dark, however, a group of younger men marched the freedmen off in pairs for execution. Only a handful of the prisoners lived to tell the tale. . . .

The Colfax Massacre of 1873 was, in the words of Eric Foner, "the bloodiest single instance of racial carnage in the Reconstruction era." For many historians, the Easter Sunday battle has come to symbolize the extremism of post-Civil War Southern racism. . . . Upon closer examination, however, the Colfax Massacre reveals a more complex story. Less a testament to the depths of Southern extremism, the massacre is more an indication of the extreme lengths to which seemingly moderate men will go to preserve their power and authority. Although many of the participants in the Easter Sunday battle were undoubtedly hate-filled extremists resistant to any and all changes in the racial status quo, others, including much of the leadership, were racial moderates who had attempted to adapt themselves to the post-emancipation order. Some, in fact, had flirted with the Republican party, the party of emancipation and black enfranchisement. The racial moderates of the Reconstruction era hoped that black citizenship and suffrage could be reconciled with the continued political authority of the plantation elite. Only with the emergence of a militant black radicalism did these men of the center abandon the Republican party and embrace the politics of brute force. On Easter Sunday, 1873, they killed not for hate, but for power.

Grant Parish was the brainchild of Republican planter William S. Calhoun. A staunch Unionist during the Civil War, Calhoun was one of the few Louisiana planters to embrace the Republican party from the outset of Reconstruction. Calhoun rode a reputation as a defender of the freedmen's rights into the Louisiana House of Representatives in 1868. The following year, he pushed a bill creating a new parish through the Republican-controlled legislature. The parish, whose borders were drawn to ensure a narrow black voting majority, was named in honor of Ulysses S. Grant, Republican president and hero of the Union war effort. The parish seat, located on Calhoun's property . . ., was named for Grant's vice president, Schuyler Colfax.

The town of Colfax . . . lay in a former province of the antebellum South's cotton kingdom. William Calhoun's parents had owned over 700 slaves and lands that extended seven miles along the Red River. This property had made the Calhouns the parish's wealthiest planters and among the wealthiest in the state. Along the Red River and nearby bayous lay fertile alluvial land where the Calhouns and their neighbors had built a way of life upon a foundation of cotton and slavery.

Calhoun was typical of the prominent white Unionists who dominated the Louisiana Republican party in the years just after black enfranchisement. Though they had been swept into power by a promise to fight for the rights of freedpeople, Republican leaders believed that, having granted political rights to black men, they could leave the divisive issues of race and class behind. Instead, they hoped to build a truly biracial Republican party around a program of nationalism, modernization, and economic development. The chief architect of the party's centrist course was Henry Clay Warmoth, Republican governor of Louisiana. . . .

Like his namesake, the great Kentucky Whig Henry Clay, Warmoth was above all a nationalist who, like Clay, saw men of "wealth and intelligence" as the nation's political backbone. Warmoth enlisted in the Missouri militia in 1861 to fight for the Union and subsequently was mustered into the Federal army. Only reluctantly did he embrace emancipation, and then only after concluding that slavery was responsible for the Civil War. . . .

[As governor,] Warmoth sought to build a biracial Republican party by appealing to the latent Unionism of the state's agricultural and commercial entrepreneurs and by promising to work with them to build a more prosperous Louisiana. In this way, Warmoth hoped to "harmonize the two races" and to persuade them "to live together on the basis of equal civil and political rights". . . .

An earlier generation of Louisiana conservatives had come to terms with universal white male suffrage. Warmoth now sought to convince their heirs that emancipation and black citizenship could also be reconciled with economic progress and social hierarchy. Former slaves, however, had flocked to the Republican party precisely because of the challenge it posed to the hierarchical social order of the Old South. . . . The need to simultaneously satisfy the expectations of both groups furnished the Warmoth administration with its central political dilemma.

The local reaction to Warmoth's initial set of Grant Parish political appointments illustrated the governor's predicament. The creation of Grant allowed Warmoth to name a full set of parish officials to serve until Louisiana's next general election. The bulk of the offices went to the party faithful, including a number of well-known white radicals. (Black Republicans received a few minor posts.) The radical tilt of the governor's appointments angered local conservatives. The selection of two prominent radicals, Delos White and William Phillips, as sheriff and parish judge, especially incensed conservatives.

Delos White was a native of Flushing, New York, who had come south with the Union Army and later served a term as a Freedmen's Bureau agent in neighboring Winn Parish. White's experience with the Bureau had inspired in him a sense of solidarity with the former slaves. Sheriff White had found the freedpeople to be "sober and industrious" and declared their "moral character" superior to that of local white population. . . . White received several death threats while serving with the Freedmen's Bureau. A few weeks after he took office as sheriff, two armed men ordered him to leave Grant Parish within twenty-four hours, a command he refused to obey.

More hated than even Sheriff White was Judge William Phillips. An ambitious young man, Phillips was an Alabama scalawag who left his war-torn native state at the age of twenty-three and settled in Louisiana's Red River Valley. Phillips began canvassing the bottomlands for the Republican party and earned a reputation for radicalism by promising to fight for land, horses, and tools for the freedpeople. Democrats and moderate Republicans alike considered Judge Phillips an unprincipled man and accused him of filling the freedpeople with false hopes in order to further his own political career. Phillips's personal life added to his radical reputation; the judge lived for a time with a black woman by whom he fathered a son. . . .

The most extreme opposition to Republican rule in Grant Parish came from the Knights of the White Camellia, a militant white supremacist organization closely allied with the Democratic party. The Knights . . . warned of an impending race war and openly advocated the disfranchisement of black voters. The Knights, however, spoke for just a portion of Grant's white citizenry. Many others took a middle ground by rejecting the Knights' extremist message while also opposing radical Republicanism. To recruit these moderate white conservatives (often termed the "respectable" element) to the Republican party, Warmoth had to sacrifice the parish's radical office-holders. In March 1870, the governor replaced Sheriff White and Judge Phillips with two Republicans more acceptable to conservatives. One was a Confederate veteran and the other, though an outspoken Unionist, had lived in the area for over twenty years and had held parish office before the war.

With the radicals' elimination, Warmoth's policy of conciliation began to pay dividends. All three lawyers residing in Colfax joined the Republican ranks, as did several planters and merchants. The recruitment of white voters allowed the Republican ticket to carry 69 percent of the parish vote in the November 1870 election. Attracted by Warmoth's vision of harmony and prosperity, moderate white conservatives seemed willing to accept black citizenship and suffrage, so long as their own power and authority were not threatened.

Shortly after Governor Warmoth removed him as parish judge, William Phillips organized an unabashedly radical wing of the local Republican party. Many of Grant Parish's homegrown black activists joined forces with Phillips. The deposed judge also received support from a group of African American military veterans who had recently settled in Grant Parish. Chief among these "black carpetbaggers" was a former cavalryman named William Ward. Ward and Phillips became fast friends as well as political allies. Together they would destroy the governor's vision of peace and harmony.

A carpenter by trade, William Ward had been reared in slavery in Virginia. At the age of twenty-four, he ran away and enlisted in the Union Army. By the end of the Civil War, the former slave held the rank of sergeant. Ward returned to Virginia after his discharge, but he remained dissatisfied with civilian life. In the fall of 1867, he re-enlisted in the United States Army and was stationed at Ship Island, Mississippi. His military career came to an end soon afterward when he was diagnosed with tuberculosis and discharged from the army. In

1870, Ward, his wife Mary, and two friends from the service settled in Grant Parish. Ward gained an outlet for his frustrated military aspirations through an appointment as a captain in the Louisiana state militia.

Although none of the black carpetbaggers were native to Grant Parish, nor even to Louisiana, they quickly became leaders of the local Republican radicals. Ward and his comrades provided a model for a new type of militant black politics. They were uncompromising and did not shy away from confrontation. Economically independent of the plantation elite, they had a freedom of political action not shared by native black activists. The black carpetbaggers demonstrated by force of example that former slaves need not always turn to white Republicans for political leadership.

The November 1870 parish elections left Grant with a government divided between the radical and conservative wings of the local Republican party. Striking a blow at Governor Warmoth's policy of conciliating conservatives, the Grant Parish Republican party's black rank-and-file nominated and elected a slate of candidates that included radicals William Phillips for parish judge and Delos White for parish recorder. The Republicans also elected black radicals as justices of the peace and constables in two of the parish's seven wards. Conservative Republicans, however, retained control of the parish police jury.

Following the election, a bitter battle erupted between Republican radicals and conservatives. . . . A personal feud that pitted Alfred Shelby, Grant Parish's white Republican sheriff, against Delos White and William Phillips exacerbated the factional strife. By 1871, relations between the sheriff and the radicals were so sour that Shelby was reported to say that the parish was not big enough to hold both himself and White.

White and Phillips shared a house not far from Colfax. Late in the evening of September 25, 1871, the sound of approaching horsemen awakened them. Before the pair could rouse themselves, the house had been set ablaze, and guards armed with double-barreled shotguns had blocked the exits. Outside was a mob of about fifty white men. To remain inside meant certain death, so White and Phillips chose to risk the mob. As the two rushed to the door, the guards opened fire. White died instantly. . . . Phillips escaped by feigning death. . . .

The murder of White was a bipartisan event. Although much of the crowd was undoubtedly Democratic, and likely included extremists of the Knights of the White Camellia, at the helm were Republicans—representatives of the parish's "respectable" element. According to Phillips, Republican Sheriff Alfred Shelby led the mob. At his side was Deputy Sheriff Christopher Columbus Nash, a local merchant and Confederate veteran who had also joined the Republican ranks. Strife among Republicans had exploded into bloodshed.

William Phillips swore publicly that he would spare no effort to make Delos White's murderers suffer the full penalty of law. The judge fled to New Orleans, where he sought both federal and state aid in bringing the perpetrators to justice. Phillips obtained federal warrants for the arrest of eight men, including Sheriff Shelby, Deputy Nash, and two other white Republicans. The Warmoth administration dispatched a shipment of Enfield rifles to William Ward in his capacity as captain of Grant Parish's militia company.

Governor Warmoth had intended that the Louisiana State Militia be half white and half black. . . . William Ward's militia company, however, was entirely black. Knowing how provocative a show of force by an all-black militia unit would be, Ward's superiors gave him explicit instructions to keep the arms carefully stored, subject to the governor's orders. . . .

In direct violation of his orders, the captain armed and drilled his all-black militia company. To the conservatives' horror, he then arrested the eight men named in the federal warrants obtained by Phillips. The prisoners remained under militia guard awaiting the arrival of a federal marshal who would escort the men to a pre-trial hearing in New Orleans.

In late October, state district judge John Osborn, a moderate Republican, held a hearing at Colfax to determine whether the eight men in custody had, in fact, been legally arrested. Phillips and Ward were in attendance, with their prisoners in tow. Also present was a federal marshal, who had arrived to take charge of the prisoners. Over the radicals' objections, Judge Osborn refused to release the prisoners into the custody of the federal marshal. Instead, the judge claimed personal jurisdiction over the case.

As the hearing proceeded, a New Orleans-bound steamboat came within sight of Colfax. Hoping to catch the approaching vessel, the federal marshal renewed his demand for custody of the prisoners. When Judge Osborn again refused to hand them over, William Ward resolved the jurisdictional dispute in his own manner. As astonished observers watched, the captain led his militia into the courtroom with bayonets fixed and seized the eight men. Judge Osborn protested. "Damn the court," responded Ward. The militiamen marched the prisoners down to the riverbank and onto the steamboat, which carried them off to New Orleans.

Thus began what conservatives dubbed Ward's "reign of terror." In the weeks that followed, the militia, in cooperation with federal marshals, rounded up conservatives suspected of violating the federal Enforcement Act (which made conspiracy to deny any person or class of persons equal protection under the law a federal crime). One man who resisted was killed. In December, a force of sixteen federal troops arrived to assist. . . . Some men who traveled to the city to testify for the accused were themselves arrested at the instigation of Phillips.

Ward's bold action infuriated his superiors in the Warmoth administration. A board of state militia officers sent by the governor to investigate the arson and murder . . . recommended that the company be disbanded and Ward be placed under arrest. A state militia staff officer traveled to Colfax to disband the company, but Ward refused to comply.

The murder of Delos White had set off a small-scale civil war in Grant Parish. By the end of 1871, the radicals appeared to have fought this war to a successful conclusion. The radicals were better armed and better organized than their opponents, and they had the support of the federal courts and federal troops. In reality, however, the position of the radicals was actually quite weak. The radicals depended critically upon federal power, which was far away and, as it turned out, not always reliable.

At a November 1871 pre-trial hearing in New Orleans, Sheriff Alfred Shelby and Deputy Sheriff Columbus Nash were imprisoned without bail, pending a federal grand jury investigation into the murder of Delos White. . . . The grand jury refused to hand down any indictments. . . . Shelby resumed his duties as sheriff, and Nash set to work organizing a united front of those who opposed radical rule.

By the spring of 1872, neither the state nor the federal authorities in New Orleans found the Grant Parish radicals to be credible. In March, a party of radicals applied for military assistance to counter armed conservative organizations that they claimed had driven them from their homes. . . . Shortly thereafter, William Phillips abandoned his position as parish judge and fled to New Orleans. Governor Warmoth appointed in his place a conservative Republican who had served in the Confederate army.

In the summer of 1872, Warmoth made one final attempt to create a grand coalition that would harmonize the interests of black and white Louisianians. . . . [T]he governor severed his ties with the national party and declared his support for the dissident "Liberal Republican" movement. Warmoth then called for a Liberal Republican state convention to nominate a ticket for Louisiana's fall elections under the banner, "Justice to all Races, Creeds, and Political Opinions". . . . Louisiana's black and radical Republicans were unwilling to abandon the Republican party for a coalition with white conservatives, even moderate conservatives. Spurned by the radicals, Warmoth and the Liberal Republicans united with Louisiana's Democrats and together nominated a joint "fusion" ticket headed by Democrat John D. McEnery.

Rather than harmonize the races, Warmoth's break with the Republican party actually accelerated Louisiana's political polarization. In Grant Parish, disgruntled conservatives followed the governor out of the Republican party and into an alliance with the Democrats. Together, they nominated a local fusion ticket that united the parish's "respectable" element with conservative extremists. . . .

The political alignment of November 1872 lay bare the fundamental political cleavage wrought by emancipation and enfranchisement. On one side stood radicals, committed to a militant defense of freedpeople interests. On the other side stood conservatives, determined to preserve the privileged position of former slaveholders. Conservative Republicans, . . . now found themselves in league with ultra-conservative Democrats. . . .

The 1872 Louisiana state elections were so marred by fraud that, to this day, it is unclear which side actually received the most votes. Official returns were never announced for Grant Parish and both parties claimed victory there. Following the election, Governor Warmoth named the fusionist candidates to Grant Parish offices. In early January 1873, the conservatives took possession of the courthouse and began to discharge their official duties. A few weeks later, Republican William Pitt Kellogg, who had assumed the governor's office, appointed a Republican slate of local officials, giving Grant Parish rival sets of officeholders.

Although the Republicans made no immediate attempt to take office in Grant Parish, some local conservatives anticipated a confrontation. In mid-

March, they dispatched William Rutland and William Richardson, two Republican lawyers who had defected to the fusionists the previous summer, to implore Governor Kellogg to retract his recent appointments. The governor, after some vacillation, agreed to appoint some of the fusionist candidates, but he refused to name Columbus Nash sheriff. . . .

In late March, Grant Parish's Republican officeholders seized the courthouse. A day or so later, a handful of white men met at William Rutland's Colfax law office and issued a call for a mass meeting at the courthouse to take the parish offices by armed force. Rutland dispatched messengers to spread word of the meeting throughout the parish.

William Ward was home, sick in bed, on the evening of March 31, 1873, when a black man brought word that conservative planter and reputed Klan leader James Hadnot was mustering men with the intention of attacking Colfax the next day. Hadnot, the reports indicated, planned to take possession of the courthouse, replace the Republican officials with fusionist candidates, and hang Ward and other prominent radicals. The local Republican leaders quickly gathered at Ward's house and instructed the parish's white Republican sheriff to appoint a group of special deputies to defend the courthouse. By the next morning, some twenty to thirty men, mostly African Americans, had been sworn in.

On April 1, James Hadnot approached Colfax at the head of an armed party of about fifteen. . . . Two smaller bands were also seen in the town's vicinity. Finding Colfax well defended, the conservatives withdrew to await reinforcements. That evening, a group of black radicals, angered by former Republican William Rutland's role in the attempted overthrow of the parish government, compelled the lawyer to flee and ransacked his house. Two days later, Rutland's co-conspirator, William Richardson, also fled Colfax.

Indignant that he and his family had been driven from their home, Rutland ventured to the town of Montgomery and related his tale to the local justice of the peace. The magistrate issued a warrant for the arrest of fourteen radicals and appointed a special constable to proceed to Colfax to make the arrests. . . . [T]he constable departed at the head of an armed party of about thirty of Montgomery's white citizens. Upon their arrival in Colfax, they found the town defended and occupied by radicals.

In an attempt to defuse the crisis, representatives of the radicals and the Montgomery conservatives held a peace conference just outside Colfax the next morning, Saturday, April 5. The discussions proceeded productively until a black special deputy arrived bearing news that African American farmer Jesse McKinney had been murdered. A party of armed white men, explained the deputy, had encountered McKinney as he was building a fence around his yard. One of the men, without apparent provocation, had shot McKinney through the head. Enraged, the deputy drew his pistol on one of the conferees from Montgomery and accused the white men of duplicity for speaking of compromise while black people were being killed. One of the radicals intervened to prevent him from pulling the trigger. Although no blood was shed, the negotiations came to an abrupt end.

Later that day, the armed party that had murdered Jesse McKinney advanced upon Colfax. About twenty-five of the Republican special deputies, who had been sent to scout the conservatives' movements, deployed themselves in a field not far from town. As the conservatives approached, the deputies opened fire. The skirmish lasted about ten minutes before the white men withdrew. The next day, the radicals routed a detachment of the Montgomery forces.

As news of Jesse McKinney's murder spread, black people around Colfax were gripped by fear. Convinced that there was safety in numbers, they flooded into town. By Monday, April 7, some 400 men, women, and children were encamped at the courthouse.

Despite their initial victories, the radicals faced a desperate military situation. Although Colfax was overflowing with freedpeople, no more than about eighty were armed. Meanwhile, the conservatives had issued a call for help, and reinforcements were pouring in from neighboring parishes. . . .

Ward and several other radical leaders abandoned Colfax in the early morning hours of April 9 in search of assistance. Catching a New Orleans-bound steamboat, they set out for the city to enlist the aid of the state and federal authorities. Before they left, they urged their followers to hold out until help arrived. Over the next few days, the remaining white Republicans quietly slipped out of town.

By the morning of April 13, Easter Sunday, the courthouse defenders found themselves besieged by over 300 men. A bit before noon, "Sheriff" Nash, who had taken command of the "posse," demanded control of the courthouse. He promised that if the freedpeople gave up their arms and dispersed they would not be hurt. Levin Allen, a freedman who was now in command at the courthouse, replied that he could not trust Nash. Black men—particularly Jesse McKinney—had already been hurt, Allen explained. Allen declared his intention to hold out until state or federal military forces arrived. Nash then allowed thirty minutes for women and children to evacuate.

Despite the efforts of racial moderates to find a middle ground between radical Republicanism and extreme conservatism, the conflict between former masters and former slaves came to a head at the town of Colfax on Easter Sunday 1873. White moderates stood shoulder to shoulder with conservative extremists, united by a common desire to break black political and military power in Grant Parish. Against them, in a last-ditch attempt to defend their interests, their newly won freedoms, and their lives, stood black radicals. . . .

In Grant Parish, the men of the center accepted civil and political equality for black people so long as harmony prevailed. When the black people of the parish refused to play by these rules, they learned that few things are more dangerous than a paternalist[1] spurned.

Questions

1. Sipress claims that the Colfax Massacre provides "an indication of the extreme lengths to which seemingly moderate men will go to preserve their power and authority." Who were these "moderate men," and why did they feel the need to protect their "power and authority"?
2. What role did the actions of Governor Henry Clay Warmoth play in creating the context for the Colfax Massacre?
3. Was there a particular point where any one different decision might have averted the massacre at Colfax? Explain your answer.

---

[1] A "paternalist" refers to a white person who claims to watch over blacks of this time period in a fatherly manner, taking care of their needs and protecting them from more extremist whites.

FEUDING IS OUR MEANS OF SOCIETAL REGULATION: ELUSIVE STABILITY IN SOUTHEASTERN LOUISIANA'S PINEY WOODS, 1877–1910

by Samuel Hyde, Jr.

The stability that returned to many areas of the post-Reconstruction South did not revisit all regions of the Bayou State. In Louisiana, years of chaotic conditions climaxed with the dramatic collapse of the Republican government. In most of the delta and sugar parishes, the planters' vast patronage allowed them to reassert their dominance easily, but in the piney-woods region of southeastern Louisiana as well as some other marginal areas, local residents resisted the return of the prewar status quo. Voters in several southeastern piney-woods parishes demonstrated their newfound assertiveness by repudiating the old elite in the initial post-Reconstruction elections.

The decline of planter authority in the piney woods created a political power vacuum and the opportunity for new leadership. But the men who filled this void lacked both the stature of the old elite and the unifying issues that the planters had so effectively manipulated in support of their dominance. The factionalization of politics and the rapid economic transformation occurring in certain areas, particularly along the New Orleans-Jackson Railroad, rendered stability increasingly elusive. Indeed, societal equilibrium proved exceedingly difficult to secure in a region where, in the absence of a common threat, many refused to be governed. Furthermore, the fledgling political leaders faced the resentment of many of the old elite, who not only offered little assistance, but even withdrew their active support from a legal system in crisis. As a result,

Originally published in *Louisiana History: The Journal of the Louisiana Historical Association* 48 (April 2007): 133–155. Used by permission of the Louisiana Historical Association.

those who assumed positions of authority at this critical juncture possessed little experience and no regional tradition of leadership, facts well known to the public at large.

In the absence of an effective legal system, factions engaged in bitter competition to fill the political void, but none of the groups commanded the level of political and economic patronage previously enjoyed by members of the antebellum elite. Adding to the unsettled political climate, one of the most powerful factions, dubbed the "Courthouse faction" by the New Orleans press, failed to provide consistent leadership regarding racial issues, a concern that had always commanded the intense interest of the planters.

Despite the increasing factionalization of regional society and politics, racial concerns ultimately remained at the center of the Southern psyche. Although the common folk proved willing to forsake the guidance of the antebellum elite, they continued to demand of their leaders an unqualified commitment to white supremacy. But during the last years of Reconstruction, some whites advocated racial cooperation as a tool to overcome the Republican government. As early as the fall of 1874, the impassioned debate surrounding this issue had created a rift in the once-solid ranks of Florida Parish Democrats. Increasing numbers of influential white Democrats preferred to grant blacks the suffrage that they in turn would control. In return for political support, blacks would be granted limited opportunities for advancement. Some of the most important supporters of the Courthouse faction opened their doors to black labor. For these "cooperationists," black employment provided a cheap and easily exploited source of workers. Even though all the emerging factions exploited blacks in one way or another, the Courthouse faction's reliance on black labor and votes seemed to compromise its commitment to white supremacy, a situation that proved intolerable to many whites.

Opponents of cooperation, criminal elements, and others in conflict with the Courthouse faction coalesced into a tenuous alliance committed to its destruction. The press frequently referred to this group as "Branch men," a name derived from the numerous branches or streams in the northeastern Tangipahoa Parish stronghold of some of the group's more notorious lawless elements. The Branch men included some opportunistic families contemptuous of the power of the Courthouse faction. More ominously, they included the leaders of some of the more violent "whitecap groups" that terrorized the region. Usually inspired by economic competition, whitecaps menaced large areas of the rural South with their nocturnal adventures. In the piney woods of the Florida Parishes, whitecap groups boldly raided mills and towns, brutally intimidating their opponents. Although the whitecaps often served as self-appointed moral policemen, blacks remained the primary target of whitecap violence. Posting armed pickets on roads leading to targeted sites, whitecap leaders in the Florida Parishes openly professed their determination to prevent blacks from working in local sawmills and brickyards. The efforts of the Courthouse faction to contain the violence and protect its black laborers brought it into a fateful confrontation with the Branch men.

Significant differences separated the two factions. Most supporters of the Courthouse faction who participated in the ensuing armed struggle were family men, with an average age of thirty-six. Over 90 percent maintained regular positions of employment, while 60 percent owned property. Four of the eleven principal feudists supporting the Courthouse faction possessed estates valued at more than $1,000. No evidence indicates that any of them had ever been indicted on criminal charges. By contrast, single younger men made up a majority of the feudists aligned with the Branch men. Most of these men, who averaged twenty-five years of age, worked only erratically, which allowed them greater time to concentrate on the business of feuding. While 15 percent of this group owned property, only one of the thirteen primary supporters maintained an estate valued at more than $1,000. Fully 85 percent faced criminal indictments during the 1890s.

The bitter divisions separating the two factions also contained an economic dimension. By employing cheaper black labor, businessmen aligned with the Courthouse faction endured the open contempt of their opponents. Ultimately, though, the competition centered on the dilemma of racial cooperation and the corresponding political ambitions of a few men determined to secure the kind of government that best suited their interests. The opportunity created by the demise of the antebellum elite proved irresistibly attractive to some. And in their efforts to secure political power, these emerging political aspirants employed methods that proved disastrous in a region where everyone was schooled in the effectiveness of violence and where less government remained a cherished ideal. The advantages in time and mobility the single, younger, largely unemployed supporters of the Branch men commanded would be augmented by yet another benefit, the self-imposed restraints under which their opponents operated. Courthouse faction supporters consistently functioned within the limits of a legal system that commanded little popular respect and a code of honor that their enemies had already abandoned.

In the Florida Parishes the time for honor-bound resolution of conflict had passed. . . . Between 1861 and 1877, society had demonstrated a tolerance of extra-legal means to defend individual perceptions of liberty. The Courthouse faction's inability to accept this transition in the absence of an effective system of justice would spell disaster for them.

The spiraling brutality that engulfed the Florida Parishes differed from that of other regions in that the legal system there was subject to, rather than separate from, the feuding. Not only were the representatives of the legal system completely cowed by the violence, but feudists so permeated the system itself that it proved ineffective, functioning as merely another partisan tool of the combatants. In addition, Louisiana's governors, unlike their counterparts in other states, were averse to monitoring and interceding in local affairs. Only a sustained statewide cry for intervention moved a reluctant governor Murphy J. Foster to make even a feeble effort to control the violence. As a result, none of the criminal elements ever faced the consequences of their actions before a determined court of law.

With the legal system in disarray and no individuals or factions capable of providing resolute leadership, feuding emerged as the principal means of societal regulation. Multiple unrelated family feuds developed across the piney-woods region of the Florida Parishes. The bloody Lanier-Kirby feud, waged across portions of Livingston and St. Helena parishes in 1883–84, had its origin in a personal quarrel dating from the late Reconstruction period. The Ricks-Bond feud, which flared intermittently throughout the early 1890s and claimed at least five lives, resulted from a broken marital engagement. An East Feliciana Parish jury's failure to convict B. W. McClendon for the murder of Bill Overton led Overton's brother to kill McClendon with a specially-loaded shotgun. The murder, in turn, provoked additional reprisal killings. Little evidence exists to suggest that any of the feuding parties sought the intervention of the legal establishment; in essence, government remained aloof and irrelevant to the struggles. In an interview with the New Orleans *Daily Picayune*, Tangipahoa Parish Deputy Sheriff Millard Edwards noted that those not involved in the feuding remained terrified of the participants and therefore would not support the peace officers.

Although the unwillingness of some individuals to address the chaotic conditions can certainly be attributed to cowardice, this in itself does not account for the reaction of the majority. The tacit tolerance of lawlessness by the mass of the population signified instead the dominance of a corrupted perception of individual rights that served as the defining ideal of backcountry justice. In the Florida Parishes, as in other regions of the South, violent resolution of perceived injustices had become not merely an accepted, but an expected, response among much of the population. The prevailing irrelevance of apathetic legal authority promoted a kill-or-be-killed attitude among many common folk involved in otherwise trivial disagreements. The long-enduring Jolly-Cousin feud in St. Tammany Parish resulted from a petty disagreement over a piece of land, while just across the border in Franklin County, Mississippi, a bloody feud ensued when one family failed to restrain its livestock from foraging on a neighbor's property. According to the *Daily Picayune*, the prevailing chaos in the piney woods resulted from the presence of a plethora of peculiar people "who are exceedingly jealous of what they deem their rights, and it was mainly through their misconception of what those rights really were that the troubles originated". . . .

. . . The refusal of most individuals to address the lawlessness reinforced the impression that individual liberty was most effectively manifested through the barrel of a gun. In the spring of 1899, Louisiana Adjt. Gen. Allen Jumel noted that the feud-related violence had spiraled out of control because the victims "could not secure juries with the moral courage to bring in verdicts against the parties charged with crimes." As he scanned a mass meeting in support of one of the most violent group's right to eliminate those who threatened their liberty, Jumel added that "this was the fault of the people not the courts". . . .

During the period 1882–1898, news accounts and personal papers reveal that at least 133 homicides occurred in the Florida Parishes. Of the total, twenty murders resulted under criminal circumstances. These incidents ranged from bungled train robberies by the notorious Eugene Bunch to the random murders of inoffensive tramps camping along the railroad. In the same period nineteen bushwhackings occurred, as did six racially motivated murders. An additional nine murders were feud-related incidents in which the victim received wounds in the back. The remaining seventy-nine murders were virtually all feud-related "difficulties"—a term generally employed by the press and the general population to describe honorable violent confrontations.

The dramatic escalation of violence corresponded chronologically and geographically with the retreat of planter dominance in southeastern Louisiana. Complete official regional criminal statistics for the period are available only for the years 1877 and 1907. But existing records indicate that in the thirty-year period following the close of Reconstruction, the number of murders in the piney woods parishes increased dramatically while the population less than doubled. The smallest change occurred in St. Tammany, where four reported murders in 1877 increased to six in 1907. "Bloody Tangipahoa" reported the most significant change, the number of murders there increasing from three to forty-six in the same period. Attempted murder and assault showed similar increases over the 1877 level. Significantly, the plantation parishes of East Baton Rouge, East Feliciana, and West Feliciana did not experience similar increases. Violent crimes in each of the plantation parishes either decreased in number or remained about the same even though these parishes experienced population growth similar to that of the other four Florida Parishes. Despite severely chaotic conditions during Reconstruction, the return of the antebellum elite to most positions of authority in the plantation parishes allowed for the restoration of stability.

Extraordinarily high rates of violence continued to plague the piney woods parishes until a statewide demand for restoration of stability in the region arrived in the wake of World War I. The series of successive murders committed by known parties provoked a statewide demand for order in the eastern Florida Parishes. Many locals were also outraged that members of the Branch faction boldly entered Amite City during the funeral of a prominent supporter of the Courthouse faction and made threats around the town. Newspapers across the state called for action to reestablish law and order in the piney woods. The *Crowley Signal* complained that murder in Washington and Tangipahoa parishes constituted little more than a misdemeanor. The *Daily Picayune* declared: "Law has ceased to be supreme and society in the parish of Tangipahoa has degenerated to that primitive state where each individual must look out for himself as best he can. The entire state demands that the reign of law shall be restored in Tangipahoa, no matter what the cost." The *Shreveport Times* came to a similar conclusion: "Nowhere in the state does a feeling of such dread and terror exist as in Tangipahoa. Only a determined and unflinching effort to discover and punish the assassins will redeem Tangipahoa from its Baptism of Blood." The *Times* maintained that lawlessness in the Florida Parishes damaged the reputation of the entire state. Similarly, the *Plaquemine Journal* condemned those responsible for the murders: "The soil of Tangipahoa has literally been drenched with blood of late, most of those who have lost their lives being the victims of cowardly and heartless assassins. There is no coward so vile and despicable as he who strikes a fellow being from behind under the favoring shadows of night or the protecting trees of a forest. These black hearted miscreants have made the name of that fair section of the state a byword and a reproach."

The resulting calls from the press and the public for intervention by the governor, became particularly strident after the murder of Joe Reid, a prominent Amite City attorney. The *Baton Rouge Daily Advocate* insisted the governor must intervene "with firmness and decision." In an eloquent appeal the *Daily Advocate* declared, "Every instinct of humanity cries out against such monstrous criminals." The same paper urged that the sitting legal officials be forced to resign and the state place justice "in the hands of men who will enforce the law and see that these enemies of civilization are brought to the gallows." The *New Orleans Times-Democrat* insisted that Governor Foster force the resignation of the sitting sheriff, district attorney, and district judge for failure to maintain order. In an interview with the *Daily Picayune*, Deputy Sheriff Millard Edwards explained the situation in Tangipahoa and neighboring parishes: "It is well known to everyone that a terrible feud exists in the region, every other man is a friend of one side or the other and thus it would be impossible to organize a posse of 50 men to serve warrants." John King, superintendent of the Gullet Cotton Gin Company at Amite City, reaffirmed Edwards' observations: "The feud is so severe that everyone goes about armed, everyone knows who killed Joe Reid. There are two parties arrayed against each other and each has many influential friends there so that it is practically impossible to suppress the lawlessness. If the people rose in mass to suppress the violence it would be one faction against the other and a bloodbath."

Under mounting statewide pressure, Governor Foster convened a conference to discuss the violence increasingly referred to as the "Bloody Tangipahoa

Troubles." Foster expressed dismay that he had received an urgent telegram from Deputy Edwards rather than from the sheriff. The telegram stated, "Certain murderous parties having relatives scattered about the parish are safe from molestation by the law." It further indicated that Joe Reid's murderers arrived in Franklinton at 6:30 P.M. and were trailed directly to a specific house in the stronghold of the Branch men by reliable bloodhounds after the killing. But, the deputy alleged, it would take a small army to arrest the suspects. The conference convened in New Orleans on December 20, 1897, with Governor Foster and Atty. Gen. M. J. Cunningham in attendance. Prominent representatives of the Courthouse faction and the Branch men were present. The newspapers noted that the representatives of each group slept at different hotels, adding, "The relations between the two factions are not amicable." The local sheriff and several of his deputies also attended.

The meeting lasted two days, but other than a condemnation of the incompetence of the sheriff's department, the gathering achieved little of substance. The governor, who seemed baffled by the incredibly chaotic circumstances, chose to remain aloof. Other than promising troops if the violence persisted, he took no action. Commenting on the ambiguity surrounding the meeting, the *Daily Picayune* bemoaned the prevailing conditions in the piney woods. "When a community reaches that stage where they believe that whenever a few citizens get together they constitute the people, and on that ground argue that the people are superior to the law, it is pretty hard to convince them to the contrary and those who have to do the convincing will have to travel over a rocky road."

The governor's conference proved to be an unqualified victory for the Branch men. Governor Foster had failed to dispatch troops, and the remnants of the once powerful Courthouse faction had been humiliated and left seemingly without support. Some speculated that Foster's inaction resulted from his reluctance to intervene in the factional feuding lest it cost him the political support of one of the groups. Others saw his inaction as consistent with his hands-off approach to the personal quarrels of white Louisianians. Rather than attempt to conduct the scheduled trials of the Branch men accused in the murders of two prominent figures of the Courthouse faction as well as that of a young boy whom the killers may have mistaken as a witness without state support, parish officeholders canceled the January term of the district court, thereby highlighting the absolute intimidation of justice officials. They attempted to justify the cancellation of the district court on a technicality, alleging that the jury had been improperly drawn. The *Daily Picayune* lamented, "A feeling of unrest prevails here and trouble is looked for." Exasperated, the Franklinton *New Era* complained, "In Washington and Tangipahoa the law is held in contempt because it is not enforced."

In the wake of the governor's conference, attorneys supporting the Branch men helped secure the release of three of the more violent members of the faction who had been incarcerated in the New Orleans city prison to await trial. Nine new murders in the five months following the governor's conference confirmed the continuing absence of law enforcement in Bloody Tangipahoa. When the trio finally stood trial for murder in June 1898, the *Daily Picayune* reported their acquittal with the contemptuous comment "the state having made no case against them." For the piney woods parishes of southeastern Louisiana, justice and the political stability it could bring would remain elusive until a more assertive legal system answerable to determined state authority arrived in the wake of World War I.

The violence that convulsed much of the late nineteenth-century South served as a manifestation of the clash between the antiquated value system common to regions of the backcountry and the demands of a more modern world. It can be argued that the feudists represented a perverted force of modernity, one that issued forth schooled in the effectiveness of violence to challenge an archaic system that denied democratic opportunity to large segments of the population. It is perhaps more appropriate instead to view those involved in the feuding as transitional figures whose conduct exposed the need for democratic reform and an advanced system of justice in regions where individuals had few options other than violence to redress grievances. Regardless of what label they may be assigned, persons who engaged in violent behavior cast an ominous shadow over regions where their methods proved ascendant. Local legal systems were frequently rendered impotent by peace officers or juries in sympathy with their ideal of justice, or out of fear of those who adhered to its violent ways. Accordingly, the transition from traditional to modern proved less painful in regions that enjoyed strong, enlightened leadership. . . .

Questions

1. How did the collapse of Reconstruction fuel instability in the Florida Parishes?
2. What role did racism play in the bitter feuds that developed between groups of whites in the Florida Parishes?
3. Who comprised the "Courthouse faction" and its rival, the "Branch men," and what were their major differences?
4. How was feuding used as a means of social regulation, and why was it more effective than other means in the late-nineteenth and early-twentieth centuries?

AN INHOSPITABLE LAND: ANTI-ITALIAN SENTIMENT AND VIOLENCE IN LOUISIANA, 1891–1924

by Alan G. Gauthreaux

Violence against louisiana's italian population must be placed in the context of the ongoing debate regarding the "whiteness" of immigrants and how their racial classification changed over time. At the height of the white struggle to reclaim control of post-Reconstruction Louisiana, Italians challenged the nature of black and white racial bipolarity. Their unwillingness or inability to assimilate into Southern society, work ethic, low socioeconomic status, and lack of support for white supremacist politics targeted them for retribution.

The Hennessy assassination was the catalyst for anti-Italian violence in Louisiana. At approximately 11:00 P.M. on the evening of October 15, 1890, following a late dinner, thirty-four-year-old New Orleans Police Chief David C. Hennessy, accompanied by fellow police officer William J. O'Connor, made his way to the residence he shared with his elderly mother on Basin Street. Hennessey walked onto his porch, unlocked his front door, but before opening it, turned toward the street when he heard some men whispering. As he turned, shots rang out from a building and a shed at the corner of Girod and Basin streets, and bullets hit Hennessy in his chest, arm, and leg. Hennessy reached for his service revolver and returned fire, but because of his wounds, he only shot four rounds. Concerned that his elderly mother might see him

Originally published in *Louisiana History: The Journal of the Louisiana Historical Association* 51 (Winter 2010): 41–68. Used by permission of the Louisiana Historical Association.

hurt, Hennessy staggered to Mrs. Henry Gillis's residence at 189 Basin Street, where he fell onto the porch. . . .

O'Connor ran to Hennessey's house and followed the trail of blood to the Gillis's porch. O'Connor knelt and asked Hennessy if he knew who shot him. "Oh Billy, Billy, they have given it to me, and I gave them back the best way I could," was the chief's reply. O'Connor then asked, "Who gave it to you, Dave?" Hennessy whispered, "the Dagoes."

Hennessey died later that evening at Charity Hospital.

In his capacity as police chief, David Hennessey saw himself as a mediator between the warring factions of the alleged Italian organized crime organizations of New Orleans. The chief familiarized himself with the "families" in the area, and even became involved with one dispute that many historians believe led to his death. The Provenzano and Matranga factions fought for control of the New Orleans docks from 1888 to 1890 as the lucrative fruit importation business grew, in the process expanding the New Orleans economy and . . . creating revenue streams for aggressive underworld figures through graft, corruption, and extortion. This battle culminated with the Provenzano family's attempted assassination of Tony and Charles Matranga on May 1, 1890. . . . A jury later convicted the Provenzanos, but the court granted a new trial ostensibly because of Chief Hennessey's personal intervention. On January 23, 1891, a jury acquitted the Provenzanos based upon Hennessey's testimony.

Hennessey's no-nonsense style earned him a reputation which angered many in underworld circles, and New Orleans police consequently viewed reputed Mafia figures as the main suspects in his murder. . . . Police ultimately arrested and held twenty-one suspects for arraignment, all reputed associates of organized crime families that operated in the New Orleans underworld. Twelve of these suspects eventually stood trial for their alleged complicity in the death of Chief Hennessy—Charles Matranga, Pietro Natali, Antonio Scaffidi, Antonio Bagnetto, Manuel Polizzi, Antonio Marchese, Pietro Monasterio, Sebastiano Incardona, Salvador Sunseri, Loretto Comitez, Carlo Traina, and Charles Politz. Joseph Macheca, a wealthy shipping magnate and reputed Mafia kingpin, surrendered himself to authorities when he learned the district attorney had issued a warrant for his arrest.

The trial began on February 16, 1891. . . . After two days of unrelenting deliberation, the jury found eight of the defendants *not* guilty and declared a mistrial for the other three on March 13, 1891. Judge [Joshua] Baker also acquitted Charles Matranga.

The verdict . . . infuriated New Orleanians and rumors of bribery surfaced. Throughout that night, various meetings took place in the city calling for a plan of vengeance against the Italians who murdered the chief. On March 14, a notice appeared in the local newspaper calling for all good citizens to assemble near the Clay Statue on Canal Street at 10:00 a.m. A crowd of 10,000 gathered . . . [and marched] to the Old Parish Prison at Basin and Tremé streets. . . .

The March 14, 1891, issue of the *Daily States* reported the ensuing events:

> When the crowd poured down Orleans, the advance guard composed of respectable business men, armed with shotguns and improved Winchesters, and numbering about three hundred men, at once took possession of the main entrance of the prison and demanded of Capt. Lem Davis admission which he did not disposed [*sic*] to grant, and then messengers were immediately dispatched for axes and crowbars and picks which were soon at hand and then commenced a furious pounding upon the massive front gate but it did not yield to the blows showered upon it.

Captain Davis and the other guards told the prisoners to find hiding places, but the vigilantes easily located their prey. Six of the men, who hid in the women's section of the prison, ran down a corridor leading to a stairwell that opened onto the outside yard. The mob cornered Natali, Polizzi, Monasterio, Incardona, Sunseri, Comitz, and Traina in the corner of the courtyard and fired their shotguns and rifles at the men at point blank range. . . . Joseph Macheca and Antonio Scaffedi met their executioners in the wing for condemned men. Each was shot in the head. The enraged mob then removed Manuel Politz from the prison and hanged him from a lamppost along St. Ann Street. The vigilantes dragged the last of the prisoners, Bagnetto, through the main entrance of the prison and hanged him from a giant oak tree in front of the prison. Following his death, the crowd defiled his corpse, using it for target practice. . . .

In investigating the anti-Italian movement within Louisiana commencing with the Hennessey affair in 1890, most historians focus primarily upon the New Orleans area rather than the state as a whole. Outside New Orleans, a volatile political environment contributed significantly to anti-Italian sentiment and economically driven violence was the frequent result.

Italians had been lured to Louisiana by immigration associations seeking to solve the state's serious postbellum labor crisis. In Louisiana, Italian immigrants sought to escape heavy taxation, unequal land assignments, the constant threat of malaria, and exhausted lands in Italy. In rural areas, many newly arrived Italians took jobs normally relegated to blacks, and Italians and African Americans lived together and socialized harmoniously. . . .

In classing Italians as "non-white" on the basis of their extensive associations and interactions with blacks, native whites also drew upon perceptions of the immigrants that were framed by a caste system deeply entrenched in their European homeland. . . . [where] northern Italians viewed their southern neighbors as racially inferior. American policymakers embraced this longstanding distinction between northern European immigrants and southern Italians and declared that southern Italians were best suited for low-paying menial labor which African Americans usually performed. Thus, the racism southern Italians experienced in Louisiana had followed them from Italy, and in the eyes of white natives, Italians became stigmatized as the socio-economic equivalents of African Americans, which stripped them of any claim to white status. The Italians soon found themselves as surrogates for racial prejudice and violence based on ingrained Southern attitudes; hence, white supremacists targeted them and blacks simultaneously.

The 1891 lynching of Italians in Louisiana must be examined within the context of African American lynchings occurring concurrently throughout the South. Southerners responsible for lynching African Americans, especially African American males, often insisted that their victims had raped white women. Opponents of lynching argued that this vicious practice concealed a hidden agenda, and, indeed, post-lynching investigations, when they did occur, proved that rape allegations against most black men were unsubstantiated.

Contemporary sources and recent scholarly investigations offer more plausible motives for the lynchings. W. E. B. Dubois stated in *The Souls of Black Folk* (1903) that "the ignorant southerner hates the Negro, the workingmen fears his competition, the moneymakers wish to use him as a laborer, [and] some of the educated see a menace in his upward development." In *Under Sentence of Death: Lynching in the South*, historian W. Fitzhugh Brundage asserts that white male participation in lynchings became a way of maintaining the South's racial and gender hierarchy.

Southern Democratic politics served as the wellspring for such conservatism. In Louisiana, political conservatism was centered within the New Orleans political machine known as "The Ring" and among the rural "Bourbons," generally rich landholders who portrayed themselves as the guardians of Southern social paradigms. Although Italian immigrants effectively occupied the middle ground between white and black societies, the Bourbon Democrats made no distinction between them and the African Americans in social or political questions. . . .

Meanwhile, serious issues caused dissatisfaction with the economic circumstances surrounding blacks, poor whites, and even Italians in farming communities throughout the state. Economic depressions struck the United States in the 1870s and 1890s and commodity prices consequently dropped sharply, increasing surpluses overwhelmed worldwide demand, and global competition further eroded prices. In addition, prices for transportation of farm produce rose suddenly because of rail monopolies. Farmers consequently found themselves incurring ever greater debt—even as they worked ever harder.

The result of this economic turmoil was political unrest. . . . The Populist Party, which originated in the Midwest and later expanded into the South, was a response to rising costs of transporting goods to market, the lack of educational opportunities for blacks and poor whites in Louisiana, and the corruption and graft associated with the Democratic Party's struggle to maintain white power throughout the state. Populists embraced efforts to help blacks by seeking to eradicate lynching, ending the convict-lease system, and pledging to fight for African Americans' political rights. They also proposed an end to the crop-lien system through the establishment of a "sub-treasury" system, in which the federal government would guarantee the allocation of goods and services to farmers, set up "marketing and purchasing facilities," and provide "greenbacks" to "provide credit for the farmer's crops."

The Populists' intentions seemed honorable to blacks seeking equal political status with whites, but in working to elevate blacks in the South, the movement opened old racial wounds that caused more aggressive tactics on the part of white supremacists throughout the South. . . . [D]espite their public pronouncements on behalf of African Americans, the Populists failed to include blacks to any great extent and ultimately alienated them. Populists nevertheless hoped to garner the black vote in rural Louisiana, while at the same time encouraging poor whites to suppress their racism in the interest of economic and political solidarity. . . .

This provided a political opportunity to Louisiana's Democratic Party, which continued to promote the ideals of the "Lost Cause" while holding the Populist movement in check through fraudulent elections. More importantly, the Democratic Party embraced certain Populist tenets in an attempt to stifle true reform initiatives that appealed to African Americans, Italians, and other poor whites. Democratic overtures were rejected by Italians, thereby stifling Democratic attempts to rally these estranged whites to the banner of racial supremacy in Louisiana. The Democrats consequently altered their emphasis from economic to racial interests with their goal of disenfranchising the blacks of south Louisiana.

To achieve African American disenfranchisement in Louisiana, Murphy J. Foster, elected governor in 1892, proposed a suffrage amendment to the legislature based upon property and educational requirements. The state house and senate passed the amendment in 1894 and submitted it to the people through a referendum in 1896. The amendment served two purposes: first, to neutralize black support for the Populists and Republicans, and, second, to keep whites from dividing their votes among three parties. On March 24, 1896, proclaiming their solidarity with the African Americans, the Italians protested alongside Populists against the amendment in a New Orleans parade, in which they marched behind an Italian flag. . . .

Between 1892 and 1896, the Populists performed well in Louisiana elections and even ran a candidate for governor in the latter year. However, their policies appeared too progressive for the "solid South." The Populists' collapse in 1896 extinguished any hope of establishing a countervailing political force in the South. However, political memories died hard in Louisiana, and the Italians' alliances with blacks in Louisiana stigmatized them into the twentieth century.

The lynching of Italians thus became part of the ongoing battle for political control of Louisiana. Louisiana's Democratic Party unleashed forces of repression bent on disenfranchising both African Americans and Italians as the struggle reached its peak in the 1890s. . . .

In June 1896, the Louisiana legislature passed a new election law that advanced the disenfranchisement agenda, by creating assessors who acted as registrars and mandating that "persons applying to register should complete an application form in his own handwriting in the presence of an assessor or registrar." These officials could then disenfranchise black voters who failed to either write their name or "figure his age in terms of years, months, and days. . . ." With the Democrats' successful disenfranchisement of blacks, Democratic leaders needed constitutional authority to restrict foreigners, namely Italians, and persons who owned no property from voting. Louisiana legislators therefore passed a resolution calling for a constitutional convention.

Before the convention could be called, however, another Italian lynching took place. On August 8, 1896, south Louisiana newspaper headlines declared "Trio Lynched in St. Charles." The victims—Lorenzo Saladino, Decino Sorcoro, and Angelo Mancuso, who had been killed by a violent crowd just before midnight—were charged with murder. . . .

Two days later, the black residents of St. Charles Parish showed their sympathy for the victims. A Crescent City newspaper reported that "a large number of negroes and Italians were present at the burial, and [all] went home from the scene terror-stricken." The local white population feared that this show of solidarity by Italians and blacks portended violence, but the anticipated uprising never materialized. . . .

Charles Papini, the Italian consul in Louisiana, conducted an investigation. . . .

Unable to pursue criminal prosecutions, the Italian government, which demonstrated that the three Italian lynching victims had been subjects of King Humbert at the time of their deaths, sought and obtained financial compensation from the United States government in the amount of $6,000 per family. . . .

As the furor over the St. Charles lynchings subsided, the state's dominant Democratic Party moved forward with its disenfranchisement campaign against the foreigners living in Louisiana. The Constitutional Convention of 1898 convened on February 8, 1898. The Choctaw Club of New Orleans, one of the state's most powerful political organizations, sought to use the convention to "put the negro out of politics" for good. The Choctaw Club wanted to use the Italian vote to defeat the planters in predominantly black parishes. To accomplish this, they proposed a "grandfather clause" which essentially "permitted illiterate and propertyless whites to vote if their grandfather or father voted prior to January 1, 1867. . . ."

[T]he legislature adopted the revisions to the Constitution of 1898 with all its controversies. The lesson Italians learned from this political wrangling showed that they needed to adopt Southern prejudices in order to be accepted into Southern society or face political alienation like African Americans.

Such a shift was necessary because anti-Italian sentiment remained virulent in [places like] the tiny hamlet of Tallulah, in Madison Parish, . . . [where] Italian storekeeper named Joe DeFatta owned a herd of sheep that grazed behind his store on Front Street. This land abutted property claimed by a well-respected member in the community, Dr. J. Ford Hodge. Hodge repeatedly cautioned DeFatta to keep his sheep off of his land, but DeFatta ignored the warnings. On the night of July 19, 1899, Hodge shot and killed one of DeFatta's sheep. DeFatta confronted the doctor the next morning at his office and warned him not to do it again. Hodge forced DeFatta to leave and thought the matter ended. That evening as the doctor walked past DeFatta's store after dinner in the company of a Mr. Kauffman, DeFatta and his brother Charles shouted insults at Hodge. Charles then attacked Hodge, forcing him to the ground. As Hodge began to draw a pistol from his jacket, Joe DeFatta produced a double-barreled shotgun, firing both barrels into the doctor's abdomen and hands as he lay on the porch in front of the store.

Another brother, Frank DeFatta, who owned a store nearby, heard the gunshots, and he and two of his associates, Sy Deferroche and John Cereno, armed themselves with shotguns and long knives and rushed down the street toward Joe's store. Madison Parish Sheriff Coleman Lucas intercepted and subdued Frank DeFatta, Deferroche, and Cereno and then took them to the city jail. Meanwhile Joe and Charles DeFatta barricaded themselves in their home just a few blocks from Joe's store; however, they later relented and submitted to arrest by Sheriff Lucas. Shortly afterward, 250 local residents intercepted Lucas with his two charges. The mob took the two brothers to a nearby tree and hanged them. Turning their attention to the jail, the crowd broke in and seized Frank DeFatta, Deferroche, and Cereno, forced them out of their cells, and hanged them in the jailhouse yard. . . .

After the lynchings, local newspapers published reports of the victims' past criminal activities as a means of providing some justification for the murders.
. . .

The Tallulah lynching threatened to cause a third international incident between the United States and Italy. . . . Soon thereafter, rumors subsequently spread throughout Madison Parish that local officials were strongly urging Italians to leave the region, because their lives might be in danger. Many Italians fled Tallulah for their lives. At the height of the resulting panic, Italian officials visited Tallulah on July 24, 1899 as part of a fact-finding mission. . . .

The investigators reportedly issued their findings, but to no avail for federal government officials made no effort to provide compensation to the victims' families. . . . [A]nti-Italian bigotry persisted without abating. The popular stereotyping of Italians as members of criminal organizations endured well into the twentieth century, despite efforts by authorities to eradicate the practice. . . .

The violence escalated to such an extent [in southeastern Louisiana's Tangipahoa Parish] that Gov. Murphy J. Foster launched an investigation into the killings. The United States government, which also expressed concern, formed the Dillingham Commission in 1907 to investigate the assimilation of foreigners into American society over the course of four years. These efforts seem to have yielded meager, if any, positive results. Yet, despite the violence, Italians continued to migrate to the area in the hope of making their fortunes in strawberry farming. Like the Italians who migrated earlier to the area, these immigrants "fought their way inch by inch through unreasoning hostility and prejudice to almost unqualified respect or even admiration." But because of their cultural, social, and political proclivities, namely their willingness to perform menial tasks once relegated to slaves, Italians became the newest targets in Tangipahoa Parish.

Anti-Italian violence first erupted [in Tangipahoa Parish] in February 1908, when lumber mills in the Kentwood area began laying off employees, but kept Italians on the payroll. The companies running the mills justified their actions by announcing that Italians worked harder and displayed more dedication to their jobs than native whites. The resulting resentment among Tangipahoa's native population served as a catalyst for a campaign of terror. On March 1, 1908, Charles Pittaro, an Italian merchant living near Kentwood, received a letter from a local resident encouraging the immigrant and his family to leave his home before any danger befell them. . . . Gov. Newton Crain Blanchard mobilized Company I of the state militia and invested it with arrest powers. The troops arrested six men in connection with the threat.

On July 23, 1908, Joe, George, and Tony Liambisi, three Italian brothers accused of wounding Walter Simmons, a mill worker in Natalbany, were pursued by deputized posses. George and Tony made their escape, but law enforcement officials captured their brother Joe and arrested him for the shooting. The residents of Tangipahoa Parish held the Simmons family in high regard, and a mob gathered outside the jail where deputies held Liambisi. In an effort to save his life, Joe Liambisi agreed to lead deputies to locations where other Italians may have been hiding his brothers. A sheriff's posse subsequently located George and Tony near the tiny hamlet of Tickfaw. A shootout ensued, and three Italians were wounded and a ten-year-old boy named Tony Gatano was killed.

Walter Simmons subsequently died at New Orleans's Charity Hospital, but, despite continuing threats of mob violence, enraged locals did not lynch the Liambisis. On the night of Simmons's death, however, unknown assailants bombed an Italian grocery store in an effort to force Italians to reconsider their settlement plans. Even though there were no injuries as a result of the blast, Gov. Newton Crain Blanchard ordered a small detachment of National Guardsmen to the area in hope of preventing further violence. The Kentwood Vigilance Committee, formed after the shooting of Walter Simmons, nevertheless issued a proclamation ordering Italians "to leave town under pain of death." Many Italians took the warning seriously and vacated the small town, leaving behind only half their original contingent of 200. . . .

In the wake of the Tangipahoa incidents, the Italian consulate in New Orleans again became involved. But, over time, tensions eased, and eventually the threat of vigilante violence waned. Governor Blanchard consequently recalled the troops, and Tangipahoa remained quiet—for a time.

The last recorded violent incident involving Tangipahoa's Italian population was the outcome of judicial proceedings. On May 8, 1921, Mrs. Dallas Calmes, the wife of a grocery owner in Independence, heard a noise outside her back door in the early morning hours. Mrs. Calmes awoke her husband who immediately grabbed his pistol and ran to their home's rear entrance, which was adjacent to the bank. When he opened the door, gunshots rang out, and Calmes fell mortally wounded. His subsequent death engendered an intensive manhunt and an official investigation. In the wake of this inquiry, a Tangipahoa grand jury indicted Joseph Rini, Andrew Lemantia, Roy Leona,

Joseph Giglio, Joseph Bocchio, and Natale Deamore for the attempted robbery of Farmers and Merchants Bank of Tangipahoa and for the murder of Dallas Calmes.

One of the suspected killers, Natale Deamore, turned state's evidence in exchange for a reduced sentence. Deamore identified his five fellow conspirators, thereby sealing their fate; in addition, an unidentified ten-year-old boy corroborated Deamore's testimony. However, Deamore later withdrew his testimony and accepted his co-conspirators' fate. Following their indictment, the six defendants were transported to the parish courthouse at Amite, where they stood trial.

After the defendants' conviction, Judge Robert Ellis sentenced Joseph Rini, Andrew Lemantia, Roy Leona, Joseph Giglio, Joseph Bocchio, and Natale Deamore to hang for the murder of Dallas Calmes. But the sentence was delayed by an appeal based upon the refusal of Judge Robert Ellis, a leader of the local Knights of the White Camellia, to recuse himself from the case despite his alleged injudicious race bating and unethical public comments. In the appeal, eventually adjudicated by the Louisiana State Supreme Court in *State* v. *Rini, et al.*, the alleged murderers asserted that the "Hon. Robert S. Ellis has on numerous occasions discussed this case openly and publicly with the citizens of Tangipahoa Parish, Louisiana, expressing the belief that your defendants were guilty of said charge of murder and should be hanged." The defendants' counsel also alleged jury tampering, but the high court found no evidence to support their claims, and the lower court's decision was upheld.

In the early morning hours of May 9, 1924, executioners led the six convicted men to the gallows in Amite. Prior to his execution, Andrew Lemantia attempted to stab himself in order to cheat the hangman, but, bleeding profusely from a chest wound, he was hanged anyway.

Despite the passage of time since the Hennessey affair, the *Rini* case served as a reminder to Italians that Louisiana's white population remained antagonistic. At first congenial to the newcomers, native Louisianians came to perceive Italians as interlopers who threatened the established social hierarchy. The Italians' socioeconomic similarity to Southern African Americans and their lack of racial prejudice invoked the wrath of the white elite. The alliances forged by Italians with African Americans demonstrated their desire to become American citizens and their determination to use political and economic avenues to achieve those ends. But the Italians' political activism exposed them to vicious, open discrimination aimed at limiting or halting their active participation in Louisiana politics and keeping these "undesirables," whom whites regarded as racially, economically, and socially equivalent to blacks, in their place. The Italian community failed to overcome these challenges in the late nineteenth and early twentieth centuries, perhaps because the immigrants' economic success posed a threat to other white business owners in the state and because they failed to shift their political allegiance to the state's Democratic power structure. In Louisiana as in other parts of the nation, however, even nativist Americans eventually accepted the Italians as worthwhile additions to the population, legitimizing the sacrifices made by the early immigrants to this strange, inhospitable land.

Questions

1. How did Italian immigrants into Louisiana challenge "the nature of black and white racial bipolarity?"
2. What roles did politics and economics play in the emergence of anti-Italian sentiment and violence?
3. Why were Italians classified as "non-white" by native white Louisianians?

PART FIVE

PROGRESSIVES AND RACE

ॐ ॐ

Reconstruction came to an end in 1877 when Bourbon Democrats "redeemed" the state by wresting control away from the Republicans and returning the state to rule by the party that represented southern whites. Their goal was to re-establish white supremacy and disempower African Americans, but they had to move slowly so as not to alarm the federal government and risk the redeployment of federal troops to Louisiana. Thus, they proceeded incrementally. In 1890, State Senator Murphy J. Foster from St. Mary Parish—a sugar parish with a majority poor black population—shepherded through the legislature a bill to segregate the races on rail cars. Creoles of color in New Orleans decided to challenge the Separate Car Act, and they ultimately appealed their case all the way to the U.S. Supreme Court. In his essay, Keith Weldon Medley explains the circumstances that gave rise to one of the most infamous Supreme Court decisions in American history, *Plessy* v. *Ferguson*, and humanizes the people whose names became synonymous with legalized racial discrimination.

A wave of Jim Crow laws segregating African Americans swept through the South in the wake of the *Plessy* decision. At the same time, the country was in the throes of a massive campaign to win voting rights for women. The proposed "Anthony Amendment" to the U.S. Constitution (named for Susan B. Anthony) was, like all issues in Louisiana, complicated by race. Elna Green discusses Kate Gordon, who, though a leading suffragist in Louisiana, worked against passage of the Anthony Amendment. Woman suffragists like Gordon were unwilling to concede the authority of the federal government to grant voting rights to women because this would also concede the right of the federal government to guarantee voting rights for blacks. It is a great irony that just as the rest of the country was embracing the idea of enfranchising the female half of its population, southern states were in the process of disenfranchising African Americans. In Louisiana, the Constitution of 1898 required either that a prospective voter pass a literacy test or that he hold $300 in property, a substantial amount in those days and well beyond the reach of tenant farmers or sharecroppers, many of whom were black. It also mandated that voters pay $1 per year for the privilege of voting, a poll tax virtually no poor people could afford. Within a short time, 95 percent of eligible blacks and 50 percent of whites were disenfranchised. When the Anthony Amendment was ratified by three-fourths of the states (though not most southern states) and became the Nineteenth Amendment to the U.S. Constitution in 1920, women got the right to vote. However, the same state registration restrictions applied to them; thus, while many white women registered for the first time in 1920, most black women, like black men, found registering to vote in Louisiana virtually impossible. Rather than expanding democracy, Louisiana was moving away from it.

The loss of voting rights compounded the oppression of African Americans in the state in many ways. For one, jury pools were taken from voter registration rolls (although all women were excluded from jury duty). This meant that blacks accused of crimes were tried by juries composed solely of whites, and justice was not color-blind. Seldom was the outcome of a trial fair or impartial; blacks quickly learned that the justice system did not protect them. In addition, some local school funding came from poll-tax receipts collected in each district. Schools, of course, were strictly segregated, so with no blacks registered to vote, no poll-tax money went to black schools. Black education was badly underfunded by every measure, and teachers in black schools were poorly trained. By 1940, three-fourths of all "schools" for blacks in Louisiana were housed either in churches, Masonic halls, or structures built by the students and their parents from donated or salvaged building materials. There were almost no high schools for blacks until after World War II.

For blacks, then, the last years of the nineteenth century and the first decades of the twentieth saw retrogression in their status. These same years, ironically, were a time of "Progressivism" for whites, as Samuel Shepherd discusses in his lively essay. Following a national trend, white reformers in Louisiana made major advancements in public education, agricultural education, and public health, and eliminated the corrupt and barbarous convict lease system. But for these southern reformers, "progress" also meant maintaining and reinforcing white supremacy. While the standard of living and educational opportunities improved for Louisiana whites, blacks remained in substandard neighborhoods—the last to have paved streets and sanitary water and sewerage treatment—that were daily reminders of their second-class status. The only positive accomplishment in race relations, if one can view it as such, was a decline in the number of lynchings. These gruesome public acts of mob murder sullied the reputation of the South, and Progressives sought to create a better image for their region. Perhaps because blacks were by this point so thoroughly disempowered, whites no longer felt the need to turn to a campaign of terrorism to "keep them in their place."

Some African Americans responded to the new racial order by leaving the state altogether. The percentage of blacks in the population of the Pelican State declined from about 50 percent, where it had stood throughout the state's history, to about 30 percent by the end of the twentieth century. Others accommodated themselves to it and awaited the day when things would change. It would be a later generation of black Louisianians, energized by the white governor Huey Long and a new breed of Louisiana politicians, and then by the experience of World War II, who would challenge the status quo and begin to demand equalization in their status.

WHEN PLESSY MET FERGUSON

by Keith Weldon Medley

O n June 8, 1892, a New Orleans–based paper called the *Daily City Item* issued the following front page bulletin: "Yesterday afternoon at 4:15 o'clock, private detective C. C. Cain arrested from the East Louisiana train [Homer] Adolph Plessy, a light mulatto, and locked him up in the Fifth Precinct station, on a charge of violating section 2 of Act 111 of the statute of 1890 relative to separate coaches. . . . Plessy was arraigned before Judge Moulin this morning . . . and the judge committed Plessy to the Criminal District Court under a bond of $500."

Thus Homer Plessy rose from the obscurity of a nineteenth century shoemaker, defied a Louisiana segregation law, and became the pivotal figure in one of the most sweeping Civil Rights decisions in United States history. Far from happenstance, Plessy's actions climaxed a coordinated effort by a group of New Orleans Republicans known as the *Comité des Citoyens* [Citizens' Committee]. Composed of lawyers, a newspaper publisher, a French Quarter jeweler, a sail maker, politicians, former Union soldiers, educators, and descendants of veterans of the Battle of New Orleans, the *Comité* became one of the first groups in the nation to mount a civil disobedience challenge to segregation in the post-Reconstruction era.

From *Louisiana Cultural Vistas* 7 (Winter 1996–97): 52–59. Used by permission of The Louisiana Endowment for the Humanities and Keith Weldon Medley.

Homer Adolphe Plessy

Homer Plessy's birth occurred in New Orleans in the early 1860s. His parents, Adolphe Plessy and Rosalie Debergue, belonged to a group of 11,000 New Orleanians with varying degrees of African ancestry who obtained free status before the Civil War. Typically French speaking and Roman Catholic, many in the city's free black population arrived as immigrants from Haiti and Cuba. Others gained free status through manumission or purchase by a relative. Though they possessed property rights, Louisiana's *code noir* prohibited free people of color from voting, frequenting most public accommodations, or establishing organizations without permission.

While some obtained considerable wealth and prominence, census reports listed the primary trades of free men of color as carpenters, bricklayers, cigar makers, and shoemakers. Free women of color ran boardinghouses and worked as seamstresses and nurses. The 1855 city directory placed Germain, Gustave, and Adolphe Plessy at the corner of Elysian Fields and Craps (now Burgundy) in Faubourg Marigny, New Orleans' first suburban development. City indexes listed Rosalie's grandfather, Michel Debergue, as a market trader.

The Civil War spared New Orleans much of its culture and architecture, but ripped its political and social fabric with the emancipation of the city's enslaved African population and a fifteen-year occupation by Union troops. Still, before Adolphe Plessy died in 1869, he must have felt a brighter future for his six year old son. In 1867, city streetcar companies removed segregated transports from the city's tracks. Additionally, Louisiana ratified the Fourteenth Amendment granting equal protection to all, eliminated racial discrimination in juries, and extended suffrage to black males. Often taking the lead in civil rights, Louisiana became the first Southern state to allow integrated public schools. In 1870, the state removed the ban on marriages between people of different races.

Shortly after Adolphe's death, Homer's mother Rosalie worked as a seamstress marrying into the family of Victor Dupart. As a signatory to the manifesto of the 1873 Unification Movement, Dupart joined over 1800 black and white New Orleanians in a campaign to end prejudice and discrimination in Louisiana. Victor Dupart also served as president of the Catholic School for Instruction for Destitute Orphans, a school at the corner of Touro and

Dauphine Streets bequeathed by West African native Marie C. Couvent before the Civil War.

The census of 1880 listed Rosa Dupart as a mulatto head of household living on Union (Touro) Street near the corner of Marais in the New Marigny historic district. Semitropical New Orleans was a completely flat city. The incessant rains of 1880 made unpaved roads like Union impassable for days with wood boards serving as sidewalks over interminably muddy streets. Census takers also noted the presence of Homer, an older sister Ida, and half-brother Charles Dupart. While court documents described Plessy as seven eighths white, appearance rather than genetics determined these designations.

Though carpentry remained the occupation of most Plessy men throughout the second half of the nineteenth century, Homer followed in the footsteps of the Dupart clan and earned his way as a shoemaker. The 1880s found him working in the Dumaine Street concern of Patricio Brito in the French Quarter. In July of 1888, with his employer Brito as witness, the pastor of St. Augustine's Catholic Church in Treme presided over the marriage of 26-year-old Homer Plessy to 19-year-old Louise Bordenave. Shortly thereafter, the couple moved into a wooden shotgun double home fronting North Claiborne Avenue in the Faubourg Treme.

By 1890, New Orleans reigned as the South's queen city and also bore the reputation as the region's wayward sister. Twelve wood-planked wharves lining the Mississippi river banks serviced a river teeming with coal boats, barges, schooners, steamers, ferry boats, and every imaginable seaworthy vessel. Located ninety miles from the Gulf of Mexico, New Orleans exported more cotton than any other American port. In neighborhoods such as Storyville down river from Canal Street, temperance societies and Catholic convents bravely competed for souls against eight breweries and 650 saloons. An 1890 Louisiana law tried to prohibit the city's "dance houses, free and easy gambling dens, barrel houses, and shandangoes." The city also housed the Louisiana Lottery Company, a million dollar private corporation that sold chances nationwide.

Indeed, in the opening address before the 1890 legislature, Governor Francis T. Nicholls made no mention of segregated trains. Instead, he devoted the bulk of his comments calling for an end to the Louisiana Lottery. For its part, the Lottery Company offered to donate 100,000 dollars to repair the state levee system. *The Crusader* newspaper dubbed the fight between the Lottery Company and Governor Nicholls a battle of "boodle against votes." But when some black legislators joined white pro-lottery Democrats in a vote to override a Nicholls veto, debate took a racial turn. As payback, State Senator Murphy Foster called up House Bill 42, An Act to Promote the Comfort Of Passengers On Railway Trains. The bill prohibited blacks and whites from riding together on trains in the state even if they were business partners, friends, husband and wife, or parent and child. Many saw it as an attempt to return to the caste system of New Orleans' pre-Civil War years. Governor Nicholls signed the Act into law on July 10, 1890.

Despite a volatile racial climate, on September 1st, 1891, newspaper publisher and attorney Louis Martinet opened *The Crusader*'s French Quarter offices to selected New Orleanians concerned about the ramifications of the Separate Car Act. At the center of the gathering sat Alexandre Aristide Mary, a widely respected Republican, former co-chairman of the Unification Movement, treasurer of the Republican state central committee, and member of the New Orleans Freedmen's Aid Association. Educated for the law in Paris, Mary steered an inheritance from his wealthy white father toward philanthropy, financing lawsuits against segregated establishments, and promoting the Republican Party. But then, Reconstruction veteran Mary was in his late sixties and aging rapidly. As his final political act, he urged the eighteen men to build mass sentiment to fight the Separate Car law in court.

The individuals who met on that rainy September night shared deep roots in the Crescent City. Representing a cross section of professional classes, most lived and worked down river from Canal Street in the tangent neighborhoods of the French Quarter, and faubourgs Marigny, Treme, and New Marigny. A. G. Giuranovich set and cut diamonds on Royal Street, 34-year-old Pierre Chevalier brokered real estate, and Alcee Labat and Myrthil J. Piron buried the city's dead. Their president, 57-year-old Arthur Esteves, manufactured and retailed sails, awnings, and flags as a partner in Fauna & Esteves on Decatur Street. As vice-president, the *Comité* selected C. C. Antoine, Louisiana's Republican lieutenant governor from 1872 to 1876 and a prominent member of the Unification Movement. Another Unification participant, tailor and horseman Paul Bonseigneur became treasurer.

After a weekend of deliberation, the *Comité des Citoyens* emerged with an urgent twenty paragraph appeal. "No further time should be lost," it read. "We should make a definite effort to resist legally the operation of the separate car law." The statement further outlined a strategy of informing the public, raising funds, and formulating a legal strategy. Within three months, the Comité raised nearly $3000 from over 150 sources from the neighborhoods of New Orleans, small towns throughout the South, and cities as far away as Washington, D.C., Chicago, and San Francisco.

Though not an official *Comité* member, Homer connected to their cause. A number of *Comité* members joined the 1873 Unification Movement with his stepfather's family. Many on the *Comité* also devoted time and money to keep Victor Dupart's Catholic School for Indigent Orphans afloat after fires and storms. Additionally, Plessy served as an officer of Justice Protective Education and Social Club with *Comité* member and *The Crusader*'s business manager L. J. Joubert. Another one of Plessy's affiliations, the Société des Francs Amis, contributed $140 in the *Comité*'s fundraising drive. When the *Comité* sought a volunteer for the test case, Homer Plessy stepped forward.

So on June 7, 1892, Homer traveled the nearly two miles to the depot at the bustling Press Street railroad yards in Bywater—a stone's throw from the Mississippi River. He purchased a first class ticket on the East Louisiana Railroad number 8 train scheduled to depart at 4:15 P.M. . . . Plessy boarded the "White Only" car of the local East Louisiana Railroad that twice daily lumbered across a seven mile bridge spanning Lake Pontchartrain, then through Abita Springs on its 60 mile trip to Covington in St. Tammany Parish. Over 20,000 passengers made the trip in 1891.

But Homer's ride only lasted a few minutes. The conductor stopped the train and summoned private detective Captain Chris Cain who cautioned Plessy, "If you are colored you should go into the car set apart for your race. The law is plain and must be obeyed." After Plessy refused to budge, Cain and some volunteers forcibly dragged the neatly dressed Plessy from the train. Cain, who the *Comité* secretly hired to ensure filing of the proper charges, then transported Plessy to the fifth precinct jail and booked him with the array of drunks, petty larcenists, and foul-mouthed New Orleanians arrested that Tuesday evening. Members of the *Comité* met him at the precinct house after convincing a judge to release a successful if disheveled Plessy on temporary bail. The future of American civil rights rode on Homer's day in court.

John Howard Ferguson

Shortly after the 1892 elections, Louisiana's new governor, Murphy Foster, named ex-Governor Francis T. Nicholls as head of the State Supreme Court. Two months later, he appointed the judge whose name followed Plessy's throughout American legal history. Like Homer Plessy, the Civil War and Reconstruction defined John Ferguson's public life.

Born in 1838 in Martha's Vineyard, this son of a Massachusetts shipmaster worked in the office of Boston's United States attorney. At Civil War's end, he journeyed South seeking opportunity among the occupying forces in the defeated Confederacy. In July of 1866, Ferguson married Virginia Earhart, the daughter of Thomas Earhart—a staunchly pro-Union Louisiana attorney who strongly denounced slavery and the Confederacy. "Man is man," Earhart declared to an interracial 1863 Fourth of July rally of the Loyal National League, "Be the shade of his skin white, green or black." A newspaper index listed Earhart as one of the city's first attorneys to swear an oath of allegiance to the Union after the Civil War. Earhart's new son-in-law began his practice shortly thereafter.

Ferguson's legislative alliance with Francis Nicholls began in 1876 during a political crisis that resulted in the Hayes-Tilden compromise [or Compromise of 1877]. This Congressional deal extricated the remaining 600 federal troops from the South, gave Republican Rutherford Hayes the presidency, and conceded the disputed legislatures of four Southern states to ex-Confederate Democrats. In Louisiana, former Brigadier General Francis T. Nicholls assumed power and promised to protect civil liberties and "to obliterate the color line in politics." Ferguson's seat in Nicholl's legislature came at the expense of black representative Aristide Dejoie whom the Nicholls forces expelled on the second day of the session.

In the 1892 elections, Ferguson traveled to twenty different Louisiana parishes to speak in support of Murphy Foster's gubernatorial campaign and against the Louisiana Lottery. Though his brother-in-law Ferdinand Earhart served as Republican-appointed United States attorney, Ferguson had long since attached his climb to the Democratic coattails of Nicholls and Foster. He became an assistant District Attorney, and in July of 1892, with Plessy's

Separate Car case pending, Governor Foster tapped Ferguson to fill a judgeship vacancy in Orleans Parish. Ferguson's swearing-in took place in the Criminal Courts building at St. Patrick's Hall on St. Charles Avenue less than a month after Plessy's arrest.

On October 13, 1892, Homer Plessy faced Judge Ferguson in case number 19117, *Homer Adoph Plessy* v. *The State of Louisiana*. Plessy, a product of old downtown New Orleans neighborhoods, stood before Ferguson—an uptown New England transplant now allied with an ex-Confederate general. Ironically, given the nature of the case, skin color was one of their common characteristics.

On November 18, 1892, Ferguson ruled that Plessy was "not deprived of his liberty by the act of the officer of the company.... He was simply deprived of the liberty of doing as he pleased." The Nicholls State Supreme Court swiftly upheld Ferguson's ruling. In the coming years, the *Comité's* hope for a court victory withered under increasingly trying circumstances as the U. S. Supreme Court became increasingly hostile to Civil Rights cases.

But the *Comité* kept its 1891 promise to see the case to its end. In 1895, they took the final step. Attorney Albion Tourgee filed briefs for the October term in U. S. #210, *Homer A. Plessy* v. *J. H. Ferguson*. But on May 19, 1896, in a seven to one vote, the Court issued a ruling granting states the authority to forcibly segregate people of different races. Upon receiving the decision, the *Comité des Citoyens* issued its final statement: "We, as freemen, still believe that we were right, and our cause is sacred. In defending the cause of liberty, we met with defeat but not with ignominy." The *Comité* then distributed the $220 left in its reserves to a hospital, old folks homes, the Catholic School for Indigent Orphans, a sanitarium, and a testimonial for their lawyer Albion Tourgee.

On January 11, 1897, his constitutional claims dismissed, Homer Plessy returned to Section A [of the Criminal District Court in New Orleans]. The *Comité* had disbanded, *The Crusader* had closed shop, Judge Ferguson retired from the bench, and white supremacists dominated legislatures throughout the South. Plessy changed his plea to guilty, paid a $25 fine, and walked out into the brave new world of the "separate but equal" Louisiana of voter purges, separate trains and water fountains, denial of education, bans on interracial marriages, and exclusion of large numbers of citizens from Louisiana's democratic process.

Questions

1. In an act of civil disobedience, Homer Plessy volunteered to test the constitutionality of Louisiana's segregation law by willingly breaking that law and subjecting himself to arrest. In what way(s) does the history of Louisiana's free people of color suggest why this challenge to segregation laws emerged in New Orleans and not somewhere else in the South? Describe Homer's Plessy's parentage and family circumstances.

2. Describe the people who made up the *Comité des Citoyens*.

3. Explain how political shifts motivated Murphy J. Foster to submit to the Louisiana legislature a bill requiring racial segregation on railway cars.

4. Judge John Howard Ferguson was a Yankee Republican who married into a strongly pro-Unionist Louisiana family. What does the author suggest were his reasons for ruling against Homer Plessy, when his personal history indicates that in different circumstances he might have sided with Plessy?

5. What were the consequences for people of African ancestry of the Supreme Court's ruling in this case?

THE REST OF THE STORY:
KATE GORDON AND THE OPPOSITION TO
THE NINETEENTH AMENDMENT
IN THE SOUTH

by Elna C. Green

Kate gordon was an outspoken, highly visible Southern suffragist. That fact alone distinguished her from the majority of her Southern co-workers. Her extreme and inflexible position on the issues of white supremacy and states' rights also set her apart from most of her suffrage associates, and caused much conflict and tension within the Southern suffrage movement. Kate Gordon's exceptionalism has made her a natural subject for historical inquiry, and she is noted regularly in the literature on the suffrage movement. . . .

One of three socially prominent and politically active sisters in New Orleans, Kate Gordon always claimed to have come to her suffrage tendencies "through inheritance," having parents who were converted to woman suffrage before the Civil War. In 1896, Gordon and several other young New Orleans suffragists established the Era Club, whose name carried the well-kept secret meaning of "Equal Rights for All Club." Through her suffrage activities in the Era Club, Gordon came to the attention of the leadership of the National American Woman Suffrage Association (hereinafter NAWSA). President Carrie Chapman Catt, impressed with Gordon's efforts during a famous tax suffrage campaign in New Orleans, promised the Southern suffragist the next available

Originally published in *Louisiana History: The Journal of the Louisiana Historical Association* 33 (Spring 1992): 171–189. Used by permission of the Louisiana Historical Association.

position on the National board. Catt delivered on her promise in 1901, when Gordon was elected corresponding secretary for NAWSA.

The New Orleans suffragist was a likely choice. She was from a socially prominent family and her connections and status made her an important influence in the suffrage movement. As an unmarried woman with ample financial resources, Gordon was free to devote her considerable skills and talents to her chosen cause. All of these factors, plus her intelligence and lively personality, made Gordon good material for national leadership. Although inexperienced, she soon proved to be an exciting public speaker as well. According to one account, she "set the National Federation of Women's Clubs fairly aflame with Suffrage enthusiasm" in Cincinnati in 1910.

Holding a national office for nearly a decade, Gordon plunged into the internal politics of the suffrage movement. Never one to avoid dissension, in fact seeming to relish it, Gordon became an important force for generating tension within the NAWSA leadership. And she carried this penchant for factionalism with her whenever she returned home to work for suffrage in her own state. Part of the storms that surged around her were due to her outspokenness and tendency to get involved in personalities. But much of the friction that Gordon stimulated came from her controversial and inflexible ideological position.

Gordon was one of a number of Southern suffragists dedicated to obtaining the ballot through state constitutional amendments, rather than by a federal amendment. These suffragists feared that federal enactment would naturally bring federal enforcement, which would mean that the South's recently passed literacy and understanding clauses might be disallowed by the Supreme Court. Gordon maintained that the federal amendment was a trick of the Republican party to split the Solid South, and stressed that "the Democratic South is nothing else but a concise way of expressing anti-nigger." Federal action automatically meant black suffrage, an unacceptable outcome to those, like Gordon, determined to protect the South's hard-won white supremacy. As she wrote in 1915, "if Louisiana employs an understanding clause to preserve white supremacy and will grant woman suffrage, then I will not have a word to say against it. White supremacy is going to be maintained in the South by fair or foul means."

"Miss Kate" had long been outspoken on the racial issue. As early as 1901 she asserted that

The question of white supremacy is one that will only be decided by giving the right of the ballot to the educated, intelligent white women of the South. Their vote will eliminate the question of the negro vote in politics, and it will be a glad, free day for the South when the ballot is placed in the hands of its intelligent, cultured, pure and noble womanhood. . . .

In a similar vein, speaking at the NAWSA annual convention in 1907, Gordon delivered a vitriolic attack on the Reconstruction suffrage policies that had allowed the enfranchisement of "cornfield darkies" but not that of "intelligent motherhood."

Rather than turning Southern racial fears into an antisuffrage argument, Gordon attempted to harness those fears on behalf of woman suffrage. She emphasized that the enfranchisement of Southern white women would serve as a powerful tool to insure the continued numerical superiority of the white electorate. She recognized that grandfather clauses and other such subterfuges could be nullified by the federal government, but maintained that white woman suffrage would be a constitutional, irreversible form of permanent white supremacy. She believed that "there are many politicians who, while they would fight to the death the idea of women voting purely on the merits of the question, would gladly welcome us as a measure to insure white supremacy. My old point of choice between nigger or woman, and glad to take the woman, has more truth than poetry in it."

Gordon, like many others who advocated Negro disfranchisement, argued that black voters were a source of corruption in Southern politics, and that elimination of blacks from the electorate would thus be a progressive reform. Furthermore, Gordon believed that this corruptibility of black voters served to hurt the suffrage cause. As she explained after Louisiana disfranchised its black males: "Those of us who know the situation relative to the negroes' virtual disfranchisement are not regretting it, for it removes a large vote against us whenever the question of votes for women is before the people."

As it became increasingly clear that the energies of NAWSA would be directed towards passage of the federal amendment rather than state campaigns, Gordon grew disenchanted with the NAWSA, which she was also convinced was becoming a pawn of the Republican party. In fact, she resigned her office in protest over Carrie Chapman Catt's "Great Petition" asking Congress for a federal amendment in 1909. The rise of the Congressional Union led by Alice Paul and dedicated to forcing the federal amendment through Congress, showed the direction that suffrage sentiment was moving at the national level. Gordon then turned to her fellow Southerners to join her in an effort to secure state-granted suffrage. The result, in 1913, was the Southern States Woman Suffrage Conference (SSWSC), headquartered in New Orleans, headed by Gordon, and dedicated to state-controlled suffrage.

In activities, the SSWSC mirrored the NAWSA: it conducted annual conventions, lobbied state legislatures on behalf of suffrage bills, and disseminated literature. The SSWSC began publishing its own journal, called *The New Southern Citizen*, with the motto "Make the Southern States White." As its first issue made clear, *The New Southern Citizen* and the SSWSC were determined to obtain the "enfranchisement of women of the Southern States, primarily through the medium of State Legislation."

Gordon saw the new suffrage group as a "flank movement" of the NAWSA, and expected financial support from NAWSA while demanding that NAWSA keep out of the suffrage movement in the South. She insisted that Southern suffragists work only through the SSWSC, and steer clear of the tainted federal amendment philosophy of NAWSA. Privately, Gordon confessed that if the SSWSC proved unable to secure state suffrage, it could serve just as well to organize a filibuster to prevent the adoption of the federal amendment.

Southern suffragists, however, did not universally subscribe to this so-called states' rights suffrage position. Indeed, more moderate suffragists halted Gordon's efforts to incorporate the phrase "states' rights" into the name of the SSWSC. Many Southern "suffs" were unwilling to turn their backs on the very promising federal amendment. As Sake Meehan, a suffragist from New Orleans, wrote, "I don't think that 'States Rights' thing will do anybody much good. . . . But 'states rights' catches a lot of these southern women, who do not understand suffrage, anyway."

Meehan refused to join in Gordon's SSWSC, and in fact refused to participate in the Gordon-dominated Era Club any longer either. In April 1913, she and Lydia Holmes, a like-minded suffragist from Baton Rouge, formed a separate organization, the Woman Suffrage Party of Louisiana. The WSP announced its intention of working for the federal amendment, denouncing the narrow states' rights position of Gordon. In a year's time, the WSP claimed a membership of over one thousand. The women of the WSP apparently resented Gordon's heavy-handed presidency of the Era Club as much as they disagreed with her political position. . . . But creating separate organizations did not end the personality conflicts. A few months later, Meehan complained, "If Miss Kate could be silenced or eliminated some way, the cause of suffrage in La. would certainly benefit. . . . In plain words—she is a d____ nuisance."

Gordon, in turn, assailed the WSP as being nothing more than a personal attack on her, and an effort to dethrone the leader of the suffrage movement in Louisiana. When the WSP applied for affiliation to NAWSA, it was granted over Gordon's strenuous objections.... NAWSA's recognition of the new organization was an assault on Gordon's preeminence in her home state. . . .

In the summer of 1918, the Louisiana legislature took up a bill designed to send a state suffrage amendment to the public for ratification. During the session, the WSP offered to bury their differences and join forces with the Era Club in order to lobby for the bill. Less than gracious in reply, Gordon announced firmly that "we do not as a Club affiliate with any organization that does not stand for States' Rights." The two groups of suffragists worked independently for the proposal throughout the campaign.

The state amendment passed the senate by a vote of thirty-two to four, and the house by eighty to twenty-one. . . .

Gordon had little time to savor her victory, as the state suffrage amendment now had to be ratified by public referendum, in a contest that all knew would be bitterly fought. The amendment won some influential endorsements. The governor, both U.S. Senators, and all but one of the state's congressmen publicly pledged their support. The state's largest newspapers also endorsed the amendment. In the announcement of his support, Governor Pleasant stressed that "Equal suffrage, at bottom, is right and just, and it is bound to come." The *New Orleans States*, a suffrage opponent for twenty-five years, bowed to the expediency argument and endorsed the measure, saying that state suffrage was infinitely more acceptable than federal suffrage. However, even with all this powerful support, the suffragists were by no means assured of victory in the public referendum. For now, for the first time, a formal antisuffrage organization formed in Louisiana. Meeting at the Istrouma Hotel in Baton Rouge the day after the state amendment passed, antisuffrage legislators organized a Men's Anti-Woman Suffrage League, and chose Senator J. R. Domengeaux, a manufacturer from Lafayette, as president. What plans the Men's Anti-Woman Suffrage League made were not released to the press, but individual members of the League openly opposed the amendment in the public referendum.

The referendum on November 5, 1918, proved a severe blow to Kate Gordon, as Louisianians defeated the amendment by 3500 votes, with the city of New Orleans providing the necessary margin to defeat it. The *New Orleans States* reported that "Mayor Behrman was jubilant over the result of the election." His city machine had "returned a handsome majority against the amendment." The Behrman machine, operating as the Choctaw Club, regularly fought reform efforts attempted by various progressive reform groups. . . .

With the state amendment lost, Gordon turned her attention to the federal amendment, then under consideration in the U.S. Senate. Gordon wrote Louisiana's Senator Joseph Ransdell, who was a known suffrage supporter, asking that he vote against the amendment anyway on states' rights grounds. The amendment finally passed the Senate in June 1919 and was sent to the states for ratification. Kate Gordon, loath to accept such a possibility, warned the public that a federal law endangered Southern interests: "by a federal amendment negro women would be placed on the same par with white women, and . . . while white men would be willing to club negro men away from the polls they would not use the club upon black women." Apparently she believed that Southern chivalry would outweigh Southern racial prejudice, and consign white supremacy to oblivion.

Of course, Gordon was not alone in her assessment of the effects of the Anthony Amendment. Many other Southerners, male and female, saw federal enfranchisement as threatening the South's racial settlement. As Lieut. Gov. Fernand Mouton put it, "There is nothing in the form of disaster, yellow fever, cyclones, or earthquakes that could wreak the ruin of the South as effectively as the operation of the Susan B. Anthony Amendment." Gov. Ruffin Pleasant sent telegrams to the governors of all the Southern states urging them to cooperate in defeating the Anthony Amendment and enact woman suffrage by state amendment instead. He reminded them that the Nineteenth Amendment merely added the word "sex" to the Fifteenth Amendment, and Southern states had long been opposed to the Fifteenth Amendment.

Very quickly, the states [outside the South] ratified the Anthony Amendment. . . .

The Louisiana legislature took up the question in June 1920, considering both a federal and a state amendment granting women the ballot. Governor Pleasant sent a message to the legislature urging them to defeat the federal amendment, but pass the state measure instead. . . .

At first, the situation looked promising for Gordon's states' rights suffragists. The state amendment passed the house on June 2, by a resounding 93-17. But then the senate acted, defeating both state and federal amendments in quick succession. Louisiana would not join the growing column of suffrage states. . . .

But for Kate Gordon, there was no time for soul-searching and finger-pointing, for she was off to Tennessee, to fight ratification of the Nineteenth Amendment there. Since thirty-five of the necessary thirty-six states had ratified, every state contest was critical, and the eyes of the entire country were on Tennessee. "Miss Kate" and her friend Laura Clay of Kentucky embarked for Nashville under the banner of the now defunct Southern States Woman Suffrage Conference. Both Gordon and Clay insisted that they were not allied with the antisuffragists, representing instead the states' rights position. But, just as in Louisiana, they lined up on the side of the antis on the question of ratification, and for most of the "suffs" that was all that mattered. This time, however, Gordon was unsuccessful, as Tennessee provided the final approval of the Susan B. Anthony Amendment.

In conclusion, it is clear that there were powerful interests at work that opposed woman suffrage in Louisiana, including the Behrman machine of New Orleans. But these forces, powerful as they were, could not have succeeded in defeating woman suffrage in the state without the help of the suffragists themselves. Their own factionalism and jealous rivalries weakened and divided them, enabling their opponents to join forces and defeat them. The suffragists, battling over ideology, were powerless to hold their legislative supporters in line. . . .

But no evaluation of the causes of the defeat can ignore the crucial role of Kate Gordon throughout the whole drama. Gordon antagonized and alienated the leadership of NAWSA, which could have offered her effective support had she chosen to accept it. She created an atmosphere of competition and acrimony beginning as early as 1896 which escalated into open warfare. . . .

Clearly, from the fact that she travelled to other states to campaign against the federal amendment, Gordon saw the issue in terms of a united South against the rest of the country, rather than in terms of the right of the individual state to control its internal affairs. She saw no contradiction in arguing for states' rights and then entering the fracas in another state besides her own. Similarly, she expressed no resentment at out-of-state interference during the Louisiana campaigns, as long as those from outside the state opposed federal enfranchisement. So in a sense, even though she phrased her arguments in states' rights language, what Gordon actually demanded was the *South's* right to control its electorate. . . .

Although disappointed, Miss Kate still took advantage of her new enfranchisement to work for other issues of interest to her. Within a week of ratification, Gordon entered Democratic politics, and was elected president of the women's committee of her home precinct. She pledged immediately to work for the defeat of Mayor Martin Behrman and his political machine. . . .

Nor did time change Gordon's convictions about the desirability of restricting the franchise to certain "qualified" voters. In 1930, while applauding the effects of a decade of woman suffrage, Miss Kate protested that the electorate still needed refining: "What we need now is selective suffrage, the privilege of the ballot only for those who are normal and fit." She and her sister Jean lobbied the legislature to restrict the franchise from the "genetically unfit" and worked for compulsory sterilization laws so that the unfit would not produce "equally unfit children. . . ."

Kate Gordon is both a cause and a symbol of the three-sided contest over woman suffrage in the South. She deserves credit for much of the strength of suffrage sentiment in the region, having spent twenty-five years working for the cause. Yet she, and those who shared her states' rights philosophy, very nearly prevented the ultimate ratification of the Nineteenth Amendment. Even though they were smaller in numbers than the mainstream suffrage movement, the states' rights faction was the critical factor in the suffrage movement in Louisiana and in the South as a whole. The woman suffrage movement in the South should be seen as two movements, one supporting federal legislation and the other insisting on state action, which created a complex three-way contest over the enfranchisement of women. Louisiana presents the clearest example of the dynamics of this three-sided contest, and how close it came to defeating the ratification of the Anthony Amendment.

Questions

1. How did Kate Gordon's family and personal life lead her to become a suffrage activist?
2. Why did Gordon break with the National American Woman Suffrage Association and form her own rival organization?
3. What arguments did Gordon use to try to win over supporters of state suffrage for women?

IN PURSUIT OF
LOUISIANA PROGRESSIVES

by Samuel C. Shepherd

A few years ago, as a freshly minted ph.d., I joined the faculty of Centenary College, where my new duties included teaching Louisiana history. As a southern historian, I readily accepted that responsibility, acting with the glib assumption that Louisiana was much like the rest of the region. I quickly learned otherwise, and in the process benefited from an extended crash course in this state's rich heritage. Still, at the beginning of that education, I received a few jolts, most notably the discovery that progressives were virtually absent from Louisiana's historical narrative. A product of the University of Wisconsin, with that state's vaunted progressive legacy, I was startled—indeed, dumbfounded—to see so few signs of reform in early twentieth-century Louisiana. Where were the progressives? My pursuit of them took me to my textbook, where author Joe Gray Taylor advised that Louisiana governors of that period "were not completely oblivious to the Progressive movement." Where *were* the progressives? . . .

In 1900 Louisiana schools "were in a rather dismal state," recalled T. H. Harris, who later distinguished himself as state superintendent of public education. The length of the school year averaged four to five months, but was as short as one month in some places. The schoolhouses usually were poorly built, "instruction in the elementary grades was harrowing in the extreme," few high

Originally published in *Louisiana History: The Journal of the Louisiana Historical Association* 44 (Fall 2005): 389–406. Used by permission of the Louisiana Historical Association.

schools existed, and those few lacked any real standards. Only 59% of white children and 37% of African-American children between the ages of six and eighteen years of age attended public schools. Louisiana's state superintendent of public education that year deplored the low teacher salaries and observed that "much evil befalls the schools" because teachers annually moved "from place to place" in search of better pay.

Taking office in 1904, Newton Blanchard was an anomaly for a Louisiana governor—he vigorously championed the cause of public schools. James B. Aswell was elected state superintendent of education that same year, and in the words of an early historian of southern schools, "now came the great awakening in public education" in Louisiana. That awakening did not come easily. Voters rejected Governor Blanchard's proposal for a $1 million state bond issue to build schools. Undeterred, Aswell "took to the stump." By all accounts a gifted orator, Aswell traveled constantly throughout the state. According to T.H. Harris, Aswell "liked to speak, and the people liked to hear him. He induced many districts to vote building taxes and erect schoolhouses." Indeed, Aswell aroused public support for schools and persuaded individual localities to finance school buildings. The construction of more than two hundred new schoolhouses by the end of his tenure in 1908 testified to his success.

Aswell's achievements served as the foundation for even greater accomplishments by his successor, T. H. Harris. Joining him was Dr. S.E. Weber, appointed as state high school inspector, a new position funded by the New York-based General Education Board that promoted education in the South. In trips to high schools, Weber visited with principals and teachers, offered them pedagogical suggestions and instruction, and gathered information. Weber and Harris collaborated on an agenda to set uniform standards for curriculum, length of sessions, teacher qualifications, and buildings and equipment, including laboratories and libraries. The legislature helped by appropriating special funds for high schools that met the standards prescribed by the state board of education. The number of state approved high schools climbed from 67 in 1908 to 220 in 1920, enrollment quadrupled, and average teacher salaries more than doubled.

Other problems, however, troubled Harris. He later recalled his initial visits to rural schoolhouses, where he generally encountered a single "inadequately educated" teacher and short sessions. He concluded that these country schools were "as deplorable as the country roads." To alleviate this crisis caused by poor districts relying on local resources, Harris advocated consolidating schools and securing additional state funds. His campaign continued through the 1920s, but by 1923 state appropriations for all Louisiana public schools had already reached four times the amount budgeted in 1908. That money was even more essential after 1916, when the legislature enacted an effective compulsory education law.

Throughout the period urban schools made notable strides. Initiated by civic organizations, particularly women's groups, and embraced by Mayor Martin Behrman, the cause of better education in New Orleans went forward despite conflicts between the mayor and his critics. With city appropriations for education quadrupling between 1904 and 1920, school enrollment soared, new buildings were constructed, new facilities such as gymnasiums were added, and new programs such as night schools were established. In North Louisiana, Shreveport could likewise boast about its new school buildings and its climbing student enrollment. A few Louisiana communities also took advantage of the philanthropy of Andrew Carnegie and rallied their resources for the construction of nine Carnegie public libraries.

This success story did have its limitations. New Orleans's schools still lagged behind those of other major American cities, and the improvements rarely touched the lives of African Americans. T. H. Harris remembered that black churches were often used for schoolhouses and that "school authorities paid no attention" to African American schools, which operated with short terms as well as poorly paid and inadequately trained teachers. By 1916 statewide reform efforts had largely failed to help African Americans and left black schools in decrepit condition. Deploring that situation, T. H. Harris turned to northern philanthropic agencies. Between 1917 and 1922 the Julius Rosenwald Foundation subsidized the construction of 152 Louisiana schools, and by 1927 that figure more than doubled. The fund itself contributed less than one-fifth of the total costs for land, buildings, and equipment and relied on taxes and contributions from citizens for the remainder. Still, the fund did set minimum standards for these rural schools. According to T. H. Harris, the Rosenwald schools "exerted a wholesome influence for longer school terms, better equipped teachers, proper physical facilities, and a practical turn to the school program." Dr. James Dillard also secured support from the Slater Fund and the General Education Board for so-called "Negro Parish Training Schools" that gradually brought high school education to the black communities of many parishes. Agents from the Anna Jeanes Fund aided in teacher instruction. Although providing an educational boost, the Jeanes Fund and the Slater Fund maintained a commitment to vocational and agricultural training, a vision that limited the options of rural African Americans. In New Orleans any African American child seeking an education faced shabby, overcrowded schools that were limited to the first five grades. Persistent pressure from the black community brought about a summer normal school to train teachers in 1915, the opening of a high school in 1917, and a program of evening school classes in 1918.

In *The Transformation of the School: Progressivism in American Education*, Lawrence Cremin praises a man who became "an almost legendary figure," and, we might add, a man well known in Louisiana history, Seaman Knapp. Although textbooks focus on Knapp's impressive contribution to rice farming in Southwest Louisiana, his biographer celebrates him as "the schoolmaster of American agriculture." Between 1897 and 1906, the Louisiana Board of Agriculture and Immigration had tried to foster better farming practices through summer farm institutes attended by thousands of people. Knapp, however, pioneered an even better means of agricultural education: farm demonstrations.

Employed by the U.S. Department of Agriculture after 1902, Knapp used both community farm demonstrations and a growing battalion of agricultural agents to instill his "ten commandments" of farming in the South. With financial support from the General Education Board, Knapp counted thirteen Louisiana agents in 1908 and 60 agents in 1912. The early agents were responsible for geographical areas much larger than a single parish. One of them recollected that "ministers of all denominations" were "my best helpers" because they permitted him to "talk to the whole congregation in the church yard" after Sunday services and after weddings and baptisms. Knapp's program yielded results. By 1912 one Louisiana agent crowed that the hundreds of state demonstrators enjoyed average yields per acre of almost twice the size for the state as a whole in seed cotton and one-third again as much in corn per acre. Rather than being "scoffed at," agricultural agents were now welcomed by "a large majority of the farmers" who readily accepted "scientific facts." Knapp expanded his program by developing clubs for boys and girls, not the least of which was the fifty-six-member pig club in Ouachita Parish. These educational efforts among youngsters soon led to instruction of farmwomen through the work of home demonstration agents. Although Knapp died in 1911, his brother sustained his program of agricultural education that took on an even more robust form through the federal Smith-Lever Act of 1914. Thus, whether in the schoolhouses or in the fields, educational reforms constituted key parts of the Progressive Era in Louisiana.

Reformers wanted not only to get children into schools but also to keep them out of the work place. In 1908 the *Outlook* magazine hailed the new Louisiana child labor law as the "best" one "yet enacted by any Southern State." In 1913 the secretary for the southern states of the National Child Labor Committee praised Louisiana's recent legislation, but cautioned that it needed to be better enforced outside New Orleans. In fact Louisiana's earlier laws of the 1890s and 1902 had been enforced barely at all. Determined women reformers, particularly those who were members of the Era Club of New Orleans, campaigned for better laws. No one proved peskier than Jean Gordon who gathered data, drafted proposals, and lobbied state legislators. A national magazine attributed the passage of the 1908 law as "due almost solely" to her "heroic efforts." Gordon, though, did not act alone. Having assembled much of her information while serving as factory inspector of New Orleans, she had the support of Mayor Behrman, who had appointed her. At a mass meeting called to support a pending child labor law, the mayor praised Gordon. Although the 1908 law amounted to a compromise, it still prohibited children under the age of fourteen years from employment, and a 1911 law filled several gaps in the earlier statute.

Though valuable, Louisiana's child labor laws did have some imperfections. The prohibition of child actors proved a major headache for New Orleans theaters. Faced with rigorous enforcement of the laws, the theaters paid fines, removed the roles of children from some scripts and resorted to using older adolescents to play the roles of children. On at least one occasion this latter tactic displeased a drama critic who complained that it "spoiled what in other respects was a first-class production." After four years of such problems, the theaters succeeded in gaining an exemption in 1912. In an excellent study, *One Hundred Years of Child Welfare in Louisiana, 1860–1960*, Robert E. Moran delineates numerous weaknesses with the state's child labor laws, including weak enforcement in the canning industry. These facts should not be overlooked. But, on the other hand, Moran notes that the legislature passed a better law in 1926. And it should be appreciated that the number of children reported as working in Louisiana fell from almost 60,000 in 1910 to approximately 32,000 in 1920. Among the states of the old Confederacy only Florida and Virginia tallied fewer children at work. Whatever the defects of the Louisiana laws, progressive reformers could still claim a significant achievement.

The campaigns to improve schools and limit child labor demonstrated that Louisianians had heard "the cry of the children," an expression invoked by reformers of that era. New Orleans women repeatedly led campaigns to improve conditions for children. Their efforts extended to inaugurating kindergartens, launching a juvenile court system, and installing more and better parks and playgrounds. The women who participated in these endeavors included members of the Era Club, students and faculty of Sophie Newcomb College, and volunteers and residents of two social settlements, Kingsley House and St. Mark's settlement. This latter group deserves special recognition.

In a classic account of settlement houses, *Spearheads for Reform*, Allen F. Davis identified New Orleanian Eleanor McMain as one of several women who "made their settlements important factors for reform through the strength of their own dominant personalities." In his sweeping portrayal of southern progressivism, Dewey Grantham echoed that assessment. Crediting her leadership, Grantham recited a lengthy list of projects and reforms initiated by Kingsley House. Located in the Irish Channel neighborhood, Kingsley House originated in an Episcopal diocesan kindergarten and an assortment of social programs begun by Trinity Episcopal Church. Kingsley House was established in 1899. Eleanor McMain became its head resident in 1901. A native of Louisiana, she had been raised in Baton Rouge and was no doubt influenced by her father, a former planter and Confederate soldier who became dean and secretary of Louisiana State University. After directing her own private school in Baton Rouge, Eleanor moved to New Orleans to stay with her mother and participated in a new kindergarten-training program. To prepare for her work at Kingsley House, she spent the summer of 1901 taking courses at the University of Chicago and observing the settlement house work at Hull-House and Chicago Commons settlement. Returning to New Orleans, she reorganized Kingsley House on a nondenominational basis.

Like other social settlements, Kingsley House aimed to serve as a neighborhood center. That mission was more easily accomplished because the house offered playground facilities, a free clinic, a children's library, and apparently the only telephone for many blocks. In addition to conducting an array of classes, clubs, social activities, and a day nursery, the settlement became a focal point for reformers in New Orleans. After collaborating in a 1904 investigation of local housing conditions, McMain became the first president of the Women's League that served as an umbrella organization for female reformers. They campaigned for compulsory education, child labor laws, community recreation facilities, and public health services. Thanks to a large donation, Kingsley House moved to a much larger complex in 1925. Organized in 1909, St. Mark's Hall was created by Methodist women inspired by the ideas of social Christianity. Established to serve the nearby Italian-American community, St. Mark's featured facilities and programs similar to those of Kingsley House.

Contemporaries applauded Eleanor McMain for her role in a clean-up campaign that minimized the severity of the 1905 yellow fever epidemic in New Orleans. In a state infamous for its epidemics, McMain and other reformers understood the importance of correcting conditions that fostered the spread of diseases. Still, it took a flood in 1894 and a yellow fever outbreak in 1897 to make New Orleans tackle the area's complex drainage and sewerage problems. Another shocking development also played a pivotal role: women voters. Thanks to a limited suffrage provision in the 1898 Louisiana state constitution, thousands of New Orleans women who were property owners organized and voted for a city tax to finance these city improvements that were slowly constructed.

Historian Jo Ann Carrigan has argued that the 1905 yellow fever epidemic served as "a turning point in the public health history of New Orleans and the entire Gulf Coast." Dr. Beverley Warner, rector of Holy Trinity Episcopal Church, headed a huge volunteer group that eventually joined forces with Dr. Joseph White of the U.S. Public Health Service. They engaged in a massive, energetic, multifaceted campaign of education, inspection, clean-up, and eradication. As Mayor Martin Behrman recalled, Dr. Quitman Kohnke, chairman of the city board of health, "spoke all over the city" about needed actions and "explained the matter so clearly that only the worst 'dumb bells' did not get it." To raise funds for the yellow fever work, the Elks Club organized a festival, complete with a parade and an "ugly men's contest" and thereby interjected some fun into an otherwise serious situation. Still, President Theodore Roosevelt was warned to cancel a planned trip in October 1905 to the dangerous Crescent city. Roosevelt came nonetheless. He participated in a large parade and was welcomed by the mayor and Governor Blanchard as well as by huge crowds who celebrated the city's success in combating the epidemic.

With filtered and treated water after 1909 and a sewerage system reaching 94 per cent of premises in 1920, New Orleans also witnessed a decline in the incidence of such diseases as typhoid and malaria. To the north, Shreveport, too, conducted rigorous clean-up campaigns and offered better city services, including filtered and chlorinated water.

Public health campaigns were not confined to Louisiana cities. After 1905 the state board of health began to wage an extensive campaign to prevent conditions that fostered the spread of not only yellow fever but also many other diseases such as typhoid and tuberculosis. The Louisiana Anti-Tuberculosis League built a new sanitarium and opened a free clinic in New Orleans. For public health officials, preventing the spread of T.B. meant an array of actions from testing cows to stopping New Orleans men from casually spitting in public areas. Dr. Oscar Dowling, president of the state board of health arranged the most famous feature of the statewide educational campaign. During the winter of 1910–1911, a Louisiana Health Exhibit Train carried its message of the "Gospel of Health" to 256 cities and towns, including estimated audiences of 214,000. Anticipating inspections by Health Train personnel, communities along the route engaged in rapid, intense cleanup campaigns. According to one historian, the Health Train sparked "a public health consciousness" in towns throughout Louisiana. The Health Train continued to be a popular means of health education for more than a decade. The most significant public health effort in rural areas focused on the problem of hookworm. With the aid of the Rockefeller Sanitary Commission, Louisiana public health officials engaged in educational efforts, and between 1910 and 1914 arranged for free inspections and treatment at parish dispensaries.

Medical historian Gordon Gillson attributes many of Louisiana's public health accomplishments to "the energy and tenacity of Dr. Oscar Dowling." Gillson adds that "within weeks" of becoming State Health Officer Dowling "gained the reputation of being a hard-nosed crusader for clean dairies, clean markets, and clean restaurants." In fact, in New Orleans "public markets, bakeries, ice cream parlors, and restaurant kitchens were repeatedly under attack." Mayor Behrman allegedly quipped that compared to installing screens in public markets, it would be simpler to require all the flies to bathe. Dowling's work quickly earned him national acclaim. In addition to educating citizens, Dowling and other public health officials inspected facilities, gathered data, published information, developed policies and ordinances, enforced laws, and initiated services. Even before Dowling took office, the legislature had passed a pure Food and Drug Act in 1906. Health officials embarked upon a lengthy process of refining policies to ensure the quality of an array of products, particularly milk.

Thus, anyone in pursuit of Louisiana progressives will find ample evidence of reforms in public education, agricultural education, child labor laws, settlement house activity, and public health campaigns. Yet this list hardly exhausts the scope of reform initiatives. Historian Anna Burns has detailed Louisiana conservation activities dating to a 1904 forestry law and continuing under the aegis of a state Conservation Commission that began its work in 1910. Woman's suffrage proponents also waged an extended campaign. . . .

During the early twentieth century, Louisiana sported a lively and complex suffrage movement. Lacking the ballot, New Orleans women excelled at using other indirect methods to affect public policies. Skillful as lobbyists, organizers and campaigners, women led or played pivotal roles in securing such reforms as child labor laws, juvenile courts, and public health measures. Though a potent force, they remained vexed that male officials often ignored the views and needs of women. Organized in 1892, the Portia Club and later its more robust descendant, the Era Club, rallied women to the equal suffrage cause. As leader of the Era Club, the irrepressible Kate Gordon was so dynamic, articulate, and effective that the National American Woman Suffrage Association (NAWSA) hired her as national corresponding secretary. In 1903 New Orleans hosted the NAWSA convention and listened to an array of famous national proponents of equal suffrage. In the years before World War I, Louisiana women gathered information, mailed letters, and engaged in parades and rallies in support of suffrage. Even the so-called militant suffrage faction, the National Woman's Party, had members in Louisiana.

As historian Carmen Lindig notes, two Louisiana women were arrested and jailed for picketing the White House in 1917 and 1919.

The potential power of the Louisiana woman's suffrage movement was dissipated by racism. In addition to a strong personality, Kate Gordon exhibited a profound commitment to white supremacy. Dedicated to states' rights and state woman's suffrage legislation, she uncompromisingly opposed a federal constitutional amendment to achieve woman suffrage. . . . With the state legislature preparing to consider ratification [of the Nineteenth Amendment], suffrage proponents remained divided. Ethel Hudson, a leader of the Woman Suffrage Party, recounted that upon arriving in Baton Rouge, we "witnessed the curious spectacle of women who had worked and talked for woman suffrage for a generation allying" themselves with opponents of the amendment. Louisiana women celebrated the national suffrage victory with festivities, and throughout the 1920s they celebrated by registering to vote.

If the story of Louisiana's woman suffrage movement seems complex, it serves as a mere appetizer for the murky world of New Orleans politics. Recent historians have largely abandoned the simple approach of dividing the city's political arena between the dominant machine that consistently opposed change and its adversaries, mostly good-government reformers who wanted an end to corruption. Instead, historians now point to fluid movement of individuals between a sequence of reform organizations and the machine, the pragmatic willingness of Martin Behrman to accommodate some social reforms, and even a certain level of consensus about those progressive reforms that fostered the city's economic growth. Yet any notes of harmony came amidst cadences of discord, pounding loudly about race, class, and gender. Other accomplishments aside, the New Orleans machine threw its substantial political weight behind state disfranchisement of African-Americans and later against woman's suffrage. Avowedly a champion of ethnic working class citizens, Mayor Behrman derided some of his critics as impractical, misguided, silk stocking reformers and others as fake reformers who merely wanted to use certain issues to gain political office. When victorious, the self-proclaimed reformers did not always sustain a reform agenda, and the machine managed to smother and adapt reforms aimed at ending political corruption. With a new charter in 1912 New Orleans became one of the largest cities in the nation to adopt the commission form of government, but the reorganized government did not alter Behrman's political domination. Yet even as the mayor and his critics campaigned against each other, they still managed to create a strange type of synergy that produced valuable social reforms, most notably in the areas of public health and education.

As the stories of woman's suffrage and the assault on the New Orleans machine show, Louisiana progressive reforms did have some major limitations, a fact even more apparent in other reform endeavors. If anyone counts prohibition as a progressive reform, one historian counsels that the state Anti-Saloon League "met with stiff resistance from a large segment of the population," but managed to work its will by careful organizing and by exaggerating the level of support for its cause. More significantly, as was so often the case in the American South, African Americans derived only a smattering of benefits from new laws and services. Moreover, entire areas of social needs remained largely neglected. For example, Louisiana did sustain an energetic prison reform organization, did end its use of the convict lease system, and won some national accolades for penal reform in the early twentieth century. Yet, historian Mark Carleton has concluded that although the state "persisted in merchandising the illusion" of "sweeping humanitarian reforms," very few real improvements occurred. Nor did Louisiana help its impoverished citizens. Operating with a state tradition of neglect of such people, the city of New Orleans relied mostly on subsidies to local charitable organizations. A 1922 Municipal Survey Commission report concluded that in New Orleans "there is no plan, no policy, no organization" to deal with "the many-sided and involved problems of social welfare." Noting that "public responsibility in matters of relief has never been formulated in the legislative documents of the city," a 1933 study reported that the city lagged far behind other cities in its expenditures for various groups of needy people. Another 1935 study identified Louisiana as one of two southern states lacking any provision for relief at the parish or county level.

These weaknesses notwithstanding, anyone in search of reform activity in early twentieth century Louisiana certainly will find ample evidence of it. . . .

Questions

1. In what types of reform were Louisiana Progressives involved?
2. Which of those was the most successful, in your view?
3. In what areas did the reformers fall short? Explain your answer.

PART SIX

MODERN LOUISIANA POLITICS

❧ ☙

By the early twentieth century, the exclusively white Democratic Party dominated Louisiana's political landscape. The Constitution of 1898, with its
poll-tax and literacy requirements, had effectively disfranchised almost all
blacks—and many poor whites—in the state and rendered the Republican
Party powerless. The creation of a solidly Democratic political system did not,
however, bring about the end to political factionalism: even as the alliance of
New Orleans's "Old Regulars" and powerful rural planters controlled most
statewide elections, a reform "good government" faction had emerged by the
1910s to oppose that control.

That factionalism shifted and intensified with the emergence of Louisiana's
most polarizing, and most famous, politician, Huey Long. Long's activities
during his relatively brief political career—ten years as a member of the railroad commission, three as governor, and three as a U.S. Senator—completely
upended the nature of Louisiana's politics and its divisions.

In his day, Long fostered both bitter opposition and unquestioning support. His opponents tended to view him as not simply corrupt but as a threat
to self-government and democracy in the state and the nation. His supporters
tended to view him as a savior, a politician who for the first time in Louisiana's
history cared about and protected the common folk from the "interests"—big
business, bankers, and entrenched politicians. Historians, as they have assessed
Long and his place in Louisiana's history, have interpreted him in much the
same ways.

209

The dispute among historians over Huey Long revolves around a number of questions about him and his influence. What motivated Huey to do the things he did, a thirst for power or genuine concern for the commoners of Louisiana? Did the positive ends he created outweigh the corrupt means he used to achieve them? What was his long-term influence on Louisiana's politics, and was it beneficial? Varying interpretations of Huey Long are evident in the essays by Jerry Sanson and Glen Jeansonne. Sanson contends that although Long had deep flaws, one of the overwhelmingly positive benefits he brought about, and one of his long-term influences in Louisiana politics, was his ability to convince the people of the state that government could work for their benefit. Jeansonne, conversely, portrays a Huey Long much more sinister in his goals and his effects. He craved power first and foremost, and any benefits he may have provided for the people of Louisiana were simply a means of reaching that goal. Even then, the benefits were strictly limited. Jeansonne contends Long's Share Our Wealth proposal was little more than a sham and argues that Long expanded corruption on such a grand scale that it became a matter of course in state politics.

Anthony Badger assesses Long's lingering effects in his essay on race and corruption in twentieth-century Louisiana politics. The picture Badger paints is bleak. Louisiana's voters came to expect the benefits provided by Huey Long and his successors such as Earl Long, John McKeithen, and Edwin Edwards, as a basic service of the government, and many of them were willing to turn a blind eye to corruption in exchange. Voters concerned with ending corruption also expected those benefits, albeit with a more honest and efficient government in power, but they typically had to give their votes to "reform" candidates who championed segregation and disfranchisement. The legacy of the corruption and racism in Louisiana's politics was still being felt at the time Badger wrote his essay (2000), and it goes a long way toward explaining the state's budgetary, educational, and political crises at the turn of the twenty-first century.

Writing in the aftermath of the devastation wrought by Hurricane Katrina, Kent Germany points to a different political heritage for Louisianians. Looking at the grassroots efforts to change New Orleans' persistent poverty problem, Germany finds that the federal government's War on Poverty program in the 1960s spawned a fundamental shift in the politics and governance of the Crescent City. Although the programs were dismantled in the 1980s and 1990s, Germany posits that Katrina brought poverty back to the forefront of national consciousness and offered a sliver of hope that national policies to deal with poverty might be reinvigorated. Like Badger, though, Germany is pessimistic about the realization of those hopes.

"WHAT HE DID AND WHAT HE PROMISED TO DO . . . ": HUEY LONG AND THE HORIZONS OF LOUISIANA POLITICS

by Jerry P. Sanson

H uey long's political ambitions both challenged the status quo of Southern politics and created in Louisiana an expanded political system that was different from those in the rest of the South. The Southern political tradition of his era included unquestioning allegiance to candidates of the Democratic Party on both the national and state levels. In Louisiana's case, the state's electoral votes were awarded . . . to Democratic presidential candidates in the . . . seventeen presidential elections from 1880 through 1944. In 1948, Pelican State voters . . . gave their votes to Strom Thurmond of the States' Rights Democratic Party. The state elected Democratic governors for more than a century, from 1877, when Francis Nicholls took over the office, ... until 1979, when David Treen became the first Republican since Reconstruction elected to the Louisiana governorship. The state did not send a Republican to the United States Senate between the time that William Pitt Kellogg retired from that office in 1883 until David Vitter's election in 2004.

Huey Long began his political career as a Democrat even though he grew up in Winn Parish, one of the centers of Populism in late nineteenth-century Louisiana, and technically remained a member of the Democratic Party throughout his life. By 1935, the year of his assassination, however, he was willing to challenge the Democratic Party. He had campaigned for Gov. Franklin

Originally published in *Louisiana History: The Journal of the Louisiana Historical Association* 47 (Summer 2006): 261–276. Used by permission of the Louisiana Historical Association.

D. Roosevelt of New York in the 1932 presidential race and assumed that he would be a member of Roosevelt's inner circle. He was not, and that failure, added to his disdain of Republican economic policies, led him to announce his availability and willingness to lead a third-party presidential campaign in 1936, based on his advocacy of redistributing wealth in the country. Evidently, he thought that he would lose his 1936 quest, but that he would garner enough votes that otherwise would be cast for FDR to deny re-election to the president and throw the race to the Republican nominee. He . . . assumed that any Republican would so exacerbate the economic devastation that the country would eagerly turn to him as its savior in 1940.

It is also worth noting that even though he was a Democrat, Huey Long's political career reshaped the party in Louisiana to fit his political personality. His personality and his proposals so polarized the electorate that the party split into two factions creating a rivalry that dominated Louisiana politics from 1928 until 1960. . . . Bifactionalism reconfigured Louisiana politics and pushed at the boundaries of the state's political establishment. It expanded the horizons of the state's political structure and gave it an approximation of a two-party competitive political system at a time when Southern states generally had one-party dominant systems. . . .

All but the most ardent of Huey Long's supporters acknowledge that there was some element of the scoundrel about him. One way to approach that aspect of his career is to think of him not only as a participant in unsavory political activities, but also as an enabler who established a framework of government that allowed succeeding officeholders to loot the state. After the state Senate failed to convict Long on impeachment charges filed by the House of Representatives in 1929, he centralized enough power in the governor's office, which he dominated either in person or by proxy until his death, that no one could seriously challenge his control of the state again. . . .

The power that Long centralized in his own hands allowed him to appoint himself as the state's attorney to defend some of his controversial laws against legal challenges through the United States Supreme Court and to collect hefty legal fees all along the way. It also allowed him to grant lucrative oil leases on state land to a company which he co-owned and to demand that highway construction contractors buy inferior rock from a quarry that he co-owned in Winn Parish. It allowed him to collect "voluntary" political contributions from the salary of state employees. After his death, that power allowed some of his henchmen in Richard Leche's administration to loot the state of about $100,000,000.

Huey Long had not introduced corruption in Louisiana government, but unfortunately, he had expanded the horizons of Louisiana corruption. The costs of that expansion extend even into our day. The *Baton Rouge Advocate* reported in November 2005 on the concerns that many Americans harbor about sending large amounts of money to Louisiana for assistance in recovering from the massive damage inflicted on the state by Hurricanes Katrina and Rita. Editorial writers observed as part of their assessment of the situation that "the stories can go on as the ghost of Huey P. Long looks down upon a state that expected little and got less in the way of efficiency and integrity in its government."

Huey Long's legendary abuse of power is a fascinating study in politics. He fixed elections; dominated the judiciary; subdued the legislature; robbed local government of its authority; had political opponents kidnapped; appointed or had elected to office stooges who performed his bidding; and used his power to achieve his own personal goals. But, he also used that power to achieve a political agenda that was like no other in Louisiana's political history. He provided state-owned textbooks to schoolchildren, built roads, bridges, and public facilities, improved the availability of health care, and made Louisianians believe that the power of state government, long dominated by a conservative coalition of New Orleans businessmen and planters in the Mississippi and Red River Valleys, could be used in their behalf. That aspect of his career, his expansion of goals that now became possible to attain in Louisiana, might be the most lasting of all. . . .

Louisiana governors throughout the early twentieth century promised repeatedly to enhance life in the state, but always with qualifications and always within the limits that they imposed. William Wright Heard, Louisiana's governor during the first years of the twentieth century, set the tone of most of those administrations in his inaugural address. "It is the bounded duty of republican government to assist in disseminating knowledge and providing for the free instruction of youth," he said, but then cautioned, "not that we should build up a paternal government. . . ." His statement is a mixture of advocacy for enhanced educational opportunities and concern that those opportunities not disturb the status quo in state government. He also reassured his audience that his administration would not spend enough money on education or any other program to incur debt. . . .

Louisiana's governors during the early twentieth century generally followed Heard's cautious approach to government, occasionally advocating gradual improvements if they would not cost too much of the state's money. Those governors willing to spend money to improve living conditions in the state faced often insurmountable obstacles in the legislature or the electorate still dominated by conservative fiscal philosophy. . . . The state simply did not yet have a political leader with the dedication and ability to overcome these obstacles and, therefore, state services were provided half-heartedly and incompletely. The result of that lack of will and ability in Louisiana's political leaders was that many poor people "led lives of varying degrees of misery" in the description written by journalist Hamilton Basso. "They lived in mud-plastered shacks which sometimes served as both home and stable. Their women were broken at thirty, and to the horror of more than one traveler, their children often ate clay."

Huey Long explained a belief in the proper use of tax revenue during his inaugural address that was very different from that of his predecessors. "Every dollar wrung from the taxpayers of this state forms a part of a sacred fund that is pledged by the people for their own care and to provide for their children and the generations that are to come," he maintained. "On principle," he continued, "nothing is further from right than to extort money through taxation and then to use those funds for purposes and causes opposed to the public interest. . . ."

Huey Long never shied away from taxation in order to deliver the benefits that he promised to the people. Indeed, his years of control gave Louisiana impositions of, or increases in, carbon black and malt taxes, severance tax, gasoline tax, tobacco tax, corporation franchise tax, soft drink tax, taxes on the generation of electricity, chain stores, and power use, graduated individual and flat corporate income taxes, liquor and wine taxes, refined oil tax, lubricating oil tax, and sales tax. While some of these tax increases offset loss of revenue caused by reductions of other taxes, Longite administrations increased the state's income significantly. Long thought that he could get away with tax increases because people saw the tangible benefits of the revenue in the form of roads, bridges, buildings, or new services, and Louisianians became used to those benefits.

Moreover, if the state could not collect enough revenue for the "sacred fund" through taxation, Long believed, then it should incur debt rather than ignore the needs of the people. . . . Louisiana's state government debt increased from about $11,000,000 in 1928 to about $150,000,000 by 1935. Huey Long's programs of enhanced state services began to make government a relevant part of the ordinary person's life, but that presence was bought at a high cost.

It is worth noting, however, that the benefits that he provided became so ingrained in Louisiana's politics that the three Anti-Longite governors of the bifactional era, Sam Jones, Jimmie Davis, and Robert Kennon, advocated serious reductions in the level of state services only at their peril. They did not try to retreat to the days of Bourbon Louisiana. . . . They recognized that Huey Long's programs, if not always his methods, had become integral parts of the political fabric in the state and reassured voters that they would not tamper with the state network of social services.

It is also worth noting that the more conservative governors of Louisiana since the end of bifactionalism, David Treen, Buddy Roemer, and Mike Foster, generally continued high levels of state services despite often severe budget difficulties. The most significant budget reductions during these administrations occurred during Roemer's term. The same administration, however, also resurrected gambling in the state, even though it had been constitutionally prohibited since 1898, in order to avoid additional cuts or tax increases.

Edwin Edwards, the recent governor most like Huey Long, also wrestled with budget problems caused by the state's declining oil and natural gas production during his second term in office. Governor Edwards converted the severance tax rate on oil and gas from a volume basis to a value basis, a reform that resulted in Louisiana's revenue increasing during the national economic crisis caused by rising oil prices in the international markets during the 1970s. When the oil bust occurred in the early 1980s, however, Edwards had no more answers than did the more conservative governors. During his third term, he reduced state spending on social programs, even basic services, raised some taxes, and advocated the institution of a state lottery.

Louisiana voters were not kind to governors who cut services and/or raised taxes. Treen and Roemer both lost bids for second consecutive terms in office, at least in part because of the fiscal decisions that they had been forced to make by economic realities. Edwards lost a bid for a fourth term in 1987 for many personal reasons, but also in part because voters were disillusioned by reduced state services. He won his coveted fourth term in 1991 largely because he had the good fortune to be campaigning against former Ku Klux Klansman David Duke, probably the one politician in the state with a reputation more unsavory than Edwards' own. . . . All of these governors had to contend with people's vision of what was possible in Louisiana government—a high level of state services that they had come to consider as an entitlement—a vision created by Huey Long.

Huey Long also made politics relevant to the common people of Louisiana in another way. Poor Louisianians had been generally disfranchised in 1898 when the Bourbon Democrats adopted a constitution that imposed literacy or landowning requirements that a prospective voter had to meet. That disfranchisement was extended by the imposition of the poll tax in 1902 and the adoption of the direct primary method of selecting Democratic candidates for office in 1906. The conservative, white Democrats who ran early twentieth-century Louisiana generally won statewide office by obtaining support from the Regular Democratic Organization in New Orleans, which was reputed to be able to deliver about 20 percent of the vote in a general election, and from the planters and politicians who controlled the plantation parishes along the Mississippi and Red River valleys. These oligarchs realized that they could safely ignore the ordinary Louisianian, and they often did, offering only a few crumbs of improvement for the lives of the people. They also succumbed to the ideology of white supremacy during the 1920s, however, and relaxed some of the requirements that kept poor white voters off the poll lists by inserting "understanding" and "good character and reputation" clauses into the voter registration requirements so that registrars could enroll illiterate white voters while continuing to deny the franchise to black Louisianians.

Long realized the potential created by this modification of the electorate and, in contrast to the establishment candidates, brought his campaigns personally to the people. . . . Huey carefully cultivated his relationship with the ordinary Louisiana citizen. Biographers note that he often spoke directly to the voters, brought them into his confidence and shared his vision of their future. His campaign approach early in his career included his ignoring the traditional political leaders of a community because they were often allied with the Old Regulars, and speaking directly to the voters at large rallies, his powerful voice amplified by the first sound trucks used in Louisiana politics to ensure that his message reached the farthest extent of the crowd. His speeches were usually tailored to the community so he could connect more intimately with the voters. . . .

[A]fter his election in 1928, [h]is administration addressed tangible needs that poor Louisianians experienced on a daily basis. He also often reminded voters that he was accomplishing his programs designed to address their needs. Schoolchildren were advertisements for his programs every time they opened a state-owned "free" textbook at home. Highway construction sites often featured a large sign with this or similar language: "SIGN OF PROGRESS/DETOUR HERE/WE ARE PAVING ROADS/GOVERNOR LONG'S PROGRAM". . . .

Long's obituary in the *New York Times* reflected the contradictory nature of his legacy in this regard: "What he did and what he promised to do are full of political instruction and also of warning. In his own state of Louisiana, he showed how it is possible to destroy self-government while maintaining its ostensible and legal form. . . . In reality, Senator Long set up a Fascist government in Louisiana. It was disguised, but only thinly." While recognizing that Long found "material for the agitator and the demagogue" in "the lower levels of society in Louisiana," the *Times* also commented that "[h]e made himself an unquestioned dictator," and warned that "[i]f Fascism ever comes in the United States, it will come in something like that way. No one will set himself up as an avowed dictator, but if he can succeed in dictating everything, the name does not matter."

Fascist or not, communist, dictator, demagogue, or political boss, Huey Long expanded the political horizons in Louisiana. He convinced the ordinary citizen that the power of state government had been used too long for the benefit of the wealthy few when, in fact, ordinary people should be the beneficiaries of a bounty of programs provided by an activist state administration. He created in the Pelican State a new, almost unlimited, vision of the goals that could be achieved through the use of political power. He was unerring in his vision of the politics of the possible on the state level, perhaps because he reached the point of control at which if his goals could not be achieved within the extant laws, he would simply have the legislature pass new laws to accommodate his vision. . . .

Huey Long made people believe that government was their friend, that he was their protector, the guardian of their well-being. He expanded the political horizons of the state so far that they could never fully contract. . . ., Huey Long's successors in Louisiana could not ignore the changes that he had made in the relationship between the people and their government. He grasped the dreams and aspirations of generations of poor Louisianians, adopted them as his own, and made them not merely attainable, but commonplace.

Questions

1. What long-term effects did Huey Long's programs and policies have on Louisiana politics? Do you think Long's programs were beneficial to the citizens of the state? Why?
2. How did Long broaden the horizons of politics for Louisiana voters?

HUEY LONG:
A POLITICAL CONTRADICTION

by Glen Jeansonne

Huey p. long is Louisiana's most controversial citizen. Some believe that he was Louisiana's greatest governor. Others claim that he was a dictator, a thief, and a Fascist. . . . Thousands of pages have been written to substantiate both sides of the question and more than fifty years after his death politicians, historians, and ordinary citizens continue to debate the issue. Former governor Sam Jones wrote: "More bunkum has been written about Huey Long and his place in history than any man in this region I know of." He has been hailed as the first Southerner since John C. Calhoun to have an original idea and condemned as a man obsessed with personal power. John Kingston Fineran, who entitled his book about Long *The Career of a Tinpot Napoleon*, terms him, "that most extraordinary mountebank, that most mendacious liar, that eminent blackguard and distinguished sneak-thief, Huey P. Long." On the other hand, the late Professor T. Harry Williams argues that "the politician who wishes to do good may have to do some evil to achieve his goal."

No one questions Long's brilliance. James A. Farley believed Long had the best mind he had ever known, but had squandered it. Long himself quipped, "There may be smarter men than me, but they ain't in Louisiana." Perhaps the writer put it best who said of Long: "He did more good and more evil than

Originally published in *Louisiana History: The Journal of the Louisiana Historical Association* 31 (Winter 1990): 373–385. Used by permission of the Louisiana Historical Association.

any other man in the history of his state." This statement captures the paradox of Huey Long and the complexity of Louisiana.

The name "Long" has been a magic one in Louisiana. Long's widow served in Congress. His brother Earl served three terms as governor. Two distant cousins, Gillis Long and Speedy Long, served in Congress, and other relatives have held state offices. His son Russell was for many years one of the most powerful men in the United States Senate. For almost thirty years after Huey's death Louisiana was divided into Long and anti-Long factions.

Perhaps historians have gravitated too much toward the dominating figure of Huey Long, to the extent that other important figures in Louisiana's history have been neglected. Many people outside of Louisiana, asked to name an important Louisianian, can think of only one name: Huey P. Long. But history is rarely so simple as historians would have us believe. Louisiana is a complex state, and Long was as much shaped by the forces indigenous to the state as he shaped them. . . .

Louisiana has never been a typical Southern state, or a typically American state. Ethnically, geographically, economically, and religiously, Louisiana is the most complex state in the South. . . .

In South Louisiana, which was settled by France and belonged briefly to Spain, the customs and traditions are Gallic, the religion overwhelmingly Catholic. With rich deposits of oil and fertile delta soil, the south has been the most prosperous and populous part of the state.

North Louisiana, less fertile and more thinly populated, produced cotton as long as the soil would support it, but now the major products are lumber, cattle, hogs, soybeans, and corn. Anglo-Saxon, Protestant, and conservative, North Louisiana politically has had more in common with neighboring Arkansas, Texas, and Mississippi than with South Louisiana.

There are enclaves within both North and South Louisiana that are distinctive. The chief urban areas in the north, Shreveport and Monroe, are more cosmopolitan than the hinterlands. The most distinctive region in the south is the twenty-two parish area known as Acadiana, the home of Louisiana's "Cajuns". . . .

Finally, there is New Orleans, for many years the largest city in the South, with the region's only urban political machine. As Louisiana's only major city, with about one-quarter of the state's population, with its sophistication and economic clout, it has been the object of envy and suspicion by rural people. A port city and international trading center with a large foreign population, with concentrated wealth beside abject poverty, with its fine homes, urban sprawl and ghetto squalor, and with a population now more than one-half black, the metropolis differs dramatically from the state. Until the time of Huey Long, New Orleans was dominated by the Old Regular machine, also known as the Choctaws. Entrenched and corrupt, but highly organized and providing social services not available from the city or the state, the machine could deliver a bloc vote for statewide political candidates.

A state with such diversity offers endless possibilities for political factions. Voters might base their votes on class, religious, cultural, ethnic, regional, occupational, or ideological factors, or various combinations of these. Some alignments appear obvious: North v. South, Anglo v. French, Protestant v. Catholic, Agriculture v. Industry, Farmer v. Planter, Management v. Labor, Developer v. Environmentalist, Elitist v. Egalitarian, Country v. City, Nativist v. Foreigner, and Segregationist v. Integrationist. In a given election a citizen may base his vote on any of these factors, or several. . . .

Interpretations of Louisiana voting patterns sometimes ignore this complexity. For example, Huey Long's birthplace, Winn Parish, has sometimes been termed a bastion of rural liberalism because it opposed secession and in the 1908 presidential election voted Socialist by a small margin. However Winn has also voted for George Wallace, Barry Goldwater, and Ronald Reagan. If one can call the Winn Parish of Huey Long liberal because it voted Socialist many years earlier, could not one call it conservative because it voted Republican or Independent many years later? Louisiana was not a democracy before Huey Long arrived on the scene. Its entire colonial history was characterized by power struggles among public officials, nationalities, and races. Louisiana was a dumping ground for involuntary immigrants at the time John Law directed the French economy. Law deported convicts to settle New Orleans and sent over prostitutes to marry them. The life expectancy of immigrants was measured in months rather than years because of the climate and disease. Governors held power by force and fraud. Unlike English colonies there was in Louisiana no representative assembly.

In the first half of the nineteenth century Louisiana was a frontier state, unstable, violent, and corrupt. In the antebellum years the state was a battleground between Whigs and Democrats, sugar planters and cotton planters, slaveholders and small farmers. It fought in the Civil War, but fell quickly, and much of the state was occupied by Federal troops during the last three years of the war. The Reconstruction experience disillusioned the white middle class and Redeemers captured the state government by force, fraud, and economic intimidation, entrenching the Democratic party in power.

Bourbon Democrats, however, never monopolized power because the ruling class itself was divided. Because class differences frequently coincide with cultural, regional, and religious ones, historians have erroneously identified factions as deriving solely from economic disparity. However, persons living in the cotton belt voted differently from those living in the sugar belt, regardless of economic status. A South Louisiana merchant, laborer, or small farmer who was dependent upon the prosperity of the sugar industry rationally voted with the big planters when the tariff issue arose.

The issue of race also cut across class lines. Although sometimes interpreted as a false issue by which rich whites oppressed poor whites, the exclusion of blacks from the political process was in reality an issue on which all classes of white voters agreed. Historians interpreting black disenfranchisement have sometimes assumed that it was engineered by rich whites in order to prevent the poor of all races from combining to topple the Bourbons from power. Just the opposite was the case. Disenfranchisement of blacks weakened rather than strengthened the Bourbons because blacks normally were counted as having voted for the conservative Democratic candidates-regardless of how they actually voted and even if they did not vote at all. For example, the six parishes including East Carroll, Madison, Tensas, Concordia, Bossier, and West Feliciana contained 3,779 registered white voters and 19,735 black voters. In one of the watershed elections of the nineteenth century, 1896, they cast a total of 16,000 votes for the Democratic candidate for governor, Murphy J. Foster, and only 139 votes for John N. Pharr, who was running both as a Populist and a Republican. The Democrats carried twenty-three of the thirty parishes in which black voters outnumbered whites. Disenfranchising blacks diluted the planter vote.

It has been said that Huey Long did not exploit racism, but neither did other Louisiana politicians of his time, or at least no more than Long did. It is misleading to compare Long to Theodore Bilbo, racist governor and United

States senator from Mississippi, or Eugene Talmadge, Georgia's race-baiting governor and like Bilbo a contemporary of Long, because he operated in a different environment. Blacks were not a factor in Louisiana after adoption of the Constitution of 1898. The famous "grandfather clause" in this constitution was devised to preserve the vote for poor whites while black voters were removed from registration rolls. The elimination of black voters increased relatively the impact of poor whites in upcountry parishes, thus providing a favorable setting for Huey Long.

The Populist movement in Louisiana was not so much crushed as preempted. Populists collaborated in writing the 1898 constitution because they equated honest elections with an end to manipulation of black votes by Bourbon bosses. Populists and Republicans collaborated in a reform movement beginning in the 1880s and extending into the first decade of the twentieth century that brought increased stability and honesty to state politics. The Louisiana Lottery was abolished, the convict lease system terminated, a railroad commission established, and appropriations for public education increased modestly.

Between 1900 and 1920 New Orleans was dominated by a reborn machine, the Old Regulars, comprised of young businessman, experienced ward bosses from the old machine, and ethnic leaders. As machines go, it was relatively democratic, certainly not the inflexibly reactionary monolith perpetuated in legend by Huey Long. It responded to business and reform demands for more effective public services and drainage. Garbage collection, school building, and dock facilities were improved under Mayor [Martin] Behrman from 1904 to 1920. The elements that constituted the New Orleans organization resembled regimes termed "progressive" in northern major cities.

On the state level governors during this period were cautious men who lacked charisma, but they were neither reactionaries nor puppets of corporate wealth. The assertion that Louisiana's governors were chosen by a corrupt combination of the New Orleans machine and rural bosses, usually sheriffs, overlooks several factors. There was spirited opposition to the Old Regulars in New Orleans. Moreover, there was antipathy toward city candidates and toward South Louisiana Catholic candidates in North Louisiana which made city-country coalitions unstable. It is also plausible to argue that in parishes where bosses did exert influence that they represented their constituents entirely as faithfully as Long represented his. Long himself was a rural boss on a larger scale.

There were reform governors both before and after Huey Long. William W. Heard, Newton C. Blanchard, J. Y. Sanders, and Luther Hall all initiated limited reforms. John M. Parker, elected in 1920, had a reform program that rivals Long's except that he would not resort to deficit financing, which has proven in our own time a dubious device at best. Sam Jones, Robert Kennon, Earl Long, John J. McKeithan, and even Edwin Edwards are all governors who followed Long and have substantial claims to reforms. In reality Long's predecessors and successors did more than is generally recognized.

How then, did Huey Long differ? Why does he seem to tower over other Louisiana politicians? For one thing, he had precisely what almost all of them lacked: charisma. His program differed from theirs not so much in substance as in style, oratory, and notoriety. No one can deny that Long knew how to attract and hold attention. A child prodigy, he grew up in a middle-class family in Winnfield. He married at nineteen and was a lawyer at twenty-one, a public official at twenty-five, governor at thirty-five. He was dead at forty-two. No one else packed so much drama into so brief a political career.

Furthermore, Long was ambitious, aggressive, and uninhibited. On the night of his election as governor, in the midst of celebrating, he announced he would someday be president. He relished power. He enjoyed humiliating enemies. He excelled at oratory. And he recruited lieutenants who deferred to his judgment and never questioned his decisions. He was an overpowering personality.

As governor, Long set out to bring his version of a Great Society to Louisiana. When he tried to tax heavily the powerful Standard Oil Company, it proved a rallying issue to his opponents. They voted to impeach him for violation of almost every impeachable offense cited in Louisiana's constitution. He escaped impeachment by a technicality, but it made him bitter. He vowed that he would no longer say "please" but would "dynamite" opponents out of his path.

Long fulfilled enough of his promises to make credible his claim to be a champion of the poor. He provided free schoolbooks, expanded adult education, and made Louisiana State University a showcase of his administration. But in both public works and education he seemed more concerned with publicity than with substance. His activities at LSU centered on the football team and the band more than on mundane academics. He made the band the largest in the nation. In fact, during one year the university expended more money on the band than on the law school and graduate school combined.

Long hired the best football coaches money could buy and then told them how to run the team, although he had never played football himself. He housed gifted players in the Governor's Mansion, where he fattened them up on milkshakes aid sirloin steaks. He bought an airplane to use on recruiting trips and offered state jobs to athletes and their families. He even appointed a star halfback to the state legislature. When editors of the LSU student newspaper condemned the act, he had them expelled. After LSU lost one game 7–6 he had a follower introduce a bill outlawing the point after touchdown.

It is not that Long did not do some good, but that his priorities were misplaced. He built roads, which were needed, but left the problem of paying for them to future governors. His attention to LSU was salutary; the state needed a first-class university. But LSU was not the only college in the state and appropriations for other colleges declined. Salaries for elementary and secondary teachers also declined, and blacks were paid much less than whites. True, the country was in the midst of the Great Depression. But if Long could find money for roads, for LSU, and for a new capitol, why could he not find money for teachers, for other colleges, and for stipends for the unemployed.

The reason Long was so interested in making improvements that showed was that he intended to use them as a stepping-stone to higher offices. In 1930, two years before his term as governor ended, he ran for the United States Senate. He defeated the incumbent but did not take his seat until his term as governor expired because he distrusted his lieutenant governor. After 1932 he continued to control Louisiana through an amiable puppet, O. K. Allen, a Winnfield friend whom he rewarded with the governorship for having financed his first political campaign. But Huey, not Allen ran the state. When Long came down from Washington to the capitol in Baton Rouge, he took over Allen's office. Governor Allen moved out into the receptionist's office and she moved out into the hall. Someone joked that Allen was so accustomed to following Huey's orders that once when a leaf flew in his window he instinctively signed it, assuming that it was one of Long's bills.

Long was popular with his Louisiana constituents, but he was not a popular senator in Washington. He delivered long speeches, but introduced few bills. He had few personal friends in the Senate.

In 1932 Huey supported Franklin Roosevelt for president. However, soon after the inauguration, they broke. Many people thought that Roosevelt's bevy of bills to mitigate the Depression during his first hundred days in office was too much, too soon. Long thought it was too little, too late, and he had an alternative. His alternative to the New Deal was something he called the Share Our Wealth plan.

Long attributed the Depression to an unequal distribution of wealth. He promised, if his plan were enacted, to give to every American family a home, a car, a radio, a guaranteed job and income, and a free college education for their children. He would finance this simply by confiscating the fortunes of millionaires. No one but millionaires would pay any taxes at all.

The plan was a politician's dream and its appeal to the public was astounding. Long created a club he called the Share Our Wealth Society for people who supported his scheme. Within a month of its founding in 1934 it had 200,000 members; within a year, 3 million. By the early months of 1935 there were 7.5 million. Huey's mail increased enormously. He received more mail than the president and as much as all the other senators combined. Mail was delivered to the Senate in two trucks: one for Huey and one for all the other senators. Long hired a former Shreveport preacher named Gerald L. K. Smith to travel around the country signing up members for the Share Our Wealth Society.

Long frankly admitted that he wanted to be the next president. He said he could defeat Franklin Roosevelt because he could out-promise him. Huey even wrote a book entitled *My First Days in the White House.* In it he talked about millionaires surrendering their fortunes to President Long without a whimper. John D. Rockefeller signed away his entire fortune. Andrew Mellon praised Long for relieving him of a fortune he considered a burden.

It seemed unlikely that the Democratic party would deny the presidential nomination to President Roosevelt in 1936; therefore Long began to think about a third party. By mid-1935 Long had discussed a third party with such potential allies as Father Charles E. Coughlin, the influential radio priest, and Georgia governor Eugene Talmadge. He sent Gerald Smith to talk with Republican leaders. Smith reported that the Republicans would help finance

Long's candidacy because he would take votes away from Roosevelt, the likely Democratic nominee.

Long thought he could take enough votes away from the Democrats to cause a Republican victory in 1936. But he had selfish reasons of his own for desiring a Republican victory. He thought the Republicans would be thoroughly ineffectual in office and that the Depression would worsen. By 1940 the public would be tired of them. This would set the stage for Huey. He would threaten the Democrats with another third-party candidacy and, likely, a northern Republican victory. To prevent that they would offer Huey the nomination. He would accept, and proceed to defeat the Republicans. By 1940 Huey Long would be president.

The plan, of course, had flaws. For one thing, Franklin Roosevelt was a popular president, a charismatic speaker, and a manipulator of no mean ability. It was not clear that any Republican would defeat him, even with Long in the race. For another, some doubted the sincerity of Long's advocacy of sharing the wealth. For example, they said, Long did not practice in Louisiana what he preached in Washington. Louisiana did not have a system of sharing the wealth; it did not even have an income tax until 1934. When asked why he did not push for ratification by his compliant Louisiana legislature of a constitutional amendment to limit child labor, Long remarked that picking cotton was fun for kids. When questioned by labor leaders about the absence of a minimum wage law in Louisiana, Long bristled. He told them that the minimum wage on state projects was as low as he could get men to work, adding that they should be happy to get work at any salary.

Furthermore, Long's Share Our Wealth program was transparently impractical and was labeled so by every qualified economist who examined it. There was not enough money to go around. Confiscating millionaire fortunes would have yielded only one dollar and fifty cents for every poor family. There were not many millionaires in the Depression. . . . Furthermore, there would be no incentives for industrialists to continue production, and enforcement would require a police state. Long gave no explanation as to how he could liquidate tangible wealth such as factories, ships, and mines into a form that could be distributed equally. . . . The only things that could be distributed were profits, and these represented only a small fraction of the total value of any great fortune. And how would Long get his plan enacted by a Congress that considered it ridiculous? He had introduced it several times and it never got more than fourteen votes from among the ninety-six senators.

Long's Share Our Wealth plan, however, cannot be judged solely upon its feasibility and it cannot be understood in economic terms alone. It is comprehensible only if we understand that Long was a consummate politician and an ambitious individual. The economic feasibility of the plan was not important to Long. What was important was the degree to which it could bring him to national power.

The plan had undeniable appeal to people who were standing in line for bread and jobs, shivering on park benches, or being turned away from factories. His plan exploited the discontent of his constituents. Any proposal for change seemed worth a chance to them. Moreover, it appealed to the sense of justice of the underdog. Long wanted to turn the world upside down: to exchange the places of the ins and outs, the rich and poor, the powerful and powerless.

But the problems of the nation did not arise solely from materialistic causes. Long overlooked entirely problems arising from relationships between persons of different skin pigments, educational attainments, religious views, and cultural traditions. Moral questions were telescoped into a single issue; moral questions apart from material distribution were ignored.

Real economic leveling requires meticulous planning as well as vivid imagination. But it is to the imaginations and fantasies of the American people in the Great Depression that Long appealed. That is why he could practice the politics of hope, because in a hopeless situation any change seems a change for the better. Long had keen insights into the needs of his constituents. He knew their fears, their aspirations, and their jealousy of the wealthy. Hope was in short supply, and Long provided it. No logical argument could refute the simple desires of millions of hungry, discouraged Americans. Long could promise more than Roosevelt. Maybe Long was better than Roosevelt.

Long never got the chance to test his theories or to demonstrate his vote-getting ability in the nation at large. In the fall of 1935, a little over a year before the election, Long was assassinated in Baton Rouge. He was killed by a lone gunman, Dr. Carl Austin Weiss. The coroner found one bullet in Huey and sixty-one bullet holes in Dr. Weiss, whose body was shredded by bullets from Long's bodyguards.

But what if Huey Long had lived? Would the world have been a better place? Was it better because he lived? Was Louisiana? In some respects it was. Louisiana needed the roads and bridges he built; it even needed the new state capitol and the governor's mansion he built. It needed the free schoolbooks. If it also got a bigger band and better football team at LSU, and a politicized educational system, perhaps that was a part of the bargain. He gave Louisiana something to be proud of even if he gave it much to be ashamed of.

His soaring oratory was not entirely misplaced; his simple eloquence sometimes rang true. The words that mark his grave on the grounds of the capitol he built are his own:

> My voice will be the same as it has been. Patronage will not change it. It cannot be changed while people suffer. The only way it can be changed is to make the lives of these people decent and respectable. No one will ever hear political opposition out of me when that is done.

Gerald Smith lamented that Long did not live to complete his work. Smith said in his funeral oration over Long's grave:

> This tragedy fires the souls of us who adored him. He has been the wounded victim of the green goddess; to use the figure, he was the Stradivarius whose notes rose in competition with jealous drums, envious tomtoms. He was the unfinished symphony.

On the other hand, there were some who believed Long got exactly what he deserved. Those who live by the sword die by the sword. Long's gravesite on the capitol grounds was for many years protected by an armed guard. Most people thought the guard was hired to keep vandals out, but some wisecracked that it was to keep Huey in.

Louisiana had known corruption before Huey Long, but it had never been so gross or so cynical. And corruption had never been elevated to a theory for governing a state. . . .

The first half of this discussion argued that Louisiana is so complex that it is difficult to sum up the state in a slogan, a sentence, or even a book. Studies that isolate Long apart from the context in which he worked oversimplify.

There were other reform governors, before and after Long. Arguably, some accomplished more with less corruption. There are examples of other governors to demonstrate that corruption is not only inefficient, but unnecessary.

Exactly what type of person was Huey Long? That is no easier to answer than someone who asks: What type of state is Louisiana? Long had within his own personality the complexity of the state he represented; he practiced the politics of hope and the politics of hate. He was cheerful, but moody; generous, yet vindictive; ambitious, but neurotic; verbally aggressive, but physically cowardly. He was superficially assertive, yet pathetically wanted to be liked and accepted. He was Louisiana in microcosm.

Questions
1. What is "the paradox of Huey Long?"
2. What, according to Jeansonne, motivated Huey Long's political activities? How does Jeansonne's interpretation of Long's motivations contrast with Sanson's interpretation? Which of the authors do you find more convincing?
3. What were the flaws of Long's Share Our Wealth proposal, and why was it so popular?
4. In your opinion, do the ends Long achieved justify the means he took to get to them? Why or why not?

"WHEN I TOOK THE OATH OF OFFICE, I TOOK NO VOW OF POVERTY": RACE, CORRUPTION, AND DEMOCRACY IN LOUISIANA, 1928–2000

by Anthony J. Badger

From reconstruction until 1928 Louisiana was controlled by [an] alliance of planters, the business elites and city machines of New Orleans, and the representatives of the oil and gas corporations that exploited the state's natural resources. Even by southern standards, this alliance was notably conservative and corrupt. It rested on a mutual interest in low taxation and niggardly services for the bulk of the population, leaving Louisiana next to Mississippi as the worst state in the nation in terms of most welfare and quality-of-life indicators. Popular challenges were, if necessary, thwarted by raising the banner of white supremacy or by exploiting the ethnocultural divisions in the state between the Catholic South and the Protestant North.

That conservative hegemony was challenged after 1928 by the freewheeling, high-spending, popular policies of Huey Long that were accompanied also by fraud and corruption. T. Harry Williams, Long's most noted biographer, argued that, for the first time, Long brought recognition and long overdue services to the mass of Louisianans, black and white. Unlike most demagogues he eschewed the race issue. He needed to be ruthless and corrupt because that was the only way to wrest power from the hands of an equally corrupt and ruthless oligarchy. Williams's argument can be developed into a longer-term argument that the Long machine and its successors stayed in power like equivalent machines in the northern cities, not because of corruption but because of popular support and because they performed the latent function of providing order amid factional chaos and provided needed government services for the majority of the population. Reformers, by contrast, the argument would go, were conservative elitists, anxious not to expand but to restrict democracy and economically conservative. The machine politicos were racially tolerant, the reformers staunch segregationists.

How much truth is there in that argument?

Unlike the elite politicians, Huey Long deliberately identified with politically excluded lower-income voters and campaigned tirelessly, particularly at rural crossroads, which established politicians, relying on local power brokers, ignored. He persistently identified himself as a poor white. He deliberately, or maybe unconsciously, cultivated coarse manners—receiving distinguished visitors in his vest or pajamas, wandering around restaurants eating other people's food, drinking prodigiously at least until 1935, attempting to urinate between the legs of people standing in front of him in restrooms. But all the time the message was the same: I'm one of you and "Standard Oil and other predatory corporations will not be permitted to rule Louisiana."

Like Huey, his brother Earl had little difficulty in portraying himself as the common man. . . . As governor, he liked nothing better than to sit in his office with opposition newspapers spread all around him on the floor and to spend the afternoon spitting at them. He much preferred his pea patch farm with its corrugated iron roof, its bare electric light bulbs, wartime bunk beds, and a fifty-five gallon urn of coffee constantly brewing to the delights of the governor's mansion. He loved spending sprees and couldn't resist a bargain. . . . At various times he bought ropes, live goats, chickens, seed, hogs, corn, hoes, hats, hams, and earthworms, mostly items for which he had no use and which he promptly gave away. Usually he gave them away at election time. At first it was trinkets, but by the 1955-56 campaign it was hams and televisions. . . .

Later Edwin Edwards put together a formidable lower-income alliance of Cajuns, blacks, rural whites, and labor to become governor in 1971 and be elected governor four times: the first Cajun and the first Catholic governor of the state in the twentieth century.

On the stump in the old days, Huey and his successors delighted in ridiculing and personally abusing their opponents. For Huey, the bald mayor of New Orleans was "Turkey-head," the old Senator Ransdell, a crucial ally for Long in 1928, was "Old feather-duster" in 1932. Earl Long loved to ridicule the elitist pretensions of opponents. Sam Jones was "High Hat Sam, the High Society Kid, the high-kicking High and Mighty Snide Sam, the guy that pumps perfume under his arms." Robert Kennon's blood was "55% champagne, 35% talcum powder" . . . Long so convinced rural audiences that [New Orleans Mayor Delesseps] Morrison wore a wig . . . that Morrison spent time on the platform trying to tear his hair out to persuade the audience that it was real. . . .

The cultivation of a common-man appeal and a colorful, personal campaigning style were stock in trade of any southern politician in a one-party system if those politicians did not have the support of local power brokers or established elites. What distinguished the Longs and their heirs from such demagogues was that, by and large, they delivered what they had promised. They produced the reforms and the government services that the established conservative oligarchy had long denied lower-income voters.

The achievement was particularly notable for Huey Long, who provided the improved roads, schools, hospitals, and long overdue regulation of corporations and utilities during the Depression when most southern governors responded with retrenchment, cutting state services to the bone. After [World War II], Earl Long once more increased spending on education, notably teachers' pay and free school lunches, substantially improving old-age assistance, investing in hospital construction and farm-to-market roads, responding as in other southern states to the opportunities provided by 1940s prosperity and the demands of returning veterans and organized labor for a new postwar order.

Later, in 1971, Edwards showed himself to be an old-fashioned New Deal liberal who believed a beneficent government could solve people's problems. . . . Using the boom in oil and gas revenues of the 1970s Edwards built roads, bridges, hospitals, ports, and schools. He professionalized the state's administration and reduced the 250,000-word state constitution, amended 537 times, to a mere 35,000 words. . . . Even a "good government" watchdog conceded that no other politician could have modernized the constitution.

However, two caveats should be made. First, for all the populist rhetoric, the spending programs tended to invest in the infrastructure—projects that served to facilitate economic growth. In many ways the reforms of Long and his successors were in the recognized southern tradition of business progressivism. . . . Second, for all the rhetorical denunciations, particularly by Huey, of the large corporations, relations between the Long machine, its successors, and business were fairly cozy. Huey Long may have so frightened the opposition forces that they sought his impeachment, and he raised severance taxes on the oil companies, and introduced a manufacturing licensing tax surreptitiously by tacking it onto a bill which was about something totally different after the oil lobbyists had gone home unaware. But, as William Hair has shown, Long was more interested in power and domination than in substantive policy outcomes. Having demonstrated his power, he immediately moved to reach an agreement with the companies to lower the tax to the smallest rate possible, provided that Standard Oil agreed to refine 80 percent Louisiana oil. . . . Once Long was killed, business interests in Louisiana had no problems coming to terms with his successors. . . .

There is little doubt that this record of achievement brought Long and his successors popular support. It was galling to his opponents but even they recognized that Long, for all the fraud and corruption, could ultimately take his case to the people as he did when he was impeached in 1929. In that crisis he bought off the necessary votes to defeat impeachment, but then again legislators were willing enough to be bought. They knew Long was winning over their constituents. Long had addressed rallies all over the state and saturated the electorate with circulars explaining that the impeachment fight was one between Long and suffering humanity on the one side and Standard Oil and the predatory corporations on the other.

But there was more to the power base of Long and his successors than simply popular appeal and government largesse. Huey Long also relied on the traditional attributes of patronage. He controlled some 25,000 jobs, which if you take each job as worth five votes made a pretty substantial inroad into an electorate of 300,000 voters. What was unusual about Long was that he used this patronage absolutely ruthlessly and systematically. No job was too small to allow an opponent to hold. He required undated letters of resignation from most employees and required that they voluntarily contribute 10 percent of their salaries to the deduct system—a cash reserve which financed both Long's state and national political aspirations. He also moved to strip local elected politicians of power. His tame legislature had by the time of his death given his appointees power over all tax assessments, all police and fire department appointees, all district attorneys, all school teachers. Local Long supporters routinely stuffed ballot boxes under the eyes of compliant election commissioners and, when in doubt, the National Guard could be mobilized to beat down centers of resistance like New Orleans. . . .

Corruption was rife and Long routinely bought votes and legislators. His lieutenants lined their pockets too. . . . Long predicted that his followers would end in prison if they ever used the power he had accumulated. The prediction came true after Long's death. Money was no longer needed to finance their leader's national aspirations. His successors rapidly reached an accommodation with the federal government that led to federal money and projects flowing into the state, opening up the chances of local politicians lining their pockets, using state money for private purposes. The most notable victim was Governor Richard Leche. . . .

FBI files revealed that after [World War II] Earl Long received kickbacks from insurance companies, racing interests, new car dealers, and the Teamsters Union. . . . In return for allowing untrammelled slot machines in southern Louisiana, Earl Long probably received half a million dollars from [New York City mobster] Frank Costello in 1948 and a quarter of a million in 1956, and 120,000 from [New Orleans mobster] Carlos Marcello in 1955.

Persistent allegations about Governor John McKeithen's ties to organized crime culminated in two *Life* magazine articles in 1967 and 1970 alleging that Mafia boss Carlos Marcello controlled his administration. While the State Legislative Mafia Investigation committee argued that there was no evidence of Mafia involvement in the McKeithen administration, even that committee acknowledged that the Revenue Department had shown great favoritism to the Mafia boss and that Marcello had benefited from a half million-dollar contract to build a levee on his property. . . .

Edwin Edwards found himself investigated by IRS agents almost as soon as he got into office. He admitted accepting campaign contributions from corporations knowing that the businesses could not legally make those contributions under state law. "That's their business," he said. Louisiana law forbade corporations making contributions; it did not, said Edwards, forbid politicians accepting those contributions. . . . Edwards was also criticized for free airplane trips and hotel accommodations in Las Vegas paid for by the Harrah's Casino. He was also accused of having interests in insurance companies, construction companies, and architecture firms that all won contracts for state projects and from all of which Edwards received a rake-off. . . . In his third term[,] he was indicted and tried twice on fifty-one counts of racketeering and mail and wire fraud. The prosecution alleged that health care companies paid Edwards $1.9 million before 1983 in return for the granting of licenses for $10 million worth of hospital construction when he became governor. Edwards said he made that from his private law practice for the companies. Prosecutors said that he needed the money to pay off gambling debts of $686,000. The head of Harrah's Casino in Las Vegas testified that, in contrast, Edwards had won $562,000 between 1981 and 1984. In a virtuoso performance on the stand Edwards rang rings round the prosecutor, who could never make a New Orleans jury understand the fiendishly complicated arrangements that were allegedly corrupt. He was tried twice, the jury could not reach a verdict the first time, [and] he was acquitted the second.

As for vote rigging . . . Earl Long said about voting machines which were intended to eliminate vote fraud, "Give me a Commissioner I can control, and I'll make those machines play 'Home Sweet Home' every time." As late as the 1996 election there were repeated allegations that votes had been bought in New Orleans and that some voters had voted ten or fifteen times, but had complained because they had only been paid once.

A further element in the appeal of Long and his successors was their ability to bridge the ethnocultural gaps that divided the Catholic South from the Protestant North. Prohibition and the Klan had diverted Louisiana voters from economic issues in the 1920s and helped perpetuate conservative control.

Long avoided such issues as he tried to concentrate on economic matters. He claimed to have both Catholic and Protestant grandparents. He told a moving story of hitching the horse up to the wagon each Sunday to take the former to mass and the latter to church. When his friends said that they hadn't realized he had grandparents of both creeds, he replied, "Hell no, we didn't even have a horse." Earl Long had a firm rule "no hells or damns north of Alexandria," and in southern Louisiana, he arranged meetings after mass had finished and always gave the parish priest a hundred dollars for church funds.

Edwin Edwards straddled the issue equally successfully. Born and raised a Catholic, he converted to Pentecostal Nazarene, and then back to Catholicism.

The final aspect of the appeal of Long and his successors was racial moderation. T. Harry Williams praised Huey Long's racial moderation. Long, he argued, avoided the race issue as an irrelevance and concentrated on economic issues. In the 1930s he could not have done more: both blacks and whites benefited from his programs. Both Alan Brinkley and I modestly questioned this view—noting Long's routine use of racial rhetoric, the lack of black benefit from the education reforms, and Long's criticism of old-age assistance and unemployment relief because blacks would be helped by it. But William Hair, Glen Jeansonne, and Adam Fairclough have been devastatingly critical. As Jeansonne argued, Long "can hardly be given credit for not making an issue of a non-issue." They note his racist associates like G. L. K. Smith and Leander Perez, his failure to challenge local racists like Perez, the regular use of racial slurs, particularly the accusation of black blood in opponents, the persistence of lynching, and Long's opposition to anti-lynching legislation. . . ."

Earl Long . . . plumbed the depths of racism in his 1940 race against reformer Sam Houston Jones. But after [World War II], Earl Long's basic sense of fairness and appreciation of black voters came to the fore. He was particularly incensed by the callous disregard of black rights by white elites. . . . He fought for increased appropriations for black institutions, ensured that African Americans received over half the benefits of state spending programs, and strove for the equalization of black and white teachers' salaries. He recognized the futility of defiance of the Supreme Court, and he quietly supervised the desegregation of the Louisiana State University campus at New Orleans and the desegregation of the New Orleans buses. Above all, he attempted to protect the rights of blacks to vote. . . . It was under intense pressure from the segregationists that Earl Long suffered his famous personal collapse. . . .

The heir to the Long machine in the 1960s, John McKeithen, declared himself a 100 percent segregationist but not a hater. Like Earl Long, he recognized both the inevitability of some racial change and the political advantages of winning the support of black voters. In 1963 he ran as a staunch segregationist against Chep Morrison. But he courted black votes to get support for the constitutional amendment to succeed himself. And he overwhelmingly received black support in 1967 when he defeated Klan-backed congressman

John Rarick. . . . He guided the first halting steps of the state to cope with Court-ordered and legislated desegregation. Increasingly, he emphasized the importance of economic growth at the expense of racial confrontation.

His successor, Edwin Edwards, was the first governor unselfconsciously to seek black votes and to reward black supporters with large numbers of appointments to state office and patronage. . . . The first politician to exploit the full effects of the 1965 Voting Rights Act, he aligned himself with the powerful new black leaders in the Democratic Party, particularly the newly founded black political clubs in New Orleans which aimed to maximize the black vote and offered an entree to black political support to white politicians unfamiliar with that constituency. Many of the New Orleans black political organizations were based on community action projects under the War on Poverty, which gave them jobs and a sound source of patronage. They formed a mutually advantageous alliance with Moon Landrieu, the first overtly racially moderate Mayor of New Orleans. . . . Landrieu kept his promise to open up City Hall jobs to African Americans and to appoint blacks to head departments and to his most senior advisory positions. Though Dutch Morial eschewed such close personal links with the Landrieu administration, he won enough white support to get elected as the first black mayor of New Orleans in 1978.

Long and his successors therefore owed their success to their corruption, but also to a common-man appeal and an established popular record of welfare liberalism and racial moderation. . . .

What of their opponents? . . .

Economic conservatism lay at the heart of much of the reform opposition. Sam Houston Jones aimed to cut government spending, was at the forefront of southwestern business opposition to the New Deal, and was virulently anti-labor. When he failed to defeat Earl Long in 1948, business interests, appalled at the revival of tax-and-spend policies and the end of "good government reform" in the state set up the Public Affairs Research Council. The council worked closely with Robert Kennon to restore civil service provisions to state government and to secure passage of a constitutional amendment that required a two-thirds' vote in favor of any increased or new tax in both houses of the legislature. The nature of this "good government" organization is perhaps best summed up by the fact that in 1975 its chief executive left to join the Louisiana Association of Business and Industry to lobby successfully for the passage of right-to-work legislation in 1976. That law had originally passed under Kennon, but was repealed by Earl Long. Jimmie Davis . . . was tapped by Sam Houston Jones to run for governor in 1944 because Jones was anxious to see continued economic conservatism. Davis stayed out of the state making records and Hollywood films much of the time—in 1946–47 he was out of the state for almost a third of the year. Oilman Buddy Billups in 1959–60 was his chief financial backer, anxious to get favorable treatment for the petrochemical industry. Davis actually vetoed a right-to-work law in his first administration, but subsequent strikes convinced him that had been one of his worst mistakes. Later reformer David Treen was a staunch advocate of retrenchment and an enemy of organized labor.

Linked to economic conservatism was racial conservatism. Sam Houston Jones was a prominent Dixiecrat. Robert Kennon turned to support Eisenhower in 1952 because of the national Democrats' stance on civil rights, joining forces with the notorious racist Leander Perez. When the *Brown* decision was handed down in 1954, Kennon helped Perez and Willie Rainach to set up the Joint Legislative Committee on Segregation. Jimmie Davis attempted to interpose the state government between the federal courts and the New Orleans School Board in order to prevent school desegregation in New Orleans. . . . To win the governorship in the 1959-60 election, Davis made a deal with Citizens' Council leaders Leander Perez and Willie Rainach to give them jobs, a lake at Homer, an appointment on the LSU Board of Supervisors, and control of a state sovereignty commission modeled on Mississippi. Davis accused his opponent of receiving "the appalling bloc of the negro vote." He did nothing to avert the desegregation crisis.

The mayor of New Orleans, Delesseps Morrison, who did get black support, was no racial progressive. . . . [H]e dealt with certain black leaders on a clearly defined paternalistic basis which brooked no significant erosion of segregation. He may have been a darling of the Kennedys and he may have been supported by the city's businessmen, but he made no effort to enforce or facilitate the Court-ordered desegregation of New Orleans schools. Instead, he allowed the mob to roam round the streets of New Orleans, to intimidate parents and enforce a boycott of the schools. . . . Republican David Treen was by origin an old states' rights ticket supporter in the 1950s and then a member of the elite segregationist Citizen Council groups. . . .

The persistent lament of all these reformers was that the Louisiana voters were prepared to abandon them in favor of corrupt politicians who offered their electorate government services and welfare. As [former governor] Buddy Roemer wistfully acknowledged when Edwin Edwards announced in 1994 that he would not seek a fifth term, "We're last in everything that's good and first in everything that's bad, and he [Edwards] gets elected four times. . . ."

By the mid-1980s there appeared to be a sort of equilibrium in Louisiana politics, an equilibrium that was routinely described by political scientists. . . . Voters expected a high-spending government and would tolerate a level of corruption in return for government services. The politicians who delivered this cocktail of welfare liberalism and corruption were responsive to their constituents and, because African Americans voted and were a key part of the liberal coalition, these politicians practiced and preached racial moderation. Periodically, good government reformers would get elected in reaction to excessive sleaze, but these reformers failed to respond to popular needs, were sometimes as corrupt and machine-minded as the candidates they defeated, and were old-style segregationists, rather than racial moderates. In due course, therefore, the reformers were defeated and the high-spending liberals returned.

That equilibrium was shattered in the mid-1980s, in part by forces peculiar to Louisiana—the cost of corruption in a slumping economy and the rise of Nazi and Klansman David Duke—and in part by regional and national forces—the triumph of white Republicanism manifest in Ronald Reagan.

Voters tolerated corruption as long as the resulting high cost of government services could be met by tax revenues from oil and gas, costs that in effect were met by out-of-state corporations and consumers rather than by Louisiana voters. In the 1980s the chickens came home to roost as oil and gas revenues plummeted. Louisiana would soon have an unemployment rate twice the national average. In a desperate move to avert fiscal chaos Edwards had to drive through a $730 million tax increase and, when that failed to ease the deficit, ordered cuts in government services, the antithesis of his whole political and economic philosophy. In such circumstances, voters began to find corruption much harder to tolerate. Capitalizing on this discontent was the young, clean-cut congressman Buddy Roemer, who defeated Edwards in the first primary in 1987. Edwards backed out of a second primary battle and conceded defeat.

Roemer promised Louisiana a revolution in politics and to free the state from the grip of corruption. He engineered major improvements in teachers' pay and evaluation and introduced enforcement of tough new environmental standards. But he was unable to secure the fundamental restructuring of the state's tax system that he believed would have permanently solved the state's fiscal crisis and, like so many good government reformers before him, he seemed to be unable to work with the necessary give and take of legislative politics. . . . Courted by national Republicans, he switched from the Democratic Party to the Republican Party, but the state Republican Party was less than enthusiastic about their new recruit.

Roemer described himself as "socially liberal, economically conservative." But that was precisely what was wrong with Roemer for one of the new power bases in the state Republican Party, the new Christian Right. Evangelicals in the state...pushed for the toughest anti-abortion law in the country. . . . Roemer vetoed the bill but for the first time in the twentieth century a governor's veto was overridden.

The vigorously mobilized new Christian Right was not the only feature of the new Republican strength in Louisiana. From 1968 to 1992, with the exception of 1976, the national Republican strategy depended on courting southern white votes. [The Republicans capitalized on the fact that] from the mid-1970s to the mid-1990s, the purchasing power of the median wage earner had declined in real terms. Government was no longer the beneficent friend of these taxpayers as Edwin Edwards believed; instead, government, and the welfare state in particular, was the enemy. . . . Americans who felt betrayed by this turn of events found it . . . easy to return to a competitive and harsh form of race relations. Two targets, both racially nuanced, were affirmative action and welfare. Affirmative action and minority set-asides deprived well-qualified whites of jobs, many believed, and gave them instead to less well-qualified members of the new black middle class. Welfare created an underclass of dependants, mainly blacks. Hard-earned taxpayers' dollars, so the argument went, were supporting idle and irresponsible welfare mothers. . . .

No one had a surer feel for those frustrations than former Nazi and Klansman David Duke. . . . Duke's first racial enthusiasms were for Citizens' Councils literature. But he soon moved on to be obsessed by Jews. As a history major at LSU he proclaimed himself a National Socialist. In 1973 Duke joined the Ku Klux Klan. . . . In 1980 Duke left the Klan, unable to shake its old-fashioned violent image, and formed the National Association for the Advancement of White People. But, as he said in 1985, "My basic ideology, as far as what I believe about race, about the Jewish question, is the same. . . ."

In 1989 Duke was elected to the state legislature from District B 1, next to New Orleans. In 1990 he ran for the Senate against veteran incumbent, conservative Democrat Bennett Johnston, and polled 43 percent of the vote, including 59 percent of the white vote, smashing Johnston in white working class and rural neighborhoods, the old bastions of the Long forces. The next year he pushed Governor Roemer into third place in the first gubernatorial primary. Edwin Edwards and Duke were the two leading candidates in the first primary with only two percentage points between them. If the voters who voted for other Republican candidates voted for Duke in the second primary, the former Klansman and Nazi would be easily elected governor of Louisiana.

So began what one journalist described as "the gubernatorial run-off from hell." The choice was an unenviable one-between the lizard and the wizard, between the bigot and the crook. . . .

Edwards found that much of his traditional appeal to a beneficent government that provided for the common welfare cut no ice, even with many white voters who had benefited from his largesse. But he was saved by two factors.

First, African Americans, scared by the prospect of a Duke victory, registered and then voted in record numbers for Edwards.

Second, enough white Louisianans were fearful that Duke's victory would damage the state's economy by deterring tourists, convention business, and outside investment. Focus groups had shown Buddy Roemer's aides that voters were prepared to excuse Duke almost anything that would normally disqualify a candidate—his draft evasion, his failure to pay taxes, the fact that he had never had a job, his plastic surgery. Many viewed his Nazi and Klan background with sympathy. . . . What they were worried about was a pocketbook issue—a Duke victory would cost the state jobs. Roemer had failed to exploit this issue. Edwards did not make the same mistake. Business leaders immediately offered money to the Edwards campaign—and Edwards raised massive sums outside the state from Hollywood and New York. The main newspapers abandoned any pretense of impartiality and targeted Duke. Republican leaders, however reluctantly, disowned Duke and endorsed Edwards. These developments made possible a massive media and TV blitz against Duke and an equally massive effort to get out the black vote. . . . Edwards won three out of four of Roemer's supporters, and defeated Duke by 51 percent to 39 percent, despite the fact that 50 percent of voters still thought Edwards was a crook.

But what did Edwards have to offer Louisiana from the governor's mansion? He once said that the best thing would be for him to be elected and then die. His style of pork and welfare liberalism was bankrupt, especially as it would be suicidal to raise taxes. His only answer was to legalize gaming. In Louisiana, the legislature feared to put the issue to the people, [and] many legislators feared to take a public stand in favor of gambling. But the combined impact of gambling money and some sleight of hand by legislative leaders with the voting machines—trapping some opponents with green yes lights on by closing the machines early—led to the passage of a gambling law which vested vast power in the governor who controlled the state gambling board. . . .

After 1991, Duke may have been unable to sustain a viable future in the Republican Party. But voters did not repudiate his views. The single most important fact about Duke's race for governor was that, despite all the Klan and Nazi baggage, he still had secured 56 percent of the white vote. . . . In 1991 in neighboring Mississippi Kirk Fordice had got elected on almost exactly the same platform as Duke, targeting welfare mothers and affirmative action, tough on law and order, and advocating low taxation. The difference was that he was endorsed by the national parry and did not have Duke's disreputable past. In 1995 Fordice was reelected. As veteran Mississippi white liberal Frank Smith told me, he may have been polished up a bit, but "he's still the same racist reactionary bastard he always was."

In Louisiana Mike Foster was elected at the same time in 1995 as a Republican, referring to New Orleans as "the jungle," with a platform almost identical to Duke's four years earlier and endorsed by Duke. He defeated black congressman Cleo Fields overwhelmingly. He did not repudiate the endorsement he received from Duke. Only when Duke was called before a grand jury in 1999 did it emerge that Foster had also bought Duke's mailing list for $152,000. . . .

In 1999 Foster was reelected. He was the first candidate this century in the conservative reform tradition ever to win a second election. Why?

First, he ran against a black candidate again, this time congressman William Jefferson. Second, unlike other reform/good government candidates, for all his rhetoric, he did not practice retrenchment. It was discovered after the election that the number of people on the state payroll had actually increased in Foster's first term. In January after his election, it became clear that the state faced a budget deficit next year of anywhere between $500 million and $1 billion, a deficit his opponent had predicted but which Foster and his supporters had dismissed as ridiculous.

Finally, Foster promised increased government spending. He promised to call a special session to raise teachers' pay to the regional average. When he called this special session in 2000, he blithely announced that he was not going to ask for teachers' pay raise after all. . . .

Over fifty years ago, the distinguished political scientist V. O. Key foresaw the ending of the old structures of southern politics. The collapse of segregation, the enfranchisement of African Americans, the reapportionment of state legislatures, and the arrival of a two-party system would benefit the previously excluded have-nots in the South and greatly strengthen the forces of liberalism. He envisaged a biracial coalition of lower-income whites and blacks united in common economic interests. The class-based politics of Louisiana appeared to offer promising ground for Key's optimism.

Instead, in the South, and in Louisiana in particular, we have a racially polarized politics in which the Republicans secure only white support and the Democrats receive over 90 percent of the African American vote. It has been difficult for most Democrats in statewide and presidential elections in the South to pursue the task of biracial politics. The task of maximizing the black turnout and at the same time securing 35–40 percent of the white vote necessary to win has been beyond the political skills of many southern politicians. In Louisiana the Democrats have occasionally been helped by the propensity of the Republicans to shoot themselves in the foot and nominate extremist candidates like Duke, or Woody Jenkins in 1996, "that unspeakable hypocrite," as one Republican described him to me. The open primary system, complained one Republican leader, means that "good solid candidates from the mainstream...get shunted out." But even Jenkins came within 5,000 votes of victory[,] and the 1995 and 1999 gubernatorial elections demonstrate the stark racial polarization of the state. . . .

[A] progressive biracial coalition seems a long way off in Louisiana. First, suburban whites in Louisiana seem disposed to stick with the economic conservatism and white exclusivity of the Republican Party. Perhaps because they have yet to see the dynamic growth that has shaped other parts of the South, perhaps because so few of them are in-migrants, they seem more interested in low taxes and cultural conservatism than in issues of growth and quality education. There is no sign that the Republican Party itself is going to follow the advice of its chief Baton Rouge pollster and "develop programs and messages that attract significant support from black voters."

Given the attitude of the majority of white voters, black leaders have faced an unenviable choice between a moderate policy aimed at coalition-building with moderate white Democrats and a racially exclusionary policy concentrating on black power. All too often it seems to black leaders, white politicians who court the black vote ignore their concerns, once elected, and pursue policies designed not to upset white sensibilities. However, an emphasis on black racial solidarity can bring local power but at the cost of wider influence. There are more black elected officials in Louisiana than any state in the nation other than Mississippi. African Americans have attained power in cities like New Orleans or in rural districts but they do not have the revenue base to solve the problems of the impoverished black constituents. Dutch Morial had to confront the chronic problems of the Crescent City when both the federal government and the state governments were slashing their aid—which had provided over half the city's revenue. African American male political leaders in Louisiana first gained significant political opportunities in the poverty programs in New Orleans controlled by Moon Landrieu or in the 1970s Edwards administrations. Like their white counterparts they appear to have opted for personal profit, patronage, and access to the white power structure for personal and group recognition, rather than for policy input designed to restructure Louisiana government in favor of the have-nots in the state. . . .

The future both for the have-nots in Louisiana and for the state's economy look bleak. The legacy of corrupt welfare liberalism and racial moderation has produced a system of public governance that has proved incapable of delivering a modernized economy. The legacy of good government and racial and economic conservatism has equally failed to produce a vision that can see beyond the next tax cut or the next toxic waste dump.

Questions

1. What makes Huey and Earl Long, and their successors, different from other southern politicians of their type, referred to here as "demagogues"?

2. To what does Badger ascribe the success of Huey Long and his successors?

3. How did the Anti-Longites and their fellow reformers differ from the Longites? How were they similar?

4. What long-term effects have the political corruption and racial politics of the mid-twentieth century had on Louisiana since then, according to Badger? Do you agree? Explain your answer.

THE POLITICS OF POVERTY AND HISTORY: RACIAL INEQUALITY AND THE LONG PRELUDE TO KATRINA

by Kent B. Germany

On september 2, [2005], after a series of aerial surveys, President George W. Bush . . . put his boots on the ground in the city [of New Orleans]—or at least on city-controlled property at the Louis Armstrong International Airport—and winked to the world about his fond memories of fun trips to New Orleans. He did not, however, specify *which* New Orleans was the source of his nostalgia. Surely it was not the old, segregated city of his youth that had gone through a brutal contest to reorder race, remove Jim Crow, and redress inequality. Perhaps it was the architecturally stunning Garden District version with diverse columns and antebellum dreams or the shiny New South city with its tourist-obsessed progressivism and corporate-choreographed night life. Bush's quip was an ill-advised throwaway line, but it helps underscore the role of historical understanding in establishing political priorities. The politics of the post–Hurricane Katrina recovery is in many ways a battle over history, a struggle to set the emotional and intellectual rationales that eventually dictate decisions. More than ever, conceptions of the past help decide who gets to decide.

One part of the city's history is difficult to ignore: the persistence of poverty and racial inequality. The tragic conditions exposed by Katrina were long in the making, but for a period in the 1960s and 1970s, thousands of New

From *The Journal of American History* 94 (December 2007): 743–751. Used by permission.

Orleanians tried to shift the trajectory of deprivation and exclusion. They had a difficult task. In the mid-1960s, this city of almost 650,000 residents was one of the most impoverished, most unequal, most violent, and least educated places in the United States. Three of every four black residents lived near the poverty line; one of every two lived below it. Almost 50 percent of the city's income went to the top fifth of the population, while the bottom fifth survived on 4 percent. In education, only three of every ten black men aged 25 to 44 had gone beyond middle school. The city's traditionally all-black public schools were oppressively overcrowded, and over the next decade and a half, white residents abandoned all but a few public schools. The local murder rate was almost twice the national average. The incidence of infant mortality, diphtheria, and tuberculosis rivaled any in the nation. Physical infrastructure was not much better. Perhaps half of the streets were essentially unpaved. In the predominantly black Lower Ninth Ward, almost 90 percent of the roads lacked adequate paving and drainage. Approximately one-fourth of the city's 202,643 housing units were considered to be "dilapidated" or "deteriorating." According to the mayor's office, the so-called slum areas accounted for about 25 percent of the city's homes but contributed a scant 6 percent of its tax revenue. Such areas used almost half of the city's services and were the site of half of major crimes and over one-third of reported fires. City hall was all-white except at the custodial level, and in a revealing development, white segregationists in state government fought vigorously to keep blood supplies segregated by race as late as 1970.

The reasons for those problems are numerous, but in New Orleans each of them was a direct product of a system organized by Jim Crow imperatives, and by the 1960s, that system was failing from the inside out. The failure to include African Americans adequately in the modernization of the regional economy had begun to threaten the dreams of southern capitalists and had made the South's most international city too exceptional for the world market. The complexities of racial inclusion and economic boosterism made the local fight against poverty and inequality about more than money. After 1964 the federally funded War on Poverty (defined here to include a broad range of civil rights and community development initiatives) became a multifaceted assault on exclusion and its effects: inefficiency, inequality, and alienation. It did not direct people into a life of dependency and despair, but carried forward a deeply traditional agenda to expand individualism and improve productivity. Stripped down to its barest form, the War on Poverty in New Orleans was about two things: encouraging growth (of both the local economy and the individual's personality) and maintaining social stability. The major antipoverty strategy was to make individuals more adaptable to the demands of the marketplace, to turn the poor and segregated into better capitalists and capitalism into a better system for the poor and segregated.

Instead of being a radical challenge to the status quo, the War on Poverty proved quite conventional in its intent. A variety of programs tried to reshape the market in the interest of poor people and their neighborhoods by repackaging the poor and their neighborhoods for the market. Head Start was to catch poor children early and give them tools to communicate more effectively, provide an acceptance of schedules and procedures, and make them aware of life beyond the neighborhood. Project Enable was designed to improve the skills of parents in raising their child citizens and, according to a local report, teach "self-responsibility." Adult education was to address the problems (and often the shame) of illiteracy. Upward Bound was to link aspiring high schoolers with opportunities for higher learning. Job Corps was supposed to isolate poor young people in a camp setting to teach them the secrets of being worthy workers. The Concentrated Employment program included an intensive orientation that taught the poor how to dress, how to interview, how to talk—in short, how to fit in. The food stamp program required recipients to purchase the stamps and use them as currency for specified items, imposing a budgetary regimen on those wishing to participate. Urban renewal and Model Cities were to improve public services, public infrastructure, and local participation in the hope of providing jobs, raising property values, and improving the desirability of affected neighborhoods. Similar ideas also came from amateur program planners in targeted poverty areas. . . .

What gave the War on Poverty radical potential in the South was its helping people challenge the rules that controlled the mechanisms for social order and governed how black citizens took part in the local economy. In the post–Jim Crow South, using the government to integrate and assimilate black citizens instead of to segregate and alienate them represented a dramatic historical departure. In this climate of political and social reorganization, the Great Society replaced some of the managerial functions of Jim Crow, establishing structures and policies that shaped black inclusion. As such, it became part of an effort to reorient individual and social psychology to support post–Jim Crow citizenship, pressing forward individual-centered therapeutic solutions to broad political problems. Before the riots in Watts in 1965 and certainly before those in Detroit and Newark in 1967, New Orleans's civic progressives, both white and black, were deeply concerned about disorder. This small, diverse group of leaders largely supported the end of Jim Crow and hoped for a smooth transition from segregation, but they fretted about the poor—in most cases, specifically the black poor—with almost every breath, characterizing them as alienated, isolated individuals who had lost contact with the real world. The poor were hopeless, helpless beings poised to destroy the larger world if nothing were done. The solutions to this civic problem were complicated, but rehabilitating the minds of the poor topped the priority list. *characterized*

The therapeutic visions for inclusion had a wide audience, far beyond the coterie of civic boosters and corporate captains. Commentary from a variety of local War on Poverty participants showed that they wanted to belong, wanted to be included, wanted to be more competitive, and wanted to get assistance from anywhere they could. Countless contributions to grassroots neighborhood newspapers from the late 1960s called for residents to improve their self-esteem and self-reliance, thereby giving employers a reason to respect them. As the War on Poverty unfolded on the streets, messengers in the neighborhoods invoked this vision of self-improvement and community empowerment. One Algiers neighborhood activist argued that the poor could overcome their problems with "courage and fortitude" and could develop the "strength to control our lives. . . ."

Federal policies stimulated grassroots political development and helped incorporate assertive black voices into the evolving, post–Jim Crow state. That growth of the state apparatus emerged amid a fragmented, decentralized hybrid of public and private efforts that arose from the margins of local politics and from the largess of the Great Society. The Great Society's antipoverty and antisegregation initiatives were not matters of autocratic social engineering from Washington, D.C., but a complicated fusion of local, state, and federal arrangements that in New Orleans often had relatively little oversight from above. This flexibility allowed locals to tailor the use of federal dollars and control the political benefits derived from them. This quiet bureaucraticization and political entrepreneurialism represented an innovative experiment in racial inclusion. It provided a way to try to compensate for the stridently unequal Jim Crow state without having to pay for much of the change locally, and it made the state a vital place to expand economic opportunities, especially for well-positioned entrepreneurs and job seekers.

In New Orleans, the broad War on Poverty helped a coalition of progressive interests move from the fringes of political power in the early 1960s to the center of it by 1970. One of the key vehicles for this political development was Total Community Action (TCA), a federally funded nonprofit agency founded just before Christmas in 1964. Consisting of representatives from the local Social Welfare Planning Council, the Urban League, local universities, local churches, progressive business circles, and key local Jewish families, TCA brought in several million dollars worth of Great Society community development money. TCA's leadership secured authority over federal grants by careful selection of its oversight board and creative use of federal rules designed to bypass traditional sources of power. During TCA's first three years of community organizing, an estimated five thousand residents participated in over eighty neighborhood groups in the five black target areas of Central City, Desire, St. Bernard, Algiers-Fischer, and the Lower Ninth Ward. The vast majority of those residents had not been civil rights activists, but they benefited from the tone set by leaders such as Richard Haley, an African American organizer who had once been the southern field director for the Congress of Racial Equality (CORE). As the director of this community organization effort, he oversaw the construction of what he termed the white progressive community's "direct line to the ghetto." Under his leadership, organizers in black target areas built enough power to take control of the multimillion-dollar TCA from progressive white leaders by 1968.

In the later 1960s, the massive Model Cities program, urban renewal projects, the Concentrated Employment program, the food stamp program, and several other smaller programs added over $20 million to black neighborhoods and used grants to expand the state's capacity to address demands from black communities. While white employers proved resistant to hiring black workers for jobs traditionally held by whites, the Great Society helped form a parallel marketplace for ambitious African Americans, and that marketplace sustained a generation of black political and business leaders. Contracts and pinstripe patronage associated with Community Action, Model Cities, and urban renewal offered desperately needed sources of capital, income, and political power. Men such as Sherman Copelin, Donald Hubbard, and Theodore Marchand were able to develop long-term, lucrative careers at those intersections of the public and private marketplaces. After the Voting Rights Act of 1965, the number of black voters in New Orleans almost doubled. Those votes became crucial to securing control of the new Great Society–linked apparatus as the 1967 Green Amendment to the Office of Economic Opportunity appropriation bill gave mayors and city councils the authority to take over Community Action programs from nonprofit boards. The winners in this process were neighborhood-based political organizations led by bureaucratically savvy, college-educated leaders. The most prominent of these groups were the Ninth Ward's Southern Organization for Unified Leadership (SOUL), Central City's Black Organization for Leadership Development (BOLD), and the Creole-dominated Seventh Ward's Community Organization for Urban Politics (COUP). Winston Lill, the original TCA director, said that those neighborhood-based groups "came out of our [TCA's] community organization [component] without question." The capacity of the largely private groups to organize and to win elections gave them great authority to control policies and positions in antipoverty programs in black target areas, while the power from those programs helped them organize and win elections, particularly at the mayoral and gubernatorial levels.

While leaders of political groups proved adept at playing racial-bureaucratic politics, other grassroots leaders had less success. Welfare rights activists, radical students, the Black Panthers, neighborhood activists, and an organization called Thugs United Incorporated flourished in the competitive, democratic flux after 1968. By 1971 most of them had collapsed. Internal friction, the lack of effective bureaucratic structures, and their exclusion from key parts of the local Great Society marketplace kept them outside a newly forming magic circle of local political power. Part of the reason that the acronym groups became the kings of local politics was the urban crisis signaled by civil disorders in many cities. In New Orleans the groups became keepers of the Great Society's "line to the ghetto." In short, they were the quintessential political fixers.

In the 1970s this fight against poverty and inequality seemed to have been a worthwhile experiment. New Orleans had not exploded, and its cadre of powerful black leaders and black organizations helped project a progressive image. Following national trends, its poverty rate was falling quickly. Downtown New Orleans got a building so grand they called it the Superdome and made it look like a big brass spaceship—or a twenty-five-story trumpet shouting up from a historic piece of ground. . . . The oil economy was booming, and its profits further changed the architecture of downtown, producing a vertical New Orleans that turned the once-quaint Poydras Street into a mirrored canyon. This futuristic New Orleans looked away from the poverty of its past, and its political battles shifted from the search for equality to the search for usable political power. As one activist stated, the new era was about "politics, not civil rights" and was about getting "the most you can from whoever you can."

In the 1980s two primary engines of the local boom failed. The oil market went bust, which compounded problems associated with a long-term decline in the number of jobs at the port of New Orleans and left the metropolitan area in a depression from which it has never fully recovered. Almost at the same time, the federal pipeline to the cities almost shut down. The Reagan administration, following earlier trends, proposed in 1985 to cut support to cities by 50 percent and other relevant federal programs by 80 percent. To Mayor Ernest N. "Dutch" Morial of New Orleans, this signaled "the beginning of the end of the historical federal-city partnership." This economic and political trauma raised serious questions about a central premise of state-sponsored inclusion after Jim Crow. A rising tide, it turned out, did not lift all boats. Instead, that tide seemed to flow mostly out to the suburbs, and New Orleans, like other American cities, had experienced an epic exodus of white residents and many middle-class black residents. When out-migration began to slow in the late 1980s, the city had almost 200,000 fewer white residents. The white percentage of the population had steadily declined from 62 percent in 1960 to 40 percent in 1980, reaching 28 percent by 2000.

In the 1980s and 1990s, city leaders had to come to grips with the reality that the city's post–Jim Crow system for managing poverty and racial inequality had become a shell of its intended self. The community action–oriented War on Poverty had effectively been over since the mid-1970s, and even that had been less a war than a politically charged policy experiment dependent on grassroots insurgency. Some War on Poverty programs, such as Head Start, Medicaid, and Upward Bound, continued their role of assisting individuals on the economic margins, but the once-invigorating Community Action program had evolved into a set of fairly traditional social service delivery agencies, often overseeing Head Start programs. The mainstays of the remaining antipoverty framework were the means-tested, New Deal–era cash transfer programs. This situation was clearly not limited to New Orleans. In 1988 the resurgent problems of race and inequality led Ronald Reagan to declare that "poverty won" the War on Poverty. He was right in some ways because the War on Poverty was no match for larger and far more powerful economic and demographic trends. The reality was not so much that poverty had won as that the forces of privatization and the search for security and stability—usually in white-dominated, if not white-only, areas—had been the victors. In 2005 Hurricane Katrina revealed how far the country had come from the optimism and idealism of the 1960s.

Katrina dramatically exposed this fragile state of race and poverty and highlighted a complicated political bargain made by leaders responsible for cities at every level—and by implication, most other Americans. They had made peace with poverty. Unable or unwilling to stop it, they mostly hoped to contain it, and their uneasy compromise depended largely on the vast law-and-order apparatus that had emerged in the late 1960s and the vast distances between the poor and the rest of society, whether geographical, psychological, or institutional. . . . Poverty had slipped so far off the national radar that it took the worst storm in a century to put it back on the political screen, and then for only a short while. . . .

Katrina created poignant images and left a liquid arc of almost unparalleled destruction, but it has not effectively nationalized the issue of inequality or significantly altered the civic debate over social and economic rights and privileges. Sympathy and compassion awaken people's attention, but they usually do not last long enough to set national agendas. In the 1960s and 1970s, the transformation related to the War on Poverty did not arise so much from compassion as from black political power, from fear, and from the momentum generated by the civil rights movement. Since Katrina, the dispersion of New Orleans's population, especially its black middle class, has hampered the opportunities to have a mass local response that could stimulate grand action. Activists have worked feverishly, but they have struggled to gain much ground.

If history is any guide, until poverty and inequality threaten growth or become too much for the law enforcement–industrial complex to handle, the poor and marginalized will remain at the mercy of the market and the remnants of the welfare state. As time passes, the chance of turning the power of the Katrina crisis into long-term national policy slips away—if it ever existed. And if the War on Poverty offers any lessons, it is that federal policies can dramatically alter local cultures, but their impact depends on which locals implement them and on how they challenge existing sources of power and of community identity. The prevailing strategy of letting the market steer the recovery has some potential to create a better New Orleans for all, but as the War on Poverty demonstrated, citizens on the economic margins benefit from market forces most when they have a serious say in the policies that guide them and receive clear rewards from them. . . .

Questions

1. How did the War on Poverty change the political power structure of New Orleans in the 1960s and 1970s?

2. Germany claims that "In the 1970s this fight against poverty and inequality seemed to have been a worthwhile experiment." Why? What changed in the 1980s and 1990s to undermine that experiment?

3. How did Hurricane Katrina expose New Orleans's "fragile state of race and poverty" and highlight "a complicated political bargain made by leaders responsible for cities at every level—and by implication, most other Americans?" Do you think Germany is correct in making the assertion that Americans made "peace with poverty?" What evidence do you see in support of or opposition to that statement?

PART SEVEN
TRANSITIONS IN RACE RELATIONS

✺ ✺

In the twentieth century Louisiana transitioned from an agricultural to an industrial economy, a change accelerated by the massive economic stimulus provided by the federal government during World War II. These economic changes threatened the old racial and social order. Adam Fairclough's examination of racial repression in New Iberia shows how the federal government's mobilization of the economy and of the workforce during World War II strained race relations. War mobilization produced new job opportunities, and African Americans understood that the labor shortages produced by the war gave many of them their first chance to land a good job: the military was siphoning off the traditional white workforce even as factories were working overtime to fill defense orders. The ideology of the war, in which the United States stood for freedom against fascist tyranny and oppression, also energized and politicized blacks, many of whom fought overseas. The "double V" campaign launched by black leaders in the North stood for victory over tyranny abroad as well as victory over tyranny (that is, white supremacy) at home. Pressed by black leaders on this point, the Roosevelt Administration granted African Americans some help, and issued an executive order that mandated an end to racial discrimination in defense industries. Black demands for equality of opportunity did not sit well with whites, who saw the old order of race relations eroding before their eyes. Fearing both the loss of cheap labor and the increased competition for jobs, white Louisianians determined to fight back, sometimes violently.

Consider the evidence that Fairclough uses to reconstruct what happened in New Iberia when blacks demanded training for welding jobs.

In the second essay, Lesley-Anne Reed discusses the transition of African Americans from agricultural to industrial employment in the north Louisiana lumber and paper industries. The new industrial economy rewarded not just those with light skin color but also those with adequate educations. Thus, the decades of neglect of black education in Louisiana compounded African Americans' attempts to improve their circumstances as the economy transitioned from agriculture to industry.

When blacks demanded improvements in their education, as they did in New Iberia when they asked for a welding training school, whites often construed it as a threat to the racial order. Thus, demanding an education could be risky, and it did not always pay off. Since the good jobs—those that offered decent wages and the opportunity to move up the ladder—were reserved for whites in industry, acquiring an education did not automatically translate into an improved standard of living for African Americans. Blacks continually had to walk a fine line between demanding fair pay and not pushing whites so far that they might get fired or even physically harmed. Thus, poverty in the black community persisted even as the state prospered economically. The situation would not change until the Civil Rights movement of the 1960s and the imposition of federal laws against segregation and discrimination in the workplace.

RACIAL REPRESSION IN WORLD WAR TWO: THE NEW IBERIA INCIDENT

by Adam Fairclough

D
uring the week of may 15, 1944, a dozen blacks, including the leaders of the local NAACP [National Association for the Advancement of Colored People], were expelled from the town of New Iberia. Four of them suffered beatings, one so severe that the victim died soon afterward. The incident vividly illustrated the determination of many Louisiana whites to defend the racial status quo and the fury with which they sometimes reacted to wartime black militancy. It also exposed the inability or unwillingness of the federal government to protect the civil rights of black Southerners. Despite affidavits from the victims, protests from the national office of the NAACP, and an extensive FBI investigation, the Department of Justice failed to secure the indictment and prosecution of the perpetrators. The events that occurred in New Iberia serve as a reminder that the first stirrings of the modern civil-rights movement began long before the Montgomery bus boycott, during the tense, turbulent days of the Second World War. They remind us, too, of the perils that faced the obscure and all-but-forgotten pioneers of the NAACP in Louisiana.

The Second World War placed every facet of the South's racial system under pressure. Mobilization uprooted millions from homes and farms, herding them to factories, shipyards, and military bases. In the teeming cities, whites and blacks crowded together in a physical proximity unknown since slavery.

Originally published in *Louisiana History: The Journal of the Louisiana Historical Association* 32 (Spring 1991): 183–207. Used by permission of the Louisiana Historical Association.

The transience and turmoil of war ruptured traditional relationships, and the apparent certainties of the color line gave way to challenge, doubt, resentment, and fear. Beneath the blare of patriotism and propaganda, racial tensions simmered and sometimes exploded, in outbursts of violence ranging from barroom fisticuffs to full-fledged riots. And in this tinderbox atmosphere, rumor and speculation magnified anxieties: whites feared an insurrection; blacks anticipated a wave of postwar lynchings.

The war years saw a generation of blacks begin to slough off the humility and resignation with which black Southerners had formerly accepted their lot. As the conflict raged blacks clamored for fair employment, agitated for the ballot, insisted on better public facilities, denounced segregation, and protested vociferously against police brutality. The new militancy was infectious. The mere fact of being at war seemed to encourage a devil-may-care attitude that easily translated into racial assertiveness. "People were in a belligerent mood," remembered Ernest Wright, one of the most outspoken black leaders of the period. When once they would have swallowed their pride, accepting insult and injury, many blacks now stood their ground. Soldiers clashed with the military authorities; civilians argued with bus drivers and policemen; shipyard workers walked off the job. Blacks were speaking and acting in a way not seen since Reconstruction.

Some white politicians, asserting that black militancy endangered the segregated foundations of Southern society, deliberately sought to arouse white fears. In his 1942 campaign for the U.S. Senate, E. A. Stephens warned of "social equality" being "forced down the throats of white people," and alleged that "colored organizations are sitting around midnight candles" plotting the overthrow of white supremacy. Although Stephens lost, this kind of rhetoric prompted Senator Allen Ellender to underline his segregationist credentials so as to avoid being outflanked. Congressman F. Edward Hebert of New Orleans played a similar tune, denouncing a plan to convert the Senator Hotel into a seamen's hostel as a "diabolical scheme" to "equalize the negroes and the whites" and promote "a permanent mixture of the races." Even liberal whites stressed that segregation was sacrosanct.

The prospect of blacks voting also filled whites with grave misgivings. In 1940 the Southern Negro Youth Congress, which met in New Orleans that year, launched a "Right to Vote" campaign, flooding the South with pamphlets urging blacks to register. A few months later a group of black Creoles sought the blessing of state senator Joseph Cawthorn, a prominent Longite, for the creation of a "colored Democratic party." Gubernatorial candidates Earl Long and Sam Jones each accused the other of supporting black voting; both vehemently denied the charge. In 1941, however, the prospect of blacks gaining the ballot increased when the U.S. Supreme Court ruled that the Democratic primary was an integral part of Louisiana's election machinery; this made it, by implication, subject to the ban on racial discrimination contained in the Fourteenth and Fifteenth amendments.

As the NAACP prepared to challenge the "white primary" in various Southern states, blacks in Louisiana stepped up their agitation for the ballot. In New Orleans, Ernest J. Wright, a CIO [Congress of Industrial Organizations] organizer and SNYC vice president, founded the People's Defense League, which soon became, in the FBI's estimation, "the most powerful black organization in New Orleans," thanks to Wright's militant leadership. The city's most influential black Baptist, the Reverend A. L. Davis, joined forces with Wright, and the two men addressed right-to-vote rallies in Shakespeare Park under the auspices of the Louisiana Association for the Progress of Negro Citizens. In 1942 a few blacks in New Orleans attempted to vote in the Democratic primary: most, including Wright, were turned away. The following year the NAACP laid plans to file suit against Louisiana's registration laws. In April 1944, word finally came from Washington that the Supreme Court had struck down the white-only primary. Hailing the decision as "the Negro's Second Emancipation," black organizations prepared for a statewide campaign of voter registration and political mobilization.

Blacks also moved against white supremacy on the economic front. Determined to share in the prosperity of war, they sought jobs in the burgeoning defense industries and pressed for admittance to wartime training programs. Pressure from Northern blacks, in the form of A. Philip Randolph's March on Washington Movement, induced President Roosevelt to establish a federal Fair Employment Practices Committee. Even black teachers, traditionally the most docile of groups, developed signs of assertiveness: by 1944 teachers in Orleans, Jefferson, and Iberville parishes had filed suit in federal court to challenge salary discrimination. Under the leadership of J. K. Haynes, the Louisiana Colored Teachers Association worked ever more closely with the NAACP, which was itself establishing new branches, expanding its membership and organizing on a statewide basis.

Outside New Orleans, particularly in the cotton and sugar parishes, white planters saw their traditional supply of cheap black labor in jeopardy. Attempts by the Louisiana Farmers Union to organize sharecroppers and farm laborers had already provoked threats, beatings, arrests, and near-lynchings. The Farm Security Administration, which helped set up black tenants as independent farmers, also incurred the enmity of planters. In Natchitoches Parish, threats and political pressure caused the FSA to withdraw its black officials from the area in 1942. The following year, in Caldwell Parish, a black FSA official was slain. Now the war threatened to drive up agricultural wages by luring blacks to the cities and drafting large numbers into the armed services. The *Louisiana Weekly* [a black newspaper published in New Orleans] alleged that blacks in Alexandria were being "picked up off the streets" and forcibly dispatched to the cane and cotton fields. In 1943 the Department of Agriculture forbade farm workers to leave their home counties unless a "labor surplus" had been officially declared. By 1944 sugar planters were employing 4600 German prisoners-of-war—labor that had the added benefit of causing black workers to worry about being displaced. "As a result," one planter reported, "the negroes are working better and are staying on the job throughout the week."

The events that occurred in New Iberia in the spring of 1944 portrayed, in microcosm, the racial tensions that gripped Louisiana during the Second World War. They also provide a fascinating case study of the first, fumbling attempts by the federal government to protect the civil rights of black Southerners.

Blacks in New Iberia organized a branch of the NAACP in the summer of 1943, apparently unaware of the white hostility they were arousing. In August, several prominent whites received invitations to attend a mass meeting to mark the installation of the new branch officers. But city and parish officials had no intention of sanctioning the activities of the NAACP, and they asked a Roman Catholic priest, the pastor of a black parish, to discreetly warn the blacks that they would gain nothing by pushing for their rights too assertively. Shortly after the mass meeting, the branch officers were summoned before Sheriff Gilbert Ozenne and another white official, who sternly warned that the NAACP activists would be "personally held responsible for anything that may happen in New Iberia." In December Sheriff Ozenne confided to an FBI agent that he NAACP was stockpiling ammunition; the agent dismissed this allegation as fantastic. Nevertheless, the newly elected sheriff, a former highway patrolman, began to gird himself for an armed confrontation.

In March 1944, seemingly oblivious to the mounting tension, the NAACP held a rally addressed by Ernest Wright, who stressed the vital urgency of obtaining the ballot. At a mass meeting on April 28, hard on the heels of the Texas primary decision, branch president J. Leo Hardy declared that the United States had the first honest Supreme Court and the first honest president since Abraham Lincoln. As the audiences echoed their approval with "Amens," Hardy decried the fact that white children rode to school while black children had to walk; and that white neighborhoods boasted paved roads and sidewalks while the streets fronting black homes comprised dirt and mud. Now was the time, he concluded, for blacks to secure the same rights as white people, including the ballot.

It was the NAACP's demand for a welding school, however, that prompted white leaders to rid New Iberia of the emerging militant leadership in one fell swoop. Why did this issue prove so contentious and occasion such drastic action?

Industrial training had assumed great importance for blacks, symbolizing their determination to break down the employment discrimination that confined them to menial and agricultural jobs. But although the docks and shipyards were crying out for skilled labor, management and unions colluded to exclude blacks and recruit untrained whites. In New Orleans, for example, welding jobs were controlled by the white-only Brotherhood of Boilermakers, Iron Shipbuilders and Helpers of America. Operating through the powerful Metal Trades Council, the AFL [American Federation of Labor] unions kept black welders, carpenters, and other skilled tradesmen out of the giant Delta shipyard. Blacks made some limited gains elsewhere: a survey of 175 firms in New Orleans revealed that by June 1943 twenty-seven had dropped their color bar, and nineteen others now employed blacks in previously white-only jobs. The shipyards, however, were still drastically understaffed because of their refusal to recruit skilled black labor.

Faced with a national manpower shortage, the federal government funded an industrial training program, but each state retained tight control over the money. In New Orleans, for example, the parish school board offered courses to blacks in printing, shoe repairing, and motor mechanics, but it refused to run courses in welding. State and local officials believed that industrial training would draw blacks away from the agricultural areas and place them in direct competition with white workers. And the consequences of the latter were explosive. In May 1943, under pressure from the FEPC [Roosevelt's Fair Employment Practices Committee], the Alabama Dry Dock Company in Mobile placed twelve newly upgraded black welders alongside white workers. The white work force erupted in violence, and federal troops had to quell the outbreak. The following month white shipyard workers rioted in Beaumont, Texas. In the Delta shipyards in New Orleans, blacks organized a mass walkout after two of their number suffered beatings. Despite such conflicts, the FEPC stepped up pressure on the Southern states to train and upgrade black workers. According to historian Merl Reed, "To many Southern whites the committee [FEPC] was no less feared and hated than the enemy overseas."

In 1941 the State Department of Education set up a welding school in New Iberia for whites; when blacks asked for similar opportunities they were rebuffed. Faced with a complaint from a local black that had been forwarded by the federal government, Lloyd G. Porter, the superintendent of schools for Iberia Parish, called in a group of hand-picked blacks and, in the company of the sheriff, confronted them with the complaint. The blacks nervously assured Porter that they knew nothing about the offending letter; one pointed out that it could not have been written by the black complainant, Lawrence Viltz, because he was barely literate. Despite the presence of an FEPC official, the blacks denied any desire for a welding school, suggesting that "some white trash" had probably sent the complaint "in an attempt to cause friction between the whites and the blacks."

Viltz pressed his complaint, however, and the newly organized NAACP branch backed him up. On March 6, 1944, a field examiner from the FEPC, Virgil Williams, visited New Iberia to resolve the dispute; he left with the understanding that the school board would establish a welding school for blacks, with the State Department of Education providing the equipment and Gulf Public Service Co. furnishing the power. [Superintendent of Schools] Porter undertook to operate the school on two six-hour shifts, five days a week. [NAACP New Iberia branch president] Hardy gave him a list of over one hundred prospective trainees.

When the welding school opened on May 7, however, it operated one shift only, and at 8 P.M., two hours after the first class began, Porter told the instructor to finish the class at 10 P.M. because white residents were complaining about the noise of the machinery. The following day the school began operating a daytime shift that ended at 7 P.M., causing several trainees to drop out. The NAACP sent a deputation to ask that the welding class be moved to a black neighborhood, but Porter, allowing only one of them into his office, pointed out that the black school had no electric power and that he had no money to run in cables. Hardy asked the FEPC, which was closely monitoring the progress of the welding school, to intercede again, alleging that the school's current location on the edge of a white neighborhood was a deliberate attempt to deter blacks.

Precise responsibility for the ensuing expulsions is difficult to establish, but the sequence of events is reasonably clear. On the afternoon of Monday, May 15, two sheriff's deputies picked up Hardy at the welding school. Within minutes, Hardy found himself standing in the sheriff's office, facing Sheriff Ozenne and Superintendent Porter. According to the account written by Hardy a few days later—the only evidence directly linking Ozenne and Porter to the expulsions—the sheriff began to browbeat him. Did Hardy know who was talking to him? Did he realize that his letters to Porter (one of which had demanded "an immediate answer") were insulting? Terrified, Hardy became obsequious. He apologized and punctuated every sentence with "yassuhs."

Then Porter spoke. Hardy would not be writing any more letters to the FEPC, the War Manpower Commission or any other "outsiders." He, Porter, would run the welding school as he saw fit—not even the president of the United States could make him do otherwise—and he would close the school down if he chose to. Hardy's repeated "yassuhs" seemed merely to infuriate Porter. "You yellow son of a bitch," he shouted. "You are saying 'yes sir,' but deep down in your heart you would cut my throat." Hardy was the very one organizing the blacks to overthrow the whites. He had in mind to kill Hardy, and if he weren't too old he would do it with his own hands. With Porter's assent, Ozenne gave Hardy until ten the next morning to get out of town.

Unable to complete his arrangements for leaving, Hardy lingered in New Iberia throughout the next day, despite warning from friends not to spend the night in his home or stay with any of his relatives. At about eight in the evening he was chatting with friends outside Uncle Tom's Saloon at French and Robertson streets when a black sedan carrying four deputy sheriffs drew up. The men ordered Hardy into the car and took him to the sheriff's office. After threatening to kill him, one of the deputies asked Hardy where he wanted to go. When Hardy suggested that they take him by his house, the deputy retorted, "Hell, no. Do you want to go east or west?" Ozenne then proceeded to curse, pommel and kick Hardy while two deputies held his arms. After half an hour in a cell, he was bundled into a car and driven out of town; a deputy in the back seat grabbed hold of his necktie and punched him in the face. Dumped in the road, he was ordered to walk fast, not look back, and never return. The deputies drove behind him for a time, one of them firing a parting shot. When he reached the hamlet of Burke, Hardy phoned Dr. Howard Scoggins, a New Iberia physician and druggist, for help. Scoggins found Hardy standing by the roadside about five miles from town, bleeding from the nose and mouth. After applying first aid, he took his injured friend to Lafayette. The following day, the doctor drove back to Lafayette with clean clothes. Hardy took an overnight train to Monroe, two hundred miles distant.

But the expulsions had only just started. On the evening of Wednesday, May 17, Walker and two other deputies picked up, in turn, Dr. Ima A. Pierson, a dentist; Dr. Luins H. Williams, a physician; and Herman Joseph Faulk, a teacher. Like Hardy, they were driven out of town and dumped by the roadside. All suffered beatings of varying severity. . . .

News of the expulsions spread through New Iberia's black community like electricity. Others who had been involved in the NAACP's welding school campaign also fled. Octave Lilly, Jr., an insurance salesman, . . . Franzella Volter, a schoolteacher and NAACP branch secretary . . ., Dr. E. L. Dorsey, who owned a clinic, an insurance company, and a funeral home . . ., Dr. Scoggins . . ., and Roy Palmer, the black welding instructor. . . . Blacks were paralyzed by fear. . . .

FBI Agent Dill learned from a member of the Sheriff's Department that some deputies had employed "strong methods against some of the local negroes" because "the negroes were becoming very sassy and [they] had to keep them in order." The sheriff's department had also planned a raid on black bars and nightclubs to confiscate "razors, knives, guns and other weapons," but the crackdown had been cancelled because Sheriff Ozenne decided that local blacks were sufficiently intimidated already. Ozenne and other white officials had talked to the blacks "and apparently scared them plenty"; further repression might cause the blacks to "fold up or leave town" and would not leave any colored help for the merchants and planters. . . ."

The [investigation by the] FBI failed to identify the men responsible for the expulsions. . . . Leo Hardy visited Washington to relate his experience to Victor Rotnem [of the Civil Rights Section of the Justice Department], a meeting that apparently helped convince the Justice Department to present the case to a federal grand jury. . . . On January 16, 1945, when U.S. Attorney Herbert W. Christenberry presented the evidence to a federal grand jury in New Orleans, the government's case collapsed when the jurors refused to return any indictments. . . . White jurors were loath to indict and even more reluctant to convict whites accused of violence against blacks, especially when the accused included law-enforcement officers.

The Justice Department's dependence on the FBI posed another difficulty: the Bureau's performance in the New Iberia investigation typified its palpable lack of enthusiasm for civil rights cases. [FBI Director J. Edgar] Hoover disliked civil rights cases because, in part, they were difficult to prosecute and too many failures marred the Bureau's public image. In addition, police-brutality probes endangered the FBI's close relations with local law enforcement agencies, jeopardizing its investigations in other areas. It has to be admitted that the FBI's reluctance to take on civil rights cases reflected, more generally, the low status of the black in the Roosevelt administration's hierarchy of political concerns. But it also stemmed from the political conservatism that suffused the FBI and the thinly veiled racism that could be found in Bureau personnel from top to bottom. The main activities of the New Orleans office in the field of race relations were the monitoring of "foreign inspired agitation among negroes," the investigation of black and leftist organizations for "Communist influence," and the surveillance of such alleged "Communists" as Ernest Wright. It pursued the New Iberia investigation only because of continual prodding from the Justice Department.

To be sure, FBI agents faced problems in gathering evidence about the expulsions. Although many whites in New Iberia admitted that the black leaders had been run out of town, none would sign a statement confessing direct knowledge of the affair. Blacks were loathe to testify for an entirely different reason: fear. A man who witnessed Hardy's abduction refused to name the deputies "because if he did he would be found dead in a gutter somewhere. . . ." Against the government was arrayed virtually the entire white community of Iberia Parish, including its men of wealth, status, and political influence. . . . For local whites, the welding-school controversy symbolized a growing challenge to the traditional pattern of race relations that carried profound social, economic, political, and sexual implications. They detected racial threats all about them: in black demands for the vote, for skilled training, and for industrial jobs; in the shift in black leadership from docile teachers and preachers to independent businessmen and professionals; above all, in the assertive demeanor of ordinary blacks. Again and again, whites used the words "arrogant" and "sassy" in complaining of black behavior; they were unnerved and felt physically threatened by blacks who failed to display the traditional signs of deference and humility. . . .

Who ordered the expulsions? . . . The evidence—admittedly circumstantial—points to a carefully planned operation, approved by local bigwigs and acquiesced in by state officials, to rid New Iberia of selected black activists. This was not the indiscriminate violence of a mob. On the contrary, the people who ordered the expulsions wished to avoid the kind of mob action that might cause blacks to flee the area, accentuating the labor shortage. Ozenne's deputies knew who they were looking for and expelled the victims with cool, clinical efficiency. The mayor boasted that not a single black family had left New Iberia apart from those involved in the incident. . . . The expulsions achieved their desired end: the "troublemakers" left town but there was no general black exodus. . . .

Yet brutal as the expulsions were, the perpetrators exercised a degree of circumspection that would have been unusual fifty or even twenty years earlier, when lynching had been commonplace. Between 1900 and 1919 these atrocities claimed at least 158 victims in Louisiana alone. After the "red summer" of 1919, however, lynchings declined throughout the South: during the 1920s, they claimed fourteen victims in Louisiana. The death toll rose again during the early 1930s, but thereafter fell sharply. By the 1950s, writes historian Howard Smead, "ritualized public executions were a thing of the past," with lynchers becoming "considerably more surreptitious. . . ."

But if the New Iberia incident illuminated a wider pattern whereby whites were increasingly wary about employing violence against blacks, it also furnished a measure of the formidable white resistance to racial equality. The Second World War did not lead to the decisive breakthrough against white supremacy that blacks in Louisiana and elsewhere hoped for. The defense of segregation did not depend primarily upon violence and brute force: it rested on political power, economic strength, and legal stratagems—and was no less effective for that. The foundations of segregation remained intact as Louisiana's white leaders, in concert with their fellow Southerners, voted to abolish the FEPC, helped to wreck President Truman's civil rights program, attempted to suppress the NAACP, and proceeded to stymie school desegregation.

In New Iberia itself, race relations remained frozen for a decade and more. In August 1948 six blacks attempted to register to vote only to be turned away. Gus Baronne, the leader of the group and NAACP branch president, left town after receiving threatening phone calls. The NAACP lingered on, but when the state of Louisiana obtained an injunction against the Association in 1956, the ailing branch finally expired. It did not revive until 1964 when, with the civil rights movement at its zenith, Dr. James H. Henderson, a black dentist who hailed from North Carolina, recruited two hundred members and secured a new charter from the national office. Under Henderson's leadership, the New Iberia branch established itself as one of the strongest and most effective in Louisiana. At Henderson's right hand was Franzella Volter, the branch secretary, who twenty years earlier had fled New Iberia after the beating of J. Leo Hardy.

Questions

1. What changes produced by World War II strained the system of segregation?
2. Besides the welding school, what other demands did African Americans in New Iberia make for the first time during the war?
3. Why was a welding training school so important to blacks and so feared by whites?
4. In what ways did the federal government assist blacks in New Iberia?
5. Which blacks were expelled or fled New Iberia in the wake of the crisis? Why those? Consider the impact those expulsions might have had on the blacks who remained in New Iberia. How might this have affected the black community for years to come?
6. Why was the Justice Department unable to secure a conviction in this case?

TRANSITIONAL GENERATIONS: AFRICAN AMERICAN WORKERS, INDUSTRIALIZATION, AND EDUCATION IN THE NORTHERN LOUISIANA LUMBER AND PAPER INDUSTRIES, 1930–1950

by Lesley-Anne Reed

R. d. belton already worked full-time for Southern Advance Bag and Paper Company in 1930, the year his son R. L. was born inside a three-room shotgun house perched atop a hill in Jonesboro, Louisiana. The house lay just a few miles east of the town of Hodge, home of the Southern Advance paper mill. As his son later recalled, R. D. Belton worked for wages six days a week, often in twelve-to-fourteen-hour shifts, in the "common labor pool" of Southern Advance's wood yard, "unloading boxcars of wood and truckloads of wood . . . and feeding [wood] chips." Although the elder Belton raised his children in a small industrial town, he, like many others of his generation, began his life at the turn of the twentieth century as the son of African American sharecroppers, picking cotton and growing peanuts on a farm in rural Sabine Parish.

The limited employment opportunities available to African Americans in the paper and lumber industries mirrored the equally limited opportunities on the farms from whence they came. In 1927, when R. D. Belton moved his family to Jonesboro, the twenty-two-year-old farmer's education consisted of only a few years spent in a small, church-run "school," where the academic term ran in lock step with the cotton harvesting season. Only approximately 27 percent of Louisiana's African Americans even attended

Originally published in *Louisiana History: The Journal of the Louisiana Historical Association* 50 (Winter 2009): 25–56. Used by permission of the Louisiana Historical Association.

school regularly according to the 1910 census, while only 7 percent went to secondary school. Like many African American families in Louisiana and throughout the South, R. D. Belton's sharecropper parents required his labor when he was as young as six or seven years of age. For the Beltons, and for most contemporary African American families in the South, work responsibilities were tied inextricably to a family's subsistence, and the needs of basic survival commonly overrode their children's pursuit of anything above a rudimentary education. Lacking a formal education and industrial skills, male African American workers in northern Louisiana, and all across the South's piney woods, were often reduced to filling the fluctuating labor needs of emerging industries, in exchange for the cash wages that could help support their families. R. D. Belton and many African American men who made the permanent transition into a wage-labor workforce in the 1920s and 1930s fit this labor profile.

Members of the elder Belton's generation considered both farming and household duties as family traditions, and they instilled that belief in their children. Although these children—born after roughly 1930 and reared in small industrial towns—received an education far superior to that of their parents, they still worked extensively within the home. The younger Belton remembers, for example, milking cows each morning before walking to school and washing out his only set of clothes in the evenings before going to bed. "Sometimes, I'd be late for school in the morning," Belton remembers, "runnin' to get there, but the teachers knew why[;] . . . they understood." Thus, R. L. Belton, like many of his contemporaries, found himself performing farming and household duties in order to support his family.

The social process of industrialization, what historian Adam Fairclough has called the general "transformation of the South's black population from a rural peasantry to an urban proletariat," produced two groups of male workers—those like R. D. Belton and then those like his son R. L.—that may indeed be labeled "transitional." What the workers of these transitional generations inherited from their ancestors, despite inhabiting an increasingly industrial environment, was the elemental connection of family to traditional work and basic survival strategies. Industrialization, customarily held by historians to alienate workers from the home, did just the opposite in many Southern mill towns, at least in its primary stages. In northern Louisiana, many men of both transitional generations, in fact, chose to live and work in industrial communities in large part because doing so increased the quality of their home lives. . . .

Both geographic isolation and regional patterns of racial segregation produced limited employment opportunities for African American men in small lumber and paper mill towns in northern Louisiana. Owners of lumber and paper companies typically built mills in remote locales with substantial acreage and water sources. Hodge, situated in the rural north-central portion of the state and the site of Hodge-Hunt Lumber Company during the first two decades of the twentieth century, was incorporated in 1903. Both Hodge and the adjacent town of Jonesboro became home to a large number of former African American sharecroppers and their families beginning in 1927, when Hodge-Hunt Lumber sold out to Southern Advance Bag and Paper Company, a northeastern corporation. Before the influx of African American workers in the late 1920s, blacks constituted roughly 30 percent of rural Jackson Parish's population. Both blacks and whites, and even several dozen single white women, worked at the Southern Advance mill, but regional patterns of segregation still dictated the workers' daily lives. From the outset, as former mill worker R. L. Belton recalls, African American workers resided exclusively "east of the [railroad] tracks" in Jonesboro, experienced little interaction with white workers, even at the mill, and rarely appeared in the decidedly "white" downtown Jonesboro area. Proprietors of lumber and, later, paper industries, although primary employers of African American labor in the early twentieth century, did nothing to upset geographical segregation in rural northern Louisiana. Northeastern corporations typically bought sections of the South "as they were," meaning that, in the process, they acquired both extensive tracts of unused land and huge populations of poor, uneducated workers.

As early as 1890, lumber corporations, mostly from the Northeast, had purchased large tracts of forest, built sawmills and rail roads and began exporting lumber while employing African American men throughout northern Louisiana on a seasonal basis. But not until the 1920s and 1930s, after these lumber companies had stripped the region of raw timber, did paper processing and manufacturing also become lucrative industries requiring access to a permanent and cheap labor force, one which the region's African American men would fill. By the 1950s, Jackson Parish had upwards of forty integrated sawmill and paper-manufacturing entities, most of which had been in operation since the early 1930s, when they began their corporate existences as lumber companies. And by the 1960s, one-third of all Jonesboro residents were African American, most of whom were either employed by the mill at Hodge or related to someone who was. For African American men in northern Louisiana, filling a burgeoning paper industry's need for a cheap and permanent labor force meant partially sacrificing the personal autonomy afforded by farming or sharecropping.

In the early twentieth-century South, African Americans had traditionally equated personal success with economic independence. Before the 1930s, African Americans in northern Louisiana frequently gained autonomy by working on small, isolated farms in rural areas, where they largely avoided interaction with whites. In 1930, half of the African American male workforce still labored in agriculture, although mostly as sharecroppers laboring for white landlords. Only a paltry 11 percent of African American farmers owned the land they tended. Despite their overall lack of actual capital, African American men sought economic stability and independence by choosing to sell their labor, which in northern Louisiana before 1930 meant hiring out for seasonal lumber and saw mill work. Many African American men commonly defined this seasonal saw and lumber mill employment, along with government-commissioned jobs on public road and building projects, as "public work," which paid an average of $2.00 per day in the 1920s and 1930s. "That [public work] would mean you would quit farming [temporarily]," explained former sharecropper Harvie Johnson, "and you'd go and haul logs [and] cut logs [or] you would work on the roads." Sharecropping, farming, and "public work" helped African American workers in northern Louisiana and their families maintain economic independence. But a large number of African American men in rural northern Louisiana, those of the first transitional generation who first supported their families with sharecropping, seasonal lumber work, and "public work," chose to make the permanent move to industrial towns once mills offered steady wage work.

Availability of steady farm work was, by the 1920s and 1930s, quickly declining. Cotton remained a staple crop in the South through the 1920s, but cultivation of this staple proved an insurmountable problem during the Great Depression as planters compensated for falling cotton prices by expanding their output. In response to the resulting overproduction—considered a national economic crisis—the New Deal's Agricultural Adjustment Act (AAA) paid Southern farmers to cut back on their crop yields, and the ensuing market correction raised prices. Unfortunately for black sharecroppers, white planters and landlords, who acted as gatekeepers for these federal funds, retained the payments and ejected sharecroppers from the land. Many African American families whose livelihood had depended upon sharecropping suddenly found themselves out of work. Harvie Johnson recalls how it felt to watch mature cotton remain unpicked on the land he and his uncle had previously tended in rural Bienville Parish. "They [planters] said 'well, we're gonna have to tie up twelve acres'" although the cotton "was all up and blooming," says Johnson, "and they [the planters] paid for it." With little land left to farm, many sharecroppers and subsistence farmers viewed industrial wage work as the only viable means for their family's survival.

"People would leave the farm whenever they could [afford it]," recounts former mill worker R. L. Belton, but the move did not necessarily mean that their basic way of life changed fundamentally. African American men could maintain, even as they gradually moved into permanent wage work, some level of private farming, a compromise that many of them counted as a personal success. Henry Kimp remembers that his father, a member of the first transitional generation who moved with his wife and children to Jonesboro to work for Southern Advance in 1938, handled the permanent move into industrial labor by maintaining an intimate connection to the land. "For the time he worked there [at the mill], my daddy was an outdoor man," Kimp recalls, "[H]e liked to hunt and fish," and did so when he was not out driving mules in the paper mill's wood yard.

African American men did not move into permanent industrial employment in mill towns like Hodge and Jonesboro simply because of economic factors but because the move to an industrial town promised to enhance their families' overall quality of life. In northern Louisiana, this meant that African American men made the decision not to migrate by themselves, but to uproot their entire families, moving from isolated rural areas into towns like Hodge and Jonesboro. Locating housing, however, often proved troublesome. The limited number of company housing units that Hodge-Hunt had erected shut down unceremoniously when Southern Advance bought out the company. With little cash on hand, the men built or rented homes on the outskirts of the towns. These structures, "little shotgun houses" as former mill worker R. L. Belton recalls them, often lacked the most basic utilities, including electricity or running water, as late as the 1940s. But, remembers former mill worker Henry Kimp, "town life was more economical and better [than farm life]" overall, and it provided "a better opportunity for them [his family] to survive."

Families, however, were often initially excluded from the original migration to company towns. Not all African American mill employees had families, nor were all of them even at the appropriate age to have families. At age thirteen, Harvie Johnson started his first wage labor job, cutting and hauling wood, at Davis Brothers Lumber Company in the tiny village of Ansley, located just nine miles north of Hodge and Jonesboro. Even at his young age, Johnson had all the schooling he would ever receive and was acquainted with hard work: "You see, on the farm back there," recalls Johnson, "we was sharecroppers," and his father had put him to work cutting "the bushes [and] clean[ing] off the fence, those types of things." Possessing only a rudimentary education, former sharecroppers like Johnson were consigned to the grueling "black" jobs, which typically involved hauling and cutting logs in the mills' wood yards, tasks that did not require any formal education and, therefore, did not hinder their entrance into labor-intensive wage work at young ages. Of course, work assignments involved another glaringly obvious factor: "Black" jobs were degraded by whites.

Both rural whites and blacks who entered the industrial workforce in the 1920s and 1930s viewed heavy, manual labor as exclusively "black" work, proof that notions of white supremacy lingered heavily in northern Louisiana. White workers might have performed traditionally "black" labor during times of economic hardship. Most of them were poor white yeomen who engaged in subsistence farming while their wives and daughters labored as domestics in the piney woods of northern Louisiana, a place Lance Hill deems "a hostile refuge for the poor and dispossessed." But these whites saw performance of "black" work as a temporary hardship. As soon as more lucrative, less labor-intensive jobs at the mills became available, mill managers hired only whites for the skilled and well-paying positions.

Southern Advance adhered to this pattern of occupational segregation from the time it built its paper plant in Hodge in 1927 and the first transitional generation of African American men entered its workforce. Like other Southern lumber and paper companies, Southern Advance relied on a large and steady supply of cheap manual labor, consisting primarily of black male workers whom the company hired to cut and trim the timber and then transport it to the mill. White men, on the other hand, filled the management and skilled-labor positions in the mills. Historian Timothy Minchin contends that white managers believed African American men possessed a certain "abundance of physical energy," but not enough intelligence to handle skilled mill positions. Many of the whites entering mill work lacked formal education themselves, but mill managers considered white workers trainable. "[Whites] gave us the jobs they didn't want," recalls former mill worker Harvie Johnson, "[and] Negroes had to do all the hard work." White workers generally subscribed to the notion that education and skill, or the capacity to achieve such things, were all that separated them from black workers and what they regarded as the shame of performing "black" jobs.

Beginning with the establishment of the northern Louisiana's first paper mill, racially segregated "lines of progression" severely limited African American workers' opportunities for promotions or advancement. "Black" work was hard and laborious and required little skill except the strength to dig a ditch or to push a cross-cut saw. Black workers' "lines of progression" started in the wood yard and usually ended, with jobs as aids at pulp mill stations, right where the white "lines of progression" traditionally began. While the lumber industry provided one of the most substantial employment opportunities to African Americans, especially when compared to other Southern industrial sectors, it still restricted them to a set of undesirable jobs. Segregation in the workplace served as a social tool of white supremacy all across the South in the form of what Jacquelyn Hall terms "racial capitalism," which ensured that the economic domination of white workers would prevail. These "segregated lines of job assignment and seniority," argues historian Herbert Hill, became "rigid and enforceable" because whites wanted industrial roles delineated across racial lines only. As a testament to the strict racial division based on "lines of progression" within the industrial workplace, even those African American workers promoted into skilled positions during the mills' World War II-era labor shortage and increased production schedules were promptly demoted once the war ended and enough white men returned from military service to retake their jobs. At Southern Advance, Harry Mims engaged in carpentry work—a skilled position traditionally reserved for whites—during World War II, "when all the skilled men left [for military] service," but he found himself assigned to the "common labor pool" at the war's end. "We tried [to move up]," recalls former Hodge mill worker Harvie Johnson, who "asked [his] plant manager" repeatedly for promotions in the 1940s and 1950s but, like the majority of black workers in the paper mills of northern Louisiana, never received them.

Thus, the first transitional generation of African American men in northern Louisiana, sharecroppers and "public workers" who left farm life behind in the 1920s and 1930s for mill wages that they believed would better support their families, found themselves employed in jobs that paid relatively well but required nothing past a rudimentary education and offered no hope of promotion. African American paper mill workers in northern Louisiana would not gain permanent entry into jobs that required education until the mid-1960s, when a series of lawsuits in the wake of the 1964 Civil Rights Act slowly began to desegregate "lines of progression." By then, the second transitional generation of African American mill workers—the sons of those men who first made the permanent transition into wage work and town life—would come to gauge their own success against their ability to earn a cash wage that could support a family, a task that would eventually require education as much as it did fair and equal workplace practices.

The second transitional generation of African American mill workers in northern Louisiana, born after 1930, still faced life in a "family wage system," in which family members of all ages worked to contribute to the household income. On farms, families labored side by side as sharecroppers, and fathers and sons even performed "public work" together. Putting food on the table required a collective effort, and it remained so when the earliest generation of African American mill workers settled into town life. Schooling in rural areas had actually disrupted family farming traditions in the early twentieth century South. Town life, in contrast, offered African American children more formal and permanent, albeit segregated, educational networks. However, still faced with duties at home closely resembling those of farm life, these first-generation mill children were painfully familiar with the agrarian traditions of their fathers and the economic hardships tied to "black" work.

Yet many African American men of the first transitional generation had managed to carve out occupational niches for themselves and their families

in paper mill towns such as Hodge and Jonesboro by adapting rural traditions to industrial life. As long as the lumber and paper industries prospered,
and therefore continued to demand a steady supply of unskilled black labor,
African American workers could attain some level of financial success. Members of the first transitional generation often remained attached to the notion
that autonomy denoted success. For example, R. L. Belton remembers that
his father, who worked full-time in the Southern Advance wood yard in the
1930s, also tended his "backyard" produce garden extensively during his limited amount of free time, an activity that not only supplemented the family's
food allowance but also gave him immense personal satisfaction. "My daddy
loved to garden," recalls R. L. Belton. "He didn't want no one to mess with
his garden." The produce R. D. Belton grew in his garden, which actually
resembled a small farm, made its way onto the Belton family table as well as
into numerous other households throughout their neighborhood by way of
a community barter system. Thus, as the Belton family's experience demonstrates, African American men applied earnings from permanent wage work
to the maintenance of agrarian traditions, yet they did so as they established
family households in an industrializing community.

African Americans born as sharecroppers in the early twentieth-century
South often grew up believing that education, to which they had very limited
access, had no bearing on economic success. The sharecropping culture of the
early twentieth-century South was believed, by many historians, to have produced one of the country's most ineffective public education systems, one in
which a majority of students dropped out as early as the first or second grade
to help support their families. Moreover, in many cases, public schools for African Americans in the early twentieth-century South were largely nonexistent.
Harvie Johnson, born in 1918, briefly attended a makeshift school inside a
local church while growing up in the Sandhill community of rural Bienville
Parish, but he often left classes early or skipped them entirely to help his family farm or pick cotton. The cotton season still shaped the African American
school year, and, consequently, the annual school term ran for only three to
four months per year for African American students. Many African American
men of the first transitional generation thus failed to recognize any correlation
between educational levels and their family's subsistence.

In the first two decades of the twentieth century, educational facilities for
African American children in rural northern Louisiana were crude at best. In

1915, less than half of all African American children in Louisiana were enrolled in a state-registered public school, and not even a quarter of those children attended classes on a daily basis, as former sharecropper, and later Hodge mill worker, Harvie Johnson attests. "Sometimes, there would be a nice crowd [at school]," Johnson remembers, "but if it rained" fewer children would attend. Moreover, Johnson contends, in any given year, "we weren't going to school but for four months, that's all." African American children like Harvie Johnson also bore the burden of frequent uprootings, having been forced to move with their parents when seasonal employment became available, which prevented regular school attendance. Parents also hired out their children on a seasonal basis to relatives, or even to white planters. As children, members of the first transitional generation never enjoyed sustained access to education, and their economic decisions, therefore, typically hinged primarily on familial obligations.

Harry Mims, who was born in 1914 and grew up on a cattle farm in Pleasant Hill, situated in the northwestern corner of the state, watched his father labor seven days a week for an income that, in essence, merely put food on his family's table, with no cash left over. The Mims family supplemented their father's meager wages by relying mainly on neighbor-to-neighbor trade. "We used to kill cows and we didn't salt them down," Mims recalls. "We took them around to all the neighbors." So when Mims moved northeast to Hodge in the 1930s to join an older brother already at work in the Southern Advance wood yard, the prospect of a permanent wage position appealed to the former farmer. "I preferred living in a town, working a job," adds Mims, "[because] I always wanted to do something for myself." Mims did get married a few years later, but the home life he would go on to establish with his own nuclear family in Hodge looked much different from the farm life he had known in Pleasant Hill.

The switch to wage labor represented what Jones terms a renegotiation of "responsibilities to families and communities." When African Americans began to establish family households in small industrial towns like Hodge and Jonesboro, work was no longer directly rooted within the home and family structure, as it had been on the farm. But although husbands and fathers now headed to the mill each morning for work and not to the backyard, the traditions of rural life were not immediately abandoned, but instead entered a transitional phase in which they influenced the educational opportunities for children of the second transitional generation.

Educational opportunities also entered a transitional phase beginning in the 1930s as African American children in northern Louisiana paper mill towns began attending school more regularly. The first generation of children who grew up entirely within the towns of Hodge and Jonesboro received a more stable public education than had their parents or any of their ancestors. But while these children benefited from a new community emphasis on formal education, they continued to help support their families' basic survival needs. R. L. Belton's primary school, for example, stood only five blocks from the three-room shotgun house he shared with his parents and five siblings in Jonesboro, but before he could walk to school in the mornings, he was responsible for milking the family's cow (kept in the backyard) and helping his mother bake the morning bread. All of his duties were completed in a house, notes Belton, with "no running water, no lights, no telephone, [and] no gas." Henry Kimp, born in 1932, started working odd jobs when he was just thirteen years old, in order to contribute to his family's income. "I shined shoes, downtown, in Jonesboro," Kimp remembers. Three years later, Kimp began a full-time job and never graduated from Jackson High School, Jonesboro's segregated high school. "I was about sixteen years old," Kimp recalls, "when I started working for a [local] funeral company" for whom he "drove around [and] picked up bodies." African American workers had quickly adapted to a life of wage labor, but most of the work available to them still required no more than a rudimentary education. Well into the mid-twentieth century, young black men "could drop out of school," Belton remembers, "and get a job that could put bacon on the table." Belton's reference to "bacon on the table," not education or even material wealth, as the measure of a worker's success, shows that members of the second transitional generation remained heavily influenced by their parents' rural ideals and customs.

African Americans' educational networks in the early twentieth century had been, after all, socially-dependent institutions, not entities independently capable of cultural change. The sharecropping culture, and the period of Southern industrialization that followed it, did not witness the emergence of a viable public school system for its students largely because white employers required of them no education or job-specific training. In 1934, educational historian Horace Mann Bond had already posited that "the [American] school has never built a new social order," but has instead been the "product and interpreter" of social problems, such as the proliferation of racial capitalism in northern Louisiana. African Americans' demands for education in the early twentieth-century South, for example, often remained dependent on occupational opportunities. In Hodge and Jonesboro, for example, Southern Advance took great pains to establish training programs at the local high schools.

White managers at the Southern Advance paper mill in Hodge, like their counterparts in mills throughout the piney woods South, ultimately failed to promote any improvement in African American education. By all accounts, white employers were implicitly hostile to black educational advancement, a claim R. L. Belton supports. "[If] you were black," Belton recalls, "they [administrators] didn't like you to be successful." According to Minchin, many African American paper mill workers employed in the first half of the twentieth century understated their level of education because they knew their white employers held fast to a "strong back and weak minds" mentality that devalued education and intelligence. Harvie Johnson remembers the day he was recruited by a Southern Advance agent, right off a street in Hodge as he walked to buy breakfast at a local café: "He [the agent] says 'what grade were you'," Johnson recalls, "and I told him third grade when I quit school, he says 'that's all?'" and gave Johnson an application for employment. Johnson started wage work for Southern Advance soon afterward in a manual-labor position, unloading logs in the wood yard, a job which required no schooling whatsoever. "[If you were] taking a stack of lumber down to the mill," Johnson adds, "you didn't need to have no education."

Although black workers received little formal education in the early twentieth century, one African American tradition—house-to-house visitation between neighbors in a community—actually encouraged education among African American mill children in Hodge and Jonesboro. In the early 1920s, African American educator G. L. Hawk arrived in Jonesboro to help school-building efforts in the area. Hawk had been trained at Coleman College in Gibsland, located thirty miles northeast of Jonesboro and Hodge. In 1922, Hawk founded Jonesboro Colored School, which would later be known as Hawk Elementary School. While only a few children could actually afford to attend the school, a large number of African American children also benefited from Hawk's vast private library, which numbered over 1,000 volumes at the time of his death in 1953. Henry Kimp remembers that, as a small child in the early 1940s, he walked several miles from his home to Hawk's on a regular basis, an activity his parents encouraged. "I was six, seven years old," Kimp recalls, and Hawk "had already retired, but we would go up to his house in the summer and read in his library." However, Hawk's encouragement of education within the home proved exceptional in a community that still explicitly defined employment and occupational opportunities according to race, not education.

By the 1940s, African American public schools in northern Louisiana had improved only marginally since the turn of the century, when most had been run haphazardly by local black churches because of the dearth of governmental support. In 1940, notes Adam Fairclough, "the amount allocated [by the government] for each black child [in Louisiana] amounted to twenty-four percent of the amount allocated to whites." In addition, the African American school year still ran, on average, thirty-seven days shorter than the white school year. Lumber and paper corporations often donated money toward school-building efforts in local African American communities, but Jim Crow restrictions usually prevented the money from being used properly in even primary educational institutions. Davis Brothers Lumber Company in Ansley, Louisiana, for example, bequeathed land to the Jackson Parish School Board in the early 1940s for new African American primary schools. But a decrease in enrollment followed the onset of American involvement in World War II, which coincided with the need for children to take on increased responsibilities within their homes and an exodus of children accompanying their parents to the Northern cities where well-paying war production jobs were available. The declining enrollment resulted in the closure of the black primary schools that had been built with Davis Brothers' money. Meanwhile, the all-white Jackson Parish School Board closed none of the area's white primary schools. White school authorities, argued economist William H. Gray in his 1941 study of African American teachers in Jackson Parish, assumed a "laissez faire attitude" when it came to managing both the school terms and the curricula of African American schools.

Jackson Parish's Jim Crow school board, like many school boards in the early- to mid-twentieth-century South, helped ensure that educational opportunities for members of the second African American transitional generation remained inferior to those of white children well into the 1950s. For example, in 1941, 50 percent of the teachers employed by Jackson Parish's African

American schools were natives of the parish, and most had received only a limited local education themselves. Only one-third of the teachers possessed a college degree. The parish failed to attract more highly qualified employees because it paid African American teachers, on average, only 47 percent of what it paid white teachers. In the early- to mid-twentieth century, the only members of the Hodge and Jonesboro African American communities heavily encouraged to pursue a degree were women who attended African American institutions of higher learning including nearby Grambling College. At Southern African American colleges, "there was only two [career paths] you could take," remembers R. L. Belton, either "to be an elementary school teacher" or "to come out to be a coach."

Northern Louisiana's African American workers often chose industrial work because they could earn a higher income in blue-collar jobs that required no education than black professionals in white-collar jobs. In the 1950s, permanent wage employment offered economic stability in jobs that paid relatively well but required little schooling. As a result, although education was more readily available to African American children growing up in the 1940s and 1950s, work at the mill was still strongly encouraged by family members and teachers. "We made more [money at the mill] than some professional folk," recalls R. L. Belton, "because the only professional people we had were [relatively poorly paid] school teachers."

Many members of the second transitional generation became determined, early in their educational careers, to enter the industrial workforce because the curriculum at segregated schools in northern Louisiana, as throughout the South, offered few alternatives. Jonesboro's African American Jackson High School offered vocational classes only in home economics and agriculture. School-building efforts, backed by the Chicago-based Rosenwald Fund and other philanthropic organizations, drew distinct racial lines in the educational community. These lines were clearly evident at Jackson High School, where the newly built library, added in the 1950s, housed dozens of empty bookshelves. Across town, the exclusively white high school had a fully-stocked library. Thus, although African American students had schools, they lacked educational and professional opportunities equal to those of whites. In May 1954, the United States Supreme Court ruled in favor of public school integration in *Brown* v. *Board of Education*. In northern Louisiana, however, and all across the South, the enforcement of *Brown* would be, through the 1950s and 1960s, gradual at best.

Still, African American workers like R. L. Belton and other members of the second transitional generation, could enter the industrial workforce at the local mill, which in 1955 transferred ownership from Southern Advance to the Continental Can Company, without a high school or college degree and make enough money to afford a house, and even an automobile, while supporting a family. Although African Americans remained tied to those low-paying industrial jobs labeled "black" until the 1964 Civil Rights Act, the demands of earning a family wage often took precedence over the push for integration in the community, at schools, and at the mill. "You wanted more money," reasons Belton, "because you wasn't thinking about integrating." Belton, who had dropped out of Grambling College after only one term, found no professional opportunities locally, like many members of the second transitional generation. "I didn't really want to go [to college]," Belton recalls, and, moreover, "most of us went [only] a year, two years, six months."

Although some African Americans in Hodge and Jonesboro, especially those whose parents made the permanent transition into industrial wage work in the 1920s and 1930s, could afford a college education, a degree carried with it few advantages within the black community. As R. L. Belton attests, employment at the paper mill paid more than any professional occupation, particularly education, which was the only career track available at Grambling and the other African American colleges in the region. One of Belton's younger sisters, however, enrolled in a nursing program at a college in Denver, Colorado, the nearest institution that would admit an African American student. Those who wished to pursue professional careers, as the experience of Belton's younger sister makes evident, had to leave northern Louisiana far behind.

Into the 1950s, African American men of the second transitional generation, who received a more extensive primary and secondary education than their fathers, still faced life in a local and national economy that confined them to "black" jobs. Much like their fathers, sharecroppers who had moved into the local industrial economy on a seasonal basis in the first two decades of the twentieth century, Belton and many other men of his generation migrated in the mid-1950s when a slump in the paper industry led to numerous layoffs. African Americans were "especially vulnerable to layoffs," Fairclough points out, because "they were less educated and less skilled [than whites]" and because white workers claimed "black" work in hard times. Belton lost his job as a log tumbler in the Continental wood yard around that time and moved to Detroit in search of industrial work, the only kind of work he knew how to do. "We thought that the North was the Promised Land," Belton recalls, "but it wasn't." Northern cities offered African American workers steady industrial wage work, but many migrants returned to northern Louisiana after only a few years, usually to reunite with family members.

Men who returned from the North found that mechanization was rapidly eliminating the "black" jobs that they had traditionally performed. Lacking any education, "black employees began to feel full force," argues historian Jacqueline Jones, "the technological changes that would gain widespread attention only when they began to affect white[s]." Blacks would not achieve workplace integration or the elimination of the discriminatory "lines of progression" until the late 1960s.

The first transitional generation of African American male workers in northern Louisiana came to an initial realization that moving toward permanent industrial employment would better support their families, while the second transitional generation came to the realization that remaining successful in the industrial workforce required education. Harvie Johnson, born in 1918, advocated education for his children because of his own limited opportunities to attend school as a child. Johnson wanted his children's education "to be better than mine." "They went [to school], if they weren't sick, they went." Johnson also recalls his own childhood, spent working as a sharecropper on a farm in rural northern Louisiana, and the acts of racial discrimination that he experienced firsthand. "The white folks," Johnson recalled recently, "was bused to school even before there was a bus, in wagons," and they would "yell [and] shout [insults] at us" through the windows. Johnson never rode on a school bus or sat in an integrated classroom, but his children, members of the second transitional generation, eventually did.

Over two distinct generations in the early twentieth century, African American men in northern Louisiana made the permanent transition from farm life into industrial life in large numbers. The first transitional generation worked primarily to support their families through unskilled wage labor in the lumber and paper industries, still partially clinging both to the ideals of their former agrarian existence and the belief that work involved the efforts of every member in a family unit, even the children. Those children, members of a second transitional generation, struck a delicate balance between familial obligation and limited educational and occupational opportunities in an industrial economy dominated by notions of "whiteness."

But once the lumber and paper industries in northern Louisiana began to mechanize operations in the 1950s, they no longer required a large, uneducated labor force and, therefore, no longer recruited many illiterate, unskilled African American workers. Education, which had never been an economic necessity for African Americans in the local industrial wage workforce, began to pay financial dividends for those workers who had remained in school. Members of the second transitional generation, who eschewed educational opportunities for industrial employment, ultimately found themselves out of work. Beginning in the 1950s, and certainly by the 1960s, there were "no more ditches to be dug [and] no more cotton to be picked," recalls R. L. Belton, who eventually trained for skilled positions at the Hodge mill in the 1960s and survived mechanization. Belton, a member of the second transitional generation, admittedly rewrote his own definition of personal success as he aged, and it no longer included his father's benchmarks—rural independence, land ownership, or even a cohesive family unit living under one roof. "All [my children] have experienced, or are experiencing, what I call the 'American Dream'," Belton recently explained, "and that is to have your own transportation and your own home, and a job." For African American workers and their families in northern Louisiana, as Belton's statement implies, the common definition of economic success had changed—from what a family worked toward together, to what set its individual members apart.

Questions
1. How did the first generation described in this piece define success?
2. How did employment opportunities change for African Americans from the first transitional generation to the second?
3. Describe the ways in which employment opportunities were defined and limited by race.
4. How did low pay and limited employment opportunities affect educational choices for African Americans?
5. What was the impact of limited education on African Americans after the lumber and paper industries began to mechanize in the 1950s?

PART EIGHT

CULTURE AND ENVIRONMENT
IN MODERN LOUISIANA

Louisiana's economy in the late twentieth century increasingly revolved around attracting tourists to the state. Although the legalization of gambling in certain locales played a role in bringing in outsiders, many, if not most, of the travelers who came to Louisiana sought either some form of cultural experience or, increasingly, an encounter with parts of the state's natural history. Hundreds of thousands of tourists arrived annually to hear Louisiana's music, eat its food, and visit its museums, and thousands more trekked there to take swamp tours, go on fishing or hunting trips, bird watch, and engage in many other types of outdoor activities.

Tourism put Louisianians to work, provided customers to business owners, and grew Louisiana's state treasury through tax dollars. Along with those positives, however, often came negatives. The first two essays in Part Eight, Mark Souther's examination of jazz music as a mechanism for enhancing tourism in New Orleans, and Marcelle Bienvenu, Carl Brasseaux, and Ryan Brasseaux's study of the commercialization of Cajun cuisine, consider both the positive and negative aspects of outside interest in two of Louisiana's cultural hallmarks. Souther shows that jazz teetered on the edge of extinction in New Orleans before its revival as a means of attracting tourists after World War II, while Bienvenu and the Brasseauxs show that the Cajun food craze that swept the United States in the late twentieth century reflected a much longer trend in the commercialization of southern Louisiana food products. Both essays also point to the potential pitfalls—jazz musicians simply pandering for a buck and

Cajun culture becoming a caricature of itself—inherent in creating outside interest in living cultural forms.

Finally, we consider a vulnerable and valuable ecosystem, one that previous generations misunderstood. Louisiana's coastal wetlands provide hurricane protection for coastal communities, shelter a vast array of wildlife, provide resting places for migrating waterfowl, and nurture unique cultural traditions. Today, those wetlands are being lost at an alarming rate, endangering not only the burgeoning eco-tourism industry but entire ways of life. In the final essay of this collection, Tyler Priest and Jason Theriot survey the losses and assess some of the causes of wetlands depletion. They show that no single factor has led to the decline. In fact, not all of the losses are attributable to human causes. Nevertheless, the loss of wetlands is a potentially catastrophic development for Louisiana's economy, natural environment, and people.

MAKING THE "BIRTHPLACE OF JAZZ": TOURISM AND MUSICAL HERITAGE MARKETING IN NEW ORLEANS

by J. Mark Souther

This article traces the revival of new orleans-style jazz in the five decades after 1940, focusing on the renewal of local interest in a dying artistic tradition, the impact of tourism on jazz, the popularization of the Dixieland tradition through marketing, concerts, tours and festivals, the modern brass band movement, and the use of the music by various groups in shaping public memory and packaging it for tourist consumption. Like the preservation of the French Quarter, the resurrection of Dixieland triggered a contest for control over public memory, although in the case of jazz it took much longer for any degree of consensus on the value of the music to crystallize. The influence of tourism both set jazz apart from its cultural moorings and induced a renewed grassroots interest, eventually creating a sustainable cultural resource that enriched the community and fueled further tourism development. If the French Quarter's transformation into a "plastic" outdoor history shrine and freak show represented tourism run amok, the renaissance of local jazz reflected the power of tourism to pollinate and nurture the city's cultural heritage. The checkered effect of tourism on the revival of New Orleans jazz complicates the common scholarly assumption that tourism simply corrodes or adulterates local culture. . . .

Originally published in *Louisiana History: The Journal of the Louisiana Historical Association* 44 (Winter 2003): 39–73. Used by permission of the Louisiana Historical Association.

[By World War II] New Orleans had long been known as the birthplace of jazz. Widely held to have sprung from the more primitive sounds accompanying African American dances in Congo Square in the nineteenth century, in the first two decades of the twentieth jazz matured in the famous Storyville red-light district. . . . Attracting jazz musicians as well as gamblers and prostitutes, Storyville solidified among tourists the perception of what New Orleans was supposed to be. Jazz figured prominently in that image. storyville

Prior to 1940, musicians found ample employment. Most played outside the city's identifiable tourist areas. . . . Mardi Gras parades afforded the one sure way for jazz musicians to be paid for their work and for younger players to enjoy the spotlight. . . . Any tourists who viewed such a spectacle doubtless assumed that New Orleans jazz continued to thrive.

Storyville's closure during World War I and the concurrent exodus of many African Americans seeking better employment and freedom from the harsher manifestations of racial prejudice set jazz music on a long decline. Prohibition and especially the Great Depression brought the demise of many clubs that maintained performing jazz bands, and by World War II jazz was moribund. In the 1940s few musicians could find steady employment. . . . [F]or many of the city's best musicians, leaving New Orleans afforded the only hope of realizing their potential. decline of jazz

Far from recognizing jazz as a potential tourist attraction, prominent white New Orleanians usually . . . dismissed it as little more than a suitable dance music. . . . Upper-class New Orleanians connoted jazz with the crime, vice, and libidinous carousing that had characterized Storyville. . . .

Important trends in the second quarter of the twentieth century dealt a sharp blow to the continued vitality of jazz music. By World War II, New Orleans had the smallest proportion of African Americans of any major Southern city, paving the way for a dilution of black cultural forms that had roots in an earlier period when the Crescent City had a majority-black population. The war-induced transition from merchandising to manufacturing prompted a considerable influx of rural, Protestant Southerners into a city long dominated by Roman Catholics. Such newcomers often favored hillbilly music and had little regard for jazz or the permissive atmosphere in which it had flourished. No longer appreciated, jazz musicians usually had to take up other jobs to supplement meager earnings from performing. Club jobs typically demanded long hours and provided abysmal wages. In addition, increased attention to war and commerce lessened the city's traditional penchant for revelry. Mardi Gras parades, perennially a major source of income for the city's musicians, were suspended for the duration of the war. . . .

By World War II, jazz had practically disappeared from the areas of New Orleans most commonly frequented by tourists. The growing popularity of radio fostered the standardization of national popular music tastes, and French Quarter bars increasingly installed jukeboxes to save the expense of hiring local musicians. Leading New Orleans hotels had once employed local talent in jazz concerts, vaudeville acts, or programs . . . [but] by 1940, national acts had almost thoroughly replaced local talent in New Orleans' primary hotels. To be sure, plenty of talented musicians continued to play jazz in New Orleans, but tourists were unlikely to find them. . . .

Although jazz appreciation stood at low ebb in the 1940s, the coalescence of eager jazz pilgrims from around the world with a cadre of local white elite jazz enthusiasts triggered a chain of events that eventually rendered the art form practically synonymous with New Orleans. Prior to that time, Crescent City bands seldom recorded their music in New Orleans, usually venturing north instead and recording in bands mixed with Northern musicians. . . . With the exception of Baby Dodds, none of the city's biggest figures, including Louis Armstrong, Freddy Keppard, Jelly Roll Morton, Johnny Dodds, and Kid Ory, recorded in New Orleans. Not one New Orleans recording session in the 1930s featured African Americans. In fact, one 1936 Sharkey Bonano record constituted the entire repertoire of 1930s New Orleans jazz recording.

By the Second World War, outsiders began taking an interest in encountering New Orleans jazz on its own turf. In 1940, Heywood Hale Broun, editor of the New York-based Hot Record Society's newsletter H.R.S. Rag, traveled to New Orleans in hopes of recording the remaining vestiges of traditional jazz before the old musicians died. . . . William Russell, a classically trained violinist, percussionist, and composer, was among the jazz scholars who came to the Crescent City beginning in the late 1930s to collect material for the pioneering book Jazzmen. Russell "discovered" trumpeter Bunk Johnson on a farm in New Iberia. . . . After helping Johnson get a new set of teeth and a trumpet, Russell recorded him in 1942. . . .

The influx of servicemen during World War II also played an important role in stimulating interest in New Orleans jazz. Many soldiers stationed on bases around Louisiana, Mississippi, and Alabama, as well as industrial workers employed by Higgins Industries spent their weekends exploring the Crescent City's elusive and vestigial jazz scene. . . . More often than not, these sojourners found less jazz than they expected, and some later returned to ameliorate the problem. Richard Binion "Dick" Allen . . ., a Georgia native, discovered New Orleans jazz during World War II while serving in the Navy at nearby Gulfport, Mississippi. In his spare time, Allen went to New Orleans, where he befriended longtime drummer Monk Hazel, who introduced him to the city's music scene. Four years after the war ended, Allen moved to New Orleans and worked tirelessly for the cultivation of the city's living jazz traditions, eventually serving as the first curator of the William Ransom Hogan Jazz Archive at Tulane University.

The transformation of New Orleans jazz took about twenty-five years to accomplish. Jazz clubs, comprised mostly of the city's prominent citizens, along with foundations, museums, archives, and concert halls, initially provided the most effective vehicles for the jazz revival. The first New Orleans-based jazz club, the National Jazz Foundation (NJF), formed in May 1944 to preserve and promote the city's music. The NJF was a broad-based organization, but it tended to draw most heavily from the old elite. . . . The organization intended to stage concerts and band competitions as well as to open a jazz museum. It also assisted tourists who went to New Orleans in search of jazz music. . . . However, the organization focused more heavily on national performers than local musicians. Recalling his difficulties in getting support from the NJF, Crescent City jazzman Johnny Wiggs later wrote, "I learned that this fine group had no use for local musicians. No, they had to have big names like Benny Goodman, [Eddie] Condon, Louie. They spent thousands of dollars on these bands while the New Orleans musicians stayed buried under rocks." Although the NJF failed to start a museum and disbanded in April 1947, it set in motion a determined effort by some leading New Orleanians to resurrect jazz.

Less than a year later, on Mardi Gras Day, a small group of jazz enthusiasts gathered along the Zulu parade route and decided to establish the New Orleans Jazz Club (NOJC) to continue the agenda of the defunct NJF. The founders called upon many former NJF members. Like its predecessor, the

NOJC served primarily as a social vehicle for an upper-class group having in common a passion for jazz music, but it also furthered the resurrection of the art form through publicity and the employment of languishing musicians for concerts, festivals, and recording sessions. . . .

Just as jazz enthusiasts from around the world awakened well-positioned New Orleanians to the possibilities the music offered their city, the rise of tourism shaped the course of the jazz revival. What had started as a reinvigoration of a black music genre by jazz enthusiasts gradually became a cash cow for tourism promoters. The tourist trade fostered jazz in much the same haphazard fashion that the white business community had always treated the music, exploiting it with little regard for the musicians' welfare. Even after the recrudescence of jazz, it remained difficult for most musicians to find work more than three nights a week unless they were fortunate enough to sign on at one of the relatively few hotels or nightclubs that kept a house band or performer.

Although jazz had flourished through the constant replenishment of musicians with young talent, the tourist trade devoted inordinate attention to the oldest musicians. . . . In addition, jazz tended heavily toward New Orleans-style, or Dixieland, because that fit tourists' conception of what the music should be.

While the enthusiasm of outsiders and the formation of local clubs devoted to the furthering of jazz contributed heavily to the jazz revival by awakening native and tourist appreciation for the music, locally-orchestrated dissemination of jazz music across the nation proved a similarly important catalyst for harnessing the art form to the city's tourist trade. For many years New Orleans passively exported jazz through the emigration of its most promising young musicians to such cities as New York, Chicago, Kansas City, and Los Angeles. There the music adapted to progressive, ever changing tastes while New Orleans remained more insular. Because New Orleans stood relatively isolated from mainstream American culture into the 1940s, its jazz music remained less changed than that played elsewhere. The city served as the cradle of music forms that evolved and developed after they left.

The retention of a distinctive, traditional New Orleans style seemed an ideal springboard for cultural tourism. Yet New Orleanians had failed to assert themselves for decades, allowing New York-based record labels to dominate the marketing of jazz music and cities. In the 1950s, New Orleans watched as cities like Newport, Rhode Island, began staging jazz festivals that attracted international attention. Furthermore, because jazz became exceedingly rare in New Orleans' main tourist areas by the 1940s, visitors seldom experienced New Orleans-style jazz. Before New Orleans could lay claim to being the birthplace of jazz and become a Mecca for jazz pilgrims, it had to find a way of taking Mecca to the pilgrims.

A succession of local initiatives in the two decades following 1948 brought New Orleans jazz squarely into the national consciousness. Radio broadcasting, recording, and touring proved essential in stimulating the city's cultural tourism effort. Shortly after the New Orleans Jazz Club formed, the organization began sponsoring a weekly jazz show broadcast on radio station. . . .WWL, a 50,000-watt clear-channel radio station [that] could be heard in nationwide in the evenings. . . . In 1950, radio station WDSU partnered with the United States Treasury and the American Broadcasting Corporation to feature a weekly jazz broadcast called "Dixieland Jambake" to help sell United States Defense Bonds during the Korean War. All ABC radio affiliates in the United States and Hawaii carried "Dixieland Jambake," giving New Orleans jazz another major boost. . . .

The establishment of traditional jazz as a major tourist attraction in the French Quarter has often been attributed to the founding of Preservation Hall, a jazz venue that opened in 1961 to reintroduce a number of old, long-forgotten jazzmen. Preservation Hall built its reputation not simply by providing an authentic atmosphere that appealed to Americans' growing nostalgia for an imagined past, but also by sending its musicians around the world on tours. Although Preservation Hall's promoters truly saw themselves as breaking new ground, the Preservation Hall model actually had its antecedent in the efforts of Joe Mares, Jr. Along with his brother, trumpeter Paul Mares, Joe Mares operated Mares Brothers Furs, purveyors of furs, pelts, and alligator skins . . . in the French Quarter. In 1953, Mares started Southland Recording Studio and the Southland Records label in the fur company building. . . . Mares's Southland recordings found their way into national distribution, putting the first real dent in the "colonial" co-opting of local talent by New York and Chicago labels. Mares intended Southland to give New Orleans musicians, passed over by outside recording companies and unable or unwilling to leave the city, a chance to be heard. Mares recorded many musicians who later achieved national fame, including Pete Fountain, Al Hirt, Jack Delaney, Johnny Wiggs, Sharkey Bonano, and Santo Pecora.

In addition to recording New Orleans musicians, Mares took them to perform on the West Coast beginning in 1954, laying the groundwork for what eventually became a favored tool of the city's tourism officials for invoking interest in visiting the Crescent City. . . . By 1961, Mares's affiliation with the Dixieland Jubilee had led entertainment tycoon Walt Disney to take notice. That year Disney hired a six-piece New Orleans jazz band fronted by St. Cyr to play aboard the stern wheeler Mark Twain as it plied the Disneyland River in the Magic Kingdom, replacing the rather lackluster sounds of wild animals and the crackling flames of a log cabin supposedly set afire by Indians. . . . By 1964, Dixieland at Disneyland featured several Dixieland bands in a floating Mardi Gras parade on the Disneyland River. As each raft passed, a history of the nationwide dissemination of jazz unfolded from the narrator's script. Sharkey Bonano and His Kings of Dixieland belted out the "Bogalusa Strut" and other tunes aboard a raft decorated to represent Bourbon Street. For the finale, all the musicians congregated on Tom Sawyer Island as the riverboat Mark Twain sailed in with more than two hundred park guests holding sparklers. Roman candles and other fireworks exploded in the night sky above the island as Louis Armstrong blew "When the Saints Go Marching In." After the show, various jazz bands played throughout the California theme park. . . . The New Orleans Jazz Club of California, one of several such West Coast organizations dedicated to Crescent City music, observed, "To jazz fans, this is like Mecca coming to the pilgrim." In 1966 Walt Disney opened New Orleans Square, a three-quarter scale replica of the French Quarter, in his Magic Kingdom, affording a more evocative setting for jazz music. The Disney shows in the 1960s reflected more than the personal tastes of Walt Disney, who acknowledged his fondness for the Crescent City. In addition, the shows reflected the growing popularity of New Orleans culture across the nation as the media made the Crescent City known in most every household. . . . *Disney*

If Joe Mares, assisted by Disney, supplied the prototype of touring to market jazz to potential tourists, the founders of Preservation Hall brought the model to perfection. Although it would be an exaggeration to suggest that outsiders' enthusiasm for the city's musical legacy stirred New Orleanians from their apathy, there is some truth in such a statement. Just as the influx of servicemen and jazz devotees in the 1940s provided essential ingredients for the first wave of the jazz revival, newcomers determinedly provided an exception to the rule of the proliferation of strip shows and other cheap thrills in the French Quarter in the late 1950s and after. E. Lorenz "Larry" Borenstein, the son of Ukrainian immigrants to Milwaukee and grand-nephew of Leon Trotsky, came to New Orleans in 1941 on the heels of an early career in circuses and sideshows in the Midwest. Borenstein, an avid collector, opened a succession of small shops in the French Quarter and eventually started Associated Artists' Gallery in 1954 . . ., adjacent to famous Pat O'Brien's courtyard bar. Unable to leave his shop in the evenings to hear jazz shows, he encouraged musicians to play informal sessions in the back of his gallery. Borenstein supplied beer and passed a kitty to pay the jazzmen. Although he insisted he was simply a patron of the arts and expected no profit, Borenstein did use the concerts as a vehicle to make business contacts.

Borenstein's sessions evolved into Preservation Hall, essentially a jazz cooperative, which officially opened to the general public on June 10, 1961. . . . Early audiences included mostly locals and Tulane University students, in contrast to the tourist traps on nearby Bourbon Street. Unlike the gaudy Bourbon Street clubs, Preservation Hall's interior was essentially unadorned except for a few Belgian paintings. The Hall served no drinks and provided only a few chairs for patrons. Advertisements billed the club as having "No Drinks—No Girls—No Gimmicks—Just Real Music!"

Although Preservation Hall failed to turn a profit in its first two years, it soon soared in popularity as tourists became its main clientele. In 1962 Borenstein turned the Hall over to Allen and Sandra Jaffe, jazz enthusiasts who had come to New Orleans from Philadelphia the previous year. Allan Jaffe, the son of a mandolinist and music teacher and grandson of a French hornist in a Russian Imperial Army band, was born in Pottsville, Pennsylvania, in 1935. After studying cornet and piano as a child, Jaffe settled on the tuba, which he played in the Valley Forge Military Academy marching band before enrolling in the University of Pennsylvania. He and his wife Sandra enjoyed listening to jazz phonograph records and decided to move to New Orleans to pursue their interest. After relocating to the Crescent City, Allan worked as assistant controller for the D. H. Holmes department store on Canal Street, while

Sandra took a job at a local market research firm. They searched for good jazz in the evenings and were dismayed by the paucity of music they found. . . . Disillusioned by the commercialized music catering to tourists on Bourbon Street, one night the Jaffes found themselves invited to Borenstein's gallery after a concert by the Eureka Brass Band outside the Cabildo, a couple of blocks away. They soon worked their way into Borenstein's circle and helped form the New Orleans Society for the Preservation of Traditional Jazz, whose key endeavor was promoting Preservation Hall.

Immersing themselves in the timeless milieu of the French Quarter, the Jaffes moved into the former apartment of Pop Weitzel, a famed jazzman, on St. Peter Street near their jazz hall. Allan began sitting in on tuba, while Sandra passed the kitty. . . .

The Jaffes observed that tourists believed erroneously that Preservation Hall had been in operation since the halcyon days of jazz and that the musical style remained unchanged since that time. Understanding that perception often was more important than reality when building a tourist attraction, the Jaffes studiously avoided making any changes to either the building or the performances. Further, the couple wanted their jazz hall to provide an alternative to the many gaudy tourist traps then proliferating throughout the neighborhood. Indeed, the wilder the French Quarter became, the more authentic Preservation Hall seemed.

Preservation Hall's popularity relied not only on its perceived authenticity, but also on promotion through the news media and tours. Publications ranging from jazz journals to popular magazines and newspapers lavished praise on the jazz hall. . . . However, touring accomplished more than any news story, for it actually took the music to people across the country and around the world. Touring began in earnest in 1963 with a summer trip to Chicago by train. Shortly thereafter, the Jaffes took a Preservation Hall band on a three-month tour of Japan, playing ninety-two concerts for more than a quarter million people. . . . By the late 1960s, several different Preservation Hall bands were making regular tours. Through these tours, the Jaffes managed to plant Preservation Hall in people's minds as a must-see New Orleans attraction.

Preservation Hall's greatest contribution to the jazz revival lay in providing steady employment to forgotten, downtrodden New Orleans jazz players, many of whom lived in dire poverty in the sunset of their lives. The Hall also provided an after-hours meeting place for civil rights lawyers and activists, although police sometimes raided the safe haven for allowing mixed-race sessions, often using the vague charge of "disturbing the peace". . . .

Preservation Hall might have had an even more dramatic impact on tourism in New Orleans had the jazz establishment joined ranks more completely. Instead, factionalism within the establishment—including among the NOJC, Preservation Hall, the Jazz Archive at Tulane University, and others—precluded the kind of cooperation that might have led to a more comprehensive cultural tourism marketing campaign. . . .

Even though jazz promoters did not always support Preservation Hall's mission, the jazz hall succeeded beyond its founders' wildest imagination. It fed off the spectacular rise in tourism beginning in the 1960s, the ascendant American penchant for seeking the nation's cultural roots, and the increasing rarity of old jazzmen. . . .

Preservation Hall proved so successful . . . that in later years young musicians, who had come of age during the height of the civil rights struggle and associated Dixieland with segregation, hard times, and an Uncle Tom mentality, became inspired to take up the traditional style of playing. Preservation Hall was, perhaps, two decades ahead of its time, for only in the 1980s would New Orleans tourism promoters fully tap the potential of authentic heritage experiences to stimulate discretionary or leisure tourism.

The Jaffes operated under the assumption that they were helping traditional New Orleans jazz enjoy a dignified last stand before it sank into oblivion. In addition to his determination to provide a no-frills venue in which locals and tourists could enjoy Dixieland without being forced to observe an exorbitant drink minimum, Allan Jaffe supported another fading jazz tradition by sponsoring occasional Sunday afternoon French Quarter parades led by the Eureka Brass Band. In 1963 Jaffe confessed that he fully expected the revival to last only five to ten years because no younger musicians seemed to have an interest in the art form.

Jaffe was not alone in his belief that the revival of Dixieland jazz represented a golden opportunity for the world to experience New Orleans's unique cultural commodity before it died forever. Many others also sensed the passing of an era. Dr. Edmond Souchon of the NOJC observed, "The young Negroes don't want anything that smacks of Uncle Tom or minstrelsy." With the death of Onward Brass Band founder Paul Barbarin, one Tulane University student wrote, the city lost one more piece of its soul forever: "When the last New Orleans jazz musician blows the last dirge, a great era of American music will come to an end". . . .

By the mid-1970s, however, the city was sprouting a new crop of enthusiastic musicians eager to learn traditional jazz, leading Jaffe to conclude that Preservation Hall might remain a New Orleans cultural icon for many years to come.

In the late 1960s, tourism officials began using jazz bands to promote New Orleans to visitors. The Louisiana Tourist Development Commission sponsored European tours by the Olympia Brass Band in 1967 and 1968 and sent the band to the National Association of Travel Organizations convention in Detroit in 1968. The commission also distributed an album featuring the music of Al Hirt, Ronnie Kole, and Louis Cottrell to visiting VIPs. The examples of Southland Records and tours by Preservation Hall bands, then, found their way into official tourism promotion policies.

While Preservation Hall gave New Orleans a highly visible, year-round, jazz-related tourist attraction, the establishment of an annual jazz festival assured an influx of tourists into the Crescent City in the late spring, traditionally a slack time for tourism. In a city noted for Mardi Gras and the Sugar Bowl, a jazz festival would lend cultural pastiche and inform the world that New Orleans had more to offer than raucous nightlife. A festival not only would help reinforce the city's claim of being the birthplace of jazz, it would also draw attention to the music's continuing vitality in the Crescent City. What began as an unfulfilled part of the NOJC's mission in the 1950s turned into an event of international repute by the end of the next decade. However, the success of the undertaking awaited Crescent City leaders' realization of the necessity of working across racial lines. Whereas the NOJC, Southland Recording Studio, and Preservation Hall witnessed whites promoting segregated talent, the jazz festival ultimately would involve both races not only on stage but in planning.

The idea of staging a jazz festival in New Orleans originated in the New Orleans Jazz Club, which held a small event with eight concerts in Congo Square in both 1949 and 1950. By 1951 the format had evolved into one large concert with several bands playing in Municipal Auditorium. . . . Rather than building upon this promising start, however, the festival encountered difficulties for the rest of the decade. . . . largely because the NOJC tried to handle the event single-handedly. Broader civic cooperation was the essential missing ingredient. . . . The lack of an independent tourist commission before 1960 did not help matters. Instead, the New Orleans Board of Trade, the Chamber of Commerce, and the International Trade Mart—agencies whose charges extended far beyond simply promoting tourism—repeatedly held meetings trying to figure out ways of attracting tourists to New Orleans during the slack season. . . .

By the 1960s the jazz club was coordinating its annual jazz festival with the New Orleans Spring Fiesta Association's two-week festival. Significantly, this marriage of upper-class promotion of colonial and antebellum houses and gardens with twentieth-century jazz marked the first organized effort on the part of the city's ruling class to infuse the imagined romance of New Orleans' halcyon days of elite white influence with the flowering of black musical artistry. Ironically, no sooner had this meshing of cultural imagery been accomplished than the blue-blood conception of the city's proper packaging escaped their control. Indeed, the rising tide of jazz marketing combined with the rampant profiteering of entrepreneurs opening any sort of tourist-oriented business that could in any way embody the increasingly heterogeneous mixture of tourist images—including strip clubs, jazz halls, rock 'n' roll and rhythm and blues clubs, Creole eateries, and Mardi Gras-theme souvenir and trinket shops. As jazz and Mardi Gras assumed a higher position in the hierarchy of marketable tourist images, the more genteel image of moonlight and magnolias gradually retreated to a mere backdrop or stage set against which tourists simply came for sensory adventures.

The first broad-based civic effort to stage a major jazz festival in New Orleans ran aground as a result of a tense racial situation. In 1962 Harry M. England, president of the recently formed Greater New Orleans Tourist and Convention Commission, Olaf Lambert, general manager of the Royal Orleans Hotel, and Lester E. Kabacoff, a hotel developer and attorney, began discussing how to make the jazz festival realize its potential. In December 1964 a number of prominent business and civic leaders met to discuss a festival to be held in late May 1965, and within a month they had secured a producer, George Wein, who had launched the highly successful Newport festival.

On January 14, 1965, less than a week after the leaders announced that Wein would produce the show, backers suddenly tabled the event indefinitely. . . . [after] an unfortunate incident that happened a few days prior to the postponement of the festival. On January 8–10, twenty-one African American pro football players in town for the American Football League All-Star Game suffered racial discrimination when they attempted to partake of French Quarter nightlife. Some of the players reported that they had been denied admittance to Bourbon Street clubs although their white teammates experienced no harassment. Most complained that they were denied taxicab service from Moisant Field (New Orleans International Airport) to their hotels and between the hotels and the French Quarter. At the airport some waited nearly an hour before a cab picked them up. Outside the Roosevelt Hotel, several taxis lined up along the curb, but their drivers walked away to avoid serving the blacks. One Oakland Raiders player said, "Finally, we stood in the middle of the street and a cab stopped rather than run us down". . . .

After the players' poor treatment, the AFL promptly rescheduled the game in Houston. Mayor Victor H. Schiro, insisting that "you cannot change human nature overnight," quipped that the players' complaints were unwarranted, for as "educated, college men," they "should have rolled with the punch." However, the city's efforts to attract a professional football franchise necessitated a quick response that demonstrated more responsibility. Accordingly, the New Orleans Hotel Association, a number of leading hostelries, the New Orleans Restaurant Association, and the city's largest taxicab company all agreed to serve all citizens and visitors in accordance with the Civil Rights Act of 1964. Nevertheless, the disorder gave jazz festival promoters second thoughts about the advisability of hosting an event that might be marred by a similar display of racism.

The same civic and business leaders that had led the abortive effort to host a festival that year began planning for the 1968 New Orleans International Jazz Fest, which would coincide with the two hundred fiftieth anniversary of the founding of New Orleans. By the second half of the 1960s, New Orleans' public accommodations generally complied with the Civil Rights Act of 1964. Leaders were becoming more aware of the value of cultural heritage events like jazz festivals in promoting economic development, and festival backers finally acknowledged the need to involve the black community in planning the event. . . .

In keeping with the festival's new name and broader goal of stimulating tourism, the event's promoters recruited internationally known talent to augment local musicians and marketed the event worldwide. Festival backers differed over whether to emphasize national acts, and they vacillated when considering two candidates to produce the event, both of whom felt that a mixture of national and local musicians was essential for success. Believing George Wein, longtime producer of the Newport Jazz Festival, was too interested in making a personal profit off Jazzfest, promoters chose Tommy Walker instead. Walker had built an illustrious career, producing Walt Disney's Wonderful World of Color and Dixieland at Disneyland, as well as halftime shows at New Orleans Saints football games. In addition to advertising Jazzfest in European cities, promoters emphasized the French influence on New Orleans music and worked with European travel agents to bring in foreign tour groups. In cooperation with International House, the festival devoted exhibits to several countries.

After the inaugural Jazzfest attracted about 20,000 people to its events and netted just over $3,000, the 1969 Jazzfest lost nearly $24,000. The event not only proved unsuccessful on the balance sheet, it also did not satisfy critics, who noted the tremendous wage disparities between outside and local bands as well as the lack of recognition accorded the local jazzmen. While most national acts received between $2,500 and $5,000 for their performances, New Orleans acts usually got only $50 to $500. Although a number of local musicians took part in the Jackson Square and Canal Street pageantry preceding the opening of the festival, "these men were being used to advertise the music of others coming in from far corners of the jazz world".... Clearly, token black involvement proved insufficient to safeguard the interests of local musicians, even after Louis Cottrell, president of the local black musicians' union, joined the festival's board of directors in 1969. More racially balanced control of Jazzfest awaited the liberal leadership of a racially inclusive city administration and the formation of the New Orleans Jazz and Heritage Foundation in 1970. Like most tourist-oriented events in the Crescent City up to 1970, the jazz festival relied essentially on white entrepreneurs' exploitation of black talent to entertain white visitors.

In addition to stimulating a revival of recording, concerts, tours, and festivals featuring traditional New Orleans jazz, tourism helped resurrect the city's brass band tradition. New Orleans brass bands date to the antebellum period, when the German military band tradition, brought to the city during a wave of German immigration, fused with African musical traditions. For a number of years bands played from sheet music, only gradually shedding this formality. In the 1880s bands such as the Excelsior, Onward, and Reliance Brass Bands helped crystallize brass band repertoire, customs, appearance, and manner. The bands typically played dirges, marches, and hymns while marching through the city's streets.

In predominately black neighborhoods such as Faubourg Tremé, on the fringe of the French Quarter, a number of social aid and pleasure clubs organized in the nineteenth and twentieth centuries as a form of mutual benefit society, in which a member paid dues to a fund used to assist any member who faced financial straits and to provide him a funeral with brass band accompaniment. Whenever a brass band played, a crowd customarily gathered around and danced as the band wended through the streets. This contingent, often carrying brightly festooned umbrellas and waving handkerchiefs, became known as the "second line," a term that gradually became conflated with the whole spectacle. Although brass bands might be heard at most any time, the primary second-line season occurred from September to December when many social aid and pleasure clubs held their own parades. Bands also played for picnics, family reunions, building dedications, and Mardi Gras parades. Prior to World War II, the custom remained largely unknown outside New Orleans, for it tended to occur beyond the precincts of the French Quarter, where most tourists congregated.

By the 1960s most brass bands represented self-conscious attempts by musicians to revive a fading tradition for show. The dwindling number of jazz funerals tended to serve as jazzmen's memorials to fallen brethren. . . . [T]he injection of a tourist "second line" subtly altered the character and mood of the jazz funeral from an inward admixture of reverence, mourning, and jubilation, to an outward, self-conscious spectacle for consumption by an audience who could never fully comprehend the milieu from which the spectacle sprang.

Of all the new brass bands that formed concurrently with the rise of tourism, Olympia Brass Band became the most famous. Organized in 1960 by Harold Dejan, who in his earlier years had played aboard Mississippi riverboats, the predominantly black marching unit took its name from a series of earlier bands. . . . Like many New Orleans jazz bands, Olympia counted both natives and newcomers among its members. In contrast to the typical scenario, in which black musicians left the plantation South for a new life in New Orleans, Olympia took in outsiders drawn to the city purely to soak up its musical legacy. For instance, Olympia trombonist Paul Crawford, born in Atmore, Alabama, in 1925, moved to New Orleans at age twenty-six and joined the band after graduating from the prestigious Eastman School of Music in Rochester, New York. . . .

While [earlier] bands had played primarily for community functions, Olympia eagerly courted a tourist audience as well. In 1967, the band marched into Tulane Stadium (the Sugar Bowl) to play in the "Sights and Sounds of New Orleans" halftime show devised by former Disneyland producer Tommy Walker for the inaugural New Orleans Saints football game against the Los Angeles Rams. The spectacle of strutting, umbrella-toting second-liners and brass musicians drew "amused laughter and applause, [and] some comment that this was really Mardi Gras." The NAACP frowned upon the "carnival skit" after its leaders saw the televised halftime show. Less than three years later, millions of Americans saw "one of the greatest ads ever seen on television for New Orleans"–New Orleans' first Super Bowl. CBS televised the game's "Way Down Yonder" halftime show, again produced by Walker. This time trumpeter Al Hirt played "Streets of Dreams," the Southern University Marching Band from Baton Rouge performed a rendition of "South Rampart Street Parade," and "adopted natives" Lionel Hampton and Doc Severinson entertained. Following a mock Battle of New Orleans replete with cannon and cavalry, Walker trotted out the Olympia Brass Band in another staged jazz funeral.

Indeed, by prostituting this black tradition to America via national television, tourism leaders stripped it of all meaning and rendered it nothing more than one more component in the effort to exude Mardi Gras atmosphere 365 days a year for tourists' benefit. Nevertheless, it is important to recognize the complicity of Olympia's musicians in this process, for they fully understood and clearly accepted their role as cultural ambassadors for their city. Much as the Jaffes viewed themselves as preservers of a dying custom, the musicians of Olympia billed themselves as one of the last two authentic Dixieland marching bands (along with Eureka Brass Band).

Like Joe Mares's musicians and the Preservation Hall Jazz Band, the Olympia Brass Band also gained widespread attention through its touring. In 1966 and 1967, Olympia played in Washington, D.C., as part of the Smithsonian Institution's celebrations featuring American folk customs. In autumn of 1968, the band accompanied the Travel South U.S.A. mission to Europe, a delegation of tourism promoters from New Orleans and numerous other southern cities sponsored by the United States Travel Service and the Southern Travel Directors Council. . . .

Noting the irony in the South's attempt to use African American culture as the centerpiece of its ploy to attract foreign travelers to a region shackled by the iron grip of institutionalized racism and apartheid, a London writer described how the Olympia Brass Band was

> trouping all over Europe with a home-grown delegation of white chamber-of-commerce types who were trying to sell places like Mississippi, Alabama, and nine other Confederate states as tourist paradises, presumably on the assumption that Europeans don't read newspapers . . . . It makes a wonderful, horrendously funny, pitiable, sad contrast—these well-fed, pink-and-paunchy white folks 'showing off their six li'l darkies. . . .

If brass bands increasingly put on a show for growing hordes of tourists, occasionally they snubbed them in a demonstration that the music was not simply for outsiders' pleasure. The Olympia Brass Band, accompanying the Tremé Sports Social Aid and Pleasure Club's annual parade in 1967, was supposed to take a detour to Jackson Square to pick up a "second line" of tourists. From Jackson Square they would lead them to the Royal Orleans Hotel for a concert. However, the band never made it to Jackson Square, veering instead to the Caledonia Club in Tremé, where it played to a mostly local, black audience.

Despite its reputation as a leading cultural exponent of the city's tourism industry, the Olympia Brass Band did not simply forget the community from which the brass band tradition issued. On at least one occasion the bandsmen used the jazz funeral as a vehicle for social protest. After several blocks of the Faubourg Tremé were razed for the city government's Cultural Center, part of a locally funded urban renewal scheme designed to rid the inner city of impoverished neighborhoods, the Olympia Brass Band staged a mock jazz funeral to symbolize Tremé's untimely death. . . . The band accompanied a crowd huddled around a casket containing a clearly visible dummy that apparently represented the Cultural Center. When the crowd reached the old Caledonia Inn on St. Philip Street, the pallbearers shoved the coffin through a high window of the club, from which a terrific ruckus could be heard as a crowd inside set upon the "body," beating it mercilessly. Soon children began hurling stones and bottles at the building, one of those slated for demolition. . . .

As some tourists found out, venturing beyond the confines of the French Quarter to experience the second-line tradition did not come without certain risks. Tempers often flared in the crowds that gathered around the brass bands. The New Orleans Police Department, then a predominantly white force, sometimes practiced a draconian manner of crowd control, adding to blacks' distrust of them. On one occasion, a visiting reporter covering the Jolly Bunch Social Aid and Pleasure Club's parade in Tremé observed a number of white NOPD officers on horseback, "grim, unbending, clearly not enjoying the outing." They periodically rode their horses into the crowd with no regard for the people they trampled. When one child screamed after a horse stepped on her foot, the mounted officer hit her, and a second policeman roughed up another youth from atop his horse. Suddenly, on the fringe of the Lafitte Housing Project, a cop on horseback and brandishing a pistol chased a black youth through the street until he disappeared into the crowd. . . . Shortly thereafter, a rumor circulated that a cop on Tulane Avenue had killed a boy. A stone throwing match ensued that subsided only when the sounds of the Olympia band swept up the crowd once again. In another incident, a spectator shot a woman in the leg. . . .

Typical of New Orleans' attempts to tame its wild side and package it as a commodity for tourist consumption, at least one show attempted to distill the ambience of second-line jazz from the rough streets of Tremé in a lively, safe setting. In the spring of 1980, the Olympia Brass Band starred in the musical comedy "Back-a-Town," co-produced by Edgar F. Poree, Jr., and Olympia trumpeter Milton Batiste. Locals often referred to the neighborhoods of Tremé, Central City, and portions of Mid-City as "Back-of-Town." This term may have reflected the lingering black notion of the areas toward the Mississippi River as white lands and the areas away from it as black lands, for the land situated in the great crescent of the river that gave New Orleans its nickname was once comprised of slender, pie-slice-shaped sugar plantations stretching far back into cypress swamps. In antebellum days, slaves often occupied these rear portions, occasionally fleeing into the swamp as maroons. . . .

[T]he musical promised tourists a glimpse into this "Back-of-Town" neighborhood that tourism leaders warned against visiting. In the play, the character Elijah Conners sits on his front stoop and regales passing tourists with outlandish tales of old Tremé laden with racial stereotypes. In eight scenes, the play careens spatially and temporally among depictions of black life in "an African village deep in the Mother Country," a river plantation, a voodoo ritual, a parade by the "Boogie-Bunch Social Aid and Pleasure Club," and a jazz funeral for Madam Fast Sally, at which time the Olympia Brass Band fires up its second-line sounds. The play's producers apparently hoped to evoke a sense of exotic New Orleans in a safe, tourist-friendly setting. . . .

By the 1970s, the impact of tourism had shorn the declining brass band tradition of its original cultural milieu. . . . New Orleans' back streets stood increasingly silent. Jazz funerals became increasingly anachronistic as greater burial coverage by insurance policies rendered social aid and pleasure clubs less crucial. Such organizations often continued their charitable work, but focused more heavily on the component of revelry, often in conjunction with the growing popularity and proliferation of Mardi Gras parades. As outlying cemeteries became the norm, the tradition of brass band accompaniment could not bridge distances that required automobile processions. Further, the dwindling number of existing brass bands geared their activities more toward the paying public as their respective reputations grew.

Even as the custom receded, records and especially films helped spread the second-line tradition to a wide audience of potential tourists. In 1951, two Harvard students, Alden Ashforth and David Wyckoff, made the first sound recordings of a working New Orleans brass band, the Eureka Brass Band. Two years later, the Cinerama Film Corporation filmed a mock funeral featuring John Casimir and the Young Tuxedo Brass for a segment in its travelogue "Cinerama Holiday." In 1956, Frederick Ramsey, Jr., who co-edited Jazzmen, shot the Eureka Brass Band for the CBS television documentary "Odyssey." In 1958 Atlantic became the first major recording company to record a brass band when it produced a record by the Young Tuxedo Brass Band. The second-line custom found its way into major Hollywood films as well. M.G.M. filmed

Eureka for its long title sequence for the 1965 movie *The Cincinnati Kid*, and United Artists filmed a memorable scene for the 1973 James Bond film *Live And Let Die*, in which the Olympia Brass Band accompanied a jazz procession through the French Quarter. Olympia also filmed television commercials for Budweiser beer, Toyota and Pontiac automobiles, and Hushpuppies shoes. The effect of such massive international exposure to a tradition that had historically been largely sheltered from outside view in impoverished black neighborhoods cannot be overestimated.

By the 1980s, tourism paradoxically had contributed to the disengagement of traditional jazz from its historical socio-cultural milieu, yet it had also helped resurrect an art form that arguably would have died otherwise. In addition, tourism stimulated a revival of grassroots interest among young African Americans in New Orleans' inner-city neighborhoods in playing jazz by renewing older musicians' interest so that they might serve as role models for a new generation. The demands of tourism helped enshrine traditional New Orleans jazz in the tourist-frequented Preservation Hall, French Market, Café du Monde, and most notably at the annual New Orleans Jazz and Heritage Festival. Tourism also provided new milieus—conventions, football halftime shows, riverboat cruises, and festival marketplaces—in which the sounds of New Orleans brass bands might continue in the crucial years when little young talent stood ready to replace older musicians as they died.

The tourism-stoked jazz revival of the 1940s and subsequent decades, originally viewed by many enthusiasts as the final flowering of a soon-to-be bygone era, achieved something much more remarkable. More than merely arresting the demise of the music, it fertilized the soil in which a new jazz genre burst into full flower by the late 1980s. Concurrently with upsurges in the national popularity of Cajun and zydeco music, New Orleans produced two superstars, Wynton Marsalis and Harry Connick, Jr., who kept the Crescent City in the national and international spotlight. In addition to performing their own brands of jazz worldwide, Marsalis and Connick ensured through their efforts back home that New Orleans remained a musical Mecca. While Marsalis headed the University of New Orleans Jazz Studies program, Connick founded the Krewe of Orpheus, a Mardi Gras parade organization that melded the city's Carnival and jazz images and directed them toward tourists.

Like Marsalis and Connick, the New Orleans Jazz and Heritage Festival became immensely popular, achieving its first fiscal surplus in 1978. In 1985 the non-profit New Orleans Jazz and Heritage Foundation inaugurated a grant program distributing $500 to $10,000 grants to cultivate the roots of jazz and other performing arts in a city increasingly dependent upon staging a spectacle for tourists. Some of the grant money helped fund new instruments, uniforms, city parade permits, and supplies for brass bands, social aid and pleasure clubs, and Mardi Gras Indian tribes. The Foundation also sponsored WWOZ 90.7 FM, a radio station broadcasting primarily Louisiana music, the Heritage School of Music, giving free music instruction to needy children, neighborhood festivals, concert series, subsidized Jazzfest tickets for the poor, Foundation internships for inner-city youths, seed money for music-oriented start-up companies, and medical care for aging musicians. Jazzfest, then, stood out as one of New Orleans' few postwar success stories, harnessing tourism to the city's culture at a time when the city's culture generally suffered the pressures wrought by over-reliance on the tourist trade.

In the wake of the 1985 oil bust, which set New Orleans' economy on a downward spiral, the city fell upon hard times, felt most acutely by the city's poorer African Americans. The municipal government, facing grave fiscal straits, latched onto tourism as never before in hopes of keeping its beleaguered ship afloat. It worked in a close public-private partnership with tourism interests, using jazz more and more frequently in marketing efforts. An epidemic of crack cocaine abuse ripped through Tremé and other black neighborhoods, claiming the lives of many black youths and leading to an escalation of street violence. In these hard times, the example of revitalized jazz provided a degree of solace and inspiration.

Symbolic of the rekindling of young African Americans' interest in jazz musicianship was the grassroots brass band movement that blossomed in the 1980s, most notably with the spectacular rise of Re-Birth Brass Band as both role models for a black underclass and the Crescent City's newest ambassadors of cultural tourism. In contrast to elite white use of black jazz to shape public memory of New Orleans' past for tourism promotion in the 1960s and 1970s, by the 1980s, African Americans had staked a new claim to brass band music as an authentic voice of black public memory and contemporary cultural expression. Formed in 1983 by tuba player Philip Frazier and trumpeter Kermit Ruffins, who lived in Tremé and attended Joseph S. Clark High School, the teenaged Re-Birth Brass Band members used the customary brass band instrumentation. Too young to play in Bourbon Street nightclubs, the youths worked the streets of the French Quarter, entertaining passing tourists. Ironically, in its formative period Re-Birth relied on being able to play on the streets, a custom that has been periodically under attack since the effects of the jazz revival and rising tourist foot traffic in the French Quarter began clashing with affluent white French Quarter gentrifiers' notions of who took precedence in the enjoyment of the Vieux Carré's Old World charm in the 1970s.

Inspired by the innovative melding of traditional New Orleans jazz with progressive funk pioneered by the Dirty Dozen Brass Band in the 1970s and assisted by Olympia trumpeter Milton Batiste, the Re-Birth Brass Band set the streets afire with an energetic, rough-edged, high-octane fusion of jazz, funk, rhythm and blues, gospel, Caribbean, and even rap. While Re-Birth quickly positioned itself to take advantage of tourism, getting its first professional gig at a 1983 convention at the Sheraton Hotel and its first recording contract from a record company executive in town for Jazzfest in 1984, the band remained quite attuned to the community from which it sprang. The crack cocaine crisis of the 1980s stimulated a resurgence of jazz funerals as distraught families of slain victims called upon the brass band to provide a musical tribute. In 1989 Frazier averred that Re-Birth had played at more than one hundred crack funerals since 1987. Re-Birth soon made the jump from playing only neighborhood gigs, at clubs such as the Little People's Place and Trombone Shorty's, to French Quarter and Uptown venues patronized by a mostly white tourist clientele and, increasingly, international tours and contracts to produce internationally circulated compact discs. The band's innovative adaptation of traditional brass band forms to fit the preferences of a younger generation, along with the efforts of other new ensembles like Soul Rebels Brass Band, New Birth Brass Band, Li'l Rascals Brass Band, and Tuba Fats and the Chosen Few, did more than simply preserve and enshrine a timeless New Orleans sound, as Olympia and the Preservation Hall bands had done. It served as both a wellspring for the city's ongoing legacy of jazz and a key component in increasingly savvy tourism marketing efforts to woo tourists seeking cultural distinctiveness rather than standardized experiences.

Questions

1. Souther claims that "the resurrection of Dixieland triggered a contest for control over public memory." What was that contest?

2. Why had jazz "practically disappeared from the areas of New Orleans most commonly frequented by tourists" by the World War II era? What organizations prompted its reemergence as an important part of the city's cultural environment?

3. What is significant about Preservation Hall, the New Orleans Jazz Festival, and neighborhood brass bands in the preservation of the music in New Orleans and the attraction of tourists to the city? How are those two things—music preservation and tourism—at odds with one another?

COMMERCIALIZATION OF CAJUN CUISINE

by Marcelle Bienvenu, Carl A. Brasseaux,
and Ryan A. Brasseaux

P ersons with only a passing acquaintance with Cajun cuisine assume that the commercialization driving such popular fascination with the culinary genre is only a recent phenomenon, stemming from the late-twentieth century national craze, but this is not the case. Foods currently intimately associated with the Cajun tradition have been aggressively marketed both regionally and nationally for decades.

South Louisiana hot sauces, for instance, have been marketed internationally since the 1870s. In 1868, Edmund McIlhenny, a Maryland-born banker turned planter and manufacturer, began to produce his own pepper sauce—sold in cologne bottles—at Avery Island. McIlhenny's concoction proved an immediate success; indeed, it was so successful that the inventor felt compelled to obtain a patent for his recipe in 1870. By the end of the decade, the fiery Tabasco hot sauce was marketed throughout the United States and England.

By the turn of the twentieth century, Tabasco's international success spawned numerous local imitators, many of which also eventually enjoyed national and international success. . . .

The early flowering of the south Louisiana hot sauce industry coincided with the establishment of other culinary enterprises. This new phase of commercial development was technology-driven. Before railroads snaked their

From *Stir the Pot: A History of Cajun Cuisine* © 2005 by Marcelle Bienvenu, Carl A. Brasseaux, and Ryan A. Brasseaux. Used by permission of Hippocrene Books, Inc.

way through Cajun Country in the 1880s, eventually connecting the formerly physically isolated region with the East and West Coasts, local exporters shipped goods to market by steamboat or flatboat. Waterborne transportation was problematic throughout the region, for many inland ports were accessible only on a seasonable basis, when water levels permitted communications with New Orleans. Even under ideal circumstances, shipments required several days—sometimes weeks—to reach Crescent City markets. As a consequence, exporters—like Edmund McIlhenny—had to preserve food products by traditional means—smoking, salting, or, as with Tabasco, the use of vinegar. The use of these time-proven preservation techniques declined drastically after the coming of the railroad, which suddenly made New Orleans only hours away from Cajun Country depots.

The increased accessibility of Crescent City markets coincided with the introduction of refrigeration technology, the attendant establishment of ice houses, and, by the turn of the twentieth century, ice factories. . . . The ready availability of ice made possible the shipment of refrigerated perishables, which, in turn, gave birth to south Louisiana's commercial fishing and hunting industries.

Before railroads made rapid, refrigerated shipments to New Orleans possible, the Louisiana fishing industry was largely confined to the Crescent City's immediate hinterlands, particularly St. Bernard Parish. Following the establishment of the first ice houses at Morgan City around 1876, Cajun farmers displaced by the perennial flooding that followed in the wake of the Civil War, began to seek out a livelihood in the nearby Atchafalaya Basin. Some found employment as lumberjacks in the emerging cypress lumber industry others as commercial fishermen. Most of their catch was shipped by rail to New Orleans markets.

These regional exports were supplemented in the early twentieth century by shipments of ever-larger quantities of shellfish. Canneries established in the Cajun coastal parishes around the turn of the twentieth century processed shrimp and oysters for distribution to national markets. Dried shrimp, also produced by the coastal parishes, were distributed widely particularly during the Catholic Lenten season. . . .

Seafood exports were initially overshadowed in ecological and economical importance by shipments of wild game from the Cajun prairie and coastal regions. During the late nineteenth century, commercial hunter[s], most of whom were evidently Cajun—reportedly shipped more than 250,000 wild ducks to New Orleans annually. Commercial hunting appears to have reached its peak in 1909, when approximately 600,000 wild ducks and 300,000 snipe were killed in Calcasieu Parish alone. These hunters also shipped to the Crescent City large numbers of *popabottes* (upland sandpipers), prized throughout French Louisiana for their delicate flavor and reputed value as an aphrodisiac. . . .

The resulting rapid depletion of local wildlife populations and the ensuing promulgation of state and federal conservation legislation forced local entrepreneurs (many of whom had been middlemen in the game export business) to seek another exploitable resource, and the prairie region's enormous indigenous *ouaouaron* (bullfrog) population quickly filled the void.

Extant documentation makes no mention of frog leg consumption by Acadiana's established population before the 1880s, when French immigrant merchants began shipping this Gallic delicacy from Rayne, a newly established Acadia Parish railroad town, to Southern urban centers. Donat Pucheu initiated the practice of exporting frog legs to New Orleans restaurants, but, by the turn of the twentieth century, fellow Frenchman Jacques Weil had supplanted his countryman as the regional industry leader. In the 1908 season alone, Weil shipped more than 100,000 frogs, and the volume of this export trade tripled over the following two decades. . . .

Virtual armies of impoverished yeoman farmers, sharecroppers, and school children harvested these enormous quantities of bullfrogs. Desperately seeking supplementary income to improve their hardscrabble existence-made more difficult by the Southern agricultural depression of the 1920s and the national economic crisis of the following decade, lightbearing hunters combed local rice paddies and coulees on spring and summer nights in search of bellowing ouaouaron. Having mastered the art of 'gigging' bullfrogs, these modern hunter-gatherers continued to forage for the enormous amphibians long after the local export trade collapsed during World War II. The industry would never recover, and it is ironic that frog legs made their way onto prairie Cajun tables—albeit as a regional culinary anomaly—at the very time that the industry was in full retreat.

Like the frog industry, south Louisiana's agricultural export industry experienced boom and bust cycles. As a result of depressed cotton commodity prices and a rollback of federal sugar tariff support in the late nineteenth and twentieth centuries, Cajun farmers began to turn serious attention to crop diversification, particularly during the catastrophic collapse of the cotton market in the Roaring Twenties. As a consequence, hundreds of Cajuns turned to rice and sweet potato production after World War I. Cajuns had cultivated sweet potatoes (known locally as yams, a term later trademarked for identification of Louisiana sweet potato exports) for home consumption since at least the antebellum era (1812–1860). Local gardeners cross-bred this variety, a "yellow-veined" potato renowned for its taste and appealing texture, with the so-called "Honduras yam," introduced into the Cajun parishes after the Civil War. . . . The hybrid not only exhibited the best qualities of the native and imported varieties, but it was also softer, sweeter, and moister after baking than other Southern sweet potatoes. In addition, the Louisiana hybrid could be stored longer than either of the parent varieties.

Cajun farmers eagerly embraced the new hybrid before 1880 and, as a result, local sweet potato production more than tripled between 1860 and 1900. But there was no concerted effort to export the regional surplus until the early twentieth century, when enterprising local growers attempted to promote the product to the Northern market. This marketing effort coincided with the massive migration of Southern blacks—who were accustomed to eating sweet potatoes—to Northern metropolitan centers. Their nostalgic longing for foods left behind undoubtedly helped this emerging Louisiana industry to establish a foothold in the North, and, once "yams" became part of the national culinary canon for the holidays, the success of the Louisiana sweet potato industry was assured.

The resulting development of Louisiana's yam industry was most pronounced in Cajun Country's eastern prairie region, particularly within the area bounded by Church Point, Sunset, and Opelousas. Indeed, by mid-century, Sunset had proclaimed itself the "sweet potato capital of the world." The area's sweet potato industry, however, peaked by the mid twentieth century. . . .

Like their counterparts in Acadiana's sweet potato industry, south Louisiana rice growers experienced the lofty peaks and deep valleys of the twentieth-century American agricultural commodities markets, but the rice industry's decline (after peaking in the 1970s) has been more protracted. Louisianians have cultivated rice since the 1720s, when it was introduced principally as a food stock for recently imported African slaves. Cultivation of the grain was initially confined to frontier communities along the Mississippi River, where irrigation was readily available during the waterway's vernal "high water" season. Following its establishment in the bayou region during the late eighteenth century, the Acadian population experimented with rice cultivation, but the exiles and their descendants did not usually employ artificial irrigation techniques to foster crop germination. Instead, they sowed rice seeds in low-lying, flood-prone areas in hope that abundant rainfall would inundate these makeshift fields. Because the crops were almost entirely dependent upon precipitation, the local variety was called "providence rice."

Since rice production techniques were primitive and unreliable, Cajuns utilized the cereal grain primarily as a hedge against failure of the vital corn crop. The importance of rice in the Cajun diet and the crop's economic significance to rural south Louisiana changed radically following the influx of German and Midwestern immigrants into the prairie region in the last three decades of the nineteenth century. During the 1870s, the Germans experimented successfully with the commercial production of rice, which proved perfectly suited to the area's climate and topography. Between 1884 and 1894, newly arrived Midwesterners adapted for local use mechanized tools developed in the North for the cultivation and harvest of wheat, and, during the ensuing six years, the development of large-scale irrigation systems and the establishment of mills completed the infrastructure necessary for the local rice industry to blossom.

As this infrastructure matured, hundreds of Cajun farmers and ranchers rushed to capitalize upon the emerging economic opportunities. Regional rice production increased exponentially at the turn of the twentieth century. . . . Increased production helped make rice a staple of the local diet, but the local population was clearly incapable of consuming the growing supply of raw grain. As a consequence, rice commodity prices fell from $1.98 in 1905 to $1.44 five years later.

To reverse this disturbing trend, rice millers, merchants, and venture capitalists banded together during the first two decades of the twentieth century to cultivate and develop external markets for south Louisiana's rapidly growing rice surpluses. Louisiana's rice exporters initially channeled much of these exports to Cuba, but the closure of Cuban markets to American rice imports in the early 1920s forced Pelican State marketers to develop products that appealed to potato- and pasta-eating North American consumers. In perhaps the most successful of these early marketing efforts, the Louisiana State Rice Milling Company, Incorporated (LSRMCI), one of the nation's largest rice processing and marketing enterprises, launched the Water Maid and Mahatma brands in 1925 and 1932 respectively. Water Maid rice, marketed nationally in one- to three-pound cellophane bags during the Great Depression, accounted for nearly half of the company's sales between 1938 and 1939, and, by the mid-1950s, Mahatma had become the nation's "best-selling brand of regular rice."

As the success of the Mahatma brand suggests, the commercialization of Cajun foodways and commoditization of Cajun culture as a whole increased exponentially following World War II as communications improved and preservation technology advanced. Prior to the Second World War, Cajun Country's major culinary exports were not branded as "Cajun," reflecting the national obsession with socio-cultural homogenization, the regional culinary tradition's lack of a marketable identity and attendant inadequate national exposure, and the ongoing evolution of the culinary genre itself. Following America's "discovery" of Cajun cuisine in the mid-1980s, however, Cajun-branded foods took the nation by storm, leaving an indelible stamp on the national culinary landscape as they found their way onto menus and store shelves across the country. Commercial Cajun foodstuffs have also permanently changed south Louisiana cuisine by offering a convenient alternative to time-consuming, traditional methods of preparation. The post-World War II evolution of Cajun Country merchandise from generic foodstuffs (i.e., rice, "yams," frog legs, hot sauce) to the marketing of branded culinary endproducts (e.g., Hebert's Turducken or Vautrot's Cajun fried turkeys) occurred on several fronts. Three of the most historically significant developments in the recent commoditization and promotion of Cajun cuisine are explored here: the emergence of Cajun restaurants, the proliferation of packaged Cajun foodstuffs, and the appearance of culturally-based festivals.

South Louisiana's restaurant industry emerged during the antebellum era to satisfy a regional niche market catering to travelers and locals with disposable income. As early as the 1850s and '60s, taverns, inns, hotel kitchens, and bars . . . offered patrons indigenous Louisiana foods, including "Gumbo of every . . . description, Soups, Roasts, Stews, Frys [sic], Broils—Salmon, Lobsters, Sardines". . . . [O]yster bars specializing in bivalves flourished during the late nineteenth and early twentieth centuries in urban centers like Thibodaux, Houma, Lafayette, Crowley, Abbeville, New Iberia, and Opelousas. Although these restaurants offered authentic Cajun fare, owners did not incorporate ethnic designations into local eateries' formal identities until the twilight decades of the twentieth century.

Folklorist Barry Ancelet . . . concludes that naming practices and cultural identification markers—particularly the terms "Evangeline," "Acadian," and ultimately "Cajun"—shifted over time in synch with both the community's own evolving identity and shifting ascriptive stereotypes. In the early twentieth century, at the nadir of the group's modern struggle for survival, Cajuns viewed the Evangeline and Acadian labels as subtle commercial symbols accepted by, and thus marketable to, mainstream American society because of the enduring popularity of Henry Wadsworth Longfellow's *Evangeline*. The 1929 silent film *Evangeline*, starring Delores Del Rio, spurred continued public interest in the iconographic Acadian designation during the first half of the twentieth century.

"Cajun," on the other hand, connoted the pejorative "hillbilly," used to describe other poor rural whites living in the South. The term "Cajun" underwent a metamorphosis after World War II, when cultural activists helped rehabilitate the ethnic label. During the last half of the twentieth century south Louisianians attached the term to a plethora of marketable products blends. . . .

The development of the modern Cajun eatery was pioneered by the Landry family of Lafayette, who established Don's Seafood and Steakhouse in 1934. Soileau's Supper Club opened in Opelousas three years later, and comparable eateries launched operations in other regional parish seats before the beginning of the Second World War. Between the mid-1930s and the late '60s, restaurants like Don's and Soileau's, which featured limited New Orleans-influenced menus, provided what locals considered an up-scale dining experience. Meanwhile, diners providing plate lunches more representative of local culinary traditions—like Bergeron's Café in Thibodaux—catered to the urban working classes.

With the oil boom of the 1960s, a new generation of local restaurants appeared. Targeting a working-class clientele with newly acquired disposable income, these eateries, which specialized in fried seafood, simply incorporated the term Cajun into their branding to connote their culinary authenticity, to denote the content of their menus, and to appeal to the heightened ethnic consciousness on the part of their patrons. Robin's and Pat's restaurants in Henderson, a commercial fishing center on the Atchafalaya Basin's western periphery focused their advertising on their broad repertoire of Cajun dishes, ranging from crawfish étouffée to fried seafood platters.

During the 1980s, other establishments took the commercialization of Cajun cuisine a step further by fusing two distinctive south Louisiana traditions—food and music—launching in the process a revolutionary dining experience in Cajun Country. Like German beer gardens, these restaurant-dancehalls became folk dinner theaters that encouraged guests to interface with local culture by dancing to live Cajun music and imbibing local interpretations of Cajun cuisine. This new paradigm, however, could only be successful if locals were willing participants in this experiment, and the most successful of the new-breed restaurants have found the key to success in exciting new interpretations of Cajun culinary standards, which lured clients away from established seafood restaurants.

The new restaurant paradigm traces its origin to the Cajun *bal de maison* (house dance) of the nineteenth and early twentieth centuries. These intimate affairs, involving a single rural community, were generally held on weekends, and provided a genial space for social activity through musical entertainment, dancing, and refreshments. Participants developed and renewed friendships, engaged in courtship practices, and socialized either while dancing or while consuming a bowl of gumbo, which hosts traditionally served at the end of evening. By the 1940s, dancehalls had supplanted the bals de maison. Dancehalls fundamentally altered the dynamics of Cajun dances, which were no longer restricted to a single community. Although drinking was permitted inside the hall, food was not served with the same regularity as at house dances. A generation later, however, restaurant-dancehalls like Prejean's, Mulate's, and Randol's renewed the traditional marriage of food and dance.

In 1980, restaurateur Robert "Bob" Guilbeau returned to his native Louisiana after working for years in California and founded Prejean's Restaurant near the Lafayette Parish community of Carencro. Prejean's offered local cuisine and live Cajun music and attracted a large number of tourists who had the opportunity to simultaneously experience two of Bayou Country's most famous cultural exports. Over time, Prejean's chefs radically transformed hearty rural Cajun fare into *haute cuisine*. Although their marketing slogan "Simply Cajun, Simply Delicious" may imply home-style cooking, the restaurant's culinary creations are representative examples of modern innovative trends in Cajun fusion.

Mulate's Restaurant in Breaux Bridge established itself as one of south Louisiana's most famous culinary institutions by capitalizing on the Cajun craze through self-promotion as "the original Cajun restaurant." In the early 1980s, owner Kerry Boutté offered his patrons classic Cajun restaurant standards—étouffée, gumbo, fried seafood platters—and live musical performances by some of the top names in Cajun music. Mulate's has played a significant role in the preservation and promotion of Cajun music by employing legendary Cajun bands like the Grammy-award winning ensemble Beausoleil. A large wooden dance floor in the center of the building set this establishment apart from other "Cajun" restaurants. Boutté's lucrative dining concept subsequently spread across the south Louisiana landscape. . . .

By the 1990s, Cajun restaurants had become part of the American landscape, in part because of Chef Paul Prudhomme's huge impact on North American cuisine. Prudhomme's rise to fame began in 1975 at the famous New Orleans eatery Commander's Palace. . . . In 1979, Paul and his wife, K. Hinrichs Prudhomme, opened K-Paul's Louisiana Kitchen . . . in New Orleans' famed French Quarter. The restaurant generated a buzz throughout the Crescent City, the ripples of which would ultimately reverberate throughout the world. . . . Patrons often had to wait in line to sample Prudhomme's signature dishes like blackened redfish, a dish reproduced throughout the country with such frequency that it compelled the Louisiana legislature to restrict commercial redfish catches to save the species from extinction in the Gulf of Mexico. In Cajun Country, K-Paul's legacy reverberates on Cajun fusion menus.

During the 1980s and '90s, Lafayette, Louisiana, became the restaurant hub for the urbane flavors of Cajun fusion. Following Prudhomme's lead, chefs around the Lafayette area like Pat Mould and James Graham elevated traditional Louisiana foodways into a contemporary art form by fusing local ingredients, culinary aesthetics, and recipes with classical French techniques and sauces. . . .

Classical French-infused Cajun cuisine also flourished outside of Lafayette, most notably in Chef John Folse's restaurants and bed and breakfasts. Folse drew heavily from classical French, traditional New Orleans' Creole cuisine, and the foodways he experienced growing up east of the Atchafalaya Basin. His brand of cuisine celebrates the flavors from the eastern fringe of Cajun country. Folse's fusion restaurants catered to the aesthetic along the River Road that winds along the Mississippi River in Plantation Country south of the state capital, an area that traditionally boasted higher concentrations of Anglo Protestants, white Creoles, and African-Americans (Anglo-Protestant blacks as opposed to the French-speaking Catholic Afro-Creoles) when compared to the Lafayette area. . . .

As with the restaurant industry, the prepackaged Cajun food industry has undergone a long evolutionary track beginning not with local commercial agriculture, but rather with the local food-processing industry that was initially local agriculture's neglected handmaiden. Indeed, south Louisiana's canning industry laid the foundation for the local commercial packaged food industry, which has blossomed into a major export business since the mid-1980s.

Cajun Country's canning industry dates from the late nineteenth century. . . . [I]n 1887, entrepreneurs were actively soliciting venture capital to establish factories in Thibodaux and Houma. Two years later, the Lafayette Canning Company constructed a large facility in the Hub City. By the second decade of the twentieth century, commercial canneries were scattered throughout the Cajun parishes, and most proved financially successful. . . . East of the Atchafalaya Basin, most of the area's canneries processed seafood—primarily shrimp and oysters—for Northern markets. . . . The most notable of these companies, Pelican Lake Oyster and Packing Company, reputedly operated the South's largest canning plant, processing "more shrimp than any other plant in the world." Numerous additional canning factories lined lower Bayou Lafourche.

The commercial canneries were complemented by domestic cannery programs. By 1915, most Acadiana schools had "canning clubs," created to promote canning by local farm families, and home demonstration programs, established in many Cajun parishes during World War I, promoted the domestic arts in general, and gardening and canning in particular, as a means of encouraging the American war effort on the grassroots level.

Following the War-to-End-All-Wars, Cajuns became increasingly proficient at canning as facilities—both domestic and in local schools—became more readily available. Not until local restaurants, like Don's, embraced the technology to export their crawfish bisque, gumbo, and other foods did the region begin to launch a serious effort to market its distinctive local cuisine to an outside market. With the introduction of refrigeration, which became virtually universal locally in the 1950s, the focus of this burgeoning export industry shifted from canned to frozen foods.

Meanwhile, local entrepreneurs, drawing upon the success of the flourishing regional hot-sauce industry began to market packaged seasonings, and, over the course of recent decades, frozen Cajun food vendors have diversified their product lines to include seasoning mixes. As a result, seasonings are perhaps the most ubiquitous Cajun commercial products, and, in recent years, prepackaged seasoning blends have become the commercial Cajun food products most extensively used by Cajun cooks throughout south Louisiana. Hundreds of variations fill supermarket shelves along the Gulf Coast. . . .

Registered pharmacist and amateur chef Tony Chachere was an Acadiana pioneer in the packaged seasoning industry. During the 1930s and '40s, Chachere established the Louisiana Drug Company (LADCO) and marketed homemade concoctions like Mamou Cough Syrup and the insect repellent Bon Soir Bug. He traveled extensively throughout the Gulf Coast selling wholesale pharmaceuticals and later insurance. In 1972, Chachere came out of retirement to publish a recipe collection entitled *Cajun Country Cookbook*, which featured his formula for an all-purpose "Creole Seasoning" blend. A positive public response to the book—and Chachere's seasoning in particular—prompted the savvy entrepreneur to launch a line of Cajun/Creole seasonings. Today the company manufactures an assortment of products including instant roux and gravy mixes, ready-made dinner mixes (gumbo, red beans, dirty rice, jambalaya, etc.), and herb seasoning blends. Although Chachere used his trademark as a means of acknowledging his French Creole heritage, his spice mixture has found a home in thousands of Cajun pantries. "Tony Chachere's," as it is fondly referred to in south Louisiana, has indeed become a symbol of Cajun culinary traditions and Cajun ethnicity.

While Cajun seasoning blends dominate the spice shelves of Acadiana groceries and supermarkets, prepackaged Cajun foods tend to dominate the "ethnic foods" aisles of local grocery stores. Acadiana's prepackaged Cajun foods industry features offerings by mom-and-pop enterprises, including Savoie's and Richard's sausages, tasso, and dressing mixes, as well as multinational corporate giants, including Tabasco (turducken), Bruce Foods (Cajun Injector, Louisiana Hot Sauce, and Cajun King brands), Zatarain's (New Orleans-based Cajun and Creole product lines acquired by McCormick), and LSRMCI's corporate successor, Riviana Foods (established in the mid-1960s) that also produces the Mahatma rice mixes line. . . .

Mass media forever changed the cultural landscape in south Louisiana. Newspapers, cookbooks, and later television cooking programs opened communication channels and facilitated dialogues across racial and cultural boundaries and between rural enclaves and urban centers. Technological advances permitted rural residents to tap into new culinary trends, thereby stimulating new ideas and culinary possibilities.

Cajun Country newspapers began publishing recipes—most of which were derived from New Orleans dailies—at least as early as September 1877, when the Opelousas *Courier* provided local cooks with instructions for producing rice croquettes. During the 1890s, recipes were a popular feature in the weekly Lafayette *Advertiser*. They would become popular staples in . . . Acadiana's major newspapers by World War I. In addition, upper-middle class Cajun families purchased the New Orleans *Times-Picayune*, whose famous recipe section held strong appeal to innovative rural cooks who readily embraced the best ideas of food lovers from a city already world-famous for its fine cuisine. . . .These recipes had a huge impact upon turn-of-the-twentieth-century south Louisiana cooking, the formative period in which modern Cajun cuisine was born.

Cookbooks constitute the most authoritative documentation for Cajun cuisine's evolution. Recipe collections also represent a tangible example of the commoditization of Louisiana's folk culture. . . . The New Iberia *Daily Iberian* newspaper's *Creole Cajun Cookery*, published in 1952, and *First, You Make a Roux*, published by Lafayette's Les Vingt Quatre Club in 1954, two of the first explicitly "Cajun" recipe books, helped to stir a consciousness about the marketability of Louisiana foodstuffs. . . . Don's Seafood and Steak House in Lafayette's *Selected Recipes for Fine Food* promoted mail order canned meals like étouffée and bisque. Local junior leagues, church groups, and other civic societies helped to further commercialize Cajun cuisine by sponsoring cookbooks highlighting local recipes, sometimes meeting with great success. For instance, the Baton Rouge Junior League's *River Road Recipes* helped to document and disseminate the culinary traditions of Cajun and Creole settlements along the Mississippi River. The Junior League of Lafayette's cookbook *Talk About Good!*, that has sold more than 70,000 copies since its debut in 1967, features homegrown recipes from in and around one of Cajun Country's major commercial centers west of the Atchafalaya Basin.

By the late twentieth century, Cajun cookbooks had become a national phenomenon. In 1971, Time-Life's "Foods of the World" series published Peter Feibleman's *American Cooking: Creole and Acadian*, the first serious cookbook to explain in great detail the differences between Cajun and Creole cuisine. The volume presented an intelligent cross-section of representative recipes from both foodway traditions that whet the American appetite for Louisiana cuisine. More than a decade later Cajun Paul Prudhomme changed North American cuisine with the release of his debut cookbook *Chef Paul Prudhomme's Louisiana Kitchen* (1984). The book took the nation by storm and reached the *New York Times* bestseller list in 1986, subsequently increasing the national consumption of, and demand for, Cajun food products. The book's introduction set Cajun cooking in the context Prudhomme experienced growing up on a farm near Opelousas, Louisiana, and outlined the chef's culinary philosophy. The success of Prudhomme's line of cookbooks also encouraged the sale of the chef's own line of seasoning blends.

The popularity of Cajun cookbooks in the United States continued to increase during the 1990s. . . . [but] television became the major outlet for the dissemination of Louisiana's culinary treasures. The popularity of the Louisiana-flavored Food Network program "Emeril Live" exposes America's renewed interest in Cajun cuisine, in part because of [chef Emeril] Lagasse's flamboyant interpretations of classic Cajun dishes and astute use of seasonings. Long before Lagasse's ascendance as champion of Louisiana's culinary traditions, however, . . . most people in the Deep South first discovered Cajun cooking through one of the most important proponents of Cajun foodways commercialization, humorist Justin Wilson.

Born on April 24, 1914, near Roseland, Louisiana—part of the state's Anglo-American Bible Belt—comedian and celebrity cook Justin Wilson began his rise to fame by accepting a patronage job "policing the state's grain warehouse industry" during the early 1930s. His duties as a safety engineer occasionally took him into southwest Louisiana's predominately Cajun rice-producing region. During these travels, the engineer began to hone his skills as a comedic storyteller, building his humorous tales around the Cajun community. The middle-class jokester poked fun at south Louisiana's Francophone working-class by using fractured, supposedly Cajun-inflected English and malaprops as bases for humorous stories.

In the 1960s, Wilson, who claimed to have learned to cook at the age of eight as a means of avoiding field work, launched a new career as a cookbook writer. He released his first publication in 1965, a privately printed work simply entitled the *Justin Wilson Cookbook*. Three years later, Wilson's career as a comedian and writer profited immensely from the budding Cajun cultural renaissance that validated the group's identity, particularly as the community's revival gained national and, later, international notoriety. In the 1970s, Wilson capitalized upon mounting popular interest in Cajun culture by launching a popular cooking show, which was eventually syndicated on PBS. The show's success, in turn, contributed to the appeal of Wilson's comedy albums and cookbooks. . . .

Fans of the cooking show, comedy albums, and cookbooks were charmed by the comedian's "quaint" language. Indeed, non-Cajuns often took Wilson's routine at face value, not recognizing the subtleness of the humorist's ruse, and accepted him as a quirky Cajun version of Julia Child. On the other hand, some Cajuns, particularly academicians and cultural activists, took a very dim view of Wilson, regarding him as an offensive impersonator in the tradition of the nineteenth and early twentieth century black-faced minstrels and "ethnic comedians," who lampooned the nation's ethnic and racial minorities. . . .

The author of a recent Louisiana tourism study estimates that Louisiana annually hosts more than four hundred festivals, approximately half of which are held during the region's relatively mild autumn months (particularly September and October). One journalist has claimed that the Pelican State has a festival for everything that "walks, crawls, or moves." Many Louisiana festivals promote specific local or regional industries, such as rice, sugar, and cattle, but an equally large number of festivals bill themselves generally as "expressions of Cajun culture." The focus of individual festivals mirrors the prevailing mentality of the founders at the time of inception, but all Louisiana festivals—and particularly those focusing on aspects of Cajun music and foodways—are at their core well-honed promotional mechanisms, whose organizers are quite adept at cultural commoditization and commercialization.

Modern Louisiana festivals trace their origin to fund-raisers organized by civic-minded men and women. . . . during the first two decades of the twentieth century, when the national Progressive Movement (ca. 1890 to ca. 1920), a broadly based national reform campaign, advocated improved living and working conditions for poor Americans. These improvements were to be achieved by both governmental regulations and voluntary community-based efforts. On the local level, Progressivism gave impetus to fairs, which were essentially regional contests designed to promote self-improvement through the competitive selection of the healthiest babies as well as the best produce, preserves, and livestock. At the height of the Progressive era (around World War I in Louisiana), public officials at all levels encouraged such enterprises. . . .

Many Progressive era fairs were small corporations run by civic leaders; these companies often had hard assets in the form of moveable property and real estate. . . . The business orientation of the fair organizations would ultimately result in the transformation of local festivals from utilitarian educational and quasi-humanitarian enterprises to public relations and promotional operations as local organizations adjusted to precipitous changes in the local economic landscape. A severe agricultural depression gripped the Deep South throughout the 1920s and the resulting economic problems were compounded by widespread destruction wrought by the 1927 flood and the onset of the national depression in 1929. As a result, most of Cajun country's small-scale community and parish fairs were suspended in the late 1920s. Yet, during the very depths of the Great Depression (1929 to 1941), a new generation of festivals was established—usually through the influence of Anglo-American outsiders—to promote local agrarian industries. In 1937, transplanted California native Charles Stevenson organized New Iberia's Louisiana Sugar Cane Festival, while Harry D. Wilson, Louisiana's commissioner of agriculture, was reputedly the moving force behind the establishment of Crowley's Rice Festival that same year. These pioneer festivals, patterned upon harvest festivals elsewhere in the country, served as prototypes for scores of festivals established in Acadiana over the next four decades. . . .

The focus of south Louisiana festivals changed markedly in the 1970s in response to the Cajun cultural renaissance then sweeping through Acadiana. Unlike their industry-driven predecessors, festivals established between the mid-1970s and the dawn of the twenty-first century were designed to both celebrate facets of local culture—particularly music and foodways—and promote local economic development by stimulating culturally-based tourism.

The first of the new festivals was the 1974 Tribute to Cajun Music Festival at Lafayette's Blackham Coliseum. The overwhelming success of this festival, which drew crowds of unprecedented size for Cajun musical performances, revolutionized the south Louisiana festival scene. By the end of the decade, Lafayette had established Festivals Acadiens to highlight Acadiana's native music, crafts, and cuisine. In 1986, Lafayette civil leaders organized *Festival International de Louisiane* to showcase Acadiana's ties to the larger Francophone world. Recent years have witnessed the establishment of the Cajun French Music and Food Festival at Lake Charles, the Cajun Day Festival at Port Allen, the Cajun Gumbo Festival at Ville Platte, the Cajun Music Festival at Mamou, the Cajun Heritage Festival at Cut Off, the Cajun Heritage Waterfowl Festival at Larose, and the Cajun Music Festival at Eunice. . . .

The dimensions of Cajun cuisine's commercialization have taken place in two overlapping, but distinctive cultural contexts—on a national level and within a Cajun context. The United States has embraced its own interpretation of "Cajun" cuisine, which may or may not have any direct relationship to traditional foodways in Louisiana. . . . National interpretations of Cajun food have transcended the cuisine's Louisiana origins to satisfy America's hunger for indigenous American food. Separated from its natural Cajun context, Cajun food in an America environment has become a new form of gastronomy that adheres to a parallel evolution from foodways in Louisiana.

In Bayou Country, commercialization of Cajun food is part and parcel of a larger process of commoditization that is at the heart of an ongoing practice that is increasingly viewed by the larger Cajun community as a double-edged sword. After the global oil bust of 1985–86, the continuous flight of Louisiana's college-educated, white-collar workers to more prosperous areas of the nation forced the Pelican State, which struggled to become more economically diversified, toward greater dependency upon cultural tourism—of which Cajun cuisine is an integral part. Cultural tourism has helped to fill the void created by the oil industry's diminishing contribution to Louisiana's economy, while simultaneously providing employment to the state's poorly educated blue-collar work force. Indeed, government agencies now estimate that tourism is Louisiana's second most important industry. But cultural tourism also has a potentially destructive dimension: Cultural tourism's economic success hinges upon the efficacy of its promotional campaign, and, since the attendant advertising is based upon manipulation of ascriptive (often inherently negative) stereotypes, media distortions of the culture being promoted become increasingly pervasive and consequently increasingly believable and influential. The resulting challenge faced by the Cajun community—indeed, any group increasingly dependent upon cultural tourism—is thus to avoid becoming a caricature of itself.

Questions

1. What developments in transportation and food preservation allowed for the early commercialization of Cajun cuisine? What were the early products exported from "Cajun Country"?

2. How did the practice of labeling products as "Acadian" shift to "Cajun," and what does that shift tell us about the way south Louisianians viewed their own culture?

3. How has the emphasis on attracting tourists to Louisiana by using the "Cajun" label put the Cajun community in danger of "becoming a caricature of itself"? Locate at least three examples of stereotypes or caricatures of Cajuns in the media within the past year. Explain how they are caricatures.

WHO DESTROYED THE MARSH?: OIL FIELD CANALS, COASTAL ECOLOGY, AND THE DEBATE OVER LOUISIANA'S SHRINKING WETLANDS

by Tyler Priest and Jason P. Theriot

The state of louisiana possesses the world's seventh largest wetlands and 40 percent of the coastal wetlands of the United States. These wetlands provide vital habitat for abundant wildlife and fisheries, reduce the impact of storm surges on urban dwellings, serve as a filter for the Mississippi River's pollutants that might otherwise contaminate the region's water table, and are home to some of the most culturally diverse communities in the United States. Unfortunately, these wetlands are disappearing rapidly. The U.S. Geological Survey estimates that Louisiana lost approximately 1,900 square miles of coastal land from 1932 to 2000 and could lose another 700 square miles by 2050. By the 1990s, the sinking Louisiana marshes accounted for 80 percent of the nation's ongoing coastal wetland losses.

American wetlands historian Ann Vileisis claims that "wetlands have become the most controversial landscape in America." The preponderant scientific evidence demonstrating their ecological importance combined with widespread alarm at their ongoing destruction has led to efforts at restoration and preservation. But such efforts have been plagued by conflict, discord, and failure. The debate has become intense, because the stakes are so high in preserving this fragile and critical ecosystem. In some ways, the debate mirrors that over climate change and raises some of the same difficult questions: How do

From *Jahrbuch für Wirtschaftsgeschichte* (2009/2) © Akademie Verlag, Berlin 2009. Used by permission.

we weigh and account for the human and industrial causes of environmental change in comparison to, or apart from, "natural" forces? What are the most feasible and effective means of reducing the human imprint on the physical world and sustaining our environment for the future?

The rapid drowning and disintegration of the Louisiana marsh has sent people scrambling to understand the causes and effects, so that restoration, mitigation, and compensation programs can be developed. There has long been a scientific debate over the causes of this destruction, which in recent years has become increasingly a political debate, with the oil industry—the dominant economic engine in South Louisiana—singled out as a leading culprit. Oil field canals, dredged by the industry to gain access to production sites and to host pipelines that have transported oil and natural gas from coastal Louisiana to the rest of nation, have certainly contributed to wetland loss. Coastal and offshore oil and gas development, which dates back to the 1930s, has roughly coincided with the destruction of the wetlands. Each year, more than 25 percent of the petroleum consumed in the United States is transported through the Louisiana wetlands from oil and gas fields in the Gulf of Mexico. Coastal Louisiana is also home to the Strategic Petroleum Reserve and the Louisiana Offshore Oil Port, the nation's premier deepwater port for offloading foreign crude imports. Casting an eye at more than 9,000 miles of oil field canals, nearly 4,000 active platforms servicing 35,000 wells, and 29,000 miles landing across the Louisiana coast, many people have rushed to convict the oil industry as destroyer of the marsh. This verdict, however, is too simple and misleading. The coastal region along the Northern Gulf of Mexico is a complex ecosystem that has been incorporated in a multi-faceted way into the regional economy. This includes the extensive construction of levees along the Mississippi River to support settlement, in addition to the infrastructure built for oil and gas. Moreover, in recent years, scientists have begun to understand how dynamic changes in the region's geology, hydrology, and geomorphology, independent of human activity, have contributed to wetlands destruction. Humans and their technologies have clearly had a hand in this destruction over time. But there are also environmental forces at work beyond human control, and these must be taken into account in drawing historical conclusions about the relationship between oil and gas development and the disappearance of the marsh.

The Louisiana coastal wetlands are a centuries-old product of a dynamic river and delta system that drains 1,575,000 square miles of North America. The Mississippi River provided the necessary fresh water, sediment, and bed load to coastal marshes, thereby counteracting the naturally occurring subsidence [i.e., the sinking of the land] and the encroachment of natural sea level rise. The Mississippi Delta changed its course several times over the last 5,000–7,000 years. As the river migrated from west to east and back again multiple times, it increased wetland sedimentation in the active "lobes" and increased wetland loss in abandoned ones. By the mid-20th century, this dynamic system had been disrupted, and wetlands have since disappeared from South Louisiana at an alarming rate.

Prior to the 1960s, only a few scientists and the small communities living along the coast were aware of the wetland loss. The movement of all kinds of economic activity into the wetlands took place during a time when the idea of environmental protection as we know it did not exist and the concept of the marsh as a valuable resource in itself was not even considered. For much of human history, "cultures worldwide have invested marshes, bogs, and swamps with a rich, dense, and mostly eerie symbolic significance as dark and chaotic places of the earth." The words "marsh" and "mire" have a long lineage in the English language as referents to negatively perceived types of wet areas that harbored disease.

Since the earliest French settlements in New Orleans, people have continuously sought to control the direction and frequent floodwaters of the Mississippi River. In the mid-19th century, the federal government transferred federally held wetlands to Louisiana and other flood-prone states, so they could sell the land and generate funds for drainage and levee building. Swamps and wetlands, it was hoped, would be turned into farmland, bringing lightness and order out of darkness and chaos.

By the late 1870s, containing and controlling the Mississippi River, let alone draining the swamps along its banks, seemed futile. But in the wake of the deadly 1927 flood, the U.S. Army Corps of Engineers set about constructing a major flood control system to circumvent any future potentially disastrous floods. By the 1930s, the engineers had built almost a thousand miles of levees along the Mississippi. Because of these man-made structures, particularly the Old River Control Structure, which diverts a portion of the

Mississippi's waters into the Atchafalaya River, and the dam-building on all the Mississippi's main tributaries, the annual flow of sediment down the Mississippi River into the delta region by the 1960s had been reduced by 60 percent. Seventy-five years of redirecting the Mississippi's natural flow has "largely halted the delta building process" along the coast. The first studies on the Louisiana wetlands began in the 1930s and early 1940s and focused on mapping and identifying vegetation types and wildlife habitats. Early scholars reported on Louisiana's shrinking wetlands and understood the main factors that contributed to marsh deterioration: subsidence, erosion, and sea-level rise. Some of these factors were natural, subtle, geologic processes; others were man-induced, such as sediment starvation due to controlling the natural flow and sediment load of the Mississippi River. But not until the 1970s, when ecologists began to substitute "wetlands" for the pejorative terms "swamp" and "marsh," did they begin to measure the rate and extent of wetlands loss in South Louisiana. Research by Sherwood M. "Woody" Gagliano and J. L. van Beek reported land loss rates of about 16.5 square miles/year over a 30-year period, which sparked a new wave of scientific inquiry into explaining Louisiana's ever-changing coastal landscape.

Initially, scientists believed that reduced sedimentation was responsible for the disappearing wetlands. New studies published in the 1980s aimed to quantify the rate of wetland loss and identify its causes. The methods used typically involved analyzing aerial imagery, data summaries of maps, and field investigations. This new scholarship began to show that man-made structures, mainly navigation, access, and oil and gas pipeline canals, had a major influence on altering wetland hydrology. The accepted interpretation noted two types of impacts from canals: direct and indirect impacts. The direct impacts of these canals accounted for the actual conversion of marshland to open water. The indirect impacts were the "secondary or subsequent changes resulting from, for example, reductions in sediment supply or from dredging, from subsurface fluid withdrawal, or from hydrologic alterations." Beginning in the 1980s, researchers noted that these canals increased in size over time, some by more than 30 percent, depending on their location.

A close examination of the "Muskrat Line," a 355-mile large diameter natural gas transmission line built by Tennessee Gas in the 1950s, and one of the largest pipelines ever constructed through the Louisiana wetlands, illustrates the ways in which technology not only facilitated the transportation of petroleum through the nearly impassable marshes and swamps but also how it reshaped the coastal environment. Much of the pipeline was laid by dredging a 40 foot by 8 foot "flotation canal" through the marsh, which allowed for the continuous movement of pipe-laying barges and equipment. Engineers installed hundreds of concrete bulkheads and earthworks along the pipeline canal in order to keep out boat traffic and to protect the marsh from salt water intrusion. Over time, however, this pipeline canal and its many tributaries have increased in width, by as much as 150 feet in some areas, while ponding behind the spoil banks and saltwater intrusion through the outdated and weakened bulkheads have eroded the surrounding marsh.

In 1983, researchers from Louisiana State University compared coastal maps from 1955 and 1978 to assess wetland loss in South Louisiana and noted that scientists were "only beginning to appreciate" how canals influenced local ecology. The scholars, Gene Turner, William W. Scaife, and Robert Costanza, were some of the first to suggest that indirect impacts, such as salt water intrusion and soil erosion, may extend decades beyond the construction of the oil field canals themselves. In addition to quantifying the vast network of pipeline canals, the scientists also analyzed the accompanying spoil banks that were created during the dredging of the various canals. These spoil banks, particularly those built parallel to the coastline, created conditions for extensive ponding and flooding that over time drowned sections of the wetlands through altered hydrology. The scientists concluded by calling for proper mitigation techniques in future canal projects, such as restricting or rejecting dredging permits, constructing weirs to limit salt water intrusion, and backfilling the canals.

In the late 1980s, several major studies were published by scientists at LSU, the Louisiana Universities Marine Consortium, U.S. Fish and Wildlife Service, and the U.S. Minerals Management Service documenting the subtle, indirect effects over time caused by the dredging of canals for navigation as well as oil and gas pipelines. These studies helped clinch federal support of Louisiana's restoration efforts for which the state's U.S. senators had been lobbying for years. In 1990, Congress enacted the Coastal Wetlands Planning, Protection, and Restoration Act (CWPPRA)—or the "Breaux Act" after Louisiana Senator John Breaux—a joint-venture partnership between the state of Louisiana and the federal government to fund, build, and manage long-term restoration projects in coastal Louisiana. The Act appropriated $50 million annually for the federal government's 75 percent share of the costs involved. Several major restoration projects, more than half a billion dollars worth, were completed or started in the 1990s, including the Caernarvon Freshwater Diversion, the Davis Pond Freshwater Diversion, the Bonnet Carré Freshwater Diversion, and dozens of smaller projects, such as creating crevasse splays and terraces to build marsh and impoundments to protect marsh.

By the late 1990s, as the problem continued to worsen, and as CWPPRA projects seemed to have visible but negligible effects (the "proverbial finger in the dike"), some scientists and observers began to turn up the heat. In 1997, Gene Turner published a controversial article in the journal *Estuaries*. In his essay "Wetland Loss in the Northern Gulf of Mexico: Multiple Working Hypotheses," Turner argued that wetland loss resulted not from sediment starvation and subsidence, not from controlling the Mississippi River, but from extensive coastal zone canal construction, mostly by the oil and gas industry. Subsequently, in the early 2000s, Robert A. Morton and others argued that oil and natural gas extraction was reactivating subsurface faults near the reservoirs causing an increase in subsidence. Morton analyzed what he called "hotspots" in Terrebonne Parish and determined that a correlation existed between subsurface fluid withdrawal and wetland loss. He concluded that the increasing amount of subsidence in these "hotspots" was directly at-tributed to the increase of oil and gas extraction in the same area during the same period, the 1960s and 1970s. These studies, especially Turner's, set off a firestorm of controversy. In a letter to the *New Orleans Times-Picayune*, the president of the Louisiana Land & Exploration (LLE) company called Turner a "two-dimensional thinker," contrasting him with "three- and four-dimensional scientists" who "say these canals are responsible for about 10 percent of the problem." Other wetlands scientists objected to Turner's methodology and simple thesis, arguing that complex geologic processes in the delta region could not be overlooked. Subsidence and sea level rise were essential components to this environmental phenomenon, along with habitat type and condition and sediment availability in a specific region. Therefore, they argued, restoration efforts must "emphasize riverine inputs of freshwater and sediments."

Despite the challenges to Turner's thesis, his view that oil companies were the ones responsible for destroying the wetlands became common currency.

Landowners, private and public, filed lawsuits against oil companies for property damage, claiming that lease agreements obliged leaseholders to restore the marsh to its original state. Citing a lessee's obligation to act as a "reasonably prudent operator" under Article 122 of the Louisiana Mineral Code, plaintiffs alleged that oil and pipeline companies had an obligation to restore dredged marshland to its "original" state. In 2005, a Louisiana Supreme Court decision denied these claims. In a case brought by the Terrebonne Parish School Board, a landholder, versus Castex Energy, Inc. and other pipeline company defendants, the Court found that although it "was not unaware of the plight of Louisiana's coastal wetlands [. . .] imposing an implied duty to restore the surface that was clearly beyond the contemplation of the parties at the time they contracted is not a legally supportable resolution to an undoubtedly difficult problem confronting our state."

As litigation wound through the courts, a political effort was organized to fund Louisiana coastal restoration, based on, among other factors, the underlying assumption that oil field canals were responsible for a percentage of the land loss. In 1997, the Coalition to Restore Coastal Louisiana combined all the local, state, and federal restoration programs into one management plan—Coast 2050, which attempted to look at the problem from an integrated regional perspective, as opposed to local, pork-barrel type projects like those funded under CWPPRA. Louisiana's Washington political delegation hoped the federal government, which has issued most of the oil and gas leases in the Gulf of Mexico, would pick up the estimated $14 billion tab for Coast 2050. Louisiana Senator Mary Landrieu made it her mission to obtain a share of federal royalties collected from federal offshore leases to pay for it. In August 2002, coastal restoration advocates launched "America's Wetland," a massive public education initiative to spread awareness across the nation and around the world about Louisiana's shrinking wetlands. Shell Oil, one of the largest operators in the Gulf of Mexico, was the major sponsor of the $10 million campaign. In 2006, after the destruction wrought by Hurricanes Katrina and Rita in South Louisiana, some federal royalty revenues were pledged to the state, but the amount is far too small to fund Coast 2050 according to restoration advocates.

Meanwhile, scientific opinion has been moving against Turner's thesis. In 2004, LSU geologist Roy Dokka published a pathbreaking study, sanctioned by the National Oceanic and Atmospheric Administration (NOAA) and using G.P.S. technology. The study showed that for the past several decades, surveyors, floodplain managers, and levee engineers have systematically overstated elevations in coastal Louisiana. They had calculated heights using "benchmarks" which were supposedly stable, but which, as the report noted, were themselves subsiding. The big, underlying cause of wetlands destruction was regional subsidence resulting from multiple, interacting regional and local processes. Oil and gas extraction and associated canals no doubt speed the process of marsh drowning, but according to Dokka, they are neither the root cause (sediment and water load induced flexure of the lithosphere) nor the proximate cause (river leveeing, which prevents sediment deposition and accretion). In Dokka's view, the entire region, not just the wetlands, is subsiding, due to "unrelenting natural processes." According to research biologist Bill Streever: "In coastal Louisiana, where almost nothing about marsh restoration is clear, one fact stands out: elevation matters." Dokka and a growing number of others believe that merely fixing the wetlands will not save the coast, and this alone cannot provide adequate protection against storm surge. Says Dokka: "Higher and still higher ocean levees will unfortunately be needed for protection of human population if society insists on living in this dangerous environment." In Dokka's study, the environment of South Louisiana is a creation of the interaction between a complex geological, hydrological, and biological system and a complex regional economy, dominated by oil and gas extraction, but not necessarily determined by it.

Dokka's theory not only challenges the conventional wisdom about wetlands loss in South Louisiana, but it challenges some of the certainties we have about the relationship between humans and nature. Despite the alarming rate of wetlands destruction, until recently it was an article of faith, backed by controversial scientific theories, that not only had humans damaged the wetlands, but that humans had the ability to restore them. Clearly, the Louisiana ecosystem has been re-plumbed and its "natural" hydrology and geomorphology reshaped. But in recent years, and particularly since the storms of 2005, the emphasis has shifted from "restoration" and discrete scientific studies focused on the mechanisms of wetland destruction to more coordinated action by scientists, policymakers, and businesses to find ways to slow the process of destruction and protect the people, infrastructure, and economy.

A few oil companies are participating in this coordination, namely Shell Oil, the company that has dominated offshore oil development in the Gulf of Mexico since the 1950s. Some people dismiss the participation of Shell and other firms involved with coastal restoration as a publicity stunt intended to deflect criticism of the industry as a destroyer of the wetlands. Environmental advocates have openly criticized Shell for sponsoring "America's Wetland." They argue that the central mission of the non-profit initiative and Shell Oil has been to pass the liability and price tag for destroying the marsh onto the federal government and U.S. taxpayers. The critics point to the fact that "America's Wetland" has not explicitly acknowledged the thousands of miles of oil field canals that have contributed to wetland loss over the decades. On the other hand, people working in, or close to, the oil industry grumble that Shell's association with Coast 2050 is, in effect, tacit acknowledgment that pipeline canals are leading culprits in the destruction of the wetlands. In their view, Shell's management has conceded too much in the service of "political correctness" and has uncritically accepted the "junk science" produced by Eugene Turner and others.

The oil industry's long dominance in Louisiana business, its deep entwine-ment in state politics, and the notorious corruption at all political levels in the state automatically raises suspicions about oil company involvement in public initiatives such as Coast 2050. But there is ample reason to believe that oil operators have as much to protect along the coast as residents and therefore have a sincere interest in addressing the problem. Wetlands form a barrier between the open Gulf and oil fields and pipelines built inland; an estimated 3,000 wells and production facilities and thousands of miles of oil and natural gas pipelines and access canals are currently protected by marshes and barrier islands. In a 2004 congressional testimony, Ed Landgraf, environmental coor-dinator for Shell Pipeline Company, stated that coastal erosion is a "national problem with serious national implications [. . .] National energy security can be maintained only if Louisiana's coast is restored and preserved."

The massive hurricanes that ripped apart the Louisiana Gulf coast in 2005 and 2008 spotlighted the vulnerability of the nation's petroleum infrastruc-ture, most of which is located in southern Louisiana, prompting some in the industry to recognize that the long-term cost of inaction far outweighs the costs of wetland restoration. Within 50 years, an estimated 155 miles of what are now protected navigation waterways will be exposed to open water, leading to billions of dollars of losses in shipping and increased requirements for shoreline protection and dredging, not to mention repairing and relaying exposed pipelines. It is estimated that three miles of wetlands can absorb one foot of storm surge, and the loss of a one-mile strip of wetlands can increase average annual property damage by about $200,000 per acre of wetland lost. Furthermore, as the marsh sinks, insurance rates rise.

In his book *Nature's Economy*, American environmental historian Donald Worster once spoke of the shifting dialectical tension in American history between the "Arcadian" impulse to discover and preserve nature's intrinsic value and the "Imperialist" impulse to dominate and extract value from nature. The Arcadian impulse operates from the assumption that nature has its own order, its own pattern, and its own economy which humans are bound to adapt to and respect. The Imperialist ethos, by contrast, sees nature as having no economy, no concern for cost or efficiency, and thus it must be managed in the interest of "civilization." Efforts in the 1990s to "restore" the wetlands in South Louisiana may seem Arcadian in spirit, but they can also be interpreted as an Imperialist impulse to preserve habitation in an increasingly uninhabitable environment and to sustain methods of extraction that may no longer be sustainable.

In the last decade, there has been a perceptible shift to a more genuinely Arcadian perspective regarding the environmental transformation of South Louisiana. Communities, government officials, and businesses in the region are aware of their role as historical actors in this transformation, but they increasingly recognize that they do not have control over it. The best they can do is to try to accommodate the changing environment. The imperative of "restoring the wetlands" has been replaced by the objective of "protecting the coast." The Cajun people who populate much of South Louisiana derive their name from the French Acadians (exiled from Nova Scotia in 1755), and for generations they have adapted to "nature's economy" in their region. But the ongoing transformation of their natural surroundings may be the biggest adaptive challenge they have ever faced. . . .

The on-going political and academic debates about the causes of wetland loss and the direction of restoration efforts have overshadowed the public projects that have begun the actual rebuilding of the coast. According to a 2007 annual review published by the Louisiana Department of Natural Resources, 711 restoration projects have been authorized since 1989 and more than 600 have been constructed. The types of projects range from freshwater diversions to open water land terraces that trap and build up sediments. Although these projects represent only a tiny gain in the overall battle against coastal erosion, the coordinated efforts and funding by state and federal agencies have shown some sign of progress. Most people involved in the discussion believe that the small scale restoration projects can at best "hold the line" in the near-term, particularly as the Gulf hurricanes increase in size, while larger and more expensive projects, such as reintroducing Mississippi River sediment into the dying marsh and bayous using massive pipelines, might actually make a real difference in the long-term. The political, environmental, and financial issues involved in such projects, however, pose enormous challenges to the lawmakers and discouraged stakeholders of coastal Louisiana who continue to watch in disbelief as the wetlands and all that they support—energy infrastructure, coastal communities, and wildlife habitat—slowly erode toward the sea with each passing tide.

Questions

1. Why should Louisiana be concerned about wetlands loss? Why should the nation be concerned about Louisiana's wetlands loss?
2. What does the shift in the terms used to describe the coastal regions, from "swamp" or "marsh" to "wetlands," signify?
3. List the factors that help explain wetlands loss. Why are these factors contested?
4. Why is it important to ascertain what is causing the disappearance of the wetlands?